B,

isions of Jewish Education

his book is intended to stimulate the philosophical consideration of Jewish
our time as reflected in Jewish education, its alternative visions, its purposes
mentalities, the values it should serve, and the personal and social character it
foster.

ent conceptions and practices of Jewish education are neither sufficiently reflec-
thoroughgoing enough to meet the multiple challenges that the world now poses
existence and continuity. New efforts are needed to develop an education of
re that will both honor the riches of the Jewish past and grasp the opportunities
ul interaction with the general culture of the present.

omote such efforts, leading scholars formulate their variant visions of an ideal
ducation for the contemporary world. This groundbreaking book also illustrates
nslation of educational ideas into practice and reports on a sustained effort to
late such ideas as embodied in a particular school's ongoing activities.

ended to stimulate others to engage in a philosophical re-envisioning of Jewish life
arning, *Visions of Jewish Education* also should provide a new approach to reform
s in general education as well as in the education systems of various religious and
nic communities.

Seymour Fox, the author and editor of several books, including *Freud and
Education* (1975), is the Director of Program of the Mandel Foundation worldwide. He
is Professor of Education, Emeritus, at the Hebrew University of Jerusalem, where he
directed the School of Education.

Israel Scheffler is a Fellow of the American Academy of Arts and Sciences, the
Director of the Philosophy of Education Research Center at Harvard University, and the
author of *Symbolic Worlds* (1997) and several other titles.

Daniel Marom is a Senior Researcher at the Mandel Foundation, where he
works on the development of educational vision in a range of settings. He is a faculty
member of the Mandel School.

Visions of
Jewish Education

Edited by

SEYMOUR FOX

Mandel Foundation and
Hebrew University

ISRAEL SCHEFFLER

Harvard University

DANIEL MAROM

Mandel Foundation and
Mandel School

CAMBRIDGE
UNIVERSITY PRESS

PUBLISHED BY THE PRESS SYNDICATE OF THE UNIVERSITY OF CAMBRIDGE
The Pitt Building, Trumpington Street, Cambridge, United Kingdom

CAMBRIDGE UNIVERSITY PRESS
The Edinburgh Building, Cambridge CB2 2RU, UK
40 West 20th Street, New York, NY 10011-4211, USA
477 Williamstown Road, Port Melbourne, VIC 3207, Australia
Ruiz de Alarcón 13, 28014 Madrid, Spain
Dock House, The Waterfront, Cape Town 8001, South Africa

http://www.cambridge.org

First published 2003

Printed in the United States of America

Typeface Bembo 10/12 pt.   *System* LaTeX 2_ε [TB]

A catalog record for this book is available from the British Library.

Library of Congress Cataloging in Publication Data

Visions of Jewish education / edited by Seymour Fox, Israel Scheffler, Daniel Marom.
    p.   cm.
Includes bibliographical references and index.
ISBN 0-521-82147-9 – ISBN 0-521-52899-2 (pbk.)
1. Jews – Education – Philosophy.   I. Fox, Seymour.   II. Scheffler, Israel.
III. Marom, Daniel.
LC719 .V57   2003
371.82992′4–dc21   2002041244

ISBN 0 521 82147 9 hardback
ISBN 0 521 52899 2 paperback

איזהו חכם? הרואה את הנולד.

Who is wise?
He who envisions the future.

Babylonian Talmud, Tamid 32a

To Jack, Joseph, and Morton Mandel
Men of vision

Contents

vii

Preface and Acknowledgments

Jewish learning has profound roots and far-reaching implications. Yet Jewish education is often treated in local and prosaic terms, concerned with means rather than ends, with instrumentalities rather than ideas. This book represents an effort to deepen and broaden the enterprise of Jewish education by eliciting variant visions of its rationale and import, relating educational activities to their bases in the learning of the past and in reflective anticipation of the future. We hope the book will stimulate philosophical approaches to education by all, whether Jewish or not, who consider themselves stewards of a precious heritage responsible for its creative preservation and renewal.

Our book is a product of intensive and continuous collaboration over a period of many years. We are jointly and fully responsible for every chapter not signed by a particular author.

We thank the various scholars who wrote the signed chapters. Without their essential contributions, there would have been no volume at all. We are grateful to the group of Jewish educators who participated in our deliberations. We are happy to acknowledge the work of our outstanding editor, Nessa Rapoport, of the Mandel Foundation, who was an active partner in developing the plan and content of the volume as a whole; we could not have brought the book to successful completion without her acumen and dedication. We also thank these members of the staff of the Mandel Foundation: Dr. Erin Henriksen, our assistant editor, for her excellent work and unfaltering devotion; Rabbi Jeffrey Saks for his thoughtful and critical reading of the manuscript; and Chava Sagiv, for her dedicated research and technical support.

We are grateful to JoAnne Sorabella, of the Philosophy of Education Research Center at Harvard, for her superb assistance at every stage of our project from its inception.

The Mandel Foundation has been a partner from the very beginning in the development of the idea, the project, and finally a volume, all of which required great vision, deep faith, and a willingness to venture on an approach that had not been given sufficient attention in the field of Jewish education.

Other colleagues at the Foundation, in particular Annette Hochstein, president of the Mandel Foundation, Israel, encouraged us strongly throughout the many stages of the work. Many others, including educators, academic colleagues, rabbis, community leaders, and editorial assistants helped in ways too numerous to mention. We are in debt to Cambridge University Press and to our editor, Andrew Beck, for their steadfast commitment. To all, we offer our sincere gratitude.

We acknowledge permission to use material from the following books and publications:

Chapter 1. *Judaism: A Portrait,* copyright © 1960 by Leon Roth. (Passages reprinted by permission of Faber and Faber.) "Jewish Education: Purposes, Problems and Possibilities," from *Curriculum, Community, Commitment,* copyright © 1992 by Dr. Daniel J. Margolis and Rabbi Eliot Salo Schoenberg. (Passages reprinted with permission.)

Chapter 4. *Introduction to the Code of Maimonides,* copyright © 1980 by Yale University. (Passages reprinted with permission.) *Guide of the Perplexed,* copyright © 1963 by the University of Chicago. (Passages reprinted with permission.) *A Maimonides Reader,* copyright © 1972 by Isadore Twersky. (Passages reprinted with permission of Behrman House, Inc.) *Mishneh Torah* reprinted with permission of Feldheim Publishers.

Chapter 4 Supplement. "Religion and Law," from *Religion in a Religious Age,* copyright © 1974 by the Association for Jewish Studies. (Passages reprinted with permission.) "The Rov," from *Tradition,* copyright © 1996 by the Rabbinical Council of America. (Passages reprinted with permission.) "Survival, Normalcy, Modernity," from *Zionism in Transition,* copyright © 1980 by Isadore Twersky. (Passages reprinted with permission.)

Chapter 5 Supplement. "*Hiyhulim la-Ivri-Eiropi be-Sifrut ha-Ivrit be-Ma'avar ha-Meot,*" from *Migvan De'ot ve-Hashkafot be-Tarbut Yisrael,* copyright © 1992 by Menachem Brinker. (Passages reprinted with permission.) "Slavery in Freedom," from *Selected Essays of Ahad Ha-'Am,* copyright © 1960 by the Jewish Publication Society. (Used by permission.) "The Law of the Heart," "Wrecking and Building," and "The Question of Culture," from *The Zionist Idea,* copyright © 1997 by the Jewish Publication Society. (Used by permission.) "*Ahad Ha-Am, Berdyczewski, u'Brenner: Shalosh Hityahasuyot Hiloniyot le-Tekstim Mehayvim ba-Yahadut,*" from *Kivunim,* copyright © 1990 by the World Zionist Organization. (Passages reprinted with permission.) "The End of Zionism," from

by KTAV Publishing House, Inc., Hoboken, N.J. (Passages reprinted with permission.)

Chapter 11. "Remarks at Second Dialog in Israel," reprinted with permission from *Congress Monthly,* volume 30, no. 12. Copyright © 1963 American Jewish Congress.

Seymour Fox
Israel Scheffler
Daniel Marom

About the Mandel Foundation

The Mandel Foundation was established in 1963 by Jack, Joseph, and Morton Mandel, of Cleveland, Ohio. The primary mission of the Foundation is to help provide outstanding leadership for the nonprofit world. The Foundation supports leadership education programs in its own institutions and at selected universities and organizations. It has these areas of priority: higher education; Jewish education and continuity; the leadership and management of nonprofit organizations; and urban neighborhood renewal.

The Mandel Foundation approach to philanthropy is characterized by a conviction that exceptional leaders, professional and volunteer, are the critical factor in contributing significantly to community and society. Such leaders are guided by a powerful vision of the future that is inspired by profound ideas, translated into clear purposes, and energized by imaginative resolutions to today's problems. The Foundation also believes in searching for long-term, systemic solutions to problems, involving thoughtful planning, careful implementation, and rigorous evaluation.

The Foundation is committed to leadership education programs that cultivate vision and link compelling ideas to sound policy and effective outcomes. The conception and curriculum of these programs draw on ideas from a range of disciplines, including philosophy, education, Jewish studies, social sciences, policy studies, and social work, among others.

The Foundation supports the Mandel School in Jerusalem, an independent institution of higher learning whose mission is the recruitment, preparation, and placement of senior professional leaders for education and public service in Israel, North America, and globally.

Introduction

In 1991, the Mandel Foundation launched a project to stimulate the philosophical consideration of Jewish existence in our time as reflected in alternative visions of Jewish education, its purposes and instrumentalities, the values it should serve, and the personal and social character it ought to foster. *Visions of Jewish Education* is an outcome of the project.

Jewish life is currently undergoing something of a renaissance, with renewed interest by Jews in Jewish culture, religion, literature, and education. But prevalent conceptions and practices of Jewish education are neither sufficiently reflective nor thoroughgoing enough to meet the challenge of new social and cultural circumstances both in Israel and in communities elsewhere. What is needed are new efforts to develop an education of the future that will fully value the riches of the Jewish past and grasp the need for creative interaction with the general culture of the present. It is this conviction that motivates both our project and our book.

With the collaboration of the Harvard Philosophy of Education Research Center, we began our work by inviting a group of scholars concerned with Jewish life to compose written responses to the fundamental question of what a Jewish education ought to consist in under contemporary circumstances. These scholars were then convened for a first meeting at Harvard in 1992 to present their several formulations; thereafter, they met repeatedly, both in Jerusalem and at Harvard, for critical discussions of their diverse views. The overall goal of these discussions was to initiate basic thinking about the prospects of contemporary Jewish life, with primary emphasis on the education required to sustain and enhance such life.

The scholars who participated in our project were Isadore Twersky, late Professor of Hebrew Literature and Philosophy, Harvard University; Menachem Brinker, Professor of Philosophy and Hebrew Literature, Hebrew University; Moshe Greenberg, Professor of Bible, Emeritus, Hebrew University; Michael

1

A. Meyer, Professor of Jewish History, Hebrew Union College–Jewish Institute of Religion; Michael Rosenak, Professor of Jewish Education, Emeritus, Hebrew University; Israel Scheffler, Professor of Education and Philosophy, Emeritus, Harvard University, Director, Philosophy of Education Research Center, Harvard University; Seymour Fox, Director of Program, Mandel Foundation, Professor of Education, Emeritus, Hebrew University, and Project Director; and Dr. Daniel Marom, Senior Researcher, Mandel Foundation, faculty member, Mandel School, and Associate Project Director.

The three chapters in Part I explain the background and motivation of the project, provide an account of what it attempted to do and what it did, and offer a comparative introduction to the scholars' essays that follow.

The essays in Parts II and III include the visions of a halakhist and those of a biblical scholar, of a secularist and of a historian of Reform, of a pluralist concerned with community, of a philosopher treating of the educated person, of an educator studying the linkage between theory and practice, and of a participant observer who has worked to elicit and refine a particular school's vision as embodied in its daily practice. The reflections represented in these chapters, their strengths and their limitations, their disparities and their commonalities, their fundamental divisions as well as their sometimes startling convergences, their occasional scholarly surprises and their often inspiring insights into traditional as well as universal values – all of these cannot fail to invite the reader into a deeper appreciation of Jewish education, as well as the challenge to envisage its future.

We do not suppose our book to offer the last word on any of the topics with which it deals. Our project will have failed of its purpose if the reader assumes that the visions outlined in the book are final and finished projects, self-enclosed philosophical worlds. Nor should it be thought that they represent an exhaustive list of promising approaches to Jewish education or that all that is required is a judicious mix and match among them. Our hope is that the chapters to follow may initiate a continuing process of reflection and an ongoing conversation on the topics treated here. Such a process may yield unforeseen creative responses to the issues in question and in itself bring new life to the community within which it takes place. It is the strenuous effort to envision afresh the depths and the heights of Jewish learning to which our project has been dedicated.

Part I

The Visions Project

1

Envisioning Jewish Education

For more than 200 years, Jews in the Western world have aspired to civic and social equality. They have argued and worked for full political rights, for admission to universities, for access to the professions, and for the right to participate in all branches of commerce.

At the beginning of the twenty-first century, these aspirations have in large measure been realized. Jews have taken advantage of the opportunities increasingly afforded them to participate in the political, social, economic, and intellectual life of Western open societies. They have become full and active participants in the civic and political life of their communities.

Yet, paradoxical as it may seem, enhanced participation by Jews in modern society has exposed Judaism to a historic test of survival. "The occasion for this test," as the philosopher Leon Roth has described it, "was not primarily the religious one of confrontation with other faiths but the political one of being granted civil rights":

> The change of political status was the result of a long process, and its duration differed in different countries. Its more obvious landmarks were the admission into the Netherlands of some of the refugees from Catholic Spain and Portugal in the sixteenth century, the re-admission of the Jews to England in the seventeenth, the emergence in Germany of a Jewry educated on Western lines in the eighteenth. Its great symbolic manifestations were in the France of the Revolution: the tearing down of the walls of the ghettos in the first years of the Republic, the calling of a "Sanhedrin" (supreme Jewish religious court) by Napoleon in 1807.
>
> Up to this point in the history of European Jewries the previously elaborated tool of survival, religious law or *halakhah,* was astonishingly successful. It supplied the organization which kept each community a

self-contained islet in the Gentile sea; and it prescribed the type of action which, for better or for worse, satisfied the majority of individuals.

When the walls fell, however, a new situation was created, and not for Jews only but for Judaism. . . . For a score of centuries Judaism had taught the Jew how to survive political oppression. It had now to be re-adjusted to the fact of political freedom.[1]

The resulting struggle to reorient Jewish life in the modern world confronted Judaism with an enormous challenge. The dimensions of this challenge were philosophical as well as civic. The problems of Jewish education in modern society stand out sharply by contrast with the premodern period for which, as one of us has elsewhere described it,

education in the Jewish school, home, and community was one continuous entity, embodied concretely in all spheres of life. . . . Scattered in their diverse and fragile communities, Jews assuredly had no control over the world, but they had the word, and the word gave them access to the highest heavens, to which their religious life was dedicated. . . .

The Jew lived a precarious existence, but the philosophical framework of Jew and non-Jew alike was largely the same. . . .

The holiness of the Jewish Scriptures, central to this philosophical worldview, was virtually unquestioned. . . . Jewish education was thus based on systematic beliefs, of which the basic philosophical features were recognized and shared by all. . . .

Now every feature of the premodern context has been destroyed or rendered problematic in the modern period. The emancipation and entry of the Jew into the mainstream of Western life broke the tightly knit harmony of home, school and community. The general breakdown of the medieval worldview shattered the inherited conception of nature and history shared by Jew and non-Jew alike, undermined traditional attitudes to their religious Scriptures, and destroyed the uniform traditional response to Jewish existence which constituted the basis of education in the past.[2]

Compounding this continuing challenge to the internal life of Western Jewry came the unprecedented external catastrophe of the Holocaust in the twentieth century. Yet despite this incalculable trauma, which destroyed countless Jewish communities and, further, shook the foundations of traditional Jewish faith, Jewish life managed to evince remarkable strengths in its aftermath. The establishment of the State of Israel in 1948 demonstrated the durability and resilience of Judaism and the Jewish people, galvanizing Jews all over the world to support and build the state and generating in them a new sense of pride and an enhanced confidence.

In the Diaspora as well, individual Jews flourished in the free environment, striving to develop a way of life as a community that would combine Jewish loyalties with full participation as citizens of their countries. They established synagogues, schools, seminaries, hospitals, social service agencies, defense and philanthropic organizations, and they maintained strong ties with Israel. Despite such efforts, however, the erosion of Jewish loyalty continued apace as Jews became increasingly vulnerable to the pressures of a free secular environment and the inevitable weakening of inherited ideological commitments.

Such erosion has affected Israeli as well as Diaspora Jewish communities. Indeed, even before the birth of the State of Israel, prominent thinkers, such as Ḥayyim Naḥman Bialik, Yeḥezkel Kaufmann, Benzion Dinur, and Martin Buber, had foreseen that the hoped-for establishment of a secular and democratic society would lessen the commitment to traditional Jewish learning and culture. And such lessening, as predicted, has indeed been taking place.[3]

To be sure, the problems in Israel and the Diaspora are different, but they share common elements. In both cases, large segments of the Jewish population have been alienated from traditional Jewish learning and its values. Having been estranged from the Judaism of their past, they have lost commitment to a Judaism of the future. This breach in Jewish continuity poses a test arising from the very freedom for which Jews have striven. Can this breach be healed? Can Jewish loyalties thrive in an atmosphere of freedom, without the enclosure of a self-imposed ghetto?

It has been widely suggested by Jewish spokesmen that education is the answer to our problem. They have assumed – or hoped – that concerned parents, teachers, and educators can devise effective ways of stemming the tide of alienation and ensuring a creative Judaic future for the Jewish people. Many doubt, however, that education, under present-day conditions, offers a realistic solution. They are skeptical that any form of Jewish education can resist the attraction of competing ideas and ways of life pervasive in the open society. They find a paucity of new ideas that might energize educational effort and thus have little hope for educational intervention in school and community. They remind us of the low status of Jewish education as a profession, and they note that very few scholars are being trained for this profession. In short, they challenge the likely effectiveness of education as a solution to the continuity crisis.

In answer to the skeptics, various promising prospects for current Jewish education may be adduced. There is widespread recognition of the importance of informal as well as classroom settings for Jewish learning. There is a remarkable new growth of Jewish day schools. There is a growing appreciation by educators of the need for Jewish education to be comprehensive and lifelong, engaging the family and community as well as the individual, the adult as well as the child. Curricula are increasingly understood to require not only recourse to texts but also to materials drawn from the arts. Jewish educators seem increasingly to recognize the power of affective as well as cognitive learning, of experimental as well as didactic methods. They acknowledge the need to recruit and train professionals and community leaders and to place them in positions of educational responsibility. True, these prospects for Jewish education have to be strengthened, financed, and vigorously pursued in programs of action by the community at large, but at least the outlines of an answer to the continuity crisis seem to be discernible.

This reply to the skeptics is indeed forceful and persuasive. Its every element represents a necessary component of an adequate educational response to our problem. Yet the skeptic is still right to be dubious. For although the reply offers necessary conditions for an educational amelioration of the problem, it does not include every such necessary condition, leaving out, in particular, the importance of a comprehensive educational vision of the purposes and contents of Jewish education.

Even if we include the element of vision, we have no guarantees that education would in fact turn the tide against widespread erosion of Jewish loyalties. We believe, however, that without the element of vision, our educational response is guaranteed to fail. This belief has led us to undertake a project that we hope will help stimulate a discourse on alternative visions of Jewish education.

Why do we emphasize vision? Without a guiding purpose, an educational system is bound to be scattered and incoherent, incapable of consecutive effort, unable either to grasp the possibilities of effective action or to avoid the obstacles in its path. Lacking a directive guide to the future, the system becomes repetitive and uninspired, prey to past habit, incapable of justifying itself to new generations of our youth in the worlds they will inhabit. What the skeptic is responding to, among other things, is the sense that current Jewish educational practice is too often spiritless, a mere recapitulation of conventional lessons and past practices, lacking both systematic connection with the depths of Jewish lore and the energy to make such lore come alive convincingly in the hearts of contemporary youth.

Vision, as we understand it, is not simply ideological preference. It implies both comprehensive understanding and guiding purpose. It places the work of education in the setting of a present that is an outgrowth of the past but that also contains within it the seeds of a future to be grasped creatively through imagination and effort. The learning of the present is not merely a doing of the done thing, an inertial obedience to a favored ideology. It is an invitation to pupils, educators, families, and communities to create, through reflection, a desired and meaningful tomorrow. A sense of purpose is active, not passive; it is a call to engagement and thus the energizing of latent capacities. A school or community with reflective purpose is liberated from slavery to the mindless momentum of the past, as well as the fads and fashions of the present, free to pursue the lead of deliberate and self-renewing ideals.

Vision, in our sense, is not mere wishful fantasy. The guiding purposes it projects are based not only on an appreciation of the past but also on an engagement with the practical possibilities of the present. The educational activities that it guides are founded on realistic perspectives, not on prophecy or nostalgia. An educational vision offers a map of the current possibilities of action, but it also develops an itinerary that takes us from where we are, through realistic steps, to a future illuminated by our purposes. It defines overarching educational goals but also suggests strategies for approaching them.

Visions are not commands. They are not rigid, incapable of modification in course. To the contrary, they typically change and grow in the process of being acted upon. Like ordinary itineraries, they change in response to the experiences to which they lead. Their function is to energize our actions in certain directions, but they respond to the consequences of the actions they stimulate. As well, they respond, as do maps, to changes in the environments of action. A road map a decade old will be misleading, preparing the tourist to travel in an environment that no longer exists. In sum, visions need to be sensitive to relevant change; as such, they offer continuous guidance to our efforts. Rigid visions are unintelligent; actions lacking intelligent visions are blind.

The power of educational visions is amply evident in the history of educational thought, both in the general and in the Jewish sphere. One need only mention the names of Plato and Aristotle in ancient times, and those of Rousseau, Pestalozzi, Herbart, and Dewey in modern times to be aware of such power. The ideas of John Dewey, to take the most familiar twentieth-century example, responded to the new intellectual climate comprised of the modern experimental and biological sciences, as well as the new forces of urbanization and industrialization, by reconceiving the tasks of education as requiring enhanced critical thinking in the developing industrial community.[4] Such ideas helped to transform American education in a short time, promoting the creation of new educational institutions, new forms of teacher education, and new curricular approaches, and dramatically influencing every corner of the field of education.

The popular conception of Dewey's educational doctrine equates it to the idea of "learning by doing," and proceeds to vulgarize it into a mere emphasis on the pupil's unguided activity. What is insufficiently understood is the motivation of Dewey's doctrine stemming from his theory of meaning. Dewey's view, in brief, is that meaning is always a matter of connections or relations, specifically, the relations between the actions we take and the consequences that result. Acquiring a knowledge of such relations depends on our noting the effects that our activities bring about. As our sense of such effects grows, our environment continues to grow in meaning. Learning, that is, the grasp of meanings, is thus always active rather than passive. As Dewey sums up his idea, learning is a matter of trying and undergoing: We do something to nature and receive what nature does to us in return.

Experience in this light approximates experiment as practiced in modern science. Although the ancients disparaged practice as mere routine and associated it with the local knowledge of the trades and crafts, modern science sees practice as the primary source of our general knowledge of nature, for its method is one of experimentation carried out deliberately in the interest of inquiry.

The key to Dewey's idea of education is to conceive the school as an active environment for learning, encouraging the connection of the student's intentional acts with their consequences, in such a way as to promote an enhanced understanding of oneself and one's environment. The school should not oppose practice; it should intellectualize practice by putting it to systematic use in the promotion of meanings. The technical activities made possible by science are to be viewed always in light of their consequences for human life. "Learning by doing" is thus seen not only to derive from a philosophical vision of meaning, but also to respond to the twin challenges of modern science and the new social forces sweeping America. Far from a mere emphasis on unguided activity, it provides systematic depth and range to an educational practice undergoing challenge by new circumstances.

We will here cite two major visions of Jewish life, one medieval and one modern, that emerged under radically different political, social, and intellectual conditions, conditions that in each case posed radical challenges to the Jewish people. The philosophy of Maimonides (1135–1204), to take our first example, represented, among other things, his effort to meet the threat of Aristotelianism to traditional Jewish belief. In this effort, he succeeded brilliantly, forming a synthesis of the premier scientific and philosophical conceptions of his day with Jewish thought, and, at the same time, producing a radically new systematization of the content of such thought. He neither rejected the traditions of his Jewish heritage nor turned his face against the intellectual currents of his cultural environment. Consistent with his new system, he devoted significant parts of his writing to education and to the sources upon which he took education to be based.

Throughout his writings, but particularly in his major works, *The Guide of the Perplexed* and the *Mishneh Torah,* he presented his conceptions of the ideal human being, the ideal society, and the nature of knowledge and learning. These conceptions served as the foundation for his chapter on pedagogy, *Hilkhot Talmud Torah,* the *Laws of Torah Study*, in the *Mishneh Torah.* He conceived of education as character education. Based on study of the Bible, the Talmud, and the rabbinic commentaries, the practice of *mitzvot* (proper actions) shapes a person's character through habituation, "habituation" itself being a central concept of Aristotle's ethics. Habituation is, for Maimonides, a precondition for undertaking philosophical inquiry, the pinnacle of a successful Jewish education, and the way to approach and cultivate the love of God. Maimonides' writings on Jewish law and philosophy created a school of educational as well as philosophical thought, and stimulated the rise of opposing schools with alternative visions of education.

Our second example concerns the establishment of the State of Israel, commonly told in terms of the efforts of *ḥalutzim* (pioneers) in the areas of settlement, agriculture, and defense. When one learns of the role of education, however, it becomes apparent that it had no less importance – perhaps even more – in meeting the challenge of a wholly new social and political situation drastically different from the Diaspora milieu. Driven by a small group of educational leaders, early Zionist education itself was responsible for the training of the *ḥalutzim* and for their mobilization in building the infrastructure for the Jewish state. Furthermore, these educators provided a redefinition of Jewish life in terms that had widespread appeal and served as a basis of continuity for Jews around the world.

The main asset of the early Zionist educators was a clear ideological vision of education. Four major points stand out in this vision: The first point was the status of Hebrew as a living language. The aim here was to transform Hebrew so that it would provide a comprehensive linguistic basis for Jewish life. For this purpose, new words would have to be invented and diffused, textbooks in such areas as chemistry and geography would have to be written for the first time, and a whole generation of adults would have to be retrained to speak in a different language. Alongside this came the second point – the integration of the Jewish and general aspects of existence. Living Hebrew was only one means toward the attainment of this end. In addition, an attempt would be made to extend the range of meaningful Jewish existence to the diverse areas of society, politics, economics, and culture. No longer would Jewish life be limited to special institutions, such as synagogues and study houses; rather, all aspects of living, ranging from stamp collecting to municipal politics, would be seen as an expression of Jewish identity.

The natural historical setting for this comprehensive Jewish life would be the land of Israel. The third point in the early Zionist vision of Jewish education thus demanded a new perspective on Jewish history and the introduction of hitherto unknown Jewish educational practices, such as hiking and touring, that would instill love of the land. Finally, the fourth point introduced the most challenging aim: to incorporate Jewish tradition into national consciousness. This forced educators to present Judaism anew so that it could serve as a basis for good citizenship for the Jewish people in the State of Israel.[5]

These historical visions responded to the challenges of their times. They do not, however, offer appropriate guidance for the problems of Jewish education in our own times, since the social and cultural circumstances, both in Israel and the Diaspora, have changed radically. In these altered circumstances, large numbers of Jews have become ignorant of Jewish knowledge and alienated from Jewish life. Religious rifts in Israel and elsewhere have intensified, the polarization between Orthodox and secular elements of the Jewish population reaching danger levels. The split between Israeli and American Jewry over the issue of religious pluralism threatens to tear the worldwide community apart. The American Jewish population has reached unprecedented levels of assimilation. The contemporary challenge to Jewish education is clear and severe. What is required is fresh and energetic thinking about the Jewish future and its rationale, in view of the desperate circumstances we face. We need, in sum, new efforts to formulate the philosophical basis of Jewish existence in our own day.

Such an effort cannot be accomplished in one stroke. Nor is it the work of a single person or an individual essay, or even a whole set of tomes. The project that the present book inaugurates does not pretend to supply a definitive and comprehensive response to the needs we have outlined. Our purpose is, rather, to initiate a continuing discourse within the Jewish community on the vital theme of educational vision, to supplement other constructive educational efforts already in place.

We do not suppose that such a discourse is the exclusive province of educators or scholars. If it is to be effective, it should elicit the thinking of all concerned segments of the Jewish public, whatever their vocation, profession, or communal affiliation. Furthermore, such discourse should build on the plural perspectives within the community, which differ on the very issues of educational purpose and the envisaged future. We hope for a strengthening of Jewish education within such varying perspectives and for a respectful educational dialogue across their divisions, a dialogue from which all may learn.

NOTES

1 Leon Roth, *Judaism: A Portrait* (London: Faber and Faber, 1960), 216–17. For Jewish communities in Arab lands as well, emancipation began later but presented these communities with the same predicament. See Yaron Tzur, *Kehillah Keru'ah: Yehudei Morocco ve-ha Leumiut, 1943–1954* (Tel Aviv: Am Oved, 2001).

2 Israel Scheffler, "Jewish Education: Purposes, Problems and Possibilities," in *Curriculum, Community, Commitment,* ed. D. J. Margolis and E. S. Schoenberg (West Orange, NJ: Behrman House, 1992), 21–2.

3 See D. Marom, "*Haguto u-Foalo shel Benzion Dinur ke-Meḥanekh*" (Ph.D. diss., Hebrew University of Jerusalem, 2000). Since the establishment of the State of Israel, every minister of education has invested resources to strengthen Jewish studies with, however, disappointing results. In 1996, the Shenhar Commission report, sponsored by the Ministry of Education, found the teaching of Jewish studies in the general system of education to be clearly inadequate.

4 See Israel Scheffler, "John Dewey: Biographical Comments," in *Four Pragmatists* (London: Routledge & Kegan Paul, 1974), 187–96.

5 For analyses of the foundational themes of Zionist education, see B. Dinur, "*Ha-Reka ha-Histori ve-ha-Ḥevrati ha-Medini shel ha-Ḥinukh be-Yisrael,*" in *Arakhim u-Derakhim: Ba'ayot Ḥinukh ve-Tarbut be-Yisrael* (Tel Aviv: Urim, 1958), and M. Rosenstein, " 'Ha-Yehudi he-Ḥadash': Ha-Idial shel Mifal ha-Ḥinukh ha-Tzioni be-Eretz Yisrael Im Kom ha-Medinah," in *Studies in Jewish Education* 3 (1988): 75–101. (See also R. Elboim-Dror, *Ha-Ḥinukh ha-Ivri be-Eretz Yisrael*) (Jerusalem: Yad Ben-Zvi, 1986, 1990).

2

The Project in Operation

In our last chapter, we urged the critical importance of vision for a revitalized Jewish education. Accordingly, we argued for vigorous new efforts to formulate overall conceptions of Jewish life and to articulate their corresponding visions of the ends and means of Jewish learning. Our hope was that ensuing processes of reflection and debate would deepen our educational thought and enhance the quality of our educational practice. These ideas, elaborated in Chapter 1, explain the background and motivation of our project – the "why" of our efforts. Now we turn to the "what"; what did the project attempt, how was it organized, and what did it do?

The project aimed, first of all, to create a sample of what it was urging for the community at large, a serious conversation among proponents of variant conceptions of Jewish life and their attendant visions of Jewish education. It needed, thus, to elicit a number of relevant visions and create a forum within which they could be set forth and elaborated, confronted with alternatives, and debated in a collegial but critical atmosphere. Secondly, it sought to encourage analogous conversations within institutions and communities.

The initial step was to elicit the visions, and that presupposed forming a working group of those who were to supply them. To this end, the Mandel Foundation (then the Mandel Institute), represented by the project's director, Seymour Fox, and associate director, Daniel Marom, decided in 1991 to convene a group of scholars who were both learned in their special fields of study and knowledgeable about Jewish education and who, moreover, were likely to integrate these qualities into visions of Jewish learning, drawing upon comprehensive conceptions of Jewish life.

The group consisted of the following: Isadore Twersky, Menachem Brinker, Moshe Greenberg, Michael A. Meyer, Michael Rosenak, Israel Scheffler, Seymour Fox, and Daniel Marom.

The group was invited to consider such questions as "What is an educated Jew?" "What does an educated Jew need to know?" "What would you consider to be the product of a successful Jewish education?" The members of the group were then to draft an essay responding to these or related questions. In addition, they were asked to read their colleagues' drafts and to respond to them with written questions and comments.

The first meeting of the group took place at Harvard University in the winter of 1992, with Brinker, Fox, Greenberg, Marom, Rosenak, Scheffler, and Twersky. Each session during the four-day meeting followed the same format: Every member of the group began by responding to the written comments and questions of the assembled colleagues addressed to his own draft. Lively discussion of the draft ensued, which typically continued for several hours, focusing on the fundamental premises and key arguments of the draft in question. The Harvard meeting, as a whole, served the purpose of introducing the scholars to one another, giving them the chance to become acquainted with their several points of view and to measure their own ideas against those of the rest. Following the meeting, notes of the discussions, prepared by the project staff, were made available to the scholars and suggestions given to them for possible editorial changes in preparation for follow-up meetings.

A second meeting of the group took place in Jerusalem in the spring of 1992. Here, the group was supplemented by selected educators, who joined in continuing intensive discussions of the scholars' revised drafts. This supplementation accorded with the project's aim of extending the initial conversations to a wider sphere of concerned constituencies. It served the additional purpose of providing feedback from such constituencies to the scholars, thus affording them a broader sense of the import of their educational visions as initially formulated.

Further opportunities to engage others outside the group occurred as the scholars were invited to present their ideas individually to various audiences. In addition, the scholars exchanged their subsequent drafts with one another, and met regularly in individual sessions with project staff to discuss the continuing evolution of their formulations. This process of regular consultations, additional presentations, and editorial refinements continued until 1997. At this time, the scholars were asked to compose introductions to their papers summarizing their conceptions of an ideal and feasible Jewish education for our time. The point of this request was to move the project from the stage of reflection and discussion to that of projected publication for a general audience.

The span of so many years from the project's inception to the point of beginning to prepare for publication was due only in part to logistic and other practical factors. The process of organizing appropriate meetings in the United States and in Jerusalem should be mentioned in this connection, as well as the related problem of arranging the outside audiences for scholars' individual presentations. In addition, Michael Meyer joined the group later, in 1994, and the project suffered the incalculable loss of a key scholar when Isadore Twersky died in 1997.

Beyond these matters, however, was the project's premise that the most urgent need in the field of Jewish education at present is provision of the time to think. The directors thus insisted that the scholars be given sufficient time to refine their conceptions, not only in response to feedback from colleagues and outside audiences but also as a result of the internal development of their own reflections. The years of ongoing thinking and intellectual exchange gave scholars and project staff the breathing room to explore, extend, apply, and reformulate their initial responses to the key questions of the project.

A primary stimulus to the rethinking of initial positions was the series of exchanges with scholars holding opposing views. Energetic challenges by scholarly peers in open-ended discussions understandably raised the emotional temperature, but they produced light as well as heat, as they exposed fundamental differences in approach.

One example that will stand for many was the early and continuing debate over the uses to be made of the works of great Jewish thinkers of the past. Was the appropriate response to the project's central questions to be fundamentally classical or, rather, contemporary? Was it to take as its initial focus exposition of the thought of past luminaries or was it, rather, to focus from the outset on the educational dilemmas posed by the intellectual and social circumstances of our own day?

To take the historical approach seemed, on the one hand, to be the more modest course, relying on the authority of acknowledged masters of the past and eschewing bold assertions based only on present opinion. On the other hand, to rest with exposition of past writers seemed to be scanting the task of dealing with pressing problems now needing urgent attention. The continuing argumentation over this issue was vigorous as well as enlightening, and each side of the argument profited by the exchange, which led to modifications of both positions.

Another example concerned the question of ideology versus family as a basis for Jewish allegiance. Was such allegiance to be construed as acceptance of a certain set of religious doctrines or was it, rather, to be thought of as the natural result of one's having been reared in a comprehensive Jewish environment with its animating family feeling? The centrality of religious doctrine, it was argued, was peculiarly fitted to the Diaspora, where Jews lived in the midst of an open society incapable of yielding the family allegiance natural to Israeli Jews living in a majority Jewish culture. On this view, the doctrinal interpretation of Jewish allegiance in the Diaspora, though understandable, must nevertheless fail if it is to be liberal, that is, favorable to Jews' participating fully in their majority cultures.

On the contrary, argued others, a merely social construal of Jewish allegiance would lead to assimilation even in Israel, tending to degrade the moral, legal, and spiritual climate because it lacked anchorage in religious tradition. The opposition of views expressed on the question of ideology versus family proved to be a recurrent theme of project discussions, and ramified, as we have seen, into the question of Israel–Diaspora relations, as well as issues of assimilation and intermarriage. Each side, on this issue, benefited from the strong statements of the opposite position, and led to an effort, by each side, to rethink the question and accommodate emphases otherwise scanted. The group, as a whole, was united in its recognition both of the unique value of classical Jewish writings and of the need to seek new understandings of this heritage, given present realities.

A natural outgrowth of the project's educational focus was the effort to relate the central aspects of each scholar's vision to the details of practice. For example, a scholar might emphasize the need to nurture spirituality. Such an emphasis is, however, not sufficient to guide parents and other educators in generating of experiences that might be expected to foster this quality. For purposes of education, spirituality cannot remain an abstraction. Rather, it must be nurtured through specific subject matters and processes suitable both for learner and educator.

Taking the Bible as an educational resource, how can a biblical text be understood as a resource for the encouragement of spirituality? How do the words need to be perceived – as literal or metaphorical truth, as practical guide or symbolic vehicle? How do the words need to be presented by the educator – in Hebrew or translation, as truer than other religious texts or as their equal? Which passages are most relevant – the Exodus narrative, biblical laws, or the poetry of the prophets? What is the surrounding culture's approach to the Bible, and how will that affect the educational experience? Only when "spirituality" is brought down to earth – analyzed through specific educational contingencies – can it become useful to the educator.

We mentioned earlier that the second meeting of the group included educators, whose specific role it was to examine the scholars' formulations for their applications to practice. (See "The Visions Project: Participants and Forums.") The educators' guiding interest was to press the scholars with the question, "Is the vision you have articulated feasible in education?"

These educators were diverse in their Jewish commitments (from stringently Orthodox to Israeli secular) and in their subject expertise (Bible, Talmud, Jewish philosophy, Jewish history, the arts, Israel, and the Holocaust). They also varied in their academic specialties: research on Jewish education, teacher training and leadership training, educational administration and curriculum design. Finally, they varied in their developmental focus (young children, adolescents, and adults) and the settings in which they worked (both formal and informal).

Despite this range, they shared an approach to education based on practical experience, thus providing a necessary counterweight to the scholarly predilections for theory alone. All were reflective about their practice in light of philosophical issues. Asked, for example, to explain their perspective on the teaching of Jewish texts, they might cite the work of Jewish scholars, of literary theorists, of philosophers of education, and of various approaches or experiments that had been tried in the field, with the advantages and disadvantages of each. Because both the scholars and educators were committed to the importance of vision in education, the discourse between the two groups was fruitful as well as challenging.

Some queries by the educators probed the bases of scholars' visions. One query was "If you had time to teach a person only one lesson, what would its subject be?" – a variant of the famous request made to Hillel by a would-be proselyte, "Will you teach me all I need to know about Judaism while standing on one foot?" Another query was "Would you accept any of the other scholars as a teacher in your school?" – a question calculated to explore the limits of the scholars' commitment to pluralism.

Challenging the position expressed by one of the scholars, that classical Jewish texts are the basis for all Jewish education, the educators pressed for a clarification of the role of Jewish history in such education, and stimulated the scholar's subsequent efforts to rethink the matter and try to provide a more substantial role for history in a Jewish curriculum. A more dramatic challenge to the self-sufficiency of classical texts for Jewish education occurred after the massacre, by a Jewish settler, of 29 Moslems praying at a mosque in Hebron in 1994 and the assassination, by a Jew, of Prime Minister Yitzhak Rabin in 1995.

The educators had been continually criticizing the emphasis on classical texts as the exclusive focus of Jewish education, pressing the point that such texts include verses containing obsolete or potentially dangerous matter. This criticism became urgent after these tragic events, since the murderers had, in both cases, purported to be carrying out directives imposed on them by classical Jewish texts. As a result, one of the scholars published a new paper defending the classical canon as the basis of contemporary Jewish education, while guarding it from fundamentalist readings sanctioning violence.

We have said that the first aim of the project was to initiate a serious conversation among proponents of variant conceptions of Jewish life and their associated visions of Jewish education, the second aim being the encouragement of similar conversations within the wider community. Having sketched what the project did in pursuing the first aim, we turn now to some efforts undertaken in pursuit of the second.

As the various formulations of the scholars developed, the project's staff shared them with a variety of audiences: with educators, parents, school board members, community leaders, and Jewish Federation executives and planners. The codirectors then reported the responses and questions of these audiences to the several scholars concerned. In addition, arrangements were made for individual scholars to present their ideas to professional and community leaders and to leaders of training programs around the world.

These diverse audiences served to bring home the practical consequences of the project. Many participants, for example, raised questions stemming from their immediate concerns: "Should I send my child to a Jewish school?" "Which summer camp most corresponds with our family's outlook?" "What sort of educator should we hire to teach in our community high school?"

Such dialogues between the participants and the scholars were consequential for both. One community leader criticized a scholar's emphasis on text study as a lack of "Jewish heart." As a result, the scholar in question rethought his formulation, emphasizing a strong emotional dimension to his approach to Jewish education.

Sometimes it was the participants rather than the scholars who were led to reconsider their earlier conceptions as a result of the conversation. In one case, a group of Orthodox Israeli educators found themselves unexpectedly intrigued by a non-Orthodox scholar's emphasis on peoplehood in Jewish education. In another, a group of secular educators found the same paper vulnerable to the criticism that it was intolerant of nonestablishment Israelis.

One scholar's formulation emphasized the importance of focusing on minimal elements shared by all visions of Jewish education. This emphasis expressed the hope that in our fragmented and partisan era, Jews might nevertheless find that they held certain common educational convictions. The formulation persuaded a group of American community leaders and Federation planners that a serious attempt to explore common elements in their community's views might indeed evoke a positive response. Such a response, they thought, would be likely to find substantial numbers of people willing to moderate their conflicting views in order to gain a genuine community consensus. The promise of possible consensus, even on a small scale, and even within given communities, has continued to inspire project efforts to engage broader audiences in attempts to envision a Jewish education for our time.

We have, in the previous chapter, outlined the "why" of our project, while the present chapter has outlined the "what." In the next chapter we shall introduce the works of our scholars and try to indicate the variations among their several visions of Jewish education. We shall, in sum, address the question, "What difference might a vision make?"

3

Six Visions: An Overview

The purpose of this chapter is to introduce the reflections on visions of Jewish education outlined by members of the project's working group. The actual essays of these scholars will appear in succeeding chapters. What we propose to do here is decidedly not to replace those essays, but rather to provide an entry to them, sketching some of their main features, and proceeding to compare and contrast their approaches. We hope thus to facilitate a subsequent study of the essays themselves. We begin, then, with the work of Isadore Twersky.

Twersky, the historian and specialist in Jewish thought, is committed to a conception of Judaism that places philosophical understanding at the core of Jewish living. For Twersky, the practices of Judaism cannot be separated from the ideas and ideals of Judaism. If properly educated, the human being has the potential to achieve harmony between philosophy and behavior, between the practice of *mitzvot* (proper actions) and the appreciation of their meanings.

Twersky bases his conception mainly, if not exclusively, on the writings of Maimonides, the great twelfth-century scholar, rabbi, and philosopher, whom he considers to have offered the most authoritative formulation of Jewish tradition. Following Maimonides, Twersky identifies Jewish practice with *halakhah*, Jewish law, as infused with philosophical understanding. The ultimate goal of education, in brief, is to achieve both an overriding love of God and a genuine worship of God – both a deep understanding and a true piety.

To approximate this goal requires a basis in habit, achieved through a process of habituation enriched by understanding. The term that Twersky uses for this process is *hergel* (habituation, but not in the sense of routinization). Twersky supported his use of this term with Maimonidean sources. The process begins with the child's learning through mere imitation at the earliest age, continues throughout life as an internalization of Jewish practice increasingly suffused with a grasp of its rational basis, acquired through philosophical study.

Initiated in the family, proper Jewish practice is modeled by loving parents who inculcate both the discipline of action in accordance with the commandments and the habit of regular study, which provides the motivational underpinning for such action. The early development of the child in such an environment proceeds by mimesis, that is, by imitation of the parents' conduct and character. This mimetic stage provides a basis upon which the child's ensuing development can proceed, adding spontaneity and increasing sophistication.

The continuous process of *hergel* is described by Maimonides as a lifelong enterprise. Its curricular basis consists of three parts: *Mikra, Mishnah,* and Talmud. *Mikra* is the Written Law, comprising the books of the Bible, the *Tanakh. Mishnah* is the codification of the Oral Law, produced by Rabbi Judah HaNassi about 200 C.E. Talmud comprises not only the reasoning underlying *Mikra* and *Mishnah* but also the study of philosophy.

The basic content of *Mikra* is indispensable for any attempt to understand and live by the tradition. The child's early education, encouraging imitation of loving adult figures, sets the stage for the cognitive experience of learning *Mikra,* where what has been acquired by mimesis is now described and explained in biblical texts, grounded in the Written Law. Learning to read is thus a cognitive achievement of central importance for Jewish education, since it yields access to the very heart of the tradition.

The laws, narrative, and parables of *Mikra* are to be understood, at the outset, on the level of *peshat,* the plain sense of the text. Thus understood, *Mikra* is the primary source of Jewish education. However, it remains central to the education of the maturing student and the adult, for whom the philosophical aspects of the text become increasingly paramount, embodied not only in the narratives, allegories, and laws of the Bible but also in their numerous interpretations by later commentators and philosophers.

Mishnah is the authoritative code of Jewish law and practice. It provides a comprehensive formulation of the Oral Law, a summary of the whole of the tradition as embodied in decisions emerging from discussions of the rabbis from biblical times to about 200 C.E. In an extended pedagogical sense, *"Mishnah"* is to be understood as including subsequent halakhic codifications as well. It does not, in general, however, incorporate an account of the detailed reasoning upon which its decisions rest, but embodies only such culminating decisions. This emphasis, to be sure, provides a necessary guide to practice, but it cannot be sufficient, for without an understanding of the background and spirit of a decision, it is likely to deteriorate into mere dogma. Talmud provides the required supplementation by comprising the underlying dialectic – the reasoning behind the code, as well as the intellectual basis for such further elaboration of the code as may be needed in the future.

Talmud, for Maimonides, thus incorporates the rationale behind the code of the *Mishnah* as well as the discussion of the *Mishnah* within the *Gemara,* and the discourses of commentators continuing the tradition of Jewish law, early and late.

Education should, in other words, provide not only the legal product but also an understanding of the legal process leading from biblical or mishnaic texts to their elaborations and eventual decisions. Maimonides, in an original extension of the conventional notion of Talmud, understands it to include also philosophy, inclusive of the study of non-Jewish thinkers, since basic truths are discovered in a variety of frames of thought.

For Twersky, *hergel* is by no means restricted to family or school. It is a form of lifelong learning that may take place in various settings. Informal education, summer camps, trips to Israel, youth groups, adult study groups – all have the potential not only for strengthening the commitment to traditional practice but also for deepening the philosophical understanding of such practice. Nor is *hergel,* in Twersky's view, appropriate only for the select few who are thought to have the requisite ability to gain philosophical sophistication. On the contrary, every person is capable of pursuing the sophistication of Talmud in some degree, and is indeed obligated to do so in accordance with his capacity. Every person, Maimonides assumes, by nature desires to improve his or her understanding, and every person thus presents a challenge and an opportunity to the educator to help foster such understanding as far as possible.

Twersky is concerned to reach not only weaker students with traditional backgrounds but also Jews who lack such backgrounds or are estranged from Jewish learning or community altogether. His confidence in education leads him to believe it possible to initiate the majority of Jewish adults outside the circle of Jewish learning into a process of *hergel* through a philosophical treatment of key traditional texts in various settings.

All this assumes a central role for the educator. The primary importance of parents as early role models is elaborated into a further emphasis on the selection and training of teachers who can continue in this role during the years following childhood. Indeed, Twersky's vision, in accordance with what he takes to be the main emphasis of Jewish education, tends to blur the distinction between parent and educator, both involved in the process of *hergel* throughout life, not only for their students but also for themselves.

Turning now to the ideas of Menachem Brinker, scholar of Hebrew literature and philosophy, we find ourselves in quite a different conceptual territory from that of Twersky. Brinker's heroes are modern rather than medieval, his outlook secular rather than religious, his orientation pluralist rather than orthodox. Brinker's sympathies lie with the revolutionary thinkers of the East European *Haskalah* (the Jewish Enlightenment of the nineteenth century) who helped shape the ideology of Zionism and whose ideas, he believes, have continuing relevance for our own period.

The changes wrought by such thinkers as Aḥad Ha-Am, Peretz Smolenskin, Micha Josef Berdyczewski, and Yosef Ḥayyim Brenner involved a radical shift in the self-definition of Jews from the religious to the social. Rather than conceiving of Jewish allegiance as based on acceptance of theological premises or halakhic practice, Brinker bases such allegiance on the Jews' recognition of their peoplehood. Jews, for him, are those who identify themselves with the Jewish people, committing their energies, talents, and fate to the well-being of this people, according to their personal beliefs about the world.

Such commitment may have various rationales, religious, nonreligious, or antireligious. But whatever its rationale in the individual case, it implies affiliation with the historical heritage of Judaism, emotional and intellectual involvement with the Jewish people, and participation in Jewish society. The variety of Jewish rationales presupposes individual freedom of thought and decision, a freedom capable of supporting a culturally rich society and a personally enriched Jewish life. Society should therefore take an active educational role in offering individuals maximal freedom in charting their own course, and providing the tools to do so responsibly and effectively. One such tool is individuals' historical awareness of their own people, in the light of which they can participate in debates over its future.

The involvement of individuals with their own people does not, for Brinker, conflict with their concern for universal values and interests in humanity at large. Jewish peoplehood is, after all, one instance of humanity, of which other peoples represent other instances. A people offers particular idioms, languages, and styles by which its members may express themselves and communicate with others. Through active membership in the historical Jewish people, Jews may thus authentically articulate their deepest thoughts and feelings, and at the same time, enter into conversations with members of other peoples on issues of common concern.

According to Brinker, education works with what he assumes is the human being's natural need to belong. This need is an asset to the educator in helping focus learners on their particular heritage. But it is also dangerous in that too intense a feeling of belonging may lead to a narrow and stifling provincialism. The educator's task is to satisfy the learners' need to acknowledge their heritage while challenging them to make their own way through it freely and critically, choosing from its riches those elements deemed of overriding value.

In emphasizing freedom of thought and decision, Brinker conceives Jewish education as a part of liberal-humanistic education in general, empowering individuals to develop their own skills, values, and knowledge of the world, at the same time that they acquire enhanced understanding of their own heritage. Such understanding, Brinker believes, enables learners not only to improve their Jewish environment but also to communicate with other peoples and cooperate with them out of the depth of their particularism. Education must therefore refrain from presenting the Jewish world as all-inclusive and all-encompassing, building into it instead the knowledge of other worlds and the need for interaction with them. The Jewish educator, for Brinker, should be comfortable and conversant with world culture and involved in an enriching interchange between the Jewish world and what lies beyond it.

Brinker offers a variety of curricular recommendations for Jewish education. At the earliest ages, the child should acquire the Hebrew language as a basic means of expression, the calendar and customs that enable participation in living Jewish culture, and familiarity with concepts and events of Jewish history preserved in the collective memory.

Beyond this initial stage, the educative program will continue and deepen learners' prior socialization into Jewish life while maximizing their development as autonomous individuals capable of thinking freely and critically about their own Jewish environment. A program of study appropriate to this goal should, Brinker believes, contain at least three components: Jewish history, Jewish thought, and Hebrew language and literature.

Jewish history, to begin with, should give an account of Jewish life over time leading up to and informing the present. It should emphasize pluralism and tolerance of others in the Jewish world, enabling the learner to understand and empathize with alternative ways of Jewish life. To this end, Jewish education should foster awareness not only of the common experiences and epoch-making events in Jewish history, but also of the major divisions within that history, inclusive of its crises, rifts, and disintegrative events.

The second component, Jewish thought, should focus on large common themes in Jewish life – for example, Jewish self-definition, Jewish uniqueness, causes of Jewish suffering and suggestions for its relief, and relations between the ancient period of Jewish history and the present. The treatment of such themes should include not only writings by Jewish philosophers but also the ideas of political leaders, literary intellectuals, social critics, and others. Such study should deepen learners' understanding of their Jewish condition, and encourage their confrontation with problems and themes intrinsic to it.

The third component that Brinker proposes is Hebrew language and literature, aimed at enriching the capacity of Hebrew to channel the learner's interchange with the world. Brinker's suggested program draws on Hebrew texts from all periods and areas of life. Thus, for example, Talmud would be included as a resource for legal language and terminology, as well as selections from the Torah, the prophets, Midrash, Maimonides' *Mishneh Torah* and *The Guide of the Perplexed*, the secular and religious poetry of Solomon ibn Gabirol, and tales of the Hasidim.

Brinker emphasizes the last 200 years in the belief that they were more significant than all the preceding period in shaping current Jewish conditions. In his curriculum as a whole, he wants content from the modern period to comprise at least half of what is to be studied. The Jewish studies he proposes are, furthermore, to be integrated into a larger curriculum inclusive of general studies, as well as a treatment of world cultures and world history.

Brinker recognizes the need for different curricular emphases in Israel and in the Diaspora. In the latter case, conscious decisions have to be made if Jewish affiliation is to be assured. In Israel, however, the civic obligations of Jews leave them no choice as to membership in the Jewish family. Thus, Diaspora Jewish education is left with the difficult challenge of emphasizing the uniqueness and vitality of Jewish life so as to promote the learner's choosing to participate in it. In Israeli education, on the other hand, education must guard against the degeneration of the natural sense of belonging into a fascist fundamentalism that undermines Israel's democracy and liberalism. There, such education must provide an emphasis on free thought, critical thinking, and democratic values.

In brief, Brinker's vision of the positive outcome of Jewish education is the learner's involvement with Jewish life – an involvement passionate but free, capable not only of invigorating Jewish life but of contributing to the flourishing of humanity.

Before going on to discuss the work of our third scholar, we may pause briefly to contrast the visions of the foregoing two. We have already noted that Twersky's conception is essentially religious while that of Brinker is decidedly secular. Intellectual authority, for Twersky, is to be found in the classical writers of the halakhic tradition, notably Maimonides, whereas Brinker locates such authority in those modern Hebrew writers who helped form the ideology of Zionism.

What such authority provides is, however, different in the visions of these two scholars. Twersky wants the halakhic tradition to be inculcated in the learner, both ideologically and practically. The student successfully educated according to his scheme is one who has come to accept the major doctrines of the *halakhah* as well as the philosophical assumptions underpinning it, and who abides by halakhic requirements in all areas of conduct. Brinker's aim is to achieve the learner's commitment to participate in Jewish society, on the basis of an understanding of its historical roots and current problems, but to do so in any way that he or she freely chooses, without doctrinal presuppositions or uniformity of practice.

Twersky's educational aim takes perpetuation of the classical corpus of rabbinic tradition as its primary goal. By contrast, Brinker's educational program points learners toward the problems affecting contemporary Jewish life, and challenges them to deal with such problems by their own lights.

Twersky's vision of Jewish education makes no fundamental distinctions between Israel and the Diaspora. In both cases, the course of learning is to proceed by internalizing the *halakhah* in the learner and progressively sophisticating the learner's grasp of it. By contrast, Brinker's vision sharply distinguishes Jewish education in Israel from that of the Diaspora, because Israel provides an encompassing majority culture to the Jew, whereas the Diaspora does not.

This basic distinction has a number of corollaries. First, without a majority culture to support it, Diaspora Jewish education necessarily has to emphasize the religious teachings of traditional Judaism, ruling out nonreligious and antireligious construals of Jewishness. Second, Brinker's view of Diaspora Jewish education is thus pessimistic, since he holds it to be opposed to free thought and believes, further, that it cannot survive the overwhelming influence of the non-Jewish majority culture in weakening Jewish allegiance.

A consequence of the difference between Twersky and Brinker with regard to Diaspora Jewish education is that they support quite different attitudes toward Hebrew. For Twersky, while Hebrew is important as the original repository of the classics of the tradition – the Bible, the Talmud, the Midrash, the responsa, and so on – other languages used by halakhic thinkers and educators are also important, for example, Aramaic, Arabic, Yiddish, English, and so on. All are actual or potential instruments of halakhic and philosophical education, inclusive of primary writings in these languages as well as originals and translations from the Hebrew. Brinker, on the contrary, takes Hebrew as an indispensable requirement of Jewish education – as a vernacular defining the Jewish family's live culture in Israel and channeling the continuing development of such culture.

Another contrast between Twersky and Brinker has to do with the role of non-Jewish thought. For Twersky, the core of Jewish education is the *halakhah,* tempered as it is by increasing philosophical sophistication. Philosophy, whether Jewish or not, serves the function of strengthening the internalization of halakhic life by increasing its rational basis. For Brinker, Jewish education itself is but a part of a general liberal-humanistic education whose basis is free thought and democratic culture. Non-Jewish thought is not a mere force bolstering Jewish allegiance but, rather, a value in its own right. Philosophy is to be undertaken freely, without prejudging its impact on Jewish allegiance; it is to be followed wherever it leads. Non-Jewish cultural achievements are, in general, to be esteemed for their intrinsic worth, as well as brought into the circle of Jewish life through their interaction with the writings and writers of modern Hebrew.

The likely impact of all the foregoing differences on the training of the Jewish educator, the climate of the school, the curriculum of Jewish learning, the settings for such learning, and many other aspects of education should be kept in mind by the reader as useful categories in dealing with the works we have encountered and those we have yet to discuss.

The essay of the biblical scholar Moshe Greenberg presents a third conception of Jewish education. Like Twersky's conception and unlike Brinker's, it is religious rather than secular. But, like Brinker's approach and unlike Twersky's, it emphasizes the student's freedom of interpretation rather than the internalization of authoritative halakhic belief and practice. Greenberg sees religions not primarily as systems of ideology or ritual, but rather as responses to the universal quest for meaning and value in life – for answers to such questions as "Whence have I come and whither am I going?" and "What is the good path for one to choose?" Jewish education, in particular, aims to introduce the Jewish child to the masterworks of Judaism, as a basis for continuing the search for transcendent meaning and value in his world.

These masterworks are not monolithic; they comprise a wide variety of genres and styles, including but not limited to narratives, poetry, law, parable, and ethical maxims. The common thread in this variegated literature is its "primary purpose . . . to instruct in the way of goodness." Jewish education, offering access to this literature, provides students with a treasury of value concepts by which to infuse their raw experience with meaning and order. The success of such an education is to be measured by its capacity to remain with students as nourishment for the whole of life's journey.

The curriculum of an ideal Jewish education, for Greenberg, consists in the basic books of Judaism – Bible, Talmud, and Midrash, as well as traditional and modern commentaries, and creative works translating such books into contemporary idiom. Representative selections of such sources are to be taught in such a way as to touch students' hearts, dealing with the vital existential questions that concern them. The ultimate educational goal is for students to engage such questions through an encounter with authentic Jewish sources and to discover their own Jewish identity in the process.

Jewish education, according to Greenberg, ought in particular to foster four qualities:

1. Love of learning Torah and love of the fulfillment of the commandments between man and God: Learning Torah for its own sake constitutes contact with the inherently valuable. The commandments, such as observing the Sabbath, prayers, blessings, and so on, are symbolic of a realm that transcends the merely material and the utilitarian; they affirm the enduring validity of the good both in the universe and in human beings.
2. Acceptance of the Torah as a moral guide, along with the recognition that its moral precepts have undergone constant reinterpretation: The recognition is to be fostered that the moral precepts of the Torah can serve us as a guide in our own day, given the continual process of rethinking and reevaluation essential to such guidance.
3. A way of life that creates a community: A good many of the precepts of Judaism are social and presuppose public-communal institutions, such as schools, synagogues, loan funds, and so on. Such precepts and institutions foster a community that not only strengthens friendship, neighborliness, and self-help but also provides an ideal setting for the raising of children in a Jewish way of life.

4. A relationship to the Jewish people in all the lands of their dispersion: The unity of the people requires a consciousness of common origins, a common existential status (members of the people of the Covenant), and a common vision of the future redemption. These three components are embodied in the national-historical saga of the Bible and rabbinic literature; the internalization of this saga is essential to creating a Jewish identity.

Diaspora Jews and the Jews of Israel, facing very different problems of existence, are in danger of increasing mutual alienation. Only the cultivation of common sources of inspiration can preserve the unity of these two communities – that is, the study of Torah, the ideal of sanctity, and moral values drawn from the basic books under continual interpretation. The Hebrew language is essential for a truly meaningful Jewish education, and the cultivation of Hebrew requires special commitment by Diaspora communities.

Greenberg's fundamental claim is that the basic books of Judaism are capable of meeting the spiritual needs of the learner. Hence, there is no need for dogmatic assumptions about these works in order to justify their being studied. The literary corpus comprising the religious history of the Jews, and thus defining Judaism itself, is central for Jewish education. The material history of Jews, while obviously essential to their spiritual history, is secondary in importance and should by no means dominate the curriculum. It reinforces national consciousness, to be sure, and adds aesthetic value to the study of Jewish culture, but "when it comes to giving meaning to Jewish life . . . the basic books are our primary educational resource." Such books do not, of course, stand in isolation. Jews always have interacted, and should continue to interact, with the cultural environments in which they find themselves. In such interaction, values originating in external sources are to be assimilated into Jewish idioms, thus protecting Judaism from obsolescence and petrification.

Greenberg's approach departs from tradition in various ways. For example, he does not require that the teacher of Bible assent to the answers given in the Bible to outstanding questions: "The basic requirement of a Bible teacher is not faith but understanding, not assent but recognition of the profound issues of which the Bible treats." For another example, he regards the Genesis story not as literal truth but as a fable that, like a Platonic myth, expresses in a striking, imaginary way profound insights: "What is important is that the fabulist had the insight to light upon an aspect of moral reality, and the artistry to articulate it memorably."[1] Thus, the conflict between science and the Bible is alleviated.

Greenberg's faith in the educational power of Jewish texts does not preclude supplementary educational efforts. The capacity to undertake the sort of instruction Greenberg outlines is enhanced by settings in which the learner's peers and elders are all engaged in the study and application of Jewish texts as part of their everyday living. And he hopes that educational institutions will also use such symbols and practices as prayer, festival rituals and celebrations, acts of charity, and so on to make the spiritual realm palpable to learners. Finally, he expects Jewish education to lead to social involvement, promoting a Jewish way of life that creates community.

Greenberg's educational approach promotes a synthesis of formal and informal educational frameworks, including schools, youth movements, community centers, and summer camps, where significant portions of the total substance of Jewish education can be experienced. In such environments, the pupils will indeed study the texts, but they will also experience what it is like to abide by the import of such texts in everyday life, as developed through discussion and reflection.

Thinking back to the previous essays we have discussed, certain comparisons and contrasts emerge. We noted Twersky's accommodation of other languages along with Hebrew as vehicles of Jewish education, in contrast to Brinker's upholding of Hebrew as the live vernacular of Israeli society. Greenberg's attitude differs from both, in that he gives the Hebrew language primacy not as vernacular but as the untranslatable vessel of authentic Jewish religious thought. Where Brinker was pessimistic about the prospects of Jewish survival in the Diaspora, while Twersky was supremely confident in the survival of both Israeli and Diaspora Jewry through halakhic education, Greenberg warns that Israeli and Diaspora communities can both survive creatively only if they recognize their differing problems and place their primary emphases upon their common religious heritage.

Greenberg, like Brinker, emphasizes the importance of interaction with surrounding cultures, but whereas Brinker sees the contributions of such cultures as often having independent and intrinsic worth, Greenberg wants such contributions to be deliberately assimilated into Jewish thought so as to be attainable through Jewish sources. Finally, whereas the core of Jewish education for Twersky is halakhic thought and practice, while for Brinker it is a free and passionate involvement in modern Jewish life, Greenberg takes as his central point classical Judaism's response to the existential strivings of human beings, and envisages Jewish education as promoting a deep and continuing encounter with such response throughout life.

Michael A. Meyer, historian of Judaism, addresses those in the Reform community in particular, but his message is by no means limited to this community. He writes out of a recognition of the historical tensions that have characterized the Jewish past, from the opposition between prophets and priests in ancient times to the conflict between tradition and modernity in the present. His conception of education is directed to the autonomous individual committed to the Jewish faith, yet equally committed to the values of liberalism. He hopes to honor the individual's autonomy by eschewing dogmatic inculcation of Jewish belief and practice but yet to influence the individual's choice by educating toward core Jewish values.

The educated Jew, for Meyer, is one who has chosen Judaism out of knowledge, whose identification with Jewish tradition, nurtured in the first instance by the warmth of home experiences, flows thereafter from an ever-deepening education in the substance of that tradition. This education ought not only to strengthen Jewish identity but also to make clear the boundaries between the Jewish and the non-Jewish spheres. The diminishing social separation of Jews from non-Jews in modern America indeed makes it imperative to define the Jewish religious realm unambiguously, so as to avoid its increasing erosion. The goal of Jewish education today, declares Meyer, is the creation of Jewishly educated Jews – those whose principal identity lies in being a Jew – as defined primarily in religious terms.

Openness to the world of multiple traditions, combined with primary religious allegiance to Judaism, requires a total education, fostering an awareness of the similarities and differences between Jewish and non-Jewish values. How do Jewish texts relate to parallel texts drawn from other traditions, for example, the Greco-Roman, the Christian, the Eastern religions? Consideration of such questions would enable students to see for themselves where the boundaries between Jewish and other traditions lie, and to reject the idea that Judaism is merely an ethnic variant of universal themes.

The liberal emphasis on autonomy conflicts with the normative emphasis of the tradition. Autonomy gives the child at best a set of choices from which to select, making him or her the master of the tradition, while the tradition is itself obligatory, making the child its servant. How to reconcile both free choice and obligation, so that the child is neither master nor servant of the tradition? Meyer proposes that the solution is to recognize that the tradition is religious and not merely cultural, the religious aspect, as distinct from the cultural, aiming to direct life, not merely enhance it. Insofar as Jewish education is cultural it is, in effect, completely open to choice; insofar as it is religious, it is not neutral but aims frankly to instill Jewish values rather than simply to inform concerning them. Nor should Jewish religious texts be freely interpreted so as to bring them into harmony with contemporary liberal predilections. Such predilections must be frankly acknowledged as products of modernity, not religiosity. The texts themselves require interpretations as products of their own historical times and should not be distorted into versions of our own present-day notions.

The implementation of Meyer's conception requires primary emphasis on the home, the first community of Jewish learning. Only when common commitments to Jewish learning are forged in the home can the school then take over as the second community of learning. Entire families must be educated together under the auspices of the synagogue so that eventually the home can resume the role of primary educator. In the school communities, teachers serve as models and fellow learners, reinforcing the desired emotional commitment as well as providing the intellectual substance.

Meyer's curriculum for the Jewish school emphasizes both ethnic awareness and religious knowledge – Jewishness and Judaism. Hebrew is critical to both, being not only the chief cultural attribute of the Jewish people but also the sacred bridge between God and Israel, the language of Torah and of prayer. Ethnic awareness requires, further, the study of Jewish history and of contemporary Jewish life everywhere, bolstering solidarity. Diaspora Jews need, especially, to learn about Jewish life in Israel, while Israeli Jews must learn about the Diaspora. Familiarity with Jewish tragedy, especially the Holocaust, and with modern Jewish literature are both important in developing a sense of common fate and shared culture comprising the ethnic element of Jewish education.

Ethnicity, however, is not enough. In America, Jewish ethnicity is being speedily absorbed by the majority culture; in Israel, it is being transformed from the Jewish to the Israeli. Only an education in religious belief and practice can sustain Jewish identity. Secularism is to be abjured not alone because it threatens Jewish survival but, more importantly, because the Jewish people is "fundamentally defined by its religion." Jewish learning differs from secular learning in addressing the ultimate questions of human existence.

It follows that Jewish religious texts are especially important for education. The attitude to be taken toward these texts is that they convey religious and ethical messages that the individual can, out of religious commitment, autonomously choose to accept as binding. Dissent as to particular texts is compatible with commitment to the tradition as a whole, which itself embodies variations in belief and practice.

Young children come to the texts unreflectively and uncritically. The texts they are taught embody value-laden stories naively acquired as the basis for a Jewish identity. As the children grow, the texts become elements in an increasingly critical understanding of their contexts. Story is transformed into history; Judaism becomes understood both as a developing process and as one that differs from other religious traditions. Yet the value-ladenness of story remains as a core of the growing Jewish identity.

For adults without an early Jewish education, the movement is the reverse. Entering the Jewish community with the critical attitudes inculcated by their general education, they may come increasingly to understand and absorb the values embedded in the texts they encounter. For them, history has turned into story. In both cases, the transition is neither sharp nor sudden; a gradual dialectic bridges story and history, commitment and critique.

The texts cannot be studied in isolation. They need to be studied within a community, preferably a community that practices Judaism together. The educated Jew thus becomes the observant Jew. But such a community is not monolithic. Members who function together in a practice may well differ in their theological rationales. Collective observance is compatible with ideological variation. The envisaged result of such an education is a Jewish self securely grounded in the Jewish community and the Jewish religion, and therefore able confidently to reach outward to the whole human community, and forward to the realization of universal ethical goals.

Reflecting on Meyer's vision in the light of the earlier essays we have discussed, we may note several points of interest. The paramount emphasis on freedom and autonomy in choice closely resembles Brinker's attitude, yet Meyer rejects secularism definitively in favor of a religious conception of Jewish identity. His religious conception is, however, patently diffuse by comparison with those of Twersky and Greenberg. Where Twersky hews to the *halakhah* with heavy emphasis on Maimonides' interpretation, and Greenberg emphasizes the quest for transcendent meaning and order to which the traditional text responds, Meyer speaks of Hebrew as a bridge between God and Israel but does not elaborate. He urges the importance of religious practice but allows that common practice may subsist with a variety of theological rationales.

Meyer's emphasis on Hebrew comprehends both Brinker's and Greenberg's attitudes. That is, it is seen as important in gaining an entry to the Israeli vernacular as well as to modern Hebrew literature, as in Brinker, but it is also valued as the supreme vehicle of Jewish religious expression. Like Twersky and unlike Brinker, Meyer is not pessimistic about Jewish survival in the Diaspora, although he recognizes the difficult obstacles that need to be overcome. Like Greenberg, he emphasizes the critical need for mutual understanding by the Jewries of Israel and the Diaspora.

It is interesting that while both Meyer and Twersky emphasize the value of early childhood education in the warm home environment and speak of the gradual increase in the child's critical understanding of what has been learned unreflectively, Meyer lays particular stress on the value of the converse movement whereby the critical adult may, through a favorable Jewish education, acquire some of the warm empathic feeling of the child's naive understanding. Other points of interest will no doubt occur to the reader, who is urged to be on the lookout for further differences and similarities in the visions.

The essay by Michael Rosenak, philosopher of Jewish education, offers a conception he believes applicable to the various types of committed Jews in the world today, one that is capable of clarifying the differences among them as well as pointing out their commonalities as educated Jews. The main feature of

Rosenak's conception is the distinction between a language and its literature –
a language (e.g., the grammar and lexicon of English) comprising a vehicle
for the expression of ideas, while its literature (e.g., all novels, treatises, essays,
and poems written in English) comprehends the ideas actually expressed by its
means. It is the broadening of this distinction from its literal application to spoken
languages (such as English or French or German) to the wider realm of cultures
that enables Rosenak to identify the critical conditions for being an educated
Jew as he envisages the matter.

Thus, by the "language of a culture," he refers to its basic assumptions and
forms of thought and expression. Educated Jews are those who have been initiated into the "language" of Judaism and who are able to use its forms in
expressing their own thoughts, thus adding to its "literature" and potentially
enriching the language itself.

Rosenak's view is that to learn the language of Judaism is to learn a good deal
of its sacred literature; it is also to become familiar with what has been done "in
the language" throughout the millennia of Jewish life. Sacred literature is peculiarly "language-presenting" – that is, it comprises the basic forms of thought and
styles of expression of Jewish culture; one cannot speak the language of Judaism
without acquiring a goodly acquaintance with it, but there are differences among
Jews as to what constitutes such literature. For example, Reform Jews do not
agree with Orthodox Jews that the Talmud is sacred in the sense that the
Bible is.

The educated Jew uses Judaic language in a way that is intrinsic to personal
identity. It is not merely an instrument of description and action but a channel of
self-expression and self-understanding. Moreover, such language is a vehicle of
community affiliation, signaling the educated Jew's loyalty to those communities
that speak the language. For all but extreme ultratraditionalists, such loyalty also
embraces those who speak it differently, extending to the whole of the House
of Israel.

The educated Jew, for Rosenak, has the need and the ability to connect the
Jewish with the universal, the language of Judaism relating to all human concerns and translatable, at least in part, into other cultural languages. Historically,
neighboring cultures in particular share various needs and aspirations; openness
to other cultures, moreover, enhances one's own and promotes cultural bridges
compatible with one's own identity. The educated Jew, in consequence, aspires
to a genuine understanding of the lives and values of others while remaining
"situated" within Judaism.

Such situatedness involves the disposition to relate one's Jewishness to "ultimate concerns" as expressed in the idiom of Judaism. Traditionally, this is seen
as the service of God; the secularist may see it as finding the treasures of human
existence wherever one happens to be. Whether religious or secular, the educated Jew sees no conflict between individuality and community, viewing the

community not as a threat to personal identity but rather as the arena within which it is to be expressed. The person thus represents the community and hopes to do so in exemplary fashion. Indeed, the educated Jew finds the urge to educate and so to perpetuate such community not a mere matter of preference but rather an obligation, flowing from a love of the Judaic language.

Such love is by no means incompatible with criticism. The loyalty expected of the educated Jew in fact motivates a critical response when the Jew's ideal image of Judaism is belied by the actuality. Such response, as typically expressed within the family, betokens no disloyalty and may be a force for constructive change in the direction of the ideal.

The educated Jew takes seriously the need to address problems facing the Jewish people in the present. Such address is an essential feature of creating "literature" as a Jew. There is no conflict, in fact, between speaking the language of Judaism and resolving the practical issues of the day. To suppose such a conflict would be to underplay the comprehensiveness of the language, which clearly engages practical as well as moral issues.

Considering Rosenak's conception in the context of the others earlier discussed, it is evident that he gives a primary educational place to the sacred literature of Jews, the basic locus for acquiring the language, without which one cannot be an educated Jew. Secondarily, he gives an important role to the non-sacred literature of Jews, as providing paradigms for the continuing use of the language. Acquiring the language is not a merely passive matter. To acquire it means to use it, thus to extend the voluminous literature created by its means during the millennia of Jewish history. The education Rosenak envisages is one that, in sum, emphasizes the language of Judaism, as well as its accumulated literature of thought, action, communication, and expression.

The picture he presents is one that encompasses the variety of idioms spoken by committed Jews making different uses of the common language – all, however, recognizing such differences and according them acknowledgment and respect. His view, unlike that of Twersky, does not set down halakhic belief and practice as an essential requirement for the educated Jew. But, unlike Brinker, he does not view free thought and involvement in Jewish life as sufficient. His vision places the sacred literature of Judaism at the forefront of all Jewish educational endeavors, allowing as well that Jews may define such literature quite differently and interpret it variously. Certainly, a good portion of his implied curriculum occupies itself with the learner's gaining a serious knowledge of our inherited religious literature, however understood.

An evident feature of Rosenak's vision is his emphasis on aspects of character. His ideal is of a Jew who is animated by love of his language yet open to others, loyal to his community yet critical of its shortcomings, involved with its problems yet sensitive to ultimate concerns and responsive to the universal, proud of his identity yet secure enough not to trumpet his pride.

The essay does not spell out a detailed course of study for the Jewish school but presents, as he says, "guidelines for introductions to Jewish curricular thinking" needed by all identifiable viewpoints in contemporary Judaism. Such guidelines, he hopes, may help clarify differences among viewpoints as well as identify commonalities among them. He offers a detailed outline of such commonalities in the conviction that they are of fundamental importance for every particular vision of Jewish life and education.

Following a suggestion of the directors that Israel Scheffler treat some aspects of the general philosophy of education and then develop their relations to Jewish educational thought, Scheffler begins by outlining a concept of the educated person as it has been developed in the Anglo-American philosophy of education in recent years. The educated person, first of all, is one whose learning is valuable in itself and, further, represents a significant accomplishment. Such learning encompasses understanding in contrast to mere information, cognitive perspective as against the narrow skill learning typically associated with training.

Cognitive perspective not only requires breadth; it also demands that the knowledge of the educated person be active, not inert. Knowledge should not simply be stored as information, but should transform the educated person's perception and commerce with the environment. A corollary of such perspective is the search for explanatory principles offering a framework for particular items of belief and judgment. Moral education, as distinct from moral training, for example, promotes the learner's disposition to probe critically the principles underlying the very code of conduct being taught.

Such principles ought, further, to enter into and to transform the educated person's vision of things. Historical knowledge, for example, is not merely a list of facts governing one's potential responses to a hypothetical examination. It enriches the way the educated person looks at surrounding institutions, informing current conceptions and attitudes, enlarging one's grasp. Knowledge is, in this respect, a visual instrument, entering into and modifying whatever one sees.

The educated person is not simply well-informed or knowledgeable; he or she has acquired disciplined ways of thinking in certain areas and cares that such disciplines be properly applied. The educated person is one who has been initiated into the "great human traditions of thought – science, literature, philosophy, technology," and whose initiation promotes critical participation in them.

The development of critical participation is a product of rational exchanges in the process of teaching. These exchanges rest on a respect for the learner's judgment, offer explanations and demonstrations appealing to such judgment, and open themselves to questions arising from such appeal. Implicit in the rational exchange appropriate to teaching is a recognition that teacher and pupil are alike in respect of their positions as intellectual and moral agents. The process must, therefore, respect each participant's struggle to understand.

Treated thus, the educated person is strengthened in self-respect and respect for others, acquiring the sense of himself or herself as member of a critical community, responsible to principles of evaluation applicable to all. The educated person has in this way acquired an intellectual and moral character.

Turning from the conception of an educated person to questions of Jewish education, Scheffler emphasizes the importance of distinguishing such education from schooling. Education is not the peculiar province of the school but flows from influences deriving from various other agencies – the family, religious institutions, communication media, and the quality of human associations and cultural traditions in society. In designing school practices, we cannot rest on general concepts of the educated person but must reckon with the state of other social agencies. Current Jewish schools, for example, cannot rely on the traditionally familiar home life permeated with Jewish religious sentiments, concepts, and practices; such schools need to reconsider their potential roles under contemporary circumstances.

Schools, moreover, are limited institutions, whereas education is lifelong. School pupils need increasingly to take the initiative in directing their own efforts to become educated persons. This emphasis is a permanent feature of traditional Jewish culture, which obligates each person to continue to study throughout life. The school does not exhaust the total content of such study, which far outstrips the curriculum of any given school. The school's function is to provide the basic and indispensable impetus for an educational experience that should continue until the learner's last breath. The implication of these points is that the Jewish school needs to think through its role in current actual conditions and to promote the continuation of Jewish learning after the pupil leaves the school environment.

Given the limited scope of school influences, every curriculum choice must be made to count to the utmost. Rote learning of fundamentals, for example, must be viewed in the context of a future life of learning for the pupil; it must therefore be presented as part of a broadly meaningful curriculum capable of capturing the student's heart and growing mind. The study of texts should not only inculcate fluency and accuracy but at the same time provide an entry into their human and moral significance.

Scheffler notes the difficulty faced by the Jewish educator in the Diaspora, where a very small number of years at best are given over to most Jewish schooling. This situation creates a gap between Jewish and non-Jewish education; the latter continues to grow and mature with continuing schooling, while the pupil's Jewish understandings remain immature and wooden, preserved, if at all, only in a separate mental compartment. Rather than cognitive perspective, Jewish schooling often produces cognitive isolation, lacking connections with other aspects of learning and possessing no place within a coherent pattern of life. A basic challenge to Jewish schooling is to expand its scope, both within its own purview and within additional venues – summer camps, family programs, and adult education, for example.

Scheffler emphasizes the importance of developing the student's capacity to apply traditional Jewish concepts to personal experience. The effort to do so, however, encounters the difficulty that the concepts are woven into traditional religious belief, heavily disrupted by postmedieval intellectual thought. The challenge to Jewish education, Scheffler argues, is boldly to reinterpret traditional concepts so that they can become integral elements of the student's thinking and development throughout life.

The educated person, for Scheffler, is one who has entered into the great traditions of imaginative thought. Applied to Jewish education, this idea places Jewish learning within the stream of general history, where it can freely interact with intellectual and literary endeavors, in contact with modern scientific, philosophical, and technological thinking. But the great traditions are by no means sufficient, and here the prevalent philosophical view of the educated person is vulnerable to criticism, according to Scheffler. For it leaves out the need for pupils to acquire a knowledge of their own past, the philosophical, religious, and sociological influences that have formed them and created the historical environment within which they must now live.

Scheffler also urges the importance, for Jewish education, of taking account of other cultures. Our pupils continue to develop and grow in close contact with non-Jewish cultures, and their Jewish identity, especially in the Diaspora, needs to sustain itself in a multicultural environment. To learn about other cultures would deepen awareness of Jewish experience and values, while showing the continuities between Jewish and non-Jewish cultures among the families of mankind. Jewish pupils also need to learn about Jewish cultural uniqueness, while learning at the same time to appreciate the unique cultural features of others.

Reflecting on Scheffler's discussion in relation to the previous ones we have treated, we may note some similar emphases. Like Brinker, Scheffler conceives of Jewish education as part of a general framework of education that lays special emphasis on breadth of perspective and rational approaches to teaching. Like Meyer, he emphasizes the need to deal with non-Jewish cultures along with Jewish tradition in order to develop a sense of what differentiates such tradition and to strengthen Jewish identity. With Rosenak, he agrees on the importance of learning a vast array of traditional Jewish concepts, and along with Greenberg, he advocates the need for interpretation of these concepts and their presentation in such a way as to capture the student's heart as well as mind. Unlike Brinker and Twersky, he does not present a specific course of study, although, like both, he advocates dealing with philosophical matters that affect basic Jewish content. However, whereas for Twersky philosophical reflection is dealt with in the framework of *halakhah* and Maimonidean thought, Scheffler advocates direct confrontation with the conflict between traditional thought and contemporary philosophical understandings.

In his essay, Project Director Seymour Fox turns to an examination of the process whereby abstract formulations are brought to earth in the challenging arena of practice. We have, in our foregoing discussions, continually stressed the importance of visions of learning in offering guiding perspectives to the institutions of education. We have also insisted that visions are not commands. They purport, after all, to have purchase in the real world, a world that is not static but requires intelligent adaptation to changing circumstances. Essential for coherent activity at each juncture, visions are not therefore immune to modification, in greater or lesser degree, over time. The interplay of vision and circumstance is a continual process, engaging ideas and actions, theory and practice.

Each of the essays we have so far considered has, in fact, not only presented a philosophical conception of Jewish education in the abstract but also tried to show its feasibility and promise for the actual environments we inhabit. Thus, even Twersky, who in philosophical basics follows the twelfth-century Maimonides, implies that his regime of early *hergel* and the increasingly sophisticated learning of Jewish classics is likely to draw and retain the coming generation of Jewish youth in the twenty-first century. Similarly, Brinker implies that his conception of Jewish loyalty as based on a broad notion of family is especially congenial to the building of an inclusive community of Jews freely determining the parameters of their Jewish identities. In analogous fashion, each of the foregoing essays has offered a conception of Jewish education thought to be both possible and appropriate for the coming generations in the world we now foresee.

Yet none of the previous essays has addressed the general question as to how ideal conceptions of Jewish education may be brought into close connection with the realities of practice. Abstract philosophies of education do not, in general, allow the derivation of implications for practice without the addition of supplementary premises. What Seymour Fox calls the "translation of theory into educational practice" depends essentially on the provision, or assumption, of such premises as to the settings within which a basic philosophical emphasis is to be implemented. His essay offers a general consideration of the process of such translation, a process that applies not only to the visions discussed in this book but also to any vision that proposes to represent an ideal, as well as a practical, Jewish education for our times.

Fox, an architect of the renowned Camp Ramah, draws special attention to the variety of settings within which a conception of education may function – for example, in the family, in informal as well as formal education, in community centers, in camps, and in adult education. Each of these settings presents its own special challenges, resources, and limitations in the actualization of the guiding educational vision. The attempted translation, for example, into a curriculum – for a given array of students, in a particular school, within a certain community, with its unique cadre of teachers, and the special dispositions of its parents and community leaders – must take each of these factors into account in fitting the projected vision into the presented reality. Without such translation, the vision gains no traction in its educational work; it is the translation itself that connects the underlying conception with the specifics of the setting and thus turns it into an operational guide for practice.

To illustrate the process, Fox refers to examples from our scholars and from his own work: Greenberg, for instance, stresses the spiritual curiosity of the young child, and this emphasis requires that translation of his vision respond to the curiosity of young children about the world, about human relationships, and about the meaning of life. In turn, this suggests the desirability of collaboration among textual scholars, sensitive teachers, and psychologists concerned with spiritual development when it comes to designing a curriculum as well as appropriate teaching methods.

By contrast, Meyer emphasizes emotional attachment to Judaism as a factor of prime importance in early childhood education. To translate this emphasis into present educational practice in an environment in which the Jewish home seldom provides a rich emotional base for Jewish commitment requires educators to devise settings outside the home, replete with positive emotive elements embodied in songs, stories, and religious observances.

The recognition that contemporary Jewish homes seldom provide a sufficient base for a rich Jewish identity is shared by Greenberg as well. His educational vision, for example, looks toward a way of life that creates a community. Not only are current Jewish homes largely inadequate in this regard, but so, too, are formal school settings because they fail to provide the opportunity for students to carry into practice the precepts learned in school.

The needed translation thus involves designing settings for nurturing a way of life that creates a community, affording the student the opportunity not only to learn the lessons of the texts but also to understand, appreciate, and apply these lessons in practice along with other students in a common learning environment. Fox insists that if understanding and appreciating the meaning of an idea in the text is a challenge, understanding what is involved in acting on the idea is an even greater challenge. The experience of acting on ideas deepens and thickens the meaning of the idea, for it requires that the maturing student learn what is involved in navigating through reality with religious ideas and principles. Schools rarely make room for the experiences required in the movement from ideas to action, from theory to practice.

The province of education ideally embraces both formal and informal education. In Greenberg's view, for example, formal study of the classical texts of the Bible needs to attend not only to their literal meaning as disclosed by scholarship, but also – and especially – to the moral meaning they embody, which transcends their archaic forms and carries a timeless human message. It is this moral meaning that needs not only to be appreciated as applicable to contemporary life but also to be given the environment in which students themselves can grapple with its application in all the informal situations they confront. The goal is that formal and informal learning be melded, theory and practice brought together in the learner's experience. Here practice is not only enlightened by theory; it throws new light on theory. The texts illumine practical situations and are in turn illuminated by them.

The translation of theory into practice requires a team effort, Fox insists. The teacher, the curriculum expert, and the scholar certainly need to collaborate. In addition, the psychologist ought to assess the spiritual development of the child, the talented school administrator is needed to gauge the responses of parents to the introduction of educational change, and the wise community leader is required to advise as to how to weigh and reconcile competing community priorities. Fox provides a detailed account of the ideal requirements for the teacher and for the informal educator in the educational team.

Fox also emphasizes the experimental character of the translation process: "To make words on a page come alive in a community means to experiment, to learn from mistakes, to try a new approach, sometimes to fail, and inevitably to reformulate the initial vision in light of experience. No one can write a step-by-step manual for success. Rather, success is the consequence of the ability both to justify an idea and demonstrate its implementation."

In the remainder of his chapter, Fox explores the practical implications of educational visions in several critical areas of Jewish education, in each case suggesting how prevalent practices might be improved or even transformed. In discussing lifelong learning as variously treated by the scholars in our project, Fox notes the special problem of reaching modern-day adults, many of whom lack a strong Jewish upbringing and have little or no acquaintance with Jewish texts. He remarks on the success of Alma Hebrew College, founded in Tel Aviv by Ruth Calderon, in attracting adults to the regular study of biblical and talmudic materials, and he cites Meyer's advocacy of synagogue communities of adult learners who can enter into Jewish education with little or no prior exposure.

As to early childhood education, Fox calls attention to the firm agreement among our scholars on its critical importance, but he outlines as well their variant approaches to it, adding that all such approaches are jeopardized by the insufficient numbers of Jewish teachers in this educational area and by the dearth of relevant investment, research, and training efforts.

In analogous fashion, Fox provides illuminating discussions of the variant approaches by our scholars to informal education, the role of the text, the crucial position of the principal, and the central contribution of the teacher. In each case, he outlines significant differences in our scholars' versions of these topics along with the shared insistence on their overriding importance. He also comments on certain urgent problems to be dealt with by all, such as the need for improved teacher training and recruitment and the long-overdue upgrading of teachers' salaries and benefits.

Following additional discussion of the team approach mentioned earlier, Fox ends with an extended discussion of the role of policy makers in Jewish education. He considers as policy makers all "those people whose decisions – whether about vision, personnel, curriculum, or budget – influence Jewish education. They may be professional Jewish educators, but also Israeli ministers of education and their deputies, heads of organizations whose mission includes Jewish education, foundations and their leadership, and especially lay leaders."

Fox is particularly concerned with fostering an inclusive understanding of the class of policy makers, claiming that Jewish educators have in the past tended to minimize in particular the role of lay leaders. In fact, he argues, there have in the past been individuals and organizations outside the realm of professional educators with a strong record of impact on Jewish education. Today, their participation is even more urgent. The growth of Jewish foundations, for example, opens the possibility of increased sources of wisdom, funding, and advocacy in support of worthwhile educational causes. Intelligent and engaged lay leaders – parents, scholars, board members, business people, professional persons in different areas – all have important contributions to make in shaping a community's educational vision, steering it toward successful implementation through critical evaluation and informed advocacy based on increased levels of Jewish understanding.

The essay by Daniel Marom, Associate Project Director, offers a case study of his experience in distilling a school's vision from its practice and thus encouraging its critical examination. Visions, as Marom emphasizes, are not to be confused with vision statements. The comprehensive purposes that guide an educational enterprise may be implicit in its practice, lacking verbal formulation. Such purposes may, however, become explicit through reflection on the educational decisions taken and the actions authorized in the life of the enterprise. An approach that is sensitive to educational vision does not need to proceed "deductively," that is, from general principles to the realm of practice. It may also proceed "inductively," that is, from the realm of practice to the articulation of the principles embodied in its de facto decisions and priorities.

These principles displayed in practice may be only partial in their scope; they may be inconsistent; they are not in any case easily accessible to the persons who seem to be living by them. Moreover, once made explicit, they may be thought to require modification or even rejection by those very persons. The effort to articulate the principles implicit in practice brings them to conscious attention. Once scrutinized consciously, they may be seen to require changes to mesh with approved values, to eliminate inconsistencies, and, in general, to gain rational approval. Articulation of embodied principles thus invites their refinement as a result of conscious reflection on their scope and meaning. Whether the principles are formulated first and then confronted with practice or crystallized and refined through an initial study of practice is of little importance. The main need is to confront general principles with the details of practice, such confrontation illuminating practice while enriching our grasp of the principles in question.

The foregoing essays have, for the most part, focussed initially on substantive educational principles and then considered their bearings on practice in particular settings. The essay by Marom proceeds in the opposite direction, attempting to articulate the educational vision implicit in the practice of a particular school, and, by so doing, to enable the school to reflect on this vision and to refine it in the light of such reflection. The result is a case study of the effort by Marom to stimulate the school's reflection on the aims and goals embodied in its day-to-day practice, and to consider how these aims and goals might need revision. Marom's essay is thus a report on the process of articulating and refining an educational vision not initially verbalized, but rather implicit in its practical life.

By an arrangement between the Mandel Foundation and a non-denominational day school, Marom was able to enter into the life of the school, where he conceived his task to be to participate in its culture of practice, join its discussion of aims and goals, and encourage consideration of its implicit educational vision. The report of his experience in carrying out this task includes a description of particular characteristics of the school, an account of several of the persons involved in its operation, and portrayals of a variety of discussions relating to the generation of the school's educational vision. Included in Marom's report are vignettes intended to highlight important general points by encapsulating them in particular events or encounters.

Marom's activities at the school began in the summer of 1994 and continued through 1998. In proceeding with his work, he devised several categories to guide his efforts: a) decoding the implicit vision, b) establishing readiness, c) introducing vision as a framework for everyday practice, d) deepening vision through study, and e) developing strategies for sustaining vision in practice. These categories are not only informative as to how Marom carried out his task at the school but are also useful as bridges between what he has experienced in his work and what might be considered in other settings of Jewish education. The account of Marom's use of each of these categories is followed by one or two of the vignettes earlier mentioned, to illustrate its operation.

Marom cautions that his use of the categories should not be construed as a formula to be applied elsewhere in a mechanical fashion. The activities he describes following the stated order of these categories "were often undertaken simultaneously, sometimes in reverse order. The complex work on vision, in which the detail stands for the whole even as the whole is larger than the sum of the details, is dynamic and unceasing." The order in which the categories were applied is thus of minor importance. What is important, for Marom, is the set of features, as a whole, that were salient in his efforts. It is this set which he believes may prove useful in the work of others who may attempt similar initiatives.

One overall feature of Marom's conception is the emphasis on community. Marom viewed the school as an arena in which a community attempts to regenerate itself through the education of the young. In his view, as he states it, a school is "a setting where a compelling social drama is taking place. The main character in the drama, ever present though never fully visible, is a community, a social consensus. . . . All in all, a school is a place where the community boldly makes a promise to its youth – 'Learn as we suggest and you will fare better. We believe that what we have to teach you is profoundly significant, that if you master it you will fulfill yourself more completely, grapple better with the challenges of life, and make a contribution for the good of others in our world.' "

The result of the school's sensitivity to issues of vision in its various departments seemed increasingly to reinforce Marom's community emphasis. People in the different constituencies were talking more to one another; new programs and practices were being proposed in light of the school's larger aims. Greater inclusiveness seemed evident in various respects: "Notably, the former trustees' 'education committee' indeed became the 'educational goals committee' and now included members of the administrative and teaching staff, as well as other experts, parents, and graduates."

Marom's account of his experience concludes with a sobering critical evaluation of weaknesses and problems. Among these, he notes the absence of an evaluating mechanism to gauge relative success. As a result, it was not possible to know how many of the new initiatives at the school resulted from greater attention to the question of vision, rather than simply from Marom's personal enthusiasm. In addition, despite increased constructive initiatives, people had different understandings of what they were engaged in, and some confessed to finding the challenge simply confusing.

The effort by a complex school community to articulate its aims and goals is, in any event, a difficult and delicate matter, which should not be expected either to proceed in a perfectly clear and orderly fashion or to issue in a final conclusion once and for all. At best, it is a challenging, sometimes painful process of rethinking and consequently reshaping one's fundamental direction. Marom's rich portrait encourages us not to abandon analogous efforts but, rather, to continue to try to improve them and so to enhance and deepen our educational systems.

NOTE

1   Moshe Greenberg, "On Teaching the Bible in Religious Schools," *Jewish Education* 29:3 (1959): 45, 48.

Part II

Visions in Detail

Part II Introduction

       The preceding chapter gave an overview of our scholars' visions of Jewish education. Each of the next six chapters will be devoted to a single scholar, beginning with the scholar's essay, prepared for our project and used as a basis for the deliberations with the educators, followed by a supplementary section highlighting materials, culled from the scholar's other writings, that amplify his point of view and thus enhance the understanding of his work. Some of the supplementary sections also include notes from the scholar's meetings with the educators, focusing on the implications of the scholar's conception for the practice of Jewish education.

4

What Must a Jew Study – and Why?

ISADORE TWERSKY

Introduction

This essay[1] has two purposes: Its first purpose is to propose foundational
ideas, paradigms, and insights from a distinct educational philosophy that emerges
from Maimonides' writings in various contexts – to specify its guidelines as to
curriculum and pedagogy; to draw an ideal portrait of the teacher and the student
and the relations between them; and to identify and extol values and trends in a
religious education that is centered on the Torah. We will attempt to explicate
a worldview that is anchored first and foremost in the writings of Maimonides
(although we will also need to refer to other authoritative legalists and thinkers in
order to complete or complement his formulations), and on which it is possible
to base a comprehensive educational system.[2] It is a great challenge to understand
and explain the centrality of *halakhah* (Jewish law) and its role, and then to chart
the reciprocity of learning and observance. While education is the focus of this
essay, additional aspects of Maimonidean thought are obviously essential to this
inquiry.

The essay's second purpose is to illuminate for educators and students –
including those who do not presently identify with the spiritual-cultural content or the moral-intellectual framework of *halakhah* – portions of the Jewish
tradition, the Judaism that, in the course of generations, shaped our historical
existence and our cultural-national character. Every person ought to take an
interest in these ideas, whether because he accepts them or because he feels a
commitment to know Judaism and Jewish history. (To understate the case, each
person should learn Jewish thought and be familiar with Judaism as it shaped
the Jews and directed their activities and achievements, just as he learns Greek
culture or the history of European enlightenment. Judaism is part of everyone's
historical-cultural heritage. Clearly, there are more powerful and convincing

arguments; this minimal case is meant to be only a point of departure for the broad community of educators and no more).

It is necessary to point out here that Judaism is in the midst of a historical crisis. As religion and secularity wrestle with each other, ignorance of Judaism presides over the confrontation. The element common to the processes of secularization, which developed out of various eighteenth-century ideologies, is a reservation about the lifestyle and value system of traditional society. Until approximately 200 years ago there was a single and unified lifestyle – one that, as we shall see, can be characterized as halakhic monism and spiritual pluralism – which accompanied Judaism from time immemorial, since it appeared in the arena of history. During the eighteenth century the crisis emerged and crystallized. Still, as Jacob Katz has noted, the tension between tradition and crisis continues to be among the more significant problems of our time. The process of disengagement and estrangement from Jewish tradition persists with great force. We are becoming increasingly conscious of the fact that if we do not find a way to become attached again to the tradition and its values, if we do not succeed in helping the tradition speak in a manner that enables us to hear and absorb its meaning and echoes – its religious-spiritual message – then we will find ourselves caught in a terrible historical predicament.[3]

Of course, in the application of Maimonides' principles to education, we will have to distinguish between Orthodox and non-Orthodox settings. At the least, everyone should become familiar with Maimonides' intellectual framework, the principles of his system and its aspirations, which they can then adapt to diverse contexts.[4]

It is both important and desirable to contend with Maimonides' ideas and to examine closely their intellectual and educational implications for the following reasons:

First, there is no one like him as a magisterial legal authority with an authentic philosophical system.

Second, the confrontation with Maimonides sharpens one's sensitivity to the fundamental issues and elements underlying the contemporary crisis. He makes possible a comprehensive understanding of the traditional system of values. His philosophy is a challenge to shallow forms of modernity; to moral relativism, which negates absolute and timeless values; and to secularism, which, as one realizes that a one-dimensional existence does not grant either peace of mind or spiritual elevation, leaves a vacuum in a person's soul.

Finally, Maimonides' philosophical system is compelling. Its content and its language enrich thought and deepen inquiry, and its structure and line of argument illuminate Judaism – both its *halakhah* and philosophy – and lead to new perspectives and insights.

Our task is to understand Maimonides' ideas and what flows from them or is intimated by them with the same analytic care and intellectual discipline that guide those who inquire into the ideas of Plato or Aristotle, Kant or Moore, Whitehead or Dewey. In our opinion, Maimonides, as a classic and authoritative halakhist, demands further attention because of his stature, his genius, and his profound and continuing influence on Jewish history. Maimonides is at once a codifier of that which preceded him and a pioneer of that which followed, both a transmitter and a visionary architect looking at the present from a unique perspective and planning and shaping the future.

We do not propose Maimonides' writings, especially his *Mishneh Torah,* as a replacement for the Talmud or the sources upon which it drew. Our quoting from Maimonides is based on the knowledge that he provides an authentic summary of the tradition, as well as illuminating the sources.

It is interesting to note modern attempts to base the study of Judaism on Maimonides' *Mishneh Torah*. We will mention two of them — one from nineteenth-century Eastern Europe, at the height of the *Haskalah* (the Jewish Enlightenment) movement, and the other from *Eretz Yisrael* (the land of Israel), before the establishment of the State of Israel.

In the first example, a committee of *maskilim* (adherents of the Jewish Enlightenment) proposed a curriculum based upon the standard prayerbook, selections from the Bible, selections from the *Mishnah,* and selections from Maimonides. The Lubavitcher Rebbe, Rabbi Menachem Mendel Schneersohn, known as the "Tzemaḥ Tzedek" (1789–1866), rejected this program with the following explanation: "What interests us in particular is the fourth section."

The use of Maimonides as a replacement for Talmud does not seem to him appropriate, and he quotes from the Sages of Israel in the course of the generations — for example, Rabbeinu Asher (the Rosh) and Rabbi Shlomo Luria (Maharshal) — who forcefully claim that one cannot fully understand Maimonides' writings without knowing the exact sources on which he drew. Moreover, said the Tzemaḥ Tzedek, if the justification for the sole use of the *Mishneh Torah* is that it treats not only matters of *halakhah* but also moral and ethical issues, one can study books that address *mussar* literature and include "additional thoughts on morality and ethical dispositions" more than the *Mishneh Torah* does.[5]

In 1930, Yeḥezkel Kaufmann wrote a letter to Ḥayyim Naḥman Bialik with a somber description of education in Israel: "I was horrified to discover the terrible lack of Jewish knowledge and great ignorance that prevails [in our schools]." The corrective Kaufmann proposes is "to establish the study of *halakhah* based on a selection from Maimonides' *Mishneh Torah* in connection with a selection from the sources (the *Mishnah* and the Talmud)." He then continues to report to Bialik: "I tried [this approach] and behold the wondrous result: The dry bones came to life, learning is now a pleasure, while the study of *Mishnah* – that is, the study of '*Mishnah*' as it is undertaken in our schools – is hell for the teachers and the students alike." It is important to stress that Kaufmann's proposal does not ignore the sources on which Maimonides drew.[6]

When we speak of the "educated person," it is clear that we are discussing not only the sum total of a person's knowledge, but also, and perhaps most significantly, a system of attitudes. We attempt to establish not what a person should know, but what a person is, his nature, spiritual character, modes of behavior, spiritual and moral aspirations. Every educational philosopher admits that education intends to shape a certain kind of personality in accordance with values and beliefs. The educated person reflects, as in a mirror, the ideal person, who represents the embodiment and fruition of these values.

In discussing the educated Jew in Maimonides' philosophical system, we are required – notwithstanding the clear focus on education – to relate to the portrait of the ideal person. Education is the medium through which moral and intellectual perfection can be achieved. The desired perfection determines the contents and method of study – so as not to miss the target. It is necessary to maintain a special sensitivity to a number of fundamental terms that describe the direction of education and its outcome: *shlemut* (perfection), *tikkun ha-nefesh* (correction of the soul), *kedushah* (holiness), *da'at Hashem* (knowledge of God), *ahavat Hashem* (love of God), and *avodat Hashem* (worship of God). The understanding of these terms will illuminate the means of education.[7] We see that teleology influences phenomenology and methodology.[8]

Maimonides taught that the Torah is an educational resource whose purpose is to shape the supreme spiritual-moral character. Our inquiry will prove and emphasize that this assumption concerning the purpose of the Torah – an assumption that removes any arbitrariness about the Torah's foundations or prescriptions – is the intellectual focus of the system of *ta'amei mitzvot* (rationales of the commandments) in Maimonides' philosophy: The practice of each and every *mitzvah* contributes something to human perfection – moral and intellectual-spiritual perfection. Religious acts lead to perfection.

Maimonides repeatedly stresses that the *mitzvot* – which are derived from the highest source of authority – are not arbitrary; they have a use and purpose. This principle is emphasized in all of Maimonides' writings, not only in the *Mishneh Torah* and *The Guide of the Perplexed,* but also in the *Commentary on the Mishnah, Eight Chapters, The Epistle to Yemen, The Book of Commandments, The Essay on the Resurrection of the Dead,* and various responsa. It is worth noting the clear and succinct formulation of the teleological dimension of the *mitzvot* in *The Epistle to Yemen,* a popular source at the time:

> If he could only fathom the inner intent of the law, he would realize
> that the essence of the true divine religion lies in the deeper meaning

of its positive and negative precepts, every one of which will aid man in his striving after perfection, and remove every impediment to the attainment of excellence. These commands will enable the masses and the elite to acquire moral and intellectual qualities, each according to his ability.[9]

In my book *Introduction to the Code of Maimonides,* I summarized Maimonides' philosophical outlook in this area as follows: "One has to relate each of the 613 commandments to one of three goals: a) establishment of civilized society – principles of social utility and justice; b) development of the ethical personality – principles of goodness and love of fellow man; or c) intellectual perfection – true knowledge and experience of God."[10]

The following quotation from Maimonides' commentary on *Pirke Avot* (4:2) has a special resonance:

> "Run to do even a slight *mitzvah* . . . for the carrying out of one *mitzvah* draws another."
>
> We have already explained the interpretation of this passage in the tenth chapter of Sanhedrin. And our sages, blessed be their memory, testified to this wonderful innovative insight in the Torah, one in which there is an inducement for the carrying out of *mitzvot*. It says [in Scripture]: "Then Moses set apart three cities on the side of Jordan, which is east of the sunrise" (Deut. 4:41). Now it is known that they are of no use [i.e., these cities cannot legally provide a refuge to those who murdered unintentionally], since the law of the cities of refuge would not apply to them until the other three [cities of refuge] in *Eretz Yisrael* would be set apart. They [the Sages] said: Moses, blessed be his memory, knew that the three cities beyond the Jordan would not be able to take in [unintentional murderers] until the three [cities of refuge] in *Eretz Yisrael* would be set apart, since it is written "There shall be six cities of refuge" (Num. 35:12). Nevertheless, he set apart these [cities on the east side of Jordan], since he thought that "seeing that a *mitzvah* has come my way – I will carry it out." Now if our teacher Moses, blessed be his memory, the discoverer of truths, the most perfect among those who are perfect, was so eager to add a half of a positive *mitzvah* to his high stature and perfection – it goes without saying the same should be done by those whose soul has been infected by disease, which is intensifying and spreading.

There is value even in the practice of half a *mitzvah*. We should hasten to practice an incomplete *mitzvah* because it contributes to perfection, as we learn from the phrase *shalem she-ba-sheleimim* (the most perfect among those who are perfect). We will further discover, in various contexts, that the *mitzvah* leads to human perfection; the *mitzvah* is an expression of a religious sensibility and it enables a religious experience.

To develop this matter further: *Halakhah,* the foundation and infrastructure of Judaism, is first and foremost a system of *mitzvot* – that is, religious acts that are anchored in an irrevocable authority. Simultaneously, because of its comprehensive scope, it reflects moral assumptions and directives, historical experiences, and theological axioms. *Halakhah* is the practical manifestation of the Jewish spiritual essence. Consequently, it is within the power of *halakhah* to expose the Jew who practices it gently and loyally to a great religious force capable of awakening inner spiritual instincts and motives. The practice of *mitzvot* – which is not conditioned upon any other achievement – is intended to bring a person to supreme religious-spiritual achievements.

Halakhah describes the manner in which the practice of a *mitzvah* is to be undertaken. That is, while there are established modes of religious behavior, there are no established modes of religious sensibility, religious experience, or measures of moving ever closer to God. Here uniqueness reigns. Every halakhic act is accompanied by "practice of the heart" – a personal, subjective religious component. The objective act is standard and unchanging; the practice is various and multifaceted.

The act provokes meditation and reason – intellectual comprehension. This comprehension is not the contemplation of a *mitzvah* but rather an awakening to its understanding. The movement is from the visible to the invisible, from the sensed to the perceived.

Despite this dialectical claim concerning the relationship between the defined act and the unique nature of its practice, we must repeat and emphasize that the practice of a *mitzvah* is not conditioned upon its understanding or upon one's agreement with it – this is a first principle.

Maimonidean Aspects of the Phenomenology and Teleology of Learning

The views that I am proposing here are closely linked to particular sources and to their precise interpretation.[11] It will be necessary first to arrive at a thorough understanding of these sources. Then, only after this has been accomplished, they should be considered separately, in depth and with sensitivity, in terms of their theoretical and practical educational implications. I am not proposing a specific curriculum here, but it should be abundantly clear that Maimonides' ideas provide the basic ideas and guiding principles for a curriculum and for the understanding of its aims at various stages. Content and purpose are inseparable. We must therefore explicate Maimonides' principal formulations and terms.

A key passage, shedding valuable light on Maimonides' understanding of and approach to the vast and complex issue of what a Jew must study, is found in the *Laws of Torah Study* 1:11–12:

> The time allotted to study should be divided into three parts. A third should be devoted to the Written Law; a third to the Oral Law; and the last third should be spent in reflection, deducing conclusions from premises, developing implications of statements, comparing dicta, studying the hermeneutical principles by which the Torah is interpreted, till one knows the essence of these principles, and how to deduce what is permitted and what is forbidden from what one has learned traditionally. This is termed Talmud.
>
> For example, if one is an artisan who works at his trade three hours daily and devotes nine hours to the study of the Torah, he should spend three of these nine hours in the study of the Written Law, three in the study of the Oral Law, and the remaining three in reflecting on how to deduce one rule from another. The words of the Prophets are comprised in the Written Law, while their exposition falls within the category of the Oral Law. The subjects styled *Pardes* (Esoteric Studies) are included in Talmud. This plan applies to the period when one begins learning. But after one has become proficient and no longer needs to learn the Written Law or continually be occupied with the Oral Law, he should, at fixed times, read the Written Law and the traditional dicta, so as not to forget any of the rules of the Torah, and should devote all his days exclusively to the study of Talmud according to his breadth of mind and maturity of intellect.[12]

This unusually expansive, almost prolix, formulation is based on the following concise, almost epigrammatic, saying in the Talmud: "One should always divide his years into three: [devoting] a third to Scripture, a third to *Mishnah,* and a third to Talmud."[13] Maimonides has here dramatically inverted the usual procedure, which leads him to condense lengthy talmudic statements.

The Maimonidean paraphrase is highly problematic, and the following items require explication: (a) the nonchalant substitution of what appears to be the genus for a species, in other words, "Oral Law" for "*Mishnah*"; (b) the designation of "*Gemara*" or "Talmud"[14] as an independent unit of study, distinct from the "Oral Law," and the inclusion of metaphysics and the natural sciences in this third unit of study. A precise definition of the terms "*Mishnah*" and "*Gemara*" according to Maimonides, determination of their scope, and definition of their relations will help resolve these difficulties. It would be useful perhaps to indicate the conclusions and then provide the documentation:

First, *Mishnah* and *Gemara* are exactly coterminous in scope – complete, unabridged summaries of Oral Law.

Secondly, they differ in method and form, *Mishnah* being apodictic and popular while *Gemara* is analytic and technical, but they are alike in purpose and actual achievement. *Gemara* is to *Mishnah* what rational demonstration (*moffet*) is to traditional belief (*kabbalah*). Its essence is independent reflection, conceptualization, and interpretative elaboration or innovation.

Finally, philosophy is an integral, even paramount component of this Oral Law, and, like *halakhah* proper, can be presented either in apodictic and catechetic summary or in analytic and demonstrative elaboration.

That Maimonides equates *Mishnah* with the Oral Law in his paraphrase of Kiddushin 30a, interpreting it to mean the authoritative corpus of the entire Oral Law, is not really perplexing upon closer scrutiny. The basic text of the Oral Law in toto is the work redacted by R. Judah HaNassi, the *Mishnah*. *Every other work* – Tannaitic or Amoraic – stands in interpretative-commentatorial, but not actually innovating, relation to the *Mishnah*. Maimonides repeats this assertion, carefully and consistently, in his introductions to the *Commentary on the Mishnah* and the *Mishneh Torah*. The purpose of the *Sifra* and *Sifre* is "to explain the principles of the *Mishnah*," while the function of the *Tosefta* is "to explain the subject matter of the *Mishnah*." The same is true for the *Baraita*, whose purpose is "to elucidate the words of the *Mishnah*." This interpretative relation characterizes also the Talmud, the Palestinian as well as the Babylonian; both continue the task of explanation. One of the four goals that R. Ashi set for himself in the compilation of the Talmud was to reveal the principles, methods, and proofs utilized in the *Mishnah*. Explanation *(be'ur)* is the major feature of all these works. In light of this we may perhaps explain the fact that Maimonides frequently uses the term "Talmud" when he is actually quoting the *Tosefta*,[15] for they are generically identical. *Mishnah*, in brief, represents the entire Oral Law.

Mishnah differs from *Gemara* only in that its contents are cast in an apodictic mold – and this is the second characteristic or connotation of the term. *Mishnah* includes the normative conclusion, the obligatory *mitzvah*, without excessive explanation or review of the process of exegesis and inference. It is for this reason that in many different contexts the terms *mishnah*, *mitzvah*, and *halakhah* (or *hilkhata*) are interchangeable and used freely as equivalents.[16] The following instance is especially significant. The introduction to the *Mishneh Torah* begins: "All the precepts that Moses received on Sinai were given together with their interpretation, as it is said, '*And I will give to you the tables of stone, and the law [Torah], and the commandment [mitzvah]*' (Ex. 24:12). 'The law' refers to the Written Law; 'the commandment,' to its interpretation. God bade us fulfill the Law in accordance with 'the commandment.' This commandment refers to that which is called the Oral Law."[17] Here the equation of *mishnah*, *mitzvah*, and *Torah she-be'al peh* (the Oral Torah) is sharply delineated. That this is a conscious equation, carefully reasoned and consistently maintained, is clear from the cross-reference to it in a subsequent book of the *Mishneh Torah*. The talmudic source (Berakhot 5a) for this was noted for the first time apparently by R. Elijah Gaon of Vilna.[18] Happily, we now have the explicit testimony of R. Abraham Maimonides to the effect that this "explanation of the *tradentes* [rabbinic sages]" indeed underlies the opening statement of the *Mishneh Torah*. What is more, our general thesis, which has Maimonides equating *Mishnah* with the Oral Law as a whole (or *mishnah* and *mitzvah*), is fully corroborated by R. Abraham, who asserts very forcefully, almost dramatically, that *mishnah* refers not to a given text but to the "principles [sources] of tradition."[19] *Mishnah* refers to the traditional corpus of the Oral Law, and Talmud is its ever-expanding commentary.

As a final illustration we turn to the passage in the oft-quoted letter of Maimonides to R. Pinḥas, the judge of Alexandria:

> Furthermore, in the introduction to my composition I wrote that I had composed the work according to the method of the Mishnah and in the style of the Mishnah. But you have not paid sufficient attention to my words, nor have you understood the difference between the method of the Mishnah and the method of the Talmud. Because of your ignorance of this matter, you wrote the following criticism in your letter: "Even when I study your composition, I find in it many matters which remain unclear to me because you have not given proofs for them, while my own mind is not clear enough to comprehend them." This was the gist of your criticism; permit me now to explain.
>
> You should know that every author of a book – whether it deals with the laws of the Torah or with other kinds of wisdom, whether it was composed by one of the ancient wise men among the nations of the world or by physicians – always adopts one of two ways (structures and styles): either that of the monolithic code (*ḥibbur*) or that of a discursive commentary (*perush*). In a monolithic code, only the correct subject matter is recorded, without any questions, without answers, and without any proofs, in the way which Rabbi Judah adopted when he composed the Mishnah. The discursive commentary, in contrast, records both the correct subject matter and other opinions which contradict it, as well as questions on it in all its aspects, answers, and proofs as to why one opinion is true and another false, or why one opinion is proper and another improper; this method, in turn, is that of the Talmud, which is a discursive commentary upon the Mishnah. Moreover, if someone should object to my distinction between the code and the commentary, and claim that because the names of the Rabbis are cited in the Mishnah – as when one Rabbi holds one opinion about a law and another Rabbi holds a contradictory one – this kind of citation of names constitutes proof, it is necessary for me to point out that this

is not proof: a proof explains why one Rabbi holds a certain opinion, while another Rabbi might hold a contradictory one.[20]

In defending the purpose and nature of the *Mishneh Torah,* Maimonides defined the structural and stylistic differences between *perush* and *ḥibbur,* discursive commentary and monolithic code, justifying his own opus by characterizing it as *ḥibbur.* What has not been stressed in this passage is the telling equation of *ḥibbur* with the "way of the *Mishnah*" and *perush* with the "way of the Talmud"; in other words, two approaches to, or two presentations of, the same material. Maimonides then proceeds to equate his own work not only with the *Mishnah* but with the "way of the *Mishnah,*" which can now be paraphrased as follows: The *Mishneh Torah,* a complete summary of the Oral Law, is equal to the *Mishnah* in its comprehensive scope and apodictic method. This is further substantiated by all Maimonidean descriptions of his Code.[21] If one were to conflate them, the following characterization would emerge: An authoritative summary of and guide to the entire Oral Law, practical and nonpractical, modeled upon the genre as well as the style of the *Mishnah* and obviating the need for exacting analysis of talmudic demonstration and argumentation, and on the basis of which one will be able to know in capsule form the contents of *Torah she-be'al peh.* Especially significant is the elimination of talmudic "depth study."

From this discussion we can learn the following about the three study units:

1. At first glance the substitution of the term "Written Law" for *Mikra* (Bible) seemed simple and unproblematic, and therefore we did not find it necessary to comment on it previously. However, it is difficult to understand the relegation of the Bible (Written Law) to the elementary level of study ("the period when one begins learning"), that which is needed in order to create a reservoir of basic knowledge but which apparently does not involve interpretive effort or deep study. The implication that all that is required of a student in this area is a certain level of textual expertise demands further explanation. After all, we can easily show that Maimonides made extensive use of the Bible in many different contexts (philosophical, halakhic, ethical, historical, linguistic); likewise, mention can be made of his productive achievements in the area of biblical interpretation: original commentary and innovative application.

Maimonides assigned great importance to the precise and detailed knowledge of the Bible, and opposed the kind of preoccupation with Talmud study that left no place for the study of the Bible, "a book that is the guide of the first and the last men,"[22] "the book that has illumined the darknesses of the world."[23] He criticized those who claim to understand the Bible on the basis of "glancing through it during leisure hours . . . as one would glance through a historical work or piece of poetry."[24] He advised his beloved disciple R. Yosef ben Yehudah,[25] whom he knew to be deeply involved in study: "Nevertheless, expound the

Torah of Moses our teacher, peace be upon him, and do not depart from it . . . [for] in it you will see divine vision."[26]

In the third chapter of the *Eight Chapters*, the Torah is referred to as the "book of truth."[27] Philosophical views and matters of belief are regularly associated by Maimonides with the Bible, either by close interpretation or by direct reference. Maimonides' son, R. Abraham, cites several interpretive traditions that he received from his father orally, and often dwells on biblical interpretations found in the *Mishneh Torah* or implied by halakhic statements therein.

In the light of these facts, which point to Maimonides' constant and intense engagement with the Bible, we must return to his words quoted from the *Laws of Torah Study* 1:12, in which he seems to present biblical study as an incomplete and elementary discipline, providing neither challenge nor insight. In fact, the study of the Bible has two aspects in Maimonides' conception: the aspect of simple reading, which results in basic cognitive knowledge, and the aspect of in-depth study, which leads to philosophical enlightenment and correct opinions.

2. *Mishnah* is an independent subject for study, comprehensive in its scope and not dependent on the *Gemara* (the same holds for Maimonides' *Mishneh Torah* [cf. Maimonides' well-known comment about the scope of the *Mishneh Torah* in the last paragraph of his introduction]); this can be inferred from the author's definition of his *Commentary on the Mishnah*:

> It seems to me that if this work covers the entire *Mishnah,* as I will explain, it will have four great uses. First, that we will make known the correct interpretation of the *Mishnah* and explicate its terms; for if you were to ask the greatest of the scholars to explain a particular *halakhah* from the *Mishnah,* he would not be able to answer unless he had memorized the Talmud on that *halakhah*; or he would reach the point at which the Talmud on the topic would have to be looked at. No one is able to memorize the whole Talmud, especially when one *halakhah* in the *Mishnah* gives rise to four or five folios as [the Talmud] moves from topic to topic, bringing proofs, challenges, and solutions to the point where no one who is not a great expert in the text can possibly summarize the interpretation of a particular *Mishnah*. And this does not even take into account those *halakhhot* whose interpretation is scattered through several different tractates. Second, as to halakhic decisions: I will indicate, for each *halakhah,* whose opinion determines the final decision. Third, that it will serve as an introduction for one beginning to study, enabling him to learn all matters with precision and clarity and to encompass thereby the entire contents of the Talmud; this will greatly assist in the study of the Talmud. And fourth, it will serve

as a review for one who has already studied and learned, helping him keep all of his knowledge always accessible and organized.

And when I thought about all of these things, I was drawn to write the work of which I had conceived. My intention in this work is to explicate the *Mishnah* as it is interpreted in the Talmud, presenting only the correct interpretations and leaving out those rejected in the Talmud; I will record the reason for each particular decision, as well as the reasons, in some cases, for controversies where they arose; also, the names of the Sages according to whose position the *halakhah* was decided, as indicated in the Talmud. In all this I will strive for brevity of language so that the reader will not be left with uncertainty; for this work is not written to explain to those who cannot comprehend, but rather, to explain to those capable of understanding.[28]

The same principled position regarding comprehensive scope is also emphasized in the equation of the *Mishnah* of R. Judah HaNassi to Maimonides' *Mishneh Torah*. As we have seen, Maimonides identified his magnum opus with the *Mishnah* and with the "way of the *Mishnah*"; that is, the *Mishneh Torah* is equivalent to the *Mishnah* in its comprehensive scope and in its direct and authoritative approach. This approach, which at once presents a definitive summary of the *Mishnah* and a definitive summary of the *halakhah,* is justified in terms of its pedagogical efficiency and reliability – it facilitates quick understanding and minimizes the burden on memory. The expression, "matters of Torah that require no profound reflection, as for instance established laws,"[29] epitomizes the approach exactly. Maimonides' ideal was disciplined scholarly interest in the entire range of the Oral Law, even including those laws pertaining to matters that are not currently applicable [due to the absence of the Temple in Jerusalem or the dispersion of the Jewish people in the Diaspora]. The *Mishnah* – as with his own *Mishneh Torah* – includes everything.

In order properly to clarify this concept, we should note that here Maimonides differs from R. Bahya ibn Pakuda, who emphasized that too much occupation with the study of laws remote from current reality does not necessarily contribute to one's religious sensitivity, and may even detract from it.[30] R. Bahya and those who subscribed to his view focused their attention on matters of theological and ethical contemplation, and thereby limited the study of the Talmud to its practical portions. Maimonides' system was quite different: He sought to preserve the Talmud in its entire scope, but with new language and in a different order; he rejected only certain types of *pilpul* (subtle or oversubtle exegesis) that he viewed as empty and pointless. According to his approach, limitation of the scope of study represented an impairment – both religious and intellectual – of the historical-cultural continuity of the nation. This impairment must be prevented. Maimonides' purpose in the *Mishneh Torah* was to improve the methodology of study, without limiting its scope. And just as he refused to accept the assumption that the scope of study must be limited for external reasons, so he also rejected outright the opposing claim that the reliance on summaries and conciseness would interfere with comprehensive study. The balance between inclusiveness and condensation that characterizes the *Mishneh Torah* is most impressive, no less than other characteristics that distinguish this work, such as its brevity of language and refined literary taste.

3. The study of *Gemara,* whether according to its standard definition or according to Maimonides' special definition of it, is difficult, complex, and demanding. In the words of the introduction to the *Mishneh Torah*: "Needless to add ... the Talmud itself – the Babylonian as well as the Palestinian – ... require[s], for [its] comprehension, a broad mind, a wise soul, and considerable study."[31] Maimonides repeatedly emphasizes that the study of Talmud in and of itself is difficult, independent of historical and other auxiliary factors that burden the learner even more and that increase the Talmud's inherent difficulties.[32] Even under the most comfortable and undistracting conditions, it requires that the student dedicate himself to it "according to his breadth of mind and maturity of intellect,"[33] "for its method is exceedingly profound."[34] The difficulty of Talmud study arises both from the nature of the material and from its form: the method of argument and reasoning, the extremely associative nature of its discourse, the condensed and subtle language, the broad scope, the confusing intertwining of subjects and concepts, and, in our terms of reference, the whole range of philological, historical, and phenomenological problems – all of these weigh upon the learner. And if this description is fitting for the Talmud in general, what about those passages that are particularly difficult, to the point where the greatest scholars cannot make sense of them? On the subject of ritual purity, Maimonides says:

> And if the greatest of the scholars of the *Mishnah,* peace be upon them, found these matters very difficult, how much the more so should we [be expected to find them]. ... Today, on account of our many sins, if you were to turn to the heads of *yeshivot* – and certainly of synagogues – you would discover that the matter is very hard for them. ... Any *halakhah* dealing with purity and impurity ... and related matters is difficult even for the great scholars – how much the more so for their students.[35]

The most distinctive aspect of the *Gemara* is the deliberation that seeks to reconstruct the process of formulation of the laws. The *Mishneh Torah,* like the *Mishnah,* is described as a work, one of whose main distinctions is its elimination of the complex and exhausting deliberation of the talmudic dialectic. Maimonides' words in his *Commentary on the Mishnah* are noteworthy in this context: "There is no conflict between Rabbi [Judah HaNassi] and R. Akiva regarding the decision; they differ only regarding its proof. The appropriate place for the details of their controversy and for their proofs for their respective arguments is the deliberation in the Talmud, not here [in the *Mishnah*], so that we do not multiply words here at the expense of utility."[36]

It seems then, that a consciousness of the distinction between *Mishnah* and Talmud is always in order. As a biographical addendum, which sheds some light on this complex matter, it is important to remember that Maimonides' interest in Talmud did not end with the completion of the *Mishneh Torah*. He wrote commentaries and novellae on the *Gemara,* not limiting himself to those topics about which questions were addressed to him. This does not contradict the underlying principle of his work. We must keep in mind that on many topics it was impossible to avoid dealing with the talmudic deliberation itself. Matters on which a clear decision had not been reached required renewed examination of the talmudic sources. The same is true for controversial interpretations: These, too, required a review of the original sources for proper reevaluation. No abridgment or book of halakhhic rulings can achieve completeness or win general approval without a basis in the Talmud. With respect to certain matters, the direct study of the *Gemara* remains the ultimate authority to which all must turn. Maimonides' supporters, who directed angry or mocking criticism at those students who continued to labor over the *Talmud* instead of relying exclusively on the *Mishneh Torah,* were not faithful to their master's views. It was not accidental that Maimonides emphatically declared in his letter to R. Pinḥas Dayana: "Know from the beginning that I did not, God forbid, say not to occupy yourselves with the *Gemara* . . .'"[37]

4. A component of *Gemara* that deserved special mention alongside of that "which is forbidden or permitted, clean or unclean" is philosophy, or *Pardes*. Let us note immediately a formal resemblance between these two parts of *Gemara*: Both are uniformly described as demanding "a broad mind, a wise soul, and prolonged study." The same qualities of mind and prerequisites of knowledge are prescribed for both branches of *Gemara* study.[38]

The inclusion of philosophy in the Oral Law was already posited by Maimonides in an earlier chapter of *The Book of Knowledge,* in the *Laws of the Basic Principles of the Torah*.[39] There he restated his identification of the "Account of Creation" [Gen. 1] with physics, and of the "Account of the Divine Chariot" [Ezek. 1] with metaphysics, as set forth in his *Commentary on the Mishnah*.[40] The text of the *Commentary on the Mishnah* is as follows:

> Now listen to what I have determined according to my understanding from my study of the writings of the Sages: in the term "Account of Creation" they refer to the natural sciences and the study of cosmogony.

By the "Account of the Divine Chariot" they mean theology, i.e., the discussion of the nature of reality and of the existence of the Creator, His knowledge, His attributes, the necessity of all that emanates from Him, the angels, the soul, human reason, and the afterlife. On account of the importance of these two types of science, the natural and the divine, that the Sages rightly considered of great importance, they cautioned against studying them in the same manner as the other disciplines; for it is known that every man, be he foolish or wise, is drawn naturally toward all the disciplines. It is impossible for a man to avoid contemplating these two sciences on a primary level, directing his thought toward them, without any prior introductions and without having progressed through the stages of scientific study. Thus, [the text] warned about this in order to prevent it, seeking to discourage whoever thinks he can direct his thought towards the "Account of Creation" without proper preparation, as it is said: "Whoever gazes upon four things . . ." And as a warning to one who tries to direct his thoughts and contemplate upon matters relating to the divine with his simple imagination, without having progressed through the stages of scientific study, it is said: "Whoever is not careful about the honor of his Maker . . . it would have been better for him not to have come into the world." This means that it would have been better had he not been part of humanity, but had rather been of another species of creature, for he is seeking knowledge not appropriate to his way and his nature; for he does not understand what is above and what is below, but is foolish in matters of reality. And when a man devoid of all knowledge seeks to contemplate and thereby know what is above the heavens and what is beneath the earth, using his deficient imagination, which thinks of the heavens as though they were the attic of his house, and [to know] what was before the heavens were created and what will be after they cease to exist, this will surely bring him to despair and distraction. He who considers this wonderful, divinely inspired expression, "Whoever is not careful about the honor of his Maker . . ." [realizes] that it refers to one who is not careful about his intellect, for the intellect is the honor of God. And since such a man is not aware of the value of this thing that has been granted to him, he is given to the control of his appetites and is made animal-like. This is why it was said, " 'Whoever is not careful about the honor of his Maker . . .' refers to one who sins in secret"; and elsewhere it was said, "Adulterers do not commit adultery until a spirit of foolishness has entered into them." This is true, for when the appetite rules – any appetite – the intellect is not whole. [The *Mishnah*] mentions this matter here, because above it was stated that "these are the essentials of the

Torah"; now this text delineates the foundations of the essentials of the Torah.[41]

And here is the text from the *Mishneh Torah,* the *Laws of the Basic Principles of the Torah*:

> The topics connected with these five precepts, treated in the above four chapters, are what our wise men called *Pardes* (Paradise), as in the passage "Four went into *Pardes*" (Hagigah 14). And although those four were great men of Israel and great sages, they did not all possess the capacity to know and grasp these subjects clearly. Therefore, I say that it is not proper to dally in *Pardes* till one has first filled oneself with bread and meat; by which I mean knowledge of what is permitted and what is forbidden, and similar distinctions in other classes of precepts. Although these last subjects were called by the sages "a small thing" (when they say "A great thing, *Maaseh Merkavah* [account of the Divine Chariot]; a small thing, the discussion of Abbayye and Rava" [i.e., talmudic debate]), still they should have the precedence. For the knowledge of these things gives primarily composure to the mind. They are the precious boon bestowed by God, to promote social well-being on earth, and enable men to obtain bliss, in the life hereafter. Moreover, the knowledge of them is within the reach of all, young and old, men and women; those gifted with great intellectual capacity as well as those whose intelligence is limited.[42]

Furthermore, Maimonides' halakhic formulation, which grafts philosophy onto the substance of the Oral Law, dovetails perfectly with his view of the history of philosophy. In common with many medieval writers, Jewish, Christian, and Muslim, Maimonides is of the opinion that Jews in antiquity cultivated the science of physics and metaphysics, which they later neglected for a variety of reasons, historical and theological. He does not, however, repeat the widespread view, as does HaLevi, that all sciences originated in Judaism and were borrowed or plagiarized by the ancient philosophers. HaLevi, echoing a Philonic view, states: "The roots and principles of all sciences were handed down from us first to the Chaldeans, then to the Persians and Medes, then to Greece, and finally to the Romans."[43] That Maimonides does not subscribe to this view of the Jewish origin of all wisdom has been inferred – a kind of argument *ex silentio* – from his formulation in the *Guide,* where he merely establishes the antiquity of philosophy per se. It seems to me that this is clearly noted by Maimonides in the introduction to his *Commentary on the Mishnah,* where, in buttressing an argument, he says that this matter is known to us not only from the prophets but also from the wise men of the ancient nations "even though they did not see the prophets or hear their words." Maimonides does not care to trace all philosophic wisdom back to an ancient Jewish matrix. His sole concern is to establish *ḥokhmah* (philosophical wisdom) as an original part of the Oral Law, from which it follows that the study of the latter in its encyclopedic totality – that is, *Gemara* – includes philosophy. This is the position – a harmonistic position unifying the practical, theoretical, and theological parts of the law – that Maimonides codified in the *Mishneh Torah*.

5. Maimonides has thus unequivocally committed himself to the nobility of philosophical knowledge. The provocative statement in the *Mishneh Torah* concerning the hierarchical relationship of Talmud study to *ma'aseh merkavah* (small matters and great matters) is identical not only with the emphasis of the *Mishnah Commentary* concerning *gufe Torah* (essentials, lit. "bodies") and *yesodot gufe Torah* (principles, roots, or foundations of those essentials) but also with the axiology outlined in the famous palace metaphor:

> Those who have come up to the habitation [lit., palace] and walk around it are the jurists who believe true opinions on the basis of traditional authority and study the Law concerning the practices of divine service, but do not engage in speculation concerning the fundamental principles of religion and make no inquiry whatever regarding the rectification of belief.
>
> Those who have plunged into speculation concerning the fundamental principles of religion have entered the antechambers. People there indubitably have different ranks. He, however, who has achieved demonstration, to the extent that that is possible, of everything that may be demonstrated; and who has ascertained in divine matters, to the extent that that is possible, everything that may be ascertained; and who has come close to certainty in those matters in which one can only come close to it – has come to be with the ruler in the inner part of the habitation.[44]

6. In the *Mishneh Torah, Laws of Repentance*, Maimonides writes as follows:

> It is known and certain that the love of God does not become closely knit in a man's heart till he is continuously and thoroughly possessed by it and gives up everything else in the world for it; as God commanded us, "with all your heart and with all your soul" (Deut. 6:5). One only loves God with the knowledge with which one knows Him. According to the knowledge will be the love. If the former be little or much, so will the latter be little or much. A person ought therefore to devote himself to the understanding and comprehension of those sciences and studies which will inform him concerning his Master, as far as it lies in human faculties to understand and comprehend – as

indeed we have explained in the Laws of the Basic Principles of the Torah.[45]

On the basis of these words, also hinted at in *The Guide of the Perplexed,*[46] we can take another step, to an additional conclusion that is significant and whose implications are far-reaching. The ultimate, desired perfection is spiritual perfection: love of God anchored in the knowledge of God. We are not dealing here with intellectualism for its own sake. Philosophical knowledge is not the be-all and end-all. The ultimate purpose of all study is the exalted religious experience – love of God. Intellectual perfection, which occupies a central place in Maimonides' thought, is a necessary precondition for the love of God. Note also his words in the *Laws of the Basic Principles of the Torah,* which illuminate the topic of intellectualism and which argue that intellectual occupation and achievement are means to a higher end:

> This God, honored and revered, it is our duty to love and fear; as it is said "You shall love the Lord your God" (Deut. 6:5), and it is further said "You shall fear the Lord your God" (*ibid.* 6:13).
>
> And what is the way that will lead to the love of Him and the fear of Him? When a person contemplates His great and wondrous works and creatures and from them obtains a glimpse of His wisdom which is incomparable and infinite, he will straightway love Him, praise Him, glorify Him, and long with an exceeding longing to know His great Name; even as David said, "My soul thirsts for God, for the living God" (Ps. 42:3). And when he ponders these matters, he will recoil frightened, and realize that he is a small creature, lowly and obscure, endowed with slight and slender intelligence, standing in the presence of Him who is perfect in knowledge. And so David said "When I consider Your heavens, the work of Your fingers – what is man that You are mindful of him?" (Ps. 8:4–5). In harmony with these sentiments, I shall explain some large, general aspects of the works of the Sovereign of the Universe, that they may serve the intelligent individual as a door to the love of God, even as our sages have remarked in connection with the theme of the love of God, "Observe the Universe and hence, you will realize Him who spoke and the world was."[47]

Conceptual understanding is not complete unless it leads to the love of God. The critical role of philosophical contemplation is to bring about love of God; that is, intellectualism was in the eyes of its devotees, including Maimonides, a necessary component of the religious tradition and the religious experience. While in many cases rationalism arose in the context of an apologetic polemic ("for this is your wisdom and your understanding in the eyes of the nations"),[48] nevertheless, it was undoubtedly seen as a positive obligation, of intrinsic significance, independent of apologetic aspects directed toward an external debate.

Intellectual achievement is a vital and critical component of religious perfection. It is a religious obligation to use our intellectual powers to delve into the nature of the universe and the meaning of the Torah, both of which are revelations of the divine.

The inclusion of *The Book of Knowledge* – which includes explicit philosophical topics – in a comprehensive halakhic treatise [the *Mishneh Torah*] highlights Maimonides' conception of the unity of the philosophical and halakhic essentials of Judaism. The purpose of intellectual reflection and of the mastery of the various scientific disciplines is spiritual experience. Learning attains its pinnacle and ultimate purpose to the extent that the learner approaches a condition of a "love-sick individual" with reference to God.[49]

7. The understanding of *ta'amei mitzvot* (the rationales of the commandments) is an important component of this process. The study of all of the commandments, with their explanations and reasons, is a religious obligation. Maimonides' words suggesting this matter in the *Laws of Trespass* call for careful study:

> It is fitting for man to meditate upon the laws of the holy Torah and to comprehend their full meaning to the extent of his ability. Nevertheless, a law for which he finds no reason and understands no cause should not be trivial in his eyes. Let him not "break through to rise up against the Lord lest the Lord break forth upon him" (Ex. 19:24); nor should his thoughts concerning these things be like his thoughts concerning profane matters. Come and consider how strict the Torah was in the law of trespass! Now if sticks and stones and earth and ashes became hallowed by words alone as soon as the name of the Master of the Universe was invoked upon them, and anyone who comported with them as with a profane thing committed trespass and required atonement even if he acted unwittingly, how much more should man be on guard not to rebel against a commandment decreed for us by the Holy One, blessed by He, only because he does not understand its reason; or to heap words that are not right against the Lord; or to regard the commandments in the manner he regards ordinary affairs.
>
> Behold it is said in Scripture: "You shall therefore keep all My statutes, and all Mine ordinances, and do them" (Lev. 20:22); whereupon our sages have commented that "keeping" and "doing" refer to the "statutes" as well as to the "ordinances." "Doing" is well known; namely, to perform the statutes. And "keeping" means that one should be careful concerning them and not imagine that they are less important than the ordinances. Now the "ordinances" are commandments whose reason is obvious, and the benefit derived in this world from doing them is well known; for example, the prohibition against robbery

and murder, or the commandment of honoring one's father and mother. The "statutes," on the other hand, are commandments whose reason is not known. Our sages have said: My statutes are the decrees that I have decreed for you, and you are not permitted to question them. A man's impulse pricks him concerning them and the Gentiles reprove us about them, such as the statutes concerning the prohibition against the flesh of the pig and that against meat seethed with milk, the law of the heifer whose neck is broken, the red heifer, or the scapegoat.

How much was King David distressed by heretics and pagans who disputed the statutes! Yet the more they pursued him with false questions, which they plied according to the narrowness of man's mind, the more he increased his cleaving to the Torah; as it is said: "The proud have forged a lie against me; but I with my whole heart will keep Your precepts" (Ps. 119:69). It is also said there concerning this: "All Your commandments are faithful; they persecute me falsely, help You me" (*ibid.* 119:86).

All the (laws concerning the) offerings are in the category of statutes. The sages have said that the world stands because of the service of the offerings; for through the performance of the statutes and the ordinances the righteous merit life in the world to come. Indeed, the Torah puts the commandment concerning the statutes first; as it is said: "You shall therefore keep My statutes, and Mine ordinances which if a man do, he shall live by them" (Lev. 18:5).[50]

And in the *Laws of Substitute Offerings* we find further development of the same idea:

Although the statutes of the Law are all of them divine edicts, as we have explained at the close of Laws Concerning Sacrilege, yet it is proper to ponder over them and to give a reason for them, so far as we are able to give them a reason. The sages of former times said that King Solomon understood most of the reasons for all the statutes of the Law. It seems to me that in so far as Scripture has said: "Both it and that for which it is changed shall be holy" (Lev. 27:10) – as also in that matter whereof it has said "And if he that sanctified it will redeem his house then he shall add the fifth part of the money of your valuation" (*ibid.* 17:15) – the Law has plumbed the depths of man's mind and the extremity of his evil impulse. For it is man's nature to increase his possessions and to be sparing of his wealth. Even though a man had made a vow and dedicated something, it may be that later he drew back and repented and would now redeem it with something less than its value. But the Law has said, "If he redeems it for himself he shall add the fifth." So, too, if a man dedicated a beast to a sanctity of its body, perchance he would draw back, and since he cannot redeem it, would change it for something of less worth. And if the right was given to him to change the bad for the good he would change the good for the bad and say, "It is good." Therefore Scripture has stopped the way against him so that he should not change it, and has penalized him if he should change it and has said: "Both it and that for which it was changed shall be holy." And both these laws serve to suppress man's natural tendency and correct his moral qualities.[51]

The religious commandment needs no authority beyond itself. The obligation of obedience to it is not conditional, "for reverence is due not to the commandments themselves, but to Him who has issued them, blessed be He."[52] Nevertheless, the search for the meaning and purpose of the commandment, the fervent struggle to find its rationale, is a basic component of the knowledge of God and a means for advancing a person on the path to perfection. Only contemplation, inquiry, and constant thought regarding the meaning and purposes of each and every commandment can prevent the neglect of observance of the commandments and the fading of their importance and influence. In this context, we should read *The Guide of the Perplexed*:

> Know that all the practices of the worship, such as reading the Torah, prayer, and the performance of the other commandments, have only the end of training you to occupy yourself with His commandments, may He be exalted, and not with that which is other than He. If, however, you pray merely by moving your lips while facing a wall, and at the same time think about your buying and selling, or if you read the Torah with your tongue while your heart is set upon the building of your habitation and does not consider what you read; and similarly in all cases in which you perform a commandment merely with your limbs – as if you were digging a hole in the ground or hewing wood in the forest – without reflecting either upon the meaning of that action or upon Him from whom the commandment proceeds or upon the end of the action, you should not think that you have achieved the end. Rather you will then be similar to those of whom it is said: "You are near in their mouth, and far from their reins" (Jer. 12:2).[53]

This is the aim of all spirituality that is based on the belief in the driving and renewing power of insight and internalization. Only penetration to the intention of the commandments and their very essence can open the way for a person to attain perfection or at least to approach it. If one has no awareness of the ultimate purpose, then behavior becomes perfunctory: carrying out the commandments from mindless habit. He fulfills his obligations, but obtains no spiritual benefit from the effort. Moreover, ignorance of the true purposes of the commandments is liable to lead not only to their cheapening and mechanization, but to their distortion. A clear example of this danger can be found in the *Laws of the Mezuzah*:

> For these fools ["who write names of angels, holy names, a Biblical text, or inscriptions usual on seals within the *mezuzah*"] not only fail to fulfill the commandment but they treat an important precept that expresses the Unity of God, the love of Him, and His worship, as if it were an amulet to promote their own personal interests; for, according to their foolish minds, the *mezuzah* is something that will secure for them advantage in the vanities of the world.[54]

The fact that the commandments are not arbitrary, that rather each and every commandment has a reason and a purpose, is the focal point of all Maimonidean literature. For instance, a sentence that gives distinct emphasis to the principle that the commandments are not just decrees but that there is utility in them, to the necessity of publicizing this principle, making it known to scholars and simple folk alike, is found in Maimonides' *Epistle to Yemen*: "If he could only fathom the inner intent of the law, then he would realize that the essence of the true divine religion lies in the deeper meaning of its positive and negative precepts, every one of which will aid man in his striving after perfection."[55]

8. The deep study of the content of the commandments and their purposes is also required in order to teach us that all of the laws of the Torah are intended to elevate man to the highest possible level of morality, to the most exalted level of holiness, and to the perfection deriving from these attainments.[56] Understanding the inner intent of the commandments teaches that the *halakhah* serves as a springboard, as it were, for aspirations and actions that are beyond the specific requirements of the law. Acts that are according to the specific requirements of the law (that is, acts that the *halakhah* defined exactly and with precision) educate us and lead us toward acts that transcend those requirements (that is, moral religious behavior that is the desired ideal). We must understand Maimonides' words in the *Laws of Slaves*:

> It is permitted to work a heathen slave with rigor. Though such is the rule, it is the quality of piety and the way of wisdom that a man be merciful and pursue justice and not make his yoke heavy upon the slave or distress him, but give him to eat and to drink of all foods and drinks. . . .
>
> So it is also explained in the good paths of Job, in which he prided himself: "If I did despise the cause of my manservant, or of my maidservant, when they contended with me . . . Did not He that made me in the womb make him? And did not One fashion us in the womb?" (Job 31:13, 15).

Cruelty and effrontery are not frequent except with heathen who worship idols. The children of our father Abraham, however, i.e., the Israelites, upon whom the Holy One, blessed be He, bestowed the favor of the Law and laid upon them statutes and judgments, are merciful people who have mercy upon all.

Thus also it is declared by the attributes of the Holy One, blessed be He, which we are enjoined to imitate: "And His mercies are over all His works" (Ps. 145:9).

Furthermore, whoever has compassion will receive compassion, as it is said: "And He will show you mercy, and have compassion upon you, and multiply you" (Deut. 13:18).[57]

"Statutes and judgments" and "the quality of piety and the way of wisdom" are rightly juxtaposed here, within a varied spectrum of possibilities.

An unavoidable, natural, and spontaneous consequence of constant occupation with the study of Torah and with the observance of its commandments is that a person's actions will transcend the specific requirements of the law, thereby sanctifying God. Maimonides emphasizes this lesson in the *Laws of the Basic Principles of the Torah*:

And if a man has been scrupulous in his conduct, gentle in his conversation, pleasant toward his fellow-creatures, affable in manner when receiving them, not retorting, even when affronted, but showing courtesy to all, even to those who treat him with disdain, conducting his commercial affairs with integrity, not readily accepting the hospitality of the ignorant nor frequenting their company, not seen at all times, but devoting himself to the study of the Torah, wrapped in *tallit,* and crowned with phylacteries, and doing more than his duty in all things, avoiding, however, extremes and exaggerations – such a man has sanctified God, and concerning him, Scripture says, "And He said to me, 'You are My servant, O Israel, in whom I will be glorified'" (Is. 49:3).[58]

We can summarize by saying that the commandment is simultaneously both the cause and the result of the conceptual purpose, both advancing and forming it, just as it is concurrently both a result – and a driving force – of the love of God. Maimonides taught well the principle that the love of God brings commitment and fervor to the fulfillment of the commandments, and conversely – that fulfilling the commandments, in turn, heightens the intensity of one's longing for and love of God.

9. In his intellectual-educational view and in his teaching regarding the observance of the commandments and the understanding of their inner purpose, Maimonides makes clear his disapproval of acts that are insincere and inconsistent, of artificiality and exhibitionism, of cheap externalization and deceit.[59] Let us look at the *Commentary on the Mishnah*:

> "The afflictors of *perushim*" [i.e., the Pharisees] may be explained as follows: The Sages, peace be upon them, call themselves "*perushim*" because of their separating themselves (*perishutam*) from vices and abominations and the pursuit of worldly matters that cause men to go astray, and they turn toward the world to come and exalted matters. Now there are people who adorn themselves with these qualities; he who is among them pretends to renounce lowly and abominable things, while at the same time these very things characterize him. He distances himself from these things only for worldly interests and thus said [the Sages], peace be upon them, [about them pretenders]: "There are seven types of *perushim*." And they listed all those who act with false piety for worldly gain, such as to be honored by others or to preserve one's wealth and well-being. In the Sages' opinion, the only true *perushim* are those who worship out of love, like our father Abraham. All of the [other] six are to be condemned, for they inflate what is required of them and exaggerate the external aspects in order to deceive others. And therefore, because they add to the Torah and make it despised, they are called "afflictors"; hence the expression "the afflictors of *perushim*."[60]

And we should also consider the following passage on holiness and purity from *The Guide of the Perplexed*:

> Cleaning garments, washing the body, and removal of dirt also constitute one of the purposes of this Law [of ritual purity]. But this comes after the purification of the actions and the purification of the heart from polluting opinions and polluting moral qualities. For to confine oneself to cleaning the outward appearance through washing and cleaning the garment, while having at the same time a lust for various pleasures and unbridled license in eating and sexual intercourse, merits the utmost blame. *Isaiah* says about this: *They that sanctify themselves and purify themselves to go unto the gardens behind one in the midst, eating the flesh of swine, and so on.* He says: They purify themselves and sanctify themselves in the open and public places; and afterwards, when they are alone in their rooms and in the interior of their houses, they are engaged in acts of disobedience. . . . To sum up the dictum: Their outward appearances are clean and universally known as unsullied and pure, whereas innerly they are engaged in the pursuit of their desires and the pleasures of their bodies. But this is not the purpose of the Law.[61]

In essence, we find the same outlook and emphasis in the *Laws of Moral Dispositions and Ethical Conduct*:

> It is forbidden to accustom oneself to smooth speech and flatteries. One must not say one thing and mean another. Inward and outward self should correspond; only what we have in mind, should we utter with the mouth. We must deceive no one, not even an idolator. . . . Even a single word of flattery or deception is forbidden. A person should always cherish truthful speech, an upright spirit, and a pure heart free from all forwardness and perversity.[62]

Appendix: *Aggadah* (Nonlegal Rabbinic Literature)

In Maimonides' eyes, the *aggadah* was a source of great importance that could be studied in depth and used creatively for various purposes (e.g., reinforcing a particular *halakhah* or improving its formulation, supporting a philological argument or a linguistic supposition, and especially – modeling a moral quality or anchoring a philosophical position). Maimonides expressed interest, throughout his life, in the *aggadah,* in problems of its interpretation, carrying special meaning, which missed the point on account of false assumptions and mistaken calculations. Passages of *aggadah* that seem strange and difficult to accept require a rational-spiritual interpretation in order to set straight those who accept the words of the sages "at their face value, not interpreting them at all." His words in the introduction to *Perek Ḥelek* are well known:

> The members of this group [those who interpret *aggadah* literally] are poor in knowledge. One can only regret their folly. Their very effort to honor and to exalt the sages in accordance with their own meager understanding actually humiliates them. As God lives, this group destroys the glory of the Torah and extinguishes its light, for they make the Torah of God say the opposite of what it intended. For He said in His perfect Torah, "The nations who hear of these statutes shall say: Surely this great nation is a wise and understanding people" (Deut. 4:6). But this group expounds the laws and the teachings of our sages in such a way that when the other peoples hear them they say that this little people is foolish and ignoble.[63]

Further on in the same source, we find a hint of a definite plan to write a special commentary on the *aggadot* of the *Talmud* and *Midrash,* based on rational thought and the allegorical-philosophical method of interpretation: "I hope to write a book collecting all the Sages' teachings on this subject from the Talmud and other works. I shall interpret them systematically, showing which must be understood literally and which metaphorically, and which are dreams to be interpreted by a wakeful mind. There I shall explain the many principles of our faith of which I have discussed a few here."[64]

Even though Maimonides eventually abandoned this plan, he did devote a great deal of attention in *The Guide of the Perplexed* to the problems connected with the understanding of parables and prophecies, and to exegetical approaches allowing for the basing of fundamental beliefs on biblical and rabbinic verses. There is no doubt that he saw the *Guide* as a substitute of sorts for the commentary on the *aggadot* that he had meant to write. He made this clear in his introduction to the *Guide*:

> We had promised in the *Commentary on the Mishnah* that we would explain strange subjects in the "Book of Prophecy" and in the "Book of Correspondence" – the latter being a book in which we promised to explain all the difficult passages in the Midrashim where the external sense manifestly contradicts the truth and departs from the intelligible. They are all parables. However, when, many years ago, we began these books and composed a part of them, our beginning to explain matters in this way did not commend itself to us. For we saw that if we should adhere to parables and to concealment of what ought to be concealed, we would not be deviating from the primary purpose. We would, as it were, have replaced one individual by another of the same species. If, on the other hand, we explained what ought to be explained, it would be unsuitable for the vulgar among the people. Now it was to the vulgar that we wanted to explain the import of the Midrashim and the external meanings of prophecy.... With regard to the meaning of prophecy, the exposition of its various degrees, and the elucidation of the parables occurring in the prophetic books, another manner of explanation is used in this treatise. In view of these considerations, we have given up composing these two books in the way in which they were begun. We have confined ourselves to mentioning briefly the foundations of belief and general truths, while dropping hints that approach a clear exposition, just as we have set them forth in the great legal compilation, the *Mishneh Torah*.[65]

NOTES

1   This essay is based on written materials by and discussions with Professor Twersky. Unfortunately, Professor Twersky died in October 1997 and did not write or see the final version. The introduction and accompanying notes were translated and edited by Daniel Marom.

2   Twersky related to Maimonides as "the mouthpiece of tradition." Aware of criticisms of some of Maimonides' formulations, Twersky referred to them in his presentations, sometimes as a check on Maimonides and sometimes as a complement to his approach.

Among the critics he cited were Rabbi Ḥasdai Crescas, who criticized the emphasis on intellectualism in Maimonides; Rabbi Tzadok of Lublin, who argued against Maimonides' inclusion of Aristotelian assumptions in *Hilkhot Yesodei ha-Torah* (*Laws of the Basic Principles of the Torah*); Rabbi Judah HaLevi, who placed greater emphasis on the historical rationale for the observance of *mitzvot* than did Maimonides; and Naḥmanides, who suggested an alternative view of the *ta'amei mitzvot* (rationales of the commandments).

3　Jacob Katz, *Tradition and Crisis: Jewish Society at the End of the Middle Ages* (New York: Schocken, 1971). For more on Twersky's views on this topic, see his "Survival, Normalcy, Modernity," in *Zionism in Transition,* ed. M. Davis (New York: Herzl Press, 1980), 347–51. Twersky elaborates on his views of halakhic monism and spiritual pluralism in "Talmudists, Philosophers and Kabbalists: The Quest for Spirituality in the Sixteenth Century," in *Jewish Thought in the Sixteenth Century,* ed. Bernard Dov Cooperman (Cambridge, MA: Harvard University Press, 1983), 431–59.

4　Given the critiques of Maimonides mentioned in note 2, Twersky saw three possible applications in the Orthodox world: (a) a comprehensive educational system based on the Maimonidean understanding of Jewish education; (b) a comprehensive educational system based on the Maimonidean understanding, with emendations that incorporated some of the critics' views; (c) one or more institutions that based their approach on the Maimonidean understanding alongside others guided by the views of his critics – all within a comprehensive educational system.

As for the non-Orthodox world, Twersky emphasized the need for everyone to be familiar with the traditional view of Jewish education before critiquing it or suggesting alternatives. Since no approach to the Jewish future could be based on a total negation of or detachment from the Jewish past, he argued, one had to begin with a serious consideration of what was proposed by Jewish tradition. He based this view on *The Guide of the Perplexed* III:51, in which Maimonides distinguishes between the "perplexed" Jew, whose confusion is still based on a knowledge of the tradition, and "someone who thinks and frequently mentions God, without knowledge, following a mere imagining." Of this kind of Jew, Maimonides said, "he is to my mind outside the habitation [of God] and far away from it and does not in true reality mention or think about God. For that thing which is in his imagination and which he mentions in his speech does not correspond to any being at all and has merely been invented by his imagination." *A Maimonides Reader,* ed. Isadore Twersky (West Orange, NJ: Behrman House, 1972), 343–44; henceforth *AMR*.

5　On this topic, Twersky referred us to R. Joseph Schneersohn, *The Tzemaḥ Tzedek and the Haskalah Movement,* trans. Zalman Posner (Brooklyn: Kehot Publication Society, 1962) and M. Stanislawski, "The Tsarist *Mishneh Torah*: A Study in the Cultural Politics of the Russian Haskalah," *Proceedings of American Academy for Jewish Research* 50 (1983): 165–83.

6　M. Ungerfeld, "*Mi-Mikhtavei Yeḥezkel Kaufmann le-Ḥ. N. Bialik,*" *Molad* 21: 183–84 (1964), 536–37.

7　For Maimonides' definitions of some of these terms, see Twersky's *Introduction to the Code of Maimonides (Mishneh Torah)* (New Haven, CT: Yale University Press, 1980). On *tikkun ha-nefesh,* see 300, 417; on *kedushah,* see 286–88; on *da'at Hashem,* see 261, 511; on *ahavat Hashem,* see 215–16, 262, 284, 363, 478.

8   Tversky's use of the term "teleology" with reference to education is illuminated by his discussion of the Maimonidean view of *halakhah* as a teleological system. In both cases (but not in the case of science), the purposes and outcomes determine the means for their attainment. See "On Law and Ethics in the *Mishneh Torah*: A Case Study of *Hilkhot Megillah* II: 17," *Tradition* 24:2 (Winter 1989), 138–39.

9   *Introduction to the Code of Maimonides*, 418.

10   Ibid., 388.

11   Since Tversky incorporated four short passages from his *Introduction to the Code of Maimonides* into the pages that follow, making changes only in the footnotes, we have included them as he wrote them originally in English. These passages appear on pages 489–93, 496–97, and 500 in Chapter 6 of *Introduction to the Code*. An earlier formulation of some ideas in this chapter was published in "Some Non-Halakhic Aspects of the *Mishneh Torah*," in *Jewish Medieval and Renaissance Studies* (Cambridge, MA: Harvard University Press, 1967), 95–118. The rest of the paper was translated from Hebrew by Marc Rosenstein and Daniel Marom. Most translations from Maimonidean sources are taken from Tversky's *A Maimonides Reader*. We thank Rabbi Jeffrey Saks for his help with the footnotes and his critical review of the translation.

12   *AMR*, 65.

13   *Talmud Torah*, i, II, 12; B. Kid. 30a.

14   The terms are interchangeable; see variants on this passage of *Talmud Torah* in the edition of *Sefer ha-Madda*, ed. S. Lieberman (Jerusalem: Mossad HaRav Kook, 1964).

15   See, for example, S. Lieberman, *Tosefta Kifshutah*, Tractate Zera'im, 637 n. 1; 642 n. 25; 645 n. 38, and so on.

16   Kiddushin 49b; *Mishneh Torah, Laws of Marital Relations* 8:4 (where Maimonides translated the Aramaic term "*hilkhata*" as "*Mishnah*"). See R. Ḥai Gaon (or R. Sherira Gaon [see Tzvi Groner, *Teshuvot Rav Ḥai Gaon* (Jerusalem: Chamol, 1974), 65, #881]), in A. E. Harkavy, *Teshuvot ha-Geonim* (reprint, New York: Menorah, 1959), #262, p. 135 (and *Otzar ha-Geonim*, ed. B. M. Lewin, vol. 5 (Jerusalem: Mossad HaRav Kook, 1993) on Megillah 28b, p. 53): "but *hilkhata* is our *Mishnah*." And see Simḥa Asaf, *Teshuvot ha-Geonim* (Jerusalem: HaMadpis Press, 1927), #58, p. 74: "And you must know that the core of all of our Sages' wisdom and of all of their teachings in the *Baraita* and the *Gemara* is the *Mishnah*." See, as well, the beginning of the *Introduction to the Talmud* attributed to R. Shmuel Hanagid: "The *Mishnah* is what is called the Oral Law."

17   *AMR*, 35.

18   *Mishneh Torah, Laws of Slaughtering* 1:4 (*AMR*, 125); see also the beginning of the introduction to the *Mishneh Torah*. R. Menaḥem Krakowski commented on this in *Avodat Hamelekh* (Vilna, 1931; reprint, Jerusalem: [n. p.], 1971), and see B. Z. Bacher, *Ha-Aggadah be-Yetzirat ha-Rambam*, trans. M. Chavatzelet, *Gesher* 9 (1985): 136, n. 1 (Moshe ben Maimon, 145, n. 1).

19   R. Abraham ben Moshe, commentary on Exodus 24:12, A. Wiesenburg edition (London: S. D. Sason, 1959), 382–84 (and note the editor's comment, 383 n. 105).

20   Translated in *Introduction to the Code*, 33–34.

21   Regarding the expression "*Mishneh Torah*" meaning "repeated study of the Torah," see R. Shlomo ben Shimon Duran, *Milḥemet Mitzvah*, 39a. He finds support for his

view in the expression "*Mishneh Tefillah,*" which appears in the *Laws of Prayer* 1:1 (cf. *Kesef Mishneh, Laws of Divorce* 2:6: "That is why the master called his book *Mishneh Torah,* as he writes in shortened form all that is written in the *Gemara.*")

22 *The Guide of the Perplexed,* I:2. The translation is from the S. Pines edition (Chicago: University of Chicago Press, 1963). This is the edition Twersky used in *AMR.*

23 Ibid., III:10.

24 Ibid., I:2.

25 The "perplexed" student, to whom Maimonides addressed his *Guide* – ostensibly in response to Yosef ben Yehudah's questions.

26 *Igrot ha-Rambam,* 16.

27 *Commentary on the Mishnah, Eight Chapters,* Chapter 3 (*AMR,* 366–67).

28 Introduction to *Commentary on the Mishnah,* section 10, ed. Y. Kappach (Jerusalem: Mossad HaRav Kook, 1963). All passages from this work, unless otherwise noted, were translated by Marc Rosenstein and Daniel Marom.

29 *Mishneh Torah, Laws of Prayer,* 4:18.

30 R. Bahya ibn Pakuda, *Duties of the Heart,* trans. M. Hyamson (Jerusalem: Feldheim, 1970), III: 4, 29.

31 *AMR,* 39.

32 See, for example, Twersky's discussion of the impinging historical circumstances in Maimonides' time in his *Introduction to the Code of Maimonides,* 62–67.

33 *Mishneh Torah, Laws of Torah Study* 1:12.

34 Introduction to the *Mishneh Torah* (*AMR,* 39).

35 *Commentary on the Mishnah,* Introduction to Toharot, 37.

36 *Commentary on the Mishnah,* Sotah 5:1.

37 *Igrot ha-Rambam,* vol. 1, 25b.

38 See also the introduction to the *Commentary on the Mishnah,* and *The Guide of the Perplexed* I:31–34.

39 Chapter 4:13.

40 For background on the "Account of Creation" and the "Account of the Divine Chariot," cf. Twersky, *Introduction to the Code of Maimonides,* 361, and *Mishnah* Hagigah 2:1.

41 *Commentary on the Mishnah,* Hagigah 2:1.

42 Chapter 4:13 (*AMR,* 48).

43 Rabbi Judah HaLevi, *The Kuzari,* II: 66.

44 *The Guide of the Perplexed* III:51 (*AMR,* 342).

45 Chapter 10:6 (*AMR,* 85).

46 III:28 and III:51 (*AMR,* 316–18, 341–49).

47 Chapter 2:1–2 (*AMR,* 45–46).

48 "Wisdom" here is a technical term equivalent to *Pardes.*

49 *Mishneh Torah, Laws of Repentance* 10:3 (*AMR,* 84).

50 *Mishneh Torah, Laws of Trespass* 8:8 (*AMR,* 145–46); see Twersky's interpretation of this passage in "*Berur Divrei ha-Rambam: Hilkhot Meilah 8:8 le-Parashat Ta'amei ha-Mitzvot la-Rambam,*" in *Perakim le-Toldot ha-Hevra ha-Yehudit bi-Yemei ha-Beinayim u-va-Et ha-Hadashah* (Jerusalem: Magnes Press, 1980), 24–33.

51 *Mishneh Torah, Laws of Substitute Offerings* 4:13 (*AMR,* 149–50). For a comprehensive discussion of these two sources, see *Introduction to the Code of Maimonides,* 407 ff.

52   *Mishneh Torah, Laws of Slaughtering* 14:16 (*AMR*, 125).

53   III:51 (*AMR*, 345).

54   Chapter 5:4 (*AMR*, 95).

55   *AMR*, 442.

56   See Twersky's *Introduction to the Code of Maimonides*, 427–30, for a fuller treatment of this topic.

57   Chapter 9:8 (*AMR*, 177).

58   Chapter 5:11 (*AMR*, 50).

59   See Twersky's *Introduction to the Code of Maimonides*, 150–53, for a fuller treatment of this topic.

60   *Commentary on the Mishnah*, Sotah 3:3.

61   *The Guide of the Perplexed*, III:33. The translation is from the S. Pines edition, vol. 2, 533.

62   Chapter 2:6 (*AMR*, 56).

63   *Commentary on the Mishnah*, Sanhedrin, Chapter 10, 201 (*AMR*, 407).

64   Ibid., 209 (*AMR*, 417).

65   Introduction to *The Guide of the Perplexed* (*AMR*, 240–41).

Supplement: Isadore Twersky

In Isadore Twersky's view, the ideal Jewish education is halakhic education as conceived by traditional rabbinic Judaism. To formulate this ideal, Twersky drew upon the writings of Maimonides, whom he saw as traditional Judaism's most articulate spokesman.[1]

Twersky analyzed Maimonides' writings on education using the same method with which he examined Maimonides' writings in other areas of halakhic life, such as prayer, charity, and the land of Israel.[2] He would begin with a very close reading of the law on a specific subject, as summarized in the *Mishneh Torah*, paying particular attention to key conceptual terms. He would then make explicit the philosophical underpinnings of the legal stipulations, drawing on all of Maimonides' work. Finally, he would return to the *Mishneh Torah* to elucidate the relationship between philosophy and the law.

This process was Twersky's attempt to rearticulate, rather than newly interpret, the classical Jewish approach to a given subject. Despite challenges from the other scholars about the impossibility of any "objective" rearticulation, Twersky remained firm in his contention that he was faithfully representing Maimonidean thought, which itself "merged imperceptibly" with the sources of traditional Judaism.[3]

Twersky applied this methodology to education by looking at Maimonides' summary of Jewish law in *Hilkhot Talmud Torah* (*Laws of Torah Study*) in the *Mishneh Torah*. Asking "What must a Jew study – and why?" he focused on a passage in which Maimonides identifies three units of the halakhic curriculum. Twersky explicated the three terms – *Torah she-bikhtav* (the "Written Law" or *Mikra*), *Torah she-be'al peh* (the apodictic summary of the "Oral Law" or Mishnah), and Talmud (the analytic summary of the "Oral Law," which includes *Pardes,* or philosophy) – and described the subject matter and pedagogies they entail.

He then disclosed the philosophical assumptions underlying these terms and sought the principles that integrated them into a conception of education. For this purpose he cited other writings by Maimonides on Judaism, ethics, science, society, and personality development – in their relationship to education. These explorations led him to a domain he called "meta-*halakhah*": an understanding that emerges from a thorough study of *halakhah* and reveals "the infrastructure and superstructure, the foundations and goals, of religious law and life."[4]

In his deliberations with the scholars and educators, Twersky identified the Maimonidean idea of *hergel* as the guiding principle of a traditional Jewish education, a principle he had not yet discussed in his published work. The term might literally be translated as "habituation," but, he argued, the sense of *hergel* – unlike routinization – was to infuse observance of *mitzvot* with philosophical understanding, so that observance would not become mechanical or perfunctory.

According to Twersky, the role of traditional Jewish education is to activate *hergel*. Turning to the *Laws of Torah Study*, he found three stages of *hergel*: from birth to the acquisition of reading, from reading to adulthood, and from adulthood to lifelong learning.

As he continued to clarify the ideals of halakhic education, he began to explore such themes as the teacher-student relationship in *halakhah,* character education, and universal education. He also considered various attempts in Jewish history to implement halakhic education and weighed the challenges of contemporary realities to traditional ideals.

At his death, Twersky had almost finished the introduction to what was to be his summary of Maimonides' conception of Jewish education, based on his years of work in our project; and had completed his initial analysis of the passage in the *Laws of Torah Study* entitled "What Must a Jew Study – And Why?" The essay offered in this chapter is comprised of these two works.

Fortunately, we were also left with the notes, sources, and commentaries from Twersky's meetings with the educators. He had read and approved these materials, intending to use them as the basis of his articulation of the classical ideal.

What follows is a selection of these notes and sources from Maimonides, with excerpts from Twersky's published writing that augment his inquiries into halakhic education.[5]

Part One: Meta-*Halakhah* and Education

Since Twersky based his vision of Jewish education on his conception of *halakhah,* some of the meetings with the scholars and educators were dedicated to clarifying his meta-halakhic principles.

On the Nature of Halakhah[6]

Twersky defines *halakhah* as "the practical manifestation of the Jewish spiritual essence." In his approach, *halakhah* is a religious system that combines the practical and spiritual aspects of religion, although he recognized that the two are often in a "coincidence of opposites."

"*Halakhah* is a tense, vibrant, dialectical system," he explained, one that both unites and brings into conflict "law and prophecy," "institution and charisma," "normativeness in action and inwardness in feeling and thought," "objective determinacy and subjective ecstasy," "conformity and spirituality."

Rather than allowing these polarities to compete and ultimately undermine one another, *halakhah* attempts to draw them together so that each can nurture and complete the other. The "dialectical pull" of *halakhah* is toward a "harmonious, mutually fructifying relationship between law and experience."

On Mitzvot

This unique synthesis of idea and behavior finds expression in each *mitzvah,* which was given with its own "teleology," or deeper religious, moral, or social purpose. Twersky presented *tefillah* (prayer) as a classic example of *halakhah bein adam la-Makom* (law between a person and God). In *tefillah,* "the Halakhah takes a thesis – spontaneity of prayer, manifest in a genuinely dialogic relationship between man and God – superimposes upon it an antithesis – standardization and uniformity of prayer – and strives to maintain a synthesis: a devotional routine." Thus, the law "attempts to balance inward experience with routinized performance, to avoid an anarchic liturgy and at the same time not to produce a spiritless stereotype."[7]

Twersky's second example, *tzedakah* (charity), related to the social or interpersonal realm, *bein adam le-ḥaveiro*:

> The *Halakhah* undertook to convert an initially amorphous, possibly even capricious act into a rigidly defined and totally regulated performance. It made charitable contributions, usually voluntary in nature, obligatory, subject to compulsory assessment and collection. However, while objectifying and concretizing a subjective, fluid state of mind, it insisted relentlessly upon the proper attitude, feeling, and manner of action. It hoped to combine the thesis of free, spontaneous giving with the antithesis of soulless, obligatory contribution and produce a composite act which is subjective though quantified, inspired and regular, intimate yet formal. . . . Here the tension is even reflected semantically in the term *tzedakah* which is both righteousness and charity, an act based on one's moral conscience as well as an appropriate course of action spelled out in detail by the law.[8]

On Observance and Spirituality

The observance of *mitzvot* allows the Jew who practices them to gain access to their spiritual dimensions – to a deeper understanding of their content and purpose. Unlike religious approaches that demand a suspension of cognition to make spiritual experience possible, Judaism invites and even obligates a Jew to incorporate understanding into observance of the law:

> It should be stated unequivocally that there is here no natural alliance between spirituality and anti-intellectualism, as is often the case in the history of religion. . . . The usual contrast between intellect and religion . . . is neither accurate nor useful for understanding the tensions in the history of Judaism. . . . Rationalism and spirituality are congenial; the cognitive gesture is not only not antagonistic but is conducive to sensitivity, subjectivity and spontaneity.[9]

There are, however, two limitations to the role of reason in *halakhah*. First, as Twersky stated in the introduction to his essay and emphasized in deliberations with the educators, "the practice of a *mitzvah* is not conditioned upon its understanding or upon one's agreement with it." The primary motivation for continued observance of the law is God's commanding authority, not one's own degree of rational identification with the law – important as it may be, particularly in the Maimonidean conception of *halakhah*.

Second, the practice of the law is a precondition for its understanding. Because the law's essence is not intellectual per se – but intimately bound to the cause and effect of its observance – one cannot grasp or identify with the law without the experience of practice. "One cannot understand the meaning of grieving on the Ninth of Av," Twersky insisted, "unless one gets down on the ground and recites *kinot* [lamentations]." As he points out in his essay, "the act awakens meditation and reason – intellectual understanding."

On the Educational Challenge of Spirituality in Halakhah

While the practice of *halakhah* is a precondition for its understanding, "the spiritual influence of the *mitzvah* on one who observes it is not automatic." A person cannot understand a *mitzvah* merely through contemplation; only by infusing study of the law into its regular practice, and bringing each to bear on the other, can one who practices *halakhah* be influenced spiritually. This dialectical interplay is "the opening for educational intervention," according to Twersky.

It is the dynamic of *hergel,* properly implemented, that precludes the compartmentalization of halakhic knowledge from halakhic practice. The more successfully *hergel* is realized, the more the halakhic Jew will infuse the practice of each *mitzvah* with a sophisticated and refined understanding of its purpose.

On the Aims of Halakhic Education

Hergel is a lifelong activity, but not an end in itself. The more profound *hergel* becomes, the closer it brings the halakhic Jew to "God's palace" and the ultimate aims of observance with understanding: *ahavat Hashem* (love of God) and *avodat Hashem* (worship of God). *Ahavat Hashem* is the spiritual aim and *avodat Hashem* the practical one.

Twersky's emphasis on *ahavat Hashem* was particularly striking to those educators who had been influenced by the common characterization of Christianity as the religion of love. As Twersky stated in his writing and exemplified in his teaching of Maimonidean sources, the aim of Jewish education is to nurture the kind of religious personality motivated in all areas of life by a true love of God. Such a state cannot be attained – as a crudely romantic conception of religion might assume – through fleeting inspiration or spontaneous experiences of wonder and ecstasy. Rather, *ahavat Hashem* arises through the disciplined implementation of *hergel*. Thus, Twersky explains, love of God is at once "the culmination and the goal of the intellectual process" and "the end-product of service."[10]

If *ahavat Hashem* produces "a stimulus to zealous and properly motivated performance of the commandments," *avodat Hashem* reflects the capacity to express love of God in practice. To reach this state, the religious personality must translate his understanding of *mitzvot* into his performance of them. When acts of worship are suffused with such comprehension, they become skillful, nuanced, sensitive enactments of one's love of God. Acts of worship not informed by a grasp of their rationale and purpose, however, can lead to distorted practice.

Part Two: Maimonidean Sources on Education

The Mishneh Torah *on the Nature of* Halakhah

In preparation for their discussion with Twersky, the educators studied his major work, *Introduction to the Code of Maimonides (Mishneh Torah),* particularly the sixth chapter, "Law and Philosophy."

For Twersky, the *Mishneh Torah* is as concerned with the spiritual aspects of *halakhah* as Maimonides' explicitly philosophic works, such as *The Guide of the Perplexed.* Quoting from Maimonides' introduction to the *Mishneh Torah,* Twersky explained that "It is clear that Maimonides intended from the outset not only to compile 'rules in respect of that which is forbidden and permitted, clean and unclean,' but also to elucidate 'Torah principles' and 'theological fundamentals,' to set forth 'true and exact opinion,' and to indicate how each person can understand 'the ultimate goal of the precepts, according to his capacity.' "[11]

This insight helped the educators understand Twersky's view of the *Mishneh Torah* as a pedagogical resource for the application of *hergel*:

> The *Mishneh Torah,* anything but a cut and dried, rigorously functional code, pays attention, as we have noted, to physics, metaphysics,

psychology, dietetics, astronomy, Messianism, and the hereafter. It contains many philosophical comments, theological principles and rationalistic directives, comments on the history of religion and prophecy, science and medicine, and a full ethical system. It also has frequent ethical digressions and interpolations, for ... Maimonides' systematization of the halakah included a good measure of ethicization and rationalization. Ethical assumptions and commandments are spelled out and made explicit. Ideals concretized in a particular law are articulated. Reasons for enigmatic precepts are suggested. Philosophical principles which provide the underpinning of legal details are identified. ... As part of the overall unity of learning which he aspired to embody in the *Mishneh Torah,* Maimonides tried to bring about the unity of practice and concept, external observance and inner meaning, visible action and invisible experience, *gufe Torah* [lit., "bodies of Torah"] and their foundations. ... Polarity recedes and yields to complementarity.

... By calling attention to certain emphases underscored time and again, some of them in Midrashic-exegetic garb, it is possible to obtain additional insight into the conceptions which predominated in Maimonides' mind when he was composing the *Mishneh Torah.* He aspired to produce a law code which instructs as well as commands, thereby providing an effective instrument of education and edification, for law itself is an educative force leading to ethical and intellectual perfection. Law must, therefore, be understood and appreciated as well as obeyed and implemented.[12]

Maimonides on Hergel

Twersky draws on three Maimonidean sources to formulate the principle of *hergel.* The first is from Maimonides' discussion of the tractate on offerings, Menaḥot, in his *Commentary on the Mishnah.* Maimonides explains the interchangeable use in the *Mishnah* of the term *ḥinukh* (here meaning "dedication" or "initiation" but a term that can also mean "education") with *hergel* (habituation) when referring to the consecration of the vessels used for ritual worship in the Temple (e.g., the altar for sacrifice, the table for the bread offering, and the menorah for the lighting of candles). In this passage, *ḥinukh* can be seen as a form of *hergel*:

> The term *ḥinukh* is used metaphorically in the case of the vessels, referring to "initial use." This term is applied here to the initial use of the vessels for the purpose of worship in a way that is similar to its application to a person. At first, he is taught a measure of wisdom or a proper disposition so as to habituate himself [*le-hargil atzmo*], until it is ingrained in him.[13]

Twersky's second source for *hergel* is Maimonides' *Hilkhot De'ot* (*Laws of Moral Dispositions and Ethical Conduct*). Within his discussion of desirable dispositions according to *halakhah,* Maimonides describes how a person may acquire them:

> How shall a man train himself [*yargil atzmo* (*yargil* comes from the same root as *hergel*)] in these dispositions, so that they become ingrained? Let him practice again and again the actions prompted by those dispositions which are the mean between the extremes, and repeat them continually till they become easy and no longer irksome to him, and so the corresponding dispositions will become a fixed part of his character.[14]

For Twersky, such dispositions cannot be attained only through study but through repeated practice. *Hergel* is not to be confused with indoctrination, however, because practice that does not engender the desired dispositions is insufficient. *Hergel* allows a person to understand the desirability of the dispositions and to continue manifesting them in practice consistently.

Twersky's third source for *hergel* is from a section in *The Guide of the Perplexed* in which Maimonides interprets a talmudic passage (Shabbat 31a). The passage claims that each person will be judged in the next world according to three questions: "Have you fixed certain seasons for the study of Torah?" "Have you delved into wisdom?" and "Have you inferred one thing from another?"

According to Maimonides, this passage demonstrates that "man is required first to obtain knowledge of the Torah, then to obtain wisdom, then to know what is incumbent upon him with regard to the legal science of the Law – I mean the drawing of inferences concerning what one ought to do."[15] In Twersky's view, Maimonides' point is that a Jew is evaluated not solely by knowledge of Torah, nor only by the recognition of its truth, but also by the ability to apply learning to practice.

If the previous sources distinguish *hergel* from the extreme of routinization, this one distinguishes it from the extreme of abstraction, or knowledge that is not applied to behavior. *Hergel* liberates halakhic practice from being a mechanical undertaking, adding to it spontaneity, subjectivity, and emotion – referred to by Twersky as *lahluhit* (succulence).

Maimonides on Ahavat Hashem *and* Avodat Hashem

Twersky conceives of the educated halakhic Jew as one whose understanding of Judaism has engendered both a love of God, *ahavat Hashem,* and the ability to express such love through the practice of *mitzvot, avodat Hashem*. This conception is based on his reading of these terms as Maimonides uses them. In his essay, he quotes from Maimonides' *Laws of Repentance* to emphasize that intellectual perfection is a means to the higher aim of *ahavat Hashem*: "One only loves God with the knowledge with which one knows Him. According to the knowledge will be the love. If the former be little or much, so will the latter be little or much."[16]

In his other writings, Twersky explains that the centrality of *ahavat Hashem* in Judaism can be traced to the figure of Abraham and to the core passage of *Shema Yisrael* in the Bible and Jewish prayer. Here, too, he quotes from the *Laws of Repentance*:

> Whoever serves God out of love, occupies himself with the study of the Law and the fulfillment of commandments and walks in the paths of wisdom, impelled by no external motive whatsoever, moved neither by fear of calamity nor by the desire to obtain material benefits – such a man does what is truly right because it is truly right, and ultimately, happiness comes to him as a result of his conduct. This standard is indeed a very high one; not every sage attained it. It was the standard of the patriarch Abraham whom God called His lover, because he served only out of love. It is the standard which God, through Moses, bids us achieve, as it is said "And you shall love the Lord your God" (Deut. 6:5) [immediately following the statement "*Shema Yisrael*"]. When one loves God with the right love, he will straightway observe all the commandments out of love.[17]

Twersky also claims that observance of *mitzvot* without the knowledge that leads to *ahavat Hashem* will result in imperfect practice: "Only contemplation and meditation – sustained reflection on the significance and objectives of every commandment – will safeguard against perfunctory performance."[18]

He emphasizes the knowledge that leads to *ahavat Hashem* for practical reasons as well:

> [O]nly knowledge of the goals of the law will enable man to achieve or approximate the desired perfection. If one is unaware of the ulti-mate objective and behaves mechanically, he is legally unassailable but nothing will rub off on him.[19] In addition, ignorance of the true goals may also result in perversion, not only vulgarization or mechanization of the commandments.

In his essay, Twersky illustrates such perversion with Maimonides' example of those who regard the *mezuzah* as a magical amulet. When he discussed this ex-ample with the educators, Twersky cited Maimonides' teachings on the *mitzvah* of *mezuzah* to demonstrate how proper understanding can enhance *avodat Hashem*:

> Whenever one enters or leaves a home with the mezuza on the door-post, he will be confronted with the declaration of God's unity, blessed be His holy name; and will remember the love due to God, and will

be aroused from his slumbers and his foolish absorption in temporal vanities. He will realize that nothing endures to all eternity save the knowledge of the Ruler of the universe. This thought will immediately restore him to his right senses and he will walk in the paths of righteousness.[20]

Twersky claimed that the reason Maimonides treats every one of the *mitzvot* is because he sees the study and practice of each *mitzvah* as a means to enhancing the reader's capacity for *ahavat Hashem* and *avodat Hashem*.

Maimonides and the Issue of Elitism

Many scholars have characterized Maimonides' educational aims as elitist.[21] The scholars and educators in our project pressed Twersky on this matter, arguing that Maimonides' approach is unfeasible for learners beyond a gifted few. He countered with Maimonides' claim that every individual has the potential to reach *ahavat Hashem* and *avodat Hashem* through *hergel,* noting Maimonides' consistent use of the addendum *kefi koḥo* (according to one's will or strength – as a matter of choice, not merely innate ability) in his legal stipulations relating to education. Even if few people achieve the ultimate, the potential to do so is open to all through the persistent engagement of spirit and mind:

> Maimonides made no secret of his spiritual elitism, but he did not seal it off from all aspirants either. Again, there seems to be a common feature of philosophical and mystical programs; any abstract, nonliteral system is esoteric. In common with kabbalists who passionately espouse esoteric teachings while hoping that these would be spread gradually among increasing numbers of people, Maimonides did not camouflage or compromise his elitist standards; the hierarchical structure of disciplines, attainments, and objectives is firm. The vision of a meaningful observance of *mitzvot* together with genuine appreciation of philosophy is consistently clear. Routine piety and unreflective behavior – the unexamined life – are denigrated. The nobility of philosophic religion (*Torah – ḥokhmah*), in which rationalism and piety are natural companions and through which man's two perfections (of body and soul) are advanced, is emphasized. Nevertheless, he hoped that these elitist standards and goals would be progressively democratized.
>
> He was fully aware of the difficulties and inevitable limitations in the process of combining the philosophic vita contemplativa with the religious vita activa, but this awareness did not blur the theoretical blueprint and did not dampen the hope that there would be ethical-intellectual mobility from the lower to the higher levels. . . .
>
> Whenever (in the *Moreh* [*Guide*], the *Mishneh Torah*, or the *Epistle to Yemen* and other small writings) he had occasion to refer to rational

analysis of religious belief or action, to emphasize the importance of understanding the purposiveness of the Commandments, or to discuss the pure motives for service of God, Maimonides noted that everyone should progress "according to his capacity." The assumption is that the "knowledge [of all] increases and they have attained a large measure of wisdom." Inasmuch as individual capabilities vary greatly, the reality would remain checkered, full of glaring gaps and inequalities. The theory and ideal were egalitarian; the reality sharpened the difference between the *hamon* [masses] and the elite. Consequently, esotericism (i.e., the use of rhetorical devices, expository skills, and instructional tricks, gradual unfolding of abstract conceptions, shaded-nuanced revelation of profound meanings and spiritual-intellectual objectives) was a pedagogic necessity but not an ideological finality.[22]

The Halakhic Curriculum in History

Toward the end of his study of the *Mishneh Torah,* Twersky moved from an analysis of its method and content to a discussion of its historical impact on Jewish education. Maimonides had very high aspirations for the pedagogical contribution of the *Mishneh Torah,* which Twersky summarizes eloquently:

> Ordinary ethical behavior would become sensitized and inspired; traditional beliefs would be individualized and rationalized through philosophic demonstration; knowledge would have fear give way to love, so that one would "occupy himself with the Torah for its own sake" or reach that special service of God described in the *Guide* [III: 51]: "After apprehension, total devotion to Him and the employment of intellectual thought in constantly loving Him should be aimed at."[23]

Twersky acknowledged that these goals were not fully realized historically, but he continued to maintain that Maimonides' halakhic curriculum, as presented in the *Laws of Torah Study*, "was capable of working a silent revolution in Jewish intellectual history":[24]

> ... it may be proposed that Maimonides' revolution remained primarily "literary"; there was maximum dissemination of the *Mishneh Torah* itself but more limited acceptance of its premise and goals: it did not basically transform modes of thought or redirect the course of codification, but it impinged, directly or indirectly, on methods of study and norms of observance and provided a nearly universal referent for discussion of halakha.
>
> This brief tale of complex and multifaceted influence, often differing drastically from the directions which the author anticipated, should not divert our attention from what is probably the central historical fact:

acknowledgment of the underlying force and the intrinsic originality of his work, its creative underived elements and innovative emphases, its rejection of mediocrity, timidity, and conventionality, the newness of its scope, structure, style, and intellectual sovereignty.[25]

One risk to the realization of Maimonides' vision was an overemphasis of some aspects of halakhic education at the expense of others:

On the one hand, Judaism is halakocentric. . . .

A major corollary of this halakocentricity is the repeated demand for and frequent achievement of a nearly exclusive emphasis on Talmud study – a curriculum oriented towards religious practice and hence weighted with Talmud, Talmud, and more Talmud. Study is the hand-maiden of practice and Talmudic lore is the prerequisite for and source of religious performance. . . . This is the program and rationale of Talmudism, the child of halakocentricity.

The other side of the ledger tells a tale of apprehension and anxiety lest the halakic enterprise become externalized and impoverished, lest that fine precision instrument with its most delicate mechanism cease to function effectively. We hear resounding calls for vigilance to assure that the halakic system remain rooted in and related to spirituality, to knowledge of God obtained through study and experience – through *both or either* of them. The spiritual concern, with its eye on the balance between essence and manifestation, will therefore trigger a sustained tendency to censure halakic intellectualism and to downgrade Talmudism which crowds sensibility and spontaneity out of the picture or even ranks a far-fetched, impracticable legal speculation higher than a theological or ethical inquiry. . . .

This is, in many respects, the bedrock of later spiritualist demands and criticisms of excessive Talmudism.[26]

Part Three: Halakhic Education in Practice

Twersky's meetings with the educators challenged him to delineate the curriculum and pedagogy of his vision. He began to address the halakhic emphasis on the craft of teaching, "the idea of a universal education," "the relationship between learning and teaching," and "character education." Regarding subject matter, he investigated the Maimonidean principles and stipulations on the teaching of Bible, a topic that concerned him because it is often under-emphasized in a traditional curriculum.[27] He also looked at the teaching of *aggadah* (the literary, nonlegal elements of the oral tradition), *ta'amei mitzvot* (rationales for the practice of *mitzvot*), Jewish history, as well as subjects in general education.

In addition, Twersky explored issues in contemporary Jewish life, especially the growing estrangement of religious, secular, and other groups within Israel and across the Jewish world.

Twersky's intention had been to assemble these inquiries into a volume on the practice of halakhic education. What follows are excerpts from notes on some of the meetings held with the educators.

The Stages of Hergel

In the first stage, from birth to literacy, the child is inducted into the observance of *halakhah* by witnessing, imbibing, and ultimately emulating the Jewish tradition exemplified by loving and supportive role models at home, in the synagogue, and in the community. Even at this early stage, Twersky emphasized, *hergel* requires that adults model not only halakhic behavior but also the deeper spiritual dimension of the law.

His attention to the passage in the *Laws of Torah Study* ought not to mislead us into thinking that the principle of *hergel* applies only from the point at which a child can read, he noted. Even a toddler has the capacity to achieve a measure of *ahavat Hashem*. Twersky directed us to the halakhic requirement that from the moment children begin to speak, parents are to teach them to say the words *Torah tzivah lanu Moshe* (Moses has commanded us to live according to the Torah) [Deut. 33:4].[28] Parents invite the children – from the very beginning of their capacity to understand – to join the great tradition of their ancestors.

The second stage is from reading to adulthood. The child moves from dependence on mimesis to the practice of Jewish law through the study of the three components of the halakhic curriculum: *Mikra, Mishnah,* and Talmud.

Mikra introduces the learner to the authority and substance of the Jewish tradition. Rigorous attention to the *peshat,* or "plain sense," of the text also allows the learner to move from imitation of religious role models to a more sophisticated insight into the tradition. Erudition, respect for revealed authority, and induction into the world of halakhic study are the goals of this unit.

Mishnah focuses on various codifications of Jewish law – from the mishnaic text through Maimonides' *Mishneh Torah* and Joseph Karo's *Shulḥan Arukh* – in order to introduce and summarize the system of *halakhah.* Through *Mishnah* the learner gains an understanding of the obligations and rationale of *halakhah* in all areas of living. This understanding should be both practical and theoretical, so that the learner infuses his regular practice of each *halakhah* with a sense of its purposes and uses the categories and guidelines of the halakhic system to organize his perception of the world.

Talmud enables the learner to deepen his understanding of *halakhah* by examining the process by which the laws are formulated in the *Gemara* and other halakhic commentaries. Here the goal is to develop a refined sense of the interplay and dialectic (*shakla ve-tarya*) between larger principles of Jewish law and their applications in specific instances – which the learner would activate in his own practice of *halakhah,* whether in recurring activities, such as prayer, or on an improvisational basis. (Twersky emphasized *bein adam le-ḥaveiro,* the interpersonal domain, in this case.) Talmud also deepens the learner's understanding of *halakhah* through the study of *Pardes,* or philosophy, as in Maimonides' formulation. Alongside the fine distinctions of the *Gemara, Pardes* allows the learner to comprehend Jewish law in its relation to the design of the universe and the purpose of Creation. Informed by this highest level of understanding, the learner's religious sensibilities and practice of Jewish law can bring him closer to God.

The final stage of *hergel* continues throughout life. In Twersky's view, the pinnacle of the halakhic curriculum is not mastery of Talmud but the learner's capacity to take responsibility for his own *hergel*. The pursuit of this goal necessitates intense and ongoing study of Talmud, but the study of other units must also continue, so that the philosophical discernment the learner brings to his practice is both disciplined and comprehensive.

The Halakhic Educator

Twersky stressed the essential role of Jewish educators and was committed to a substantial investment in their continuing training. What follows are key points from notes on his discussions with the educators.

First, he explained that the *mitzvah* of *Talmud Torah* (Torah study) was traditionally conceived in terms not of learning but of teaching, as an act of transmission. Even when a person fulfills this *mitzvah* in solitude, it is to be understood as teaching oneself rather than learning alone.[29]

The boundaries between transmission from parent to child and from teacher to learner dissolve, and society as a whole becomes engaged in an educational effort to transmit to the next generation what it deems valuable. The father is thus obligated to teach his child not only life skills and a trade but also the teachings of Jewish tradition; the teacher is obligated to relate to his students as if they were his own children; and the study of Torah becomes the basis for communal life and continuity.

Twersky also noted the laws relating to the respect that must be granted to educators above others, including parents: "Just as a person is commanded to honor and revere his father, so is he under an obligation to honor and revere his teacher, even to a greater extent than his father; for his father gave him life in this world, while his teacher who instructs him in wisdom, secures for him life in the world to come."[30]

The teacher, too, has obligations: "As pupils are bound to honor their teacher, so a teacher ought to show courtesy and friendliness to his pupils. The sages said,

'Let the honor of your disciples be as dear to you as your own' (*Ethics of the Fathers* 4:15)."[31]

General Education and Culture

No examination of Maimonides' ideas about Jewish education can ignore his commitment to the study of and participation in general culture. As is widely known, Maimonides was well-versed in Greek philosophy and Arabic culture and practiced medicine among Jews and non-Jews. In addition, as Twersky points out in his essay, Maimonides' philosophy of history did not view Judaism as the origin of all wisdom.

In discussing the integration of Jewish and general studies, Twersky referred us to Rabbi Joseph B. Soloveitchik's views on the study of general culture. R. Soloveitchik, a preeminent Orthodox rabbi, leader, and Jewish philosopher in the United States during the past century, taught many thousands of students at Yeshiva University and elsewhere who became educators in the Orthodox movement. According to Twersky, R. Soloveitchik's attitude to the study of general philosophy, science, and literature was open and unapologetic. In his eulogy of R. Soloveitchik, "The Rov," he stated:

> There is, in my opinion, no justification for debate or equivocation concerning the Rov's relation to general culture – philosophy, science, literature – but it is necessary to put this in a proper perspective. The facts are unmistakable. He achieved sovereign mastery of these fields and used his knowledge selectively, creatively and imaginatively, with great philosophic acumen and originality.
> ... If you knew nothing about the Rov's biography and merely studied the *Ish Ha-Halakhah* [*Halakhic Man*] (published in 1944) you would confront a massive, strategic reliance on the history of philosophy and science. The first two pages introduce you to Hegel, Kierkegaard, Rudolph Otto and Karl Barth, Eduard Spranger ... and Heidegger – a breathtaking list. A page later you meet Plato and Aristotle, Galileo and Newton and soon thereafter Husserl, Scheler, Berkeley and Hermann Cohen. If you persisted and made your way to the end of this remarkable philosophical-spiritual meditation, the very last note refocuses your attention on a cast of influential figures: Kant and Hermann Cohen, Kierkegaard, Ibsen, Scheler and Heidegger together with the Rambam and ibn Gabirol and then once again, after a passing reference to Duns Scotus, on to Schopenhauer and Nietzsche. These references reflect not only great erudition and precision in the history of philosophy but also a philosophic temper, a philosophic mode of thinking, a subtle, analytical mind. ...

What is distinctive is the fact that the Rov does not preach or cajole, persuade or brainwash; he does not present an elaborate rationale for the study of philosophy. The latter simply appears as part of his intellectual capital; he uses it freely and wisely and effectively in his various expositions and explorations of Jewish thought. The Rov's philosophic and homiletical corpus has *no apologetics*; there is no attempt to argue and demonstrate the importance of general learning as an abstract proposition just as there is no attempt to defend or glorify western culture. Similarly, there is no attempt to demonstrate that traditional Judaism is completely congruent with philosophy (or any part of it). This truly noteworthy feature is a result of the fact that for the Rov there was nothing essentially problematic about the *masorah* [the tradition]; he did not feel compelled to prove that Torah and philosophy or science are compatible.[32]

In the spirit of this tribute, Twersky explored various halakhic perspectives on the study of such areas as the natural sciences, arts and literature, history, and physical education – including the question of their relative priority – and was preparing to share the results with the educators.

Ahavat Yisrael *(Love of Jews for One Another)*

Twersky saw Maimonides' conception of Jewish education as important not only for traditional Jews but also for those seeking alternative visions of Jewish education. He stressed that a concern for all Jews is a halakhic obligation of central importance. Although Twersky's faith in the continuity of the Jewish people was firm, since it is promised by God and grounded in the design of His Creation, for him the urgent question was not whether Jews would survive but in what manner:

> If the answer to the question "Will Judaism survive?" is unequivocally affirmative – the pure empiricism provides a strong presumption for continuity while the divine promise is a firm guarantee – there still remains a worrisome, even awesome, question: *"mi yihyeh?"* who will survive? Will our children and grandchildren, our friends and neighbors, our cousins in all corners of the world – will we *all* survive as Jews, committed, concerned, creative? Herzl remarked: "Whole branches of Jewry may wither and fall away. The tree lives on." Who will be part of the eternal tree, the tree of life, and who, *has ve-shalom* (God forbid!) will be the transient, decaying branch? Will we survive as a large, flourishing nation or a minute, fragile entity?
>
> Here the answer is very equivocal and uncertain and therefore so terribly unsettling. Far from being escapist or complacent, the confident

awareness which was our premise, or point of departure, accentuates the apprehensiveness inasmuch as we dare not write off large segments of the Jewish People. I recognize ideological pluralism and social heterogeneity as facts of life, not necessarily as intrinsic values. Every individual is of concern to us; no effort should be spared to enlarge the group of survivors. ... The massive dimensions of assimilation and desertion, of religious and biological erosion, coming in the wake of the attempted Nazi genocide, are simply appalling. The various guises and expressions of anti-Semitism should not be glossed over or misconstrued. They must become catalysts for systematic reflection and introspection which make us move with zeal and determination on all fronts and respond vigorously to ever-changing stimuli. Crisis is enervating, conviction is energizing; the two must therefore interact and the latter must prevail.[33]

According to Twersky, the Jewish educator must never retreat in the effort to reach Jewish learners. Once more he quoted Maimonides, who said that no matter how far Jews may have strayed, attempts should be made "to draw them near by friendly relations, so that they may return to the strength-giving force, *i.e.*, the Torah."[34] Twersky planned to articulate this principle in the form of a Maimonidean oath for Jewish educators, similar to the Hippocratic oath taken by physicians. (In Israel, Jewish doctors take a Maimonidean oath.)

Twersky also devoted his energies to thinking about how the principle of *hergel* might apply to adults who did not receive a Jewish education early in their lives. He considered a pedagogy that would begin with the philosophical study of Judaism in order to induct the learner into the dialectic of *hergel* and imagined institutions designed specifically for adult learning.

On June 12, 1990, Twersky presented the Commission on Jewish Education in North America with his statement on common goals for Jewish education. The statement, later published in the Commission's report, also expresses beautifully his commitment to *ahavat Yisrael*:

> Our goal should be to make it possible for every Jewish person, child or adult, to be exposed to the mystery and romance of Jewish history, to the enthralling insights and special sensitivities of Jewish thought, to the sanctity and symbolism of Jewish existence, and to the power and profundity of Jewish faith. As a motto and declaration of hope, we might adapt the dictum that says, "They searched from Dan to Beer Sheva and did not find an *am ha'aretz!*" "Am ha'aretz," usually understood as an ignoramus, an illiterate, may for our purposes be redefined as one indifferent to Jewish visions and values, untouched by the drama and majesty of Jewish history, unappreciative of the resourcefulness and resilience of the Jewish community, and unconcerned with Jewish

destiny. Education, in its broadest sense, will enable young people to confront the secret of Jewish tenacity and existence, the quality of Torah teaching which fascinates and attracts irresistibly. They will then be able, even eager, to find their place in a creative and constructive Jewish community.[35]

NOTES

1 Unless otherwise specified, all statements or quotations are from the notes of Twersky's meetings with the educators. Twersky read these notes after each meeting to check for errors or distortions and kept the corrected copies in a separate file with the intention of using the notes to amplify his essay.

2 For more on this method, see note 12.

3 See "On Law and Ethics in the *Mishneh Torah*: A Case Study of *Hilkhot Megillah* II: 17," *Tradition* 24:2 (Winter 1989): 139–40.

4 "Talmudists, Philosophers and Kabbalists: The Quest for Spirituality in the Sixteenth Century," in *Jewish Thought in the Sixteenth Century,* ed. Bernard Dov Cooperman (Cambridge, MA: Harvard University Press, 1983), 450.

5 A bibliography of Twersky's writings appears in *Me'ah She'arim: Studies in Medieval Jewish Spiritual Life in Memory of Isadore Twersky,* ed. Ezra Fleischer, Gerald Blidstein, Carmi Horowitz, and Bernard Septimus (Jerusalem: The Hebrew University Magnes Press, 2001).

6 We quote in this section from "Religion and Law," in *Religion in a Religious Age,* ed. S. D. Goitein (Cambridge, MA: Association for Jewish Studies, 1974), 69–70, and "Some Aspects of the Jewish Attitude Toward the Welfare State," *Tradition* 5 (1963): 144–45. In the former, Twersky refers to the "classic work" by G. van der Leeuw, *Religion in Essence and Manifestation,* trans. J. E. Turner (New York: Harper & Row, 1963) as a source for the distinction between "religion in essence" and "religion in manifestation."

7 "Some Aspects of the Jewish Attitude," 144.

8 Ibid., 144–45.

9 "Religion and Law," 78–79, n. 6. Regarding Jewish sources that make this point, Twersky says that "From R. Baḥya ibn Pakuda to R. Moshe Ḥayyim Luzzatto the demand is for disciplined study, thoughtfulness and concentration and not hymn-singing, other ecstatic postures, or extreme asceticism." In the note, he also cites a long passage from Luzzatto's *Mesillat Yesharim,* Chapter 3.

10 *Introduction to the Code of Maimonides* (New Haven, CT: Yale University Press, 1980), 262, note 49.

11 Twersky, *Introduction to the Code,* 78.

12 Ibid., 371–73. Twersky's comments on the appropriate approach to the interpretation of Maimonidean halakhic formulations in the *Mishneh Torah* appear on 143–59. See also "On Law and Ethics in the *Mishneh Torah*": 138–49. For Twersky on Maimonides' interpretation of other *mitzvot,* see, for prayer, "*Ve-Yireh Atzmo keilu Omed Lifnei ha-Shekhinah: Kavanat ha-Lev be-Tefillah be-Mishnat ha-Rambam,*" in *Kenesset Ezra: Sifrut ve-Ḥayyim be-Veit ha-Kenesset – Asufat Ma'amarim Mugashim*

le-Ezra Fleischer, ed. S. Elitzur et al. (Jerusalem: Yad Ben Zvi, 1995), 47–68; and for *mitzvot* related to the Land of Israel, *"Eretz Yisrael ve-Galut be-Mishnato shel ha-Rambam,"* in *Eretz Yisrael be-Hagut ha-Yehudit bi-Yimei ha-Beinayim* (Jerusalem: Yad Ben Zvi, 1991), 90–122. This approach explains the method Twersky described in the introduction to the supplement, that used to explore the *mitzvah* of *Talmud Torah.*

13   *Commentary on the Mishnah,* Menaḥot 4:4. Translated by Daniel Marom. Note that Maimonides' definition of education [*ḥinukh*] integrates the imparting of knowledge with the development of character.

14   *Laws of Moral Dispositions and Ethical Conduct* 1:7 in *A Maimonides Reader,* ed. Isadore Twersky (West Orange, NJ: Behrman House 1972), 53; henceforth *AMR.*

15   *The Guide of the Perplexed* III:54 (*AMR,* 354). The talmudic passage is from Shabbat 31a.

16   10:6 (*AMR,* 85).

17   10:2 (*AMR,* 83–84).

18   *Introduction to the Code,* 395. Twersky bases this passage on *Guide* III:51.

19   Ibid., 396.

20   *Mishneh Torah, Laws of Mezuzot* 6:13 (*AMR,* 95).

21   See, e.g., Josef Stern, "Maimonides on Education," in *Philosophers on Education: New Historical Perspectives,* ed. A. Rorty (London and New York: Routledge, 1998), 109–23.

22   *Introduction to the Code,* 513–14.

23   Ibid., 514.

24   Ibid., 489.

25   Ibid., 536–37.

26   "Religion and Law," 70–72.

27   See Twersky's article in *Encyclopedia Ḥinukhit,* ed. Martin M. Buber and Haim Ormian (Jerusalem: The Ministry of Education and Culture and the Bialik Institute, 1964), vol. 4, 257–58.

28   *Mishneh Torah, Laws of Torah Study* 1:6.

29   Twersky refers to *Laws of Torah Study* 1:1–3.

30   *Mishneh Torah,* ibid. 5:1 (*AMR,* 69).

31   *Mishneh Torah,* ibid. 5:12 (*AMR,* 70).

32   "The Rov," *Tradition* 30:4 (Summer 1996): 30–33.

33   "Survival, Normalcy, Modernity," in *Zionism in Transition,* ed. M. Davis (New York: Herzl Press, 1980), 350–51.

34   *Laws of Rebels* 3:3 (*AMR,* 210). In this passage, Maimonides refers to *tinokot shenishbu* (Jewish children taken captive), who, being raised in other faiths, were deprived of a Jewish education. Maimonides was alluding to the Karaites, but, as Twersky pointed out, the twentieth-century halakhic authority Ḥazon Ish ruled that the term applied to all nontraditional Jews in the contemporary era.

35   *A Time to Act: The Report of the Commission on Jewish Education in North America* (Lanham, MD: The University Press of America, 1991), 19.

5

Jewish Studies in Israel from a Liberal–Secular Perspective

MENACHEM BRINKER

The approach of my essay[1] is liberal in two senses. The usual meaning of the word will be explained in my discussion of the value of freedom in education and how it comes into conflict with teachers' attempts to indoctrinate students in school.

But the liberalism I advocate has another meaning, which is evident in internal Jewish debates at the end of the nineteenth century and the beginning of the twentieth regarding the definition of Judaism or Jewishness. In contrast to the German Jewish philosophers (Moses Mendelssohn, Samson Raphael Hirsch, Hermann Cohen) who viewed Judaism as a distinct spiritual school of thought that could be defined as "a philosophy," a *Weltanschauung* or at least as "an ethics," the Eastern European Jewish writers and thinkers (Peretz Smolenskin, Moses Leib Lilienblum, Aḥad Ha-Am, Simon Dubnow, David Frischmann, Micha Josef Berdyczewski, Yosef Ḥayyim Brenner) conceived of a different model.

According to this model, Judaism is first and foremost a historical fact. The Jewish people is a collective whose continuous historical existence derives from shared memories (especially memories of a common fate); shared languages (Hebrew and many different jargons); shared destiny (determined to a great extent by anti-Semites in the present); and, sometimes, shared expectations of the future. The bonds among the generations are based on the feeling of their being part of one family. As happens in a family, beliefs and ideas change from generation to generation (including religious, philosophical, and ethical views), but identity and continuity remain, for they are not the result of a single spiritual essence that "embodies" the people's history from its beginnings until today.

Aḥad Ha-Am contributed more than any other Russian Jewish philosopher to the adoption of the family model over the spiritual model as the one that clarifies the nature and persistence of Jewish identity. However, he retreated to some extent from this approach and vacillated throughout his life between his view of Judaism as a collective existence that underwent significant religious

95

and spiritual transformations in its history and that could not be defined in "essentialist" terms, and his search for some kind of paradigm that runs through the entire history of Jewish culture – one he imagined could be found in the idea of "the Jewish spirit" and in the constant Jewish preference for morality and intellect over aesthetics and emotion.

The lack of consistency and the internal conflict between these two approaches are well known to all his readers. Several of his students, among them Berdyczewski and Brenner, were more conclusive on this subject than he was and free of his contradictions. More than others, they maintained the integrity of the family model as the most appropriate one to describe Jewish self-preservation and identity.

According to this approach, one cannot understand the history of the Jewish people as the proliferation of a singular spiritual phenomenon in historical time. Rather, one should understand it as the result of the Jewish people's ongoing interaction with its environment and adaptation to the surrounding mores (e.g., clothing). It is even possible that the continuing existence of the Jewish people as a separate nation was determined by its interaction with a non-Jewish environment that did not allow Jews to assimilate.

Since the Jewish people is solely a historical entity and is definitely not the embodiment of any spiritual essence, the determining factor for Jewish preservation in the face of assimilation throughout all the generations, including our own, was not the degree of loyalty to any abstract religious, philosophical, or spiritual principles but the binding of the individual's fate to the Jewish collective. This bond was frequently formed by powerful historical constraints but was sometimes the result of free and conscious choice.

If we want to educate our students toward any theory of "the essence of Judaism," we would have to conceal from them that what was frequently considered this essence – *ikkarim* (tenets) in Jewish philosophy of the Middle Ages and *ekronot* (principles) in contemporary thought – came to the Jewish people from the outside world. The belief in messianism, in the world to come, and in the immortality of the nation came to Judaism from Hellenistic culture, and, in the modern period, the ideologies of the supremacy of morality and "the Jewish spirit" stemmed from the philosophies of Herder, Kant, and so on.

Only the awareness that the history of the Jewish people cannot be understood according to an "internal law" and that Jewish culture offers a wide variety of ideas and beliefs, ways of life and customs, and literary styles makes it possible to reconcile an authentic liberal education with Jewish education and its responsibilities. Accordingly, students have no a priori obligation to adopt a specific "Jewish" doctrine as a condition for preserving their Jewish identity. Their responsibility for Jewish and Israeli life in the present and future is dependent only upon their will and readiness to see themselves as part of this life. Without any external coercion or obligation, they can, if they so desire, transform the fact of being born to a Jewish family into their own free choice, which can be made on an ongoing basis. Jewishness is always a given that can be changed. Only when it is continually renewed by free choice does it cease to become a fact and enter the realm of value.

Education does not occur in a vacuum. The *mithanekh* [Brinker's term for a self-educating person, coined from the reflexive of the word *hinukh* (education)] is never "pure" raw material, and the formal education system is not a production line that can shape this seemingly raw material as it wishes. The children and then young people who enter the gates of the education system have already been shaped by their family, by "the street," and by surrounding events. They respond to these influences and continue to be shaped by them even as they spend part of their day in the formal education system in all its stages: kindergarten, elementary school, high school, army, and university. In this regard, every educational program is the expression of the heartfelt wishes of the teachers and educators and always contains idealistic elements, in contrast to the broader and more dynamic influences to which the *mithanekh* is exposed beyond the educational institutions.

Of course, there is no reason to dismiss the power of the formal educational system. On the contrary. Its idealistic elements may partially balance the influences of the surrounding environment that the educators see as negative.

There is something of a paradox here, since the "environment," in the broad sense of the word, is not only a factor to be reckoned with by formal education. The "environment" also guides formal education, for at least in a democratic society, the education system needs parental support as well as consent as to what it teaches. The resolution of this paradox is that the environment always bestows upon education an ideal image of itself. In any society, however, parents themselves expect that *mithankhim* will strike a compromise between the "ideal" education and the realities of their lives.

These ideas, which I perceive as commonly accepted, are fully confirmed by the profound difference between Jewish education and Jewish studies in non-Orthodox institutions in the Diaspora and in non-Orthodox institutions in Israel.

In the Diaspora, parents and educators – with differing levels of awareness – charge Jewish studies with a difficult idealistic mission that in most cases is beyond its capacity. That mission is the preservation of the Jewishness of the *mithanekh* in a non-Jewish environment and world. Almost everywhere in the Diaspora today, a Jew lives in a dual world: a Jewish world and a general world. (Clearly, I am not referring to those whose Jewishness has already entirely evaporated or to the Orthodox circles.) At least in affluent countries, these two worlds stand in opposition to one another, and Jewish educators perceive their *mithanekh* as someone whose heart is wrestling with the attraction to both these worlds.

Since, on the one hand, today's Western liberal society offers Jews what they have never been offered before – free access to all centers of science, culture, commerce, and policy – and since, on the other hand, it is not at all clear what Judaism can offer its many children who have lost their religious faith, many Jews are in the process of losing their Jewish identity. Jewish education has the Sisyphean task of stopping or at least checking this process.

In the depths of their hearts, parents and educators know very well that ultimately the conflict in the soul, as it were, of the Jew will be resolved by conditions of life beyond the education system. But the parents' expectations and community pressure involve the educators in constructing systems of abstract reasoning in favor of a decision to be Jewish. In most cases, these arguments are intended to help the *mithanekh* see Jewish identity as stemming from something deeper than natural feelings of familial-tribal loyalty. This pressure confers a clear ideological character not only on most Jewish education but on most Jewish thought in developed countries.

Jewish studies in Israel are free of this constraint. Here, one can examine the pull of Jewish culture in all its historical depth and geographic scope without having to elevate and glorify it above general culture. The Jewish world of Israeli *mithankhim* encompasses them on all sides. Young people in Israel live in a heterogeneous Jewish-Israeli environment with various forms of culture and Jewish life. They almost never encounter anything else. The view from their window, most of the news that they hear on the radio or read about in the newspaper, and the family discussions that they are exposed to even before they can properly understand them are all or nearly all Jewish-Israeli. Jewish topics and Jewish-Israeli questions permeate the lives of Israeli *mithankhim* through all their experiences, and not necessarily through the system of formal education.

Therefore, it seems to me, the rationale for Jewish studies in Israel is obvious. Their goals should mesh with the existential need of Israeli youth to clarify the world for themselves – the world around them and the world within.

The current Jewish-Israeli reality can serve as a good point of departure. The present, whether of a person or a community, has the imprints of the past that led up to it; also sketched on it, however schematically, are certain future possibilities, some fascinating and attractive and others uninviting and even frightening. This present, in order to be understood, directs Israeli youth to the recent and remote past of Jewish history, as well as to the literary and philosophical treasures of Jewish culture. It seems to me, then, that in the souls of Israeli youth is a potential that designers of Jewish curriculum, gifted with empathy and a critical spirit, can tap in order to produce truly educated Israelis who are knowledgeable about the history, culture, and literature of their people.

Since I began with a liberal premise based on an awareness of the paradoxical task of school – to *educate* to *freedom*, that is, to educate so that the student is not required to conform to any given way of life – I would argue that we must not educate for compliance. The present should provide a starting point for *diverse* future possibilities, for both the individual and the community. The Jewish past is, at most, a matrix of future possibilities – models for self-formation, possible exemplary figures – aside from being indispensable for understanding the present.

In my view, the Jewish past is not a reservoir of binding content. It does not divulge a preferred dominant model alongside other inferior models for shaping one's life. The student in my school is not asked to be "like our forefather Abraham," "like Hillel the Elder," or "like Bar Kokhba." But he is called upon to know who these people are, just as he is required to know what Maimonides, Rabbi Judah HaLevi, Rabbi Naḥman of Bratslav, Aḥad Ha-Am, or Berdyczewski thought – but not which of them was infallibly right.

The *mithanekh* has to do his own work of clarification and evaluation to determine which one of these or other figures is a model for him and in what way. He also has to discover for himself which of the profound thoughts can help him in his philosophy of life and which do not serve him.

The secularity of this school should not be understood as requiring that the students study primarily modern secular texts. Rather, this kind of school would teach a broad selection of religious literature of the Jewish people, beginning with the Bible, *Mishnah,* and selected *midrashim* (exegetical writings on the Bible), through medieval sacred poetry and religious philosophy, and up to the most recent expressions of Jewish religious culture. There would also be generous selections of the Jewish people's secular literature, starting with the Song of Songs and Ecclesiastes through medieval secular poetry, and ending with Jewish thought and Hebrew belles lettres of the last 200 years, which are primarily nonreligious.

The "secularity" of this approach is expressed by the perspective the *mithanekh* is invited to assume toward this material. Beyond the fact that the vast pluralism of Jewish cultures will be taught and even *emphasized,* all the material studied should be presented for the *mithanekh*'s judgment. It would be artificial to demand that teachers or educators hide their opinions regarding questions of intellectual or aesthetic worth. However, the educator I have in mind must be able to reveal the aesthetic and intellectual qualities in diverse and even contradictory texts and works.

This pluralism should not be packaged as a doctrine of Judaism, which would, like all doctrines, create a hierarchy of the important and the unimportant, the crucial and the trivial, according to criteria that are always based on one or another *Weltanschauung*. It is preferable to present pluralism as it is actually found. This is especially important in the teaching of Jewish history. The dynamics and tensions in the classic thought and literature of the Jewish people are concealed, to some extent, by the rabbinical editing of the ancient texts and also by the ostracism of anyone who did not comply with the requirements of a halakhic way of life or whose thought and work did not accord with it (Spinoza, for example). Throughout Jewish history there are, in fact, contrasts and tensions among different believers: worshippers of God and worshippers of Baal; kings and prophets; Pharisees, Sadducees, and Essenes; rationalists and mystics; stringent and lenient legislators of *halakhah*; those knowledgeable in general culture and those against its study; Orthodox and Reform; neo-Orthodox and assimilated; liberal *maskilim* (followers of the Jewish Enlightenment) and socialists; Zionists and their opponents; universalists and particularists; as well as conservatives and adherents to an article or articles of faith in opposition to agnostics, and rebel-revolutionaries who want to turn the world upside down.

It is incumbent upon teachers of Jewish history to awaken the learner's understanding of the different manifestations of Jewish human life. For example, they must awaken an appreciation for both Rabban Yoḥanan ben Zakkai and for Bar Kokhba and the zealots, for both Spinoza and his excommunicators. Under no circumstance should they, for example, omit the period of polemics surrounding Zionism while teaching the period of national awakening at the end of the nineteenth century. They should not present the opponents of Zionism among the Orthodox – the autonomists (for example, Dubnow) or the Jewish socialists (the Bund) – as enemies of the people. Rather, they should aim for a thorough understanding of their position and its underlying motivations.

This inclusiveness should be encouraged not only out of respect for the independent personality of the *mitḥanekh* but also for the good of Jewish society. Religious or Zionist inner conviction should not be confused with religious, nationalist, or Zionist fanaticism. My aim is not some ideal of scientific objectivity, but to prevent in the learner a kind of fanaticism and a priori confidence or self-righteousness that block any possibility of understanding others. To understand the motives of a historical figure, whether a social activist, an artist, or a philosopher, requires a certain suspension of judgment, at least until understanding is achieved.

I do not object to a learner's deciding, after study, that he is "angry" at Yoḥanan ben Zakkai or at Bar Kokhba, that his heart is with Spinoza or his ostracizers, that he views the Reform movement or, just the reverse, Orthodox insularity as a danger to the people of Israel, provided that he has had the opportunity to understand in depth the intensity of the national, religious, or social issue that divided the involved parties. Only for the sake of that profound understanding do I insist on stretching to the limit the learner's insight and tolerance and advocate that the teacher of Jewish history in Israel instill in learners an appreciation for the considerable reasons that the opponents of Zionism had at the time – all this so that nothing will ever be automatically assumed by the learner and so that the learner's inner convictions will be attained not as a result of insularity but as a result of independent thinking that draws upon a broad education.

Once more I would like to emphasize that the term "secularity," as I use it here, is not a simple antithesis to the term "religious." It refers to a liberal openness and not to the cultivation of a militant-secular mentality for the *mitḥankhim*. Not infrequently I discover an obstinate resistance among observant or traditional Jews to their understanding of this position. From the moment they hear the word secularity they want to know which thinker is the secular person's authority and what primary texts are the basis of this secular doctrine. It is as though, after having patiently listened to a frank declaration of secularity, they nevertheless ask who the secularist's "rebbe" is and in which "sacred texts" he believes. From their vantage point, the challenge is to locate the "secular community" on the map of denominations in Judaism and to identify its leader and texts. In their view, the uniqueness of this community, the community of secularists, is that a single fundamental axiom is accepted as an article of faith – namely, the nonexistence of God.

However, the cultivation of free access to texts means that there is no foundational sacred text: Everything is open, both to commentary and to judgment. One can point to many non-Orthodox, "secular" models for assessing Jewish history and culture and to many visions of the Jewish people's future. Lilienblum, Aḥad Ha-Am, Bialik, Frischmann, Berdyczewski, Brenner, Klatzkin, Dubnow, Herzl, and Syrkin, for example, are ten Jewish critics and thinkers who had their own philosophy of the Jewish people, its culture, and its future. None of them saw Judaism as a religious-spiritual school of thought; all viewed Jewish culture as a creation of the Jewish people that underwent significant changes throughout the generations.

A liberal school would teach these ideas within the framework of Jewish studies, alongside the ideas of Orthodox or Reform thinkers, such as Hirsch, Geiger, Rosenzweig, or Rabbi Abraham I. Kook. But it would not teach secular ideas the way sacred texts are taught. On the contrary, it would encourage the students to see – that is, to discover for themselves – what in all these ideas is obsolete and what can still nourish their spirits. In an education centered on the *mitḥanekh*'s abilities to shape his own cultural-spiritual personality, there are no sacred texts that one is forbidden to criticize, doubt, determine as relevant and lasting and/or as trivial and transitory, or even totally negate. By the same token, there is no one unequivocally exemplary figure who is the exclusive model for emulation or the final arbiter in every matter.

The true test of the Israeli school that I envisage lies primarily in the teaching of the ideas of the Zionist thinkers. Herzl, Nordau, Borochov, Syrkin, Buber, Jabotinsky, Katznelson, Ben-Gurion, and others were all thinkers of a certain stature, even if they were not "professional" philosophers. They not only offered an analysis of the Jewish present; they also had a vision of the future of the nation. An examination of these visions indeed reveals that occasionally they were accurate predictions of the future (Herzl's declaration that a Jewish state would arise fifty years after the first Zionist Congress in 1897; Syrkin's vision that only through communal settlement would the pioneers realize Zionism; or Borochov's vision that, of necessity, the Hebrew language would become a spoken language in *Eretz Yisrael* [the Land of Israel]). But there were also predictions that now appear strange and even absurd (Herzl's idea of a train that would bring millions to *Eretz Yisrael*; Borochov's forecast of Arab assimilation with Jews through intermarriage; Syrkin's prediction, at the beginning of the twentieth century, that Jewish emigration to the United States would cease because it was not an idealistic choice).

The student of the liberal-Zionist school must be able to distinguish clearly between these two kinds of predictions. He must be critical of even the most venerated texts. Above all, the school must instill the feeling that he is his own *rebbe* and that Jewish culture, ancient and modern, cannot provide him with more than sources of inspiration. If he adopts texts from which he generates "beliefs" for his life, the decision is his responsibility and his own free choice. It is the task of this school to instill in the *mithanekh* the feeling that behind every act of devotion is a free person, even behind devotion to the good and the true and the beautiful or devotion to God as the exalted symbol of all of these.

Since the goal of the liberal school is to enable *mithankhim* to exercise their freedom, and since the purpose of Jewish studies is first and foremost to illuminate the Jewish-Israeli situation in which they live and breathe every day, the proportion of Jewish studies in the curriculum in Israel's state-run schools should be changed. At least half the teaching hours in Jewish history and Jewish thought should be allotted to events and texts of the last 150 years. If we want young people who are being educated in this school to know all the divisions and ideological camps in the Jewish world in the modern period in Eastern and Western Europe, in Israel and in the Diaspora, and especially in America, there is no other choice.

And what holds true for Jewish thought – that is, the Jewish being's reflecting on itself and its surroundings – also holds true for Jewish history. If the *mithankhim* are to become aware of the diverse social movements and the many faces of the Jewish people in the present, along with the main factors that acted upon them from the outside, there is no other way but through systematic and profound familiarization, as much as possible, with the Jewish *Haskalah* (Enlightenment) movement, Hasidism and its detractors, Orthodoxy and Reform, autonomism, Zionism, territorialism, the Bund, emancipation, and assimilation, as well as anti-Semitism and liberalism, socialism and communism, and the two World Wars.

In my opinion, in half the teaching hours allocated to Jewish history and Jewish thought, one can convey to the *mithankhim* a sufficiently broad sense of the ancient texts of Jewish culture. This can be done with appropriate selections from Torah, Prophets, Writings, *Mishnah,* sample pages from the Talmud and Midrash, and a few chapters of medieval Jewish philosophy. The other half of the teaching hours should be devoted to the more recent past.

What is true for the curriculum in Jewish history and Jewish thought is exponentially true for the teaching of literature. It seems to me that the teaching of poetry, fiction, and literary criticism must begin with what is currently being published in Israel. One should take advantage of the students' access to the "life-materials" of the poem and the story in order to create a vital interest in literature. Then, after the love of literature has been fostered, one can go back and learn the literature and poetry of earlier periods.

These thoughts are not based on a defined literary-poetic scale of values. I am well aware that in *all* periods of Jewish poetic creativity, there have been exceptional masterpieces worthy of being studied, and that, for example, the fiction of the early twentieth century (Berdyczewski, Mendele, Gnessin, Bialik, Brenner, Berkowitz, Shofman) does not fall short artistically of the finest contemporary Israeli literature. But precisely because I think there are outstanding works from all eras, I prefer to begin and cultivate the students' literary sensibilities with work that says something about their own world – without any barrier – before bringing them into contact with worlds more distant in time, place, and mentality.

Preference should be given to literary works that address Jewish or Israeli-Jewish themes (the Holocaust, the War of Independence, and so on) over other works, provided they are of high artistic quality. The large number of texts of such quality demands selectivity. Therefore, the study of literature should illuminate not only literature itself – as a language and a system of forms – but also the same Jewish phenomenon as it is manifest in Jewish thought and history.

The teaching of literature as art is difficult in schools everywhere. It is a heavy burden for those students not actively interested in literature. For those whose interest is piqued, however, there are never enough hours allotted to it. Therefore, my proposal helps those with no special literary interest by focusing on the themes and problems raised in the work, while for those keenly interested in literature, there is always room to organize a study group for literature and poetry that can also serve as a creative writing workshop.

The Hebrew language is one of the minimal common denominators but also one of the most ubiquitous in establishing the Jewish identity of Israelis. In contrast with the Diaspora, where the voluntary study of Hebrew proves the interest of the *mithankhim* in their Jewish identity, in Israel every boy and girl acquires knowledge of Hebrew. The main concern of Israeli education must be the level of the language, both spoken and written.

Therefore, the role of the classical texts (especially Bible and *Mishnah*) should not be neglected in enriching the Hebrew of the students. These texts can and should, in my opinion, be taught in every Jewish studies curriculum – in Jewish thought, Jewish history, and Hebrew literature – which will partly compensate for my insistence on limiting the study of premodern texts and periods to half the teaching hours.

In the Jewish present, Hebrew is only one of the languages in which Jewish experience is articulated and considered. In the fields of philosophy and history, Israeli *mithankhim* study texts that were originally written in German or Russian, Yiddish, Arabic, or English. In the realm of belles lettres, preference is clearly given to texts originally written in Hebrew. Nevertheless, in order to prevent a provincial identification of Jewishness with Israeliness, it is advisable to have the students encounter – even if only in a few minimal sessions – Jewish texts written in other languages (such as the stories of Kafka, Malamud, and Roth or the poems of Paul Celan and Edmond Jabes).

As mentioned earlier, a liberal non-Orthodox approach to Jewish studies (usually called a "secular" approach) is evident in the manner of teaching no less than in the more varied and less censored selection of texts, issues, and events studied in school. In a school based on this approach, there will be no a priori commitment to a preference for Jewish sources, opinions, beliefs, and lifestyles over those that are not Jewish. The "Jewish" dimension of the education given in this school will not be based on the isolation of Judaism as a historical, philosophical, or literary phenomenon from all other human phenomena. On the contrary, Jewish studies in this school will succeed and attain their goal to the extent that the *mithanekh* is able to draw analogies between phenomena in the realm of Jewish experience and phenomena in the world outside.

For example, if the student perceives Maimonides not only as a teacher and guide to Judaism but also as one of the important thinkers of his time, one who inherited a distinct set of philosophical issues from Islamic philosophy of the period; if he understands Rabbi Judah HaLevi's connection to Islamic mystical thought; Solomon ibn Gabirol's affinity with Neoplatonism; the Russian and general European background of Bialik's autobiographical poems; the inspiration provided by Russian liberal and socialist thought to such thinkers as Ahad Ha-Am or A. D. Gordon; the way Rav Kook used the intellectual models of Herder and Nietzsche to establish the uniqueness of Jewish ethics – in short, if the student understands that Judaism is grounded in a much wider world, and that in all its important creative periods it conducted a lively and fruitful exchange with the cultures of the world, then the main goal of Jewish studies will have been achieved.

This approach is also suitable for the teaching of classical Jewish themes, since even the heroic poetry of the Bible, as well as portions of Mosaic law, invite comparison with the texts of the ancient Middle East. The rules of Hillel, of Rabbi Ishmael, or of Yossi HaGlili for expounding the Law can be compared with the rules of logic and hermeneutics of Greek philosophy.

The aim of Jewish studies is to provide the *mithankhim* with a treasury of memories from ancient times, inspiring monuments, historical and literary associations, as well as examples of intellectual grappling with the human condition. We want this treasure to be available to them always. The *mithanekh* must not isolate these experiences from his other studies. Instead, they should be integrated with other knowledge from general humanist studies – philosophy, ethics, political science, history, and world literature – to form his spiritual world, personal culture, and *Weltanschauung* (if he needs a comprehensive, inclusive *Weltanschauung* and is able to formulate it).

Extensive observation of educational methods in Israel and their influence on the thinking and behavior of young Israelis has convinced me that this is the one and only path to take.

We do not have a tested and guaranteed cure for the superficiality, vulgarity, and gross materialism of "the street." These are not the only dangers threatening Israeli youth. Insularity, the lack of independent thinking, fanaticism, chauvinistic arrogance, and racist and paranoid states of mind are no less dangerous than a "lack of Jewish values."

If "the humanities" or humanistic studies can repair or somewhat balance negative influences, it is only by sharpening the *mithankhim*'s sense of individual freedom accompanied by a sense of responsibility for all that is happening around them. *Mithankhim* who feel the enormous burden of freedom can of course benefit from spiritual inspiration. However, spiritual inspiration must not be replaced by absolute authority of any kind. The role of Jewish studies as well as the role of general studies is to provide *mithankhim* with a wide range of potential inspirations to enable them to assume ultimate authority over their own lives, their behavior with others, and their choices as citizens.

NOTE

1   Translated by Felice Kahn Zisken.

Supplement: Menachem Brinker

Menachem Brinker's vision departs significantly from any in traditional Judaism. He seeks to change not only the subject matter and teaching methods of Jewish education, but also its assumptions and purposes. Liberated from the obligation to transmit a set of values, beliefs, or normative practices, Jewish education, in Brinker's view, can respect the learner's freedom of thought and cultivate his capacity to arrive at his own approach to Jewish life.

Brinker's version of the ideal curriculum divides the Jewish past into two periods – modern Jewish history (the eighteenth century to the present) and premodern Jewish history (from its origins to the eighteenth century). He emphasizes the study of the modern period, focusing on three areas: Jewish history, Jewish thought, and Hebrew literature.

His vision is based on the Eastern European Jewish thinkers whose writing, in Hebrew, at the turn of the twentieth century demanded a redefinition of Jewish life. They believed that a secular basis for Jewish identity would guarantee Jewish continuity and that the anchor of Jewish existence was not religious but communal. Jews' sense of belonging to a community, their desire to improve the condition of that community, and the will to fulfill themselves as human beings through participation in the community would ensure that Jews continue to define themselves as Jews.

For some of the educators and scholars, the ideas of the Hebrew writers seemed to demand too radical a reorientation of their own convictions about Jewish life. In a debate throughout the project, Brinker defended the validity of his approach with these arguments:

The ideas of the Hebrew writers have already proved themselves, for they were the ideological basis of the Zionist movement, which successfully established the State of Israel.

Given the inevitable assimilation of Jews in the Diaspora, Israel is becoming the world's major and most viable Jewish community; its secular system of

106

education is responsible for the instruction of more Jewish children than any other system of Jewish education.

Having achieved its political aims, Zionist ideology has served its purpose – which allows us to focus on questions of Jewish society and culture.

The quality of Jewish life in the next generation is a more pressing issue than the obsessive, if understandable, preoccupation with the quantity of surviving Jews.

The next step in building a stable and healthy basis for Jewish continuity is that contemporary Israel undertake a profound reorganization of Jewish life in areas such as law, economics, and education along the "secular" and pluralistic lines suggested by the Hebrew writers.

Finally, the curriculum of Israeli schools should address problems such as the growth of fundamentalism and fascism in Israeli society and the lack of dialogue between proponents of opposing views of Jewish culture.

The supplement to Brinker's essay, composed of excerpts from his scholarly writings and notes on his meetings with the educators, is divided into three parts: his exposition of the Hebrew writers' ideas about Jewish life; his application of these ideas to contemporary realities; and selected topics in liberal-secular Jewish education.

Part One: The Eastern European Hebrew Writers

Brinker summarizes the shared assumptions of the thinkers who informed his vision as follows: A nation is not an ideological camp, and its members are not subject to a strict theological or philosophical discipline. Rather, a nation more closely resembles a family, whose inner continuity and intimacy need not disappear when teachings and beliefs change. Regarding their Jewish heritage, Jews may exercise total freedom of thought and opinion; however they choose to do so, their identity will not be imperiled.

Below are selections from Brinker's writing on Ahad Ha-Am (1856–1927), Micha Josef Berdyczewski (1865–1921), and Yosef Ḥayyim Brenner (1881–1921) – each followed by excerpts of the writer's work.

Brinker on Ahad Ha-Am

Ahad Ha-Am was a pioneer of nineteenth-century Eastern European Hebrew writing. His critique of Western European Jewry is the basis of Brinker's liberal-secular approach to Jewish life:

> In his famous article "Slavery in Freedom," Ahad Ha-Am analyzed the existential constraints on Western European Jews. Having been granted equal rights, they are obligated to the nation in which they reside. (In Ahad Ha-Am's example, he refers specifically to France.) They want

to prove to the members of this nation their capacity to belong, as far as fulfilling all their civic duties is concerned, despite their stubborn adherence to the strictures of the Jewish religion. Consequently, these Jews are not ready to identify Jewishness in terms of nationality. Since they perceive what divides them from their neighbors exclusively in cultural-religious terms, they are forced to see Jewish culture – the beliefs and opinions of their ancestors – as superior so that they may justify their own adoption of it even as they remain French or German. This view compels them to glorify all that is related to Jewish tradition and obscure all that is not worthy of being glorified. Such a relationship to the Jewish tradition and the Jewish past prevents them from being free in their consideration and evaluation of their Jewish heritage, a freedom which for Aḥad Ha-Am, as for all the disciples of the *Haskalah* movement, was like air to breathe.

For Aḥad Ha-Am, however, Jewishness is first and foremost a deep feeling of belonging to an ethnic-cultural-historical family. This feeling of belonging does not obligate a modern Jew to sanctify all that is sanctified in the tradition of his people, and it does not keep him from thinking somewhat differently than his ancestors about the subjects and questions that face him. Aḥad Ha-Am wanted the Europeanization of the modern Jew – his adaptation to a rational-scientific mode of thinking and to the liberal ideals of Western culture. He was not afraid that this process would undermine the collective existence of the Jewish people at its root, because he saw Jewish existence as a solid fact that needs no philosophical justification in order to persist.[1]

From Aḥad Ha-Am: "Slavery in Freedom" (1891)

... If Western Jews were not slaves to their emancipation, it would never have entered their heads to consecrate their people to spiritual missions or aims before it had fulfilled that physical, natural "mission" which belongs to every organism – before it had created for itself conditions suitable to its character, in which it could develop its latent powers and aptitudes, its own particular form of life, in a normal manner, and in obedience to the demands of its nature. ...

To-day [sic], while I am still alive, I try mayhap to give my weary eyes a rest from the scene of ignorance, of degradation, of unutterable poverty that confronts me here in Russia, and find comfort by looking yonder across the border, where there are Jewish professors, Jewish members of Academies, Jewish officers in the army, Jewish civil servants; and when I see there, behind the glory and the grandeur of it all, a twofold spiritual slavery – moral slavery and intellectual slavery – and ask myself: Do I envy these fellow-Jews of mine their emancipation? – I answer, in all truth and sincerity: No! a thousand times No! The privileges are not worth the price! I may not be emancipated; but at least I have not sold my soul for emancipation. . . . I at least can speak my mind concerning the beliefs and the opinions which I have inherited from my ancestors, without fearing to snap the bond that unites me to my people. . . . And this spiritual freedom – scoff who will! – I would not exchange or barter for all the emancipation in the world.[2]

Ahad Ha-Am's attack on the definition of the Jews as "the people of the book" was not against their intellectual engagement with the canon of Jewish texts, but with their stiflingly apologetic approach to these texts:

From Ahad Ha-Am: "The Law of the Heart" (1894)

The relation between a normal people and its literature is one of parallel development and mutual interaction. Literature responds to the demands of life, and life reacts to the guidance of literature. . . .

But a "people of the book," unlike a normal people, is a slave to the book. It has surrendered its whole soul to the written word. The book ceases to be what it should be, a source of ever-new inspiration and moral strength; on the contrary, its function in life is to weaken and finally to crush all spontaneity of action and emotion, till men become wholly dependent on the written word and incapable of responding to any stimulus in nature or in human life without its permission and approval. . . .

We Jews have been a people of the book in this sense for nearly two thousand years; but we were not always so. It goes without saying that we were not a people of the book in the era of the Prophets, from which we have traveled so far that we can no longer even understand it. But even in the period of the Second Temple, heart and mind had not lost their spontaneity of action and their self-reliance. In those days it was still possible to find the source of the Law and the arbiter of the written word in the human heart, as witness the famous dictum of Hillel: "Do not unto your neighbor what you would not have him do unto you; that is the whole Law." If on occasion the spontaneity of thought and emotion brought them into conflict with the written word, they did not efface themselves in obedience to its dictates; they revolted against it where it no longer met their needs, and so forced upon it a development in consonance with their new requirements. . . .

But this state of things did not endure. The Oral Law (which is really the inner law, the law of the moral sense) was itself reduced to writing and fossilized; and the moral sense was left with only one clear and firm conviction – that of its own utter impotence and its eternal subservience to the written word. Conscience no longer had any authority in its own right; not conscience but the book became the arbiter in every human question.[3]

Brinker on Berdyczewski

Berdyczewski's claim against Aḥad Ha-Am was that by excluding from the Hebrew journal he edited essays on general culture unrelated to the condition of the Jewish people in the past or present, he was following the path of the Western European Jews that had so incensed him. In matters of culture, he was again dividing the Jewish soul into "human" and "Jew," exactly as had the *maskilim* [followers of the Jewish Enlightenment] of Berlin and Russia before him. . . .

The rallying cry of the "Euro-Hebrew" was coined to signal that it was now no longer possible or necessary to isolate the Jew from European culture. This notion was largely related to Berdyczewski's belief in the capacity of the Hebrew language to function as a *lashon ḥol* [vernacular; lit., a secular language, used in opposition to *lashon kodesh,* the sacred language of classical Jewish texts and rituals], capable of expressing any matter that could be communicated in the spoken languages of other nations.

Aḥad Ha-Am did not believe that Hebrew could be a language that would be spoken by Jews. He thought of it as the language of scholars and of a cultural elite, similar to Latin in the Renaissance. But when he directed his readers to read in other languages ideas and literature that did not relate to questions of exclusively Jewish concern, another aspect of his position was revealed. He was distinguishing – despite his deep-rooted secularity – between *lashon kodesh,* which was for discussions about Jewish peoplehood, and the attractive vernaculars of other nations, which were for discourse on every other subject.

In contrast, Berdyczewski wanted to see Hebrew develop and conquer a market of readers who were not limited to only one kind of issue or subject. He differed fundamentally from Aḥad Ha-Am in his certainty that Jewish culture suffered from an overabundance of unity, not from an overabundance of pluralism. It was this unity that he saw as a factor in distancing intelligent young people from Judaism and bringing them closer to assimilation. These young people moved away from Jewish culture because they did not find within it what their non-Jewish counterparts found in *their* culture.[4]

From Berdyczewski: "Wrecking and Building" (ca. 1900)

We are torn to shreds: at one extreme, some leave the House of Israel to venture among foreign peoples, devoting to them the service of their hearts and spirits and offering their strength to strangers; while, at the other extreme, the pious sit in their gloomy caverns, obeying and preserving what God had commanded them. And the enlightened, standing between, are men of two faces: half Western – in their daily life and thoughts; and half Jews – in their synagogues. Our vital forces disperse while the nation crumbles.

For all the yearning for a revival that has begun to awaken in the heart of the remaining few, we feel that such a revival must encompass both the inner and the outer life. It cannot arise other than by a total overturn, that is, by a transvaluation of the values [a common term used by the Hebrew authors for a revolution in Jewish values] which have been the guide lines of our lives in the past.

Our hearts, ardent for life, sense that the resurrection of Israel depends on a revolution – the Jews must come first, before Judaism – the living man, before the legacy of his ancestors.

We must cease to be Jews by virtue of an abstract Judaism and become Jews in our own right, as a living and developing nationality. The traditional "credo" is no longer enough for us.

We desire to elevate our powers of thought, to enrich our spirit, and to enlarge our capacity for action; but let us never force our spirits into set forms that prescribe for us what we may think and feel. . . .

Jewish scholarship and religion are not the basic values – every man may be as much or as little devoted to them as he wills. But the people of Israel come before them – "Israel precedes the Torah.". . .

We must cease to be tablets on which books are transcribed and thoughts handed down to us – always handed down.

Through a basic revision of the very foundations of Israel's inner and outer life, our whole consciousness, our predispositions, thoughts, feelings, desires, and will and aim will be transformed: and we shall live and stand fast.

Such a fundamental revision in the people's condition, the basic drive toward freedom, and the boundless urge to new life will revive our souls. Transvaluation is like a flowing spring. It revives whatever is in us, in the secret places of the soul. Our powers are filled with a new, life-giving content.

Such a choice promises us a noble future; the alternative is to remain a straying people following its erring shepherds. A great responsibility rests upon us, for everything lies in our hands! We are the last Jews – or we are the first of a new nation.[5]

From Berdyczewski: "The Question of Culture" (ca. 1900)

As a general rule, nationality enriches the individual, bestowing upon him ancient wealth, and, in turn, it becomes enriched from the

individual works and creations of its representatives in every generation; but among us all those who work or wish to work in the field
of culture find nothing from which to begin.

Other peoples demand sacrifices of their sons only in times of war,
when foreigners seek to destroy them. In peacetime, in the processes
of everyday life, the price of patriotism is rarely sacrifice – that is, the
individual is not aware that he lives, or should live, on behalf of his
people. The normal actions of the individual are themselves of benefit
to the community. But among us, every individual is required to live
always on behalf of his people and to make sacrifices for it every day,
every hour, every minute; we demand this of him because his own life
and needs strain toward a different arena than the group life, and, in
some measure, his personal goals oppose the life of the group.

We require of every Jew that he be greater than other men, while
our capacity for such greatness is severely limited.

The existence of our people, the very possibility of its existence,
depends on creating a harmonious framework for our individual lives
within the community – it depends on our capacity to be united within
a structure capable of future survival. Our people can continue to exist only if there will be created among us a spiritual atmosphere and
material possibilities for artists and builders.

Give the chance to live to a single individual, and the mass will follow
after of its own accord.[6]

Brinker on Brenner

Brinker sees Brenner as the most consistent of the Hebrew writers in
applying his ideas to modern Jewish life:

On the question of assimilation, Brenner took a position unlike Aḥad
Ha-Am's or Berdyczewski's. He blames both of them for the exagger-
ated spiritualization of Jewish history, with its overemphasis on spiritual factors as responsible for either assimilation or preservation. Both
thinkers pay scant attention to the economic, social, nonintellectual,
nonphilosophical dimensions of the assimilation phenomenon.

You debate about an overabundance of monism and an overabundance of pluralism in culture, says Brenner, but in my opinion Jewish
life in the ghetto and in the Diaspora is the cause of assimilation.
The Diaspora itself is the cause – with cultural-religious pluralism or
monism, with or without sacred texts. As long as Jewish life takes place
in a non-Jewish environment, people will be attracted to the outside
environment; and the attempt to force them to view particular texts as

sacred will not make a difference. Whatever happens, assimilation will consume everything, whether you encourage monism or pluralism. . . .

Therefore, there is no solution to the problem of assimilation as long as Jews live most of the time within frameworks that are not Jewish, even if those frameworks are Jewish one-and-a-half days a week. Any educational effort will be artificial and will not be a cure, since even when you generate a relationship to particular texts as sacred, you have no guarantee that this relationship will remain strong in the face of all the trials and tribulations of life. . . .

Can Jewish culture be anything and everything in the future and still be Jewish? This question, which is very real for Aḥad Ha-Am, is for Brenner very artificial and abstract. If there are Jews who see themselves as Jews and as belonging to the historical collective, whose history is such and such and whose expectations are such and such, whatever they create will be equivalent to Jewishness.

Therefore, to speak in contemporary terms, the kibbutz is a Jewish creation, the Israeli Defense Forces are a Jewish creation, and even a bank bonds crisis in Israel is a Jewish creation. Everything that Jews do is a Jewish creation. Not everything, of course, is worthy of being called culture. Jews do many things other than culture. When you read Aḥad Ha-Am and Berdyczewski, it seems that all there is in the world is culture. When you read Brenner, however, you feel that there are other things in life.[7]

From Brenner: "On the Threat of Assimilation" (1901)

The existence of and necessity for assimilation will not be reversed by abstract ideas. "Judaism," in quotation marks, will not offer salvation, even if it is explained in a thousand eloquent sermons. Let us leave theology, then, for those "priests" – theirs and ours – who have the time to occupy themselves with questions such as which religion is better, which has more beauty, more sanctity, more justice, more love. This field is wide open: There is room to show off, to introduce new ideas, to choose various passages from among the wealth of available sacred texts, to link them cleverly – and to be convincing.

However, the problem of our Jewish *life* is not the same as the problem of the Jewish religion – the problem of "the survival of Judaism." The linking of the two should have been severed at its very root. Aḥad Ha-Am did so and then retracted his claim.[8] But we, his liberated peers, have nothing to do with Judaism, and yet, all the same, here we are, part of the community no less than those who regularly don *tefillin* and *tzitzit* [phylacteries and "fringes" on a prayer shawl]. We say: The problem of

Jewish life is that of productive work. We Jews are strangers in every place, broken, without a territory, without a language, and so on, and so on; the gentile environment in which we live does not allow us to be complete Jews to the same extent that our counterparts who are free Russians, Poles, etc., are complete Russians and Poles. . . . Our people is *galutish* [exilic in its character], ill, it stumbles into something, falls again and again – and rises. We must help it stay upright. . . . We, the living Jews, whether we fast on Yom Kippur or eat milk with meat on that day, whether we embrace the morality of the Old Testament or are faithful apostates – we never stop feeling our Jewishness, living our Jewish lives, working and creating new modes of labor for Jews, speaking in our Jewish tongue, receiving our spiritual sustenance from our literature,[9] working to free our national culture, defending our national pride and fighting for our existence in whatever form that battle may take.[10]

Part Two: Brinker, the Hebrew Writers, and Contemporary Realities

The ideas of these writers directly influenced the pioneer leaders of the Zionist movement as they took on the enormous task of developing a viable and sovereign Jewish state. But Brinker claims that their ideas are significant beyond the context in which they were formulated and the realities they addressed. Because a national framework for Jewish life has been established, they can find ongoing expression in the social, cultural, and educational realms made possible by the Jewish state.

On the End of Zionism

The cornerstone of Brinker's commentary on the ideas of the Hebrew writers is his argument that the achievements of Zionism make its political ideology redundant. While his educational theory draws upon the ideas that provided a basis for political Zionism, he argues that to continue to appeal to this ideology after the establishment of the State of Israel only diverts energy from the real challenge – that of building a more open, complex, and pluralistic Jewish society in Israel:

Historical Zionism was not one ideology but a coalition of conflicting ideologies: liberal and religious, socialist and nationalist, joined together for one common goal. The Zionist movement was able to survive precisely because it respected differences within its ranks. It could never have grown into a mass movement if it had adopted the style of a top sergeant ordering the troops to close ranks. Yet this is the attitude we see more and more in Israel and in the diaspora. Zionism per se has nothing to say to the cultural and social issues dividing Israel's society, and we ought to admit it.

The pressing issues of today are no longer issues for which Zionism has answers. In fact, the questions that divide Zionists from one another are more vital and critical today than the rather arcane questions that separate the Zionist from the non-Zionist. In accomplishing the major tasks it set for itself, Zionism won a smashing victory. Beyond that, everything is wide open; and since Zionism never agreed on a recipe for the character of the Jewish state, its job is done. We need not mourn.

Nor should we regret that, for many Israelis, Zionist ideology has given way to a simple feeling of home and belongingness. For *this* was the Zionist goal: the creation of a new kind of Jewish life, unselfconscious, needing no ideologies to explain or justify its existence. . . .

Zionism's finest hours were in the decades preceding and following the establishment of the state, when it offered a home to masses of Jews. But whatever the future holds, as of today there are no masses of homeless or persecuted refugees knocking down the doors of the homeland. Today Zionism can have only one meaning: it is a means to an end, which itself is finally only a means. And the end of all this is something that appeals to only a select group – of which I happen to be a member. Zionism is a means to perpetuate the state of Israel; and Israel is a means to guarantee the future of the Jewish people in history.[11]

On Jewish Particularity and General Culture in Israel

According to Brinker, the path to human fulfillment is not through an abstract "universal culture" but through one's particular culture and history. In the project's deliberations, he warned against the assumption that one's humanity can be fulfilled in any way other than through one's own culture. "I doubt if what is called a 'universal culture' exists anywhere," he argued, "or that it might have any great depth."

In his view, the State of Israel has created the necessary framework for Jewish particularity, which then allows Jews to enter into dialogue with the outside world and to absorb for the purpose of the improvement of Israeli society the best of what general culture has to offer.

Brinker explains the necessity of "de-ghettoizing" Jewish life:

> The term "Euro-Hebrew" [first coined by Berdyczewski, but later used as a reference to the ideal of the new Jew suggested by the Hebrew writers] expresses an ideal that we today would be wise to understand, if we look not only at the positive message it carried, but also at that against

which it was proposed. . . . Its underlying meaning was the creation of a new Jewish person for whom nothing human would be alien and who would find his uniqueness through creativity rather than by self-isolation. The pioneers of the early *aliyot* [waves of immigration to Israel] at the turn of the century emphasized the need for Jews to connect with every aspect of life, particularly nature, physical labor, and self-defense. That is, they felt that it was important to generate in the Jew a readiness to defend himself and the fruit of his labor by force. In this way, the slogan of the "Euro-Hebrew" ennobled the Zionist movement and the renewal of Jewish life in the land of Israel.

Echoes of the debates that this slogan generated still resound in our day. We continue to hear claims about the need to preserve Jewish authenticity and uniqueness against foreign influences. We also hear about the danger of collective assimilation by Israeli Jews. In the State of Israel today, education in the public Orthodox system does not include sufficient components of general culture – for example, philosophy, history, or literature – except the study of science and technology. From this perspective, the slogan of the "Euro-Hebrew" still has the capacity to arouse heated debate. Here, one must stress that those who propounded this slogan at the end of the nineteenth and the beginning of the twentieth century did not think that it contributed to assimilation or that it endangered Jewish uniqueness. They thought only that the slogan removed the artificial walls built to fortify that uniqueness, the origins of which lay in extremism, dogmatism, and ignorance. They had an instinctive confidence in the continuity of Jewish life, entirely independent of the beliefs and opinions held by Jews. Furthermore, they were driven by the awareness that if Jews do have a uniqueness derived from their distinctive history and ancient religious culture, this uniqueness will persist even when tested by an unconstrained encounter with the cultures of other nations.[12]

On the Culture War Between Orthodox and Secular Jews in Israel

Brinker argues against the claim that Israel needs a cultural consensus in order to survive. Instead, he explains how competing approaches to the Hebrew language and Jewish culture can coexist:

It is true that the Zionist movement and the *Yishuv* [Jewish settlement] in Palestine did everything they could to bypass the debate over Jewish culture so as not to split the broad Zionist coalition in the days leading up to the establishment of the state. However, since the founding of the state, it has been impossible to blur the profound differences between the conceptions of the two camps about what is the worthwhile and desirable Jewish way of life in Israel. Once again, there is no way around the debate. . . .

This is the big question for our day: Is our shared Jewish–Israeli destiny sufficiently substantive to prevent the conflicting interpretations of Jewishness proposed by observant and secular Jews from dissolving the commonality – and turning it into a fact that is trivial and meaningless compared to the weight of its diverse and opposing interpretations? It seems to me that efforts to cultivate an awareness of their shared fate in a single historical movement so as to *eliminate and erase* the opposition and debate between them actually promote a groundless utopia. However, when the awareness of a shared fate is nurtured for the sake of establishing boundaries for a political and cultural clash between the two camps, there is, under certain conditions, . . . a chance to succeed . . . Israeli society is strong enough to contain a "culture war" between the two camps of the Jewish people in our generation – the traditional-religious one and the Jewish-secular one – provided that this battle takes place within a democratic framework and in keeping with basic rules of tolerance.[13]

In the following passage, Brinker addresses the debate over authenticity in Jewish culture:

The profound difference between the Orthodox and secular outlooks can be highlighted by the use of the terms *makor* ["source"] and *makoriyut* ["authenticity"] and by their contrasting relationship to the past. While the secular outlook will emphasize the fact and value of *authenticity* – that is, that every Jew is not only a passive transmitter of Jewish culture but a potential *source* of it – the religious-traditional view will stress that anyone who sees himself as having a Jewish identity participates in a given culture, *the source of which is not in him,* but has, according to traditional belief, an absolute *source.* According to the latter view, Jewish culture is not a historical adventure, whose future nobody can predict; rather, one can identify within it an enduring character, which persists despite changes and vicissitudes and which also somewhat shapes the future.

This difference is particularly evident in the differing conceptions of Jewish culture's relationship to the past. For the creator of secular culture – such as Bialik or the kibbutz movement – the texts, ceremonies, and customs of the past are, first and foremost, *materials* out of which a new creation will be fashioned, one that will differ, to a lesser or a greater degree, from what was created in the past. For the preserver of traditional culture, the texts, rituals, and customs of the past are *obligating modes and norms* that cannot be tampered with. The Passover *Haggadah* is not simply a random collection of texts one can edit or augment according to whatever suits the sensibilities of contemporary Jews who celebrate Passover. Whoever does that is denying and de-sanctifying rather than renewing Jewish culture. According to this view, the national-religious past of the Jewish people is not raw material out of which to shape a revitalized national consciousness.

. . . In the ideological debate on culture, secular Jews will emphasize that not only do they repudiate a Jewish culture that is closed and isolated from all that is created by other cultures, but they do not even believe that Jewish culture was ever in a state of total singularity: It is clear that the "authentic" dress that is accepted by Hasidim originates in the dress of non-Jews in the Carpathian mountains – just as the source of "authentic Jewish faith" in the resurrection of the dead originates in Eastern religions and in Hellenistic influences. . . .

In contrast, faithful observant Jews will emphasize the decisive and undeniable fact that for thousands of years any idea or practice that was assimilated into Jewish culture underwent a process of adjustment to the beliefs and way of life of the Jewish collective – a collective that saw itself both as a nation and a religious congregation characterized by an utterly unique fate and calling. This process of adjustment transformed the ideas and practices into Jewish ones; to disavow this understanding is to forgo the possibility of granting Jewish culture any positive characteristic that will differentiate it from other cultures, because the Jewish identity of those individuals who are supposed to be – according to the secular outlook – the source of all Jewish culture would be unclear.

. . . Often the superficiality of the Jewish education of secular Jews in [Israeli] public schools is emphasized, and there is a demand for greater familiarity with the tradition, so that the system will not develop "superficial Jews," "with no Jewish roots." This claim is justified in opposing a piecemeal knowledge of the history of Jewish culture, full of omissions – an outcome that was generated by Zionism itself. The claim is especially justified, in my opinion, when it reminds teachers and educators that Jewish culture does not end with the Bible.

However, one might also raise the following question: Does the public religious school give its learners an opportunity to experience the diversity and richness of Jewish culture in recent generations? A student who knows how to read or interpret a page of Talmud, but knows nothing about the nature poetry of Bialik or Tchernichovsky, or the various social movements within the Jewish world – is it so clear that he was given a profoundly more *Jewish* education than his secular counterpart?[14]

Part Three: Brinker's Vision and Contemporary Jewish Education

In these excerpts from our notes, Brinker addressed issues raised by the educators about his vision of liberal-secular Jewish education.

On Spirituality and Brinker's Vision

Brinker argued that freedom itself is a spiritual value, operating through a dialectic of internalization and selection. People internalize values from previous generations and from transmitted culture. They form values by responding to what they have internalized and *selecting* what they want.

The role of spirituality in his vision is to allow the learner to discover his own autonomy, to awaken him to reflection, to tear him away from what is natural to him and what he accepts by inertia so that he can confront the commitments he has taken for granted.

On the Dangers and Opportunities in Brinker's Vision

Some of the scholars and educators claimed that a successful implementation of Brinker's ideas would result in the dissipation of Jewish culture, estrangement from the Jewish past, or the collective assimilation of the Jewish people in Israel. They also contended that the learner would not have sufficient tools to accept the responsibility that comes with freedom, leading ultimately to nihilism.

Brinker rejected these conclusions. For him, collective assimilation is by definition impossible in an environment in which the majority is Jewish. True, the democratization of Jewish culture implicit in his approach could lead to a dilution and a "flattening out" of that culture in Israel. Nevertheless, he preferred such an educational system to one that seeks higher achievement at the expense of freedom of thought and speech.

Nor was Brinker concerned about the dangers of relativism and nihilism. "I prefer that 40 percent of my students turn out to be nihilists than 15 percent turning out to be fanatics!" he exclaimed.

Brinker did point out other risks. He saw the "passive ghettoism" of the Eastern European Diaspora easily transformed in Israel into a religious fundamentalism that jeopardizes democracy. He also condemned secular fanaticism, which he thought could evolve into a form of fascism.

Brinker was also aware of the danger to Israel of an ignorance of Jewish life. To acquire expertise in one's own history and culture is a necessity, not a luxury. Successful Jewish education, he argued, transforms one's Jewishness into a matter of choice, into a decision to participate in the world as a free and creative human being. It allows learners to convey their Jewishness in many ways, some of which cannot be anticipated. Ultimately, an educated Jew is one whose commitment to the improvement of Jewish society finds expression in everyday life. Reading the newspaper, for example, is an expression of Jewishness, as is writing a Hebrew poem, humming a rock tune by an Israeli artist, or buying apples and honey for the Jewish New Year.

On Hebrew in the Curriculum

Educators pointed out the infusion of English words into spoken Hebrew and asked Brinker if he considered this phenomenon pedagogically desirable. He replied that he saw no problem when foreign languages meet the needs of Israeli Hebrew. The foundations of Hebrew culture are strong enough to allow such phenomena as signs in English, which represent a desire for cultural expansion. In Brinker's words, "In Vienna there is a Café Paris and in Paris there is a Café Vienna."

Can Hebrew culture be taught in translation? Brinker responded that there is no entirely original creation in any culture. The impact of a translation depends on the need of the culture that receives it. A Hebrew text in translation can affect Jewish students in the Diaspora as powerfully as the original does an Israeli student – although there is, inevitably, an aesthetic loss.

Brinker's Vision and Jewish Communities Outside Israel

There was considerable debate around Brinker's assumption that only in Israel could everyday life be a basis for Jewish identity in a way that liberates Jews from having to justify their Jewishness ideologically. Jewish educators from communities around the world claimed that they could make effective use of his ideas in their educational settings without compromising the integrity of his vision. Some pointed to a tradition of American Zionist thinkers, such as Mordecai Kaplan and Horace Kallen, who saw Jewish life in America as sufficiently compelling to allow Jews to maintain their identity without requiring loyalty to a set of theological axioms.[15]

An interesting result of this debate was that the educators had more confidence in the application of Brinker's vision to communities outside Israel than did Brinker himself.

NOTES

1   "*Hiyḥulim la-Ivri-Eiropi be-Sifrut ha-Ivrit be-Ma'avar ha-Meot*" in *Migvan De'ot ve-Hashkafot be-Tarbut Yisrael* (Jerusalem: Ministry of Education, 1992), 84–85. All passages from this essay were translated by Daniel Marom.

2   *Selected Essays of Ahad Ha-'Am*, trans. Leon Simon (New York: Atheneum, 1970), 192–94.

3   "The Law of the Heart," trans. Leon Simon (1894) in *The Zionist Idea: A Historical Analysis and Reader*, ed. A. Hertzberg (New York: Atheneum, 1979), 251–55.

4   "*Hiyhulim*," 87–90.

5   "Wrecking and Building," trans. Ben Halpern and Arthur Hertzberg, in *The Zionist Idea*, 294.

6   "The Question of Culture," trans. Ben Halpern and Arthur Hertzberg, in *The Zionist Idea*, 298–99.

7   "*Ahad Ha-Am, Berdyczewski, u'Brenner: Shalosh Hityahasuyot Hiloniyot le-Tekstim Mehayvim ba-Yahadut*," *Kivunim* 39:2 (December 1990): 11, 15. Translated by Daniel Marom.

8   Brinker explains that while Ahad Ha-Am argued against definitions of Jewish life based on any particular set of ideas, he later posited a "national spirit" that defined Jewish life throughout history. On this contradictory aspect in Ahad Ha-Am's thought and its critique by his followers, see "Brenner's Jewishness," in *Studies in Contemporary Jewry*, ed. Jonathan Frankel, vol. iv (New York: Oxford University Press, 1988), 234–36.

9   Brinker pointed out that Brenner's seemingly extreme secular position can be misleading and is often distorted. For example, the curriculum used in Brenner's high school reveals that his emphasis on an open-ended definition of Jewish culture did not require the abandonment of Jewish tradition. In fact, the curriculum seems to have been designed with the aim of familiarizing the learner with a broad range of Jewish cultural resources, including traditional Jewish sources alongside modern ones and non-Jewish literature and history. See "*Ahad Ha-Am, Berdyczewski, u'Brenner*," 20.

10 Yosef Hayyim Brenner, *Ketavim*, vol. 3 (Tel Aviv: HaKibbutz HaMeuhad, 1985), 486–87. Passage translated by Daniel Marom.

11 "The End of Zionism? Thoughts on the Wages of Success," *Dissent* 32:1 (Winter 1985): 82.

12 "*Hiyhulim*," 81, 93–94.

13 "*Al Gevulot 'Milhemet ha-Tarbut' be-Yisrael*," *Sekirah Hodshit: Yarhon le-Ktzinei Tzahal* 33:6 (1986): 5, 10. All passages from this article were translated by Daniel Marom.

14 Ibid., 6–7, 10–11.

15 See Horace Kallen, *Education and the Survival of the World Jewish Community: An Address Delivered Before The Board of Governors of The American Association for Jewish Education, Detroit, March 9, 1957* (New York: American Association for Jewish Education); Mordecai Kaplan, *Judaism as a Civilization: Toward a Reconstruction of American-Jewish Life* (New York: Schocken, 1967); and Kallen, "Jewish Education and the Future of the American Jewish Community," *Jewish Education* 16:1 (September 1944): 6–11.

6

We Were as Those Who Dream: An Agenda for an Ideal Jewish Education

MOSHE GREENBERG

The Jewish component in the education of the Jewish child, in Israel as in the Diaspora, plays a decisive role in the formation of his identity. The shape of this component will determine the shape of the child's Jewishness – the awareness that he is heir to a tradition rich in values, one that invites him to fulfill himself through it.

Underlying this essay[1] is an image of the learner as a creature impelled by curiosity concerning the world about him and his own inner life – the meaning of what his senses take in. The need to know these is second only to basic subsistence needs (food, shelter, health, reproduction). The desire to know and understand is implanted in human nature from infancy, and what the child learns in school must satisfy that desire, through a curriculum crafted accordingly.

Knowledge of the facts of the nonhuman, material, natural world is necessary for human existence. The sciences, such as physics or chemistry or biology, are the great repositories of such knowledge. To achieve mastery in the sciences is to satisfy curiosity and acquire the means to benefit – or harm – civilization. But knowledge of the nonhuman realm, be it ever so profound, does not enable one to understand oneself – the structure of one's psyche: its needs, aspirations, fears and hopes, and the realms of value and significance.

The soul knows no rest until it gains some comprehension of, and makes some order in, the realm of value. This restlessness has generated spiritual creativity in every human society, a ubiquity that attests to a vital need. Moral contemplation begins with the question "What is the good path for one to choose?" Answers have been given, for the most part, in terms of some divine power charged with maintaining law and morality – in other words, in religious terms. Meaning, motivation, significance, approbation, and disapprobation have all been expressed in works inspired by a religious vision.

In the context of Hebrew culture, study of the masterworks of Judaism has provided a natural setting for discussing matters of value. To be sure, other natural settings exist, such as the study of literatures or classical philosophy. But the Jewish character of the child will be determined by its habituation to speak of such matters in terms drawn from the Jewish heritage, a literature whose primary purpose is to instruct in the way of goodness, utilizing to that end a wide variety of genres: narrative, poetry, law, parable, and more.

A Jewish education worthy of the name will address the hunger of the learner to know "whence he came and whither is he going." It will furnish him with value-concepts by which to infuse raw experience with meaning and order. The success of a Jewish education is measured by its adequacy in accompanying the learner through life as a treasury of concepts lending meaning to private and public experience.

The following essay presents a sampling of value-concepts capable of serving the learner as provisions for the whole of life's journey.

What would be the ideal product of an ideal Jewish education – an education whose goal is a person with knowledge, values, and loyalties that derive from the sources of Judaism? This "ideal product" is distinct from the broader concept of an "educated Jew" – a subspecies of the educated person, that is, a Jew who has acquired general knowledge as well as knowledge of Judaism. I assume that the person I am imagining will have acquired knowledge, values, and sensitivities in addition to those that are Jewish – for example, in the area of science (knowledge of nature and its laws), history (the development of nations and cultures), art (literature, music, painting), and thought (philosophy, other faiths, social criticism). It follows that the ideal product of an ideal Jewish education will have to deal with the tensions that arise between the two worlds in which he lives – the Jewish and the general.

What is the Jewish component in the formation of the educated Jew, the curriculum of an ideal Jewish education? It is the contents of the accepted fundamental books of Judaism – the Bible, Talmud, Midrash, and the body of "commentary" that has grown around these books in the course of generations, be it commentary in the narrow sense of the word (e.g., Rashi), or systematic thought or creative literature seeking to translate the contents of the books into a contemporary idiom (e.g., the languages of philosophy, of history, of ethics, of mysticism). These books define our relation to the universe and to our environment – the animate and the inanimate, the human, national, and familial.[2] The role of Jewish education is to transmit significant portions of these contents to the student, with "significant" having two connotations:

i. Meaningful, addressing matters of concern to students;
ii. An amount and a selection representative of the source in question, providing an authentic taste of the original, so that the student may be impressed by its power.

If the student receives portions of the basic books, "significant" in both these senses, there is a prospect that he will recognize their moral and intellectual power and resort to them throughout the years. The ultimate objective is for the student to be engaged during his school years with existential issues, and for him to discover his own Jewish identity through repeated encounters with Jewish sources. Our aspiration is for the product of an ideal Jewish education to feel that his most deeply felt values are derived from the basic books of Judaism.

Jewish education is to be evaluated according to its success in fostering in its graduates four qualities:

1. Love of learning Torah (i.e., the fundamental books and their offshoots); and love of the fulfillment of the commandments between man and God

Judaism's near deification of the Torah makes the study and practice of it a unique experience: As the words of God, mediated to Israel by a long line of prophets, the Holy Scriptures constitute an unfailing source of spiritual replenishing. Love of learning Torah is embodied in the concept of "(the study of) Torah for its own sake" (*Torah lishmah*). Such learning brings one into contact with something inherently valuable – the literary record of the encounter of Jews with a realm that transcends the visible, the earthly. *Torah lishmah* affords the student the spiritual pleasure of an activity, essentially meritorious, that activates his highest intellectual powers. One who studies Torah for its own sake experiences total self-actualization precisely as he is absorbed in a spiritual realm that is beyond the self. The commandments regulating relations between humanity and divinity are a set of symbols that point to the transcendent realm. Observing the Sabbath and taking delight in it, reciting the blessings of thanks, prayer, and refraining from forbidden foods – the whole system of sanctification (*kedushah*) – points us to the transcendent realm. Our ideal student will, at the least, understand and respect these symbols.[3]

Jewish education aims to amplify the whisper of conscience that rejects the prideful assertion that "I am, and there is none but me" (Isa. 47:8). It teaches rather that "I stand under a command, and must account to a Higher One for my actions." This whisper is endowed with a voice and a body in the study of *Torah lishmah* and in the performance of the commandments between man and God. Through these, the benign aspect of the realm beyond the material and sensory is experienced, lending meaning to the transiency of the individual and affirming the enduring validity of what is good and worthy in him. This experience is the basis for the insight that the visible world is not the be-all and end-all, nor is it the measure of all things. The successes and failures, the joys and sorrows of the visible world, are fleeting in comparison with the "eternal life He has implanted within us."

2. Acceptance of the Torah as a moral guide, along with the recognition that its moral precepts have undergone constant revision and refinement

By this I mean two things:

(a) The recognition that the moral precepts of the Torah can serve as a guide for our time. For example, the last six of the Ten Commandments – the values that they embody – and their subsequent development:

> Honoring of parents – necessary for the preservation of the family, the basic cell of society;

> "You shall not murder," an obligation that follows from "in His image did [God] make man";

> "You shall not commit adultery," an obligation that follows from the union (lit., "cleaving" – "and he cleaves to his wife so that they become as one flesh") that is to be realized in the relationship between husband and wife;

> "You shall not steal," an affirmation of the concept of property and ownership of goods, the abrogation of which leads to social chaos;

> "You shall not bear false witness against your neighbor," the basis of trust in the process of litigation and business, without which social bonds collapse;

> "You shall not covet," a preventive measure for all of the aforementioned prohibitions.

In *Sifra, Kedoshim* 4:12, the Sages identified "general principles" that governed interpretation of particulars:

> "Love your neighbor as yourself" (Lev. 19:18): Rabbi Akiva said: This is a great principle of the Torah. Ben Azzai said: "This is the book of the descendants of Adam (when God created man [*adam*], He made him in the likeness of God)" (Gen. 5:1). This is an even greater principle.

> "Her [the Torah's] ways are pleasant ways and all her paths are peaceful" (Prov. 3:17; cf. Maimonides, *Mishneh Torah, Laws of Kings*, end of Chapter 10).

Summaries in the Prophets and the Writings of the essence of God's demands of man were collected by Rabbi Simlai at the end of tractate Makkot (Babylonian Talmud):

> Rabbi Simlai preached: Six hundred and thirteen precepts were communicated to Moses. . . . David came and reduced them to eleven principles, as it is written (Ps. 15): "A Psalm of David. Lord, who may dwell on Your holy mountain? – [i] He who lives without blame, [ii] who

does what is right, and [iii] in his heart acknowledges the truth; [iv] whose tongue is not given to evil, [v] who has never done harm to his fellow, [vi] or borne reproach for [his acts toward] his neighbor, [vii] for whom a contemptible man is abhorrent, but [viii] who honors those who fear the Lord, [ix] who stands by his oath even to his hurt, [x] who has never lent money at interest, [xi] or accepted a bribe against the innocent. The man who acts thus shall never be shaken."

... Isaiah came and reduced them to six [principles], as it is written (Isa. 33:15–16): "[i] He who walks in righteousness, [ii] speaks uprightly, [iii] spurns profit from fraudulent dealings, [iv] waves away a bribe instead of grasping it, [v] stops his ears against listening to infamy, [vi] shuts his eyes against looking at evil."

... Micah came and reduced them to three [principles], as it is written (Mic. 6:8): "He has told you, O man, what is good, and what the Lord requires of you: [i] Only to do justice, and [ii] to love goodness, and [iii] to walk modestly with your God."

... Isaiah came again and reduced them to two [principles], as it is said (Isa. 56:1): "Thus said the Lord: [i] Observe what is right, and [ii] do what is just."

Amos came and reduced them to one [principle], as it is said (Amos 5:4): "Thus said the Lord to the House of Israel: Seek Me, and you shall live."

These attempts to epitomize the elements of the virtuous life should be presented to the pupils early in their formation, together with the prophetic visions of their fulfillment, so that they will be able to find in Judaism answers to their aspirations for a good society and for a meaningful and just way of life. They will not need to turn to foreign sources for principles of morality.[4]

(b) One of the chief tasks of Jewish education is to show the interpretation of the moral laws of the Torah and their detailed applications as an ongoing process. In this process, there is a continuous tension between particular-national and universal-human trends in the Torah. Similarly, there is a continuous tension between the mysterious element of sanctity (*kedushah*), embodied in symbols used in the worship of God, and the emphasis on the rational, moral element. This tension is apparent in the Prophets' assertion of the primacy of the moral element over the ritual element in the Covenant between God and His people, and it continues through the generations in Bible commentaries and in other Jewish sources.

At times, the Bible takes a broad view and the Sages narrow it. For example, the death penalty for murderers, in Genesis 9:5-6, applies to all the descendants of Noah; but the Sages limited it to the case in which the victim is a Jew. They deemed a Jew who murders a gentile to be exempt from human judgment and left his fate to "heaven" (*Mekhilta* to Exod. 21:14; cf. the reservation of Issi ben Yehuda, ibid.). The Sages differed with respect to the scope of the term "human" (*adam*) in the Bible: Rabbi Meir included gentiles, basing his position on the text ". . . [these are laws] by observing which humans (*ha-adam*) shall live" (Lev. 18:5), which he takes to imply that "a gentile who occupies himself with the Torah, is equal [in status] to the high priest" (Bava Kama 38a). In opposition to this view, Rabbi Shimon bar Yoḥai declared that "You are called *adam*; the gentiles are not called *adam*" (Yevamot 61a). Later scholars were divided in their interpretation of this declaration: Did R. Shimon mean to say that the gentile lacks a human essence that the Jew has (as is the opinion of certain mystics), or did he mean to say only that in the specific system of law in the Torah the term *adam* refers to "a person"; and since in any legal system "person" refers to one who is under its jurisdiction, *adam* in the Torah must refer to Jews, who alone are under the Torah's jurisdiction (as is the opinion of Rabbi Zvi Hirsch Chajes in his novellae to Yevamot).

Proper Jewish education will call the student's attention to the conflicts in the works of biblical commentators between *halakhah* and the plain sense of Scripture, the latter supported by conscience. Maimonides ruled (following the Talmud) that the law against cheating does not apply to the cheating of a non-Jew, as it is written: "You shall not wrong [lit., "cheat"] one another [lit., "each one his brother"] – (Lev. 25:17; see *Mishneh Torah, Laws of Sale* 13:7). But then Rabbi David Kimḥi, in his commentary to Psalm 15 (cited earlier) taught differently:

> "Nor do evil to his fellow (*re'ehu*), nor take up a reproach against one near to him (*krovo*)." "His fellow" and "one near to him" mean someone with whom one has business, or a neighbor. And in saying, "nor do evil to his fellow," the text does not imply that he did so to others [who are not his fellows or neighbors]; but the text describes ordinary circumstances [i.e., one ordinarily is in a position to do evil – or good – to one with whom he has some business, or to a neighbor]. Similarly, "You shall not wrong one another" [lit., 'each his comrade (*amito*)'] does not mean that one is allowed to cheat him who is not his comrade. Similarly, "You shall not bear false witness against your fellow" (*re'akha*, Exod. 20:16) does not mean that against another who is not your fellow you are allowed to bear false witness. Rather this applies to [a person with whom one ordinarily has] business and contact; that is the usage of the language in many cases.

One of the obstacles to our students' acceptance of the tradition is its petrified appearance. They are ignorant of the history of biblical interpretation and of the conflicting trends within it, and are therefore unaware of the ongoing reciprocal influence of the text on its interpreters, and interpreters on the text. Authentic Jewish culture can arise only from the dialogue between the source and the members of each generation, a dialogue in which both the loyalty of the people to the text and their adjustment of it to the culture of the present find expression.[5]

3. A way of life that creates a community

Our ideal product will want to live in a Jewish environment, since many precepts of Judaism are social:

> These are the things of which a person enjoys the fruits in this world, while the stock remains for him in the world to come: honoring father and mother, deeds of loving-kindness, timely attendance at the house of study morning and evening, hospitality to wayfarers, visiting the sick, dowering the bride, attending the dead to the grave, devotion in prayer, and making peace between persons; and the study of Torah is equal to them all.[6]

Almost all of these behaviors bind people to one another, and some of them require public-communal institutions – "deeds of loving-kindness," which are carried out (for example) by establishing an interest-free loan fund; "rising early to attend the house of study," assuming the existence of a house of study – a synagogue; "the study of Torah," which requires the employment of teachers and the maintenance of institutions of learning for adults and children. The more we undertake such enterprises, the more relations of friendship and neighborliness develop, as private resources are shared in order to establish the public institutions needed to carry out precepts such as those referred to here. Thus, a community of Jews is created, participating in one another's joys and sorrows, aiding one another in time of need, constituting an environment for the raising of children in a Jewish way of life.[7]

4. A relationship to the Jewish people in all the lands of their dispersion

Like is attracted to like. In the past, Jews in the Diaspora shared a consciousness of unity as members of a people covenanted with God, committed – more or less – to a traditional way of life. Regarded as "others" by the general population, Jews held what was shared among themselves as greater than that which they shared with their gentile "hosts." The scattered Jews were united by a common "language" in relationship to Jew and gentile, a common feeling of oppression in the present and hope for a future redemption, a common calendar of holidays, and an idea of a common "tribal" origin. Since the Holocaust and the establishment of the State of Israel, the unity of the people has been based on a common memory of national tragedy, a sense of tribal bond, and a common interest in the building and future of the state. These factors are not constantly evident to the individual, nor are they sufficient to ensure the continued connections among the various Jewish Diasporas. Only a systematically cultivated consciousness of 1) common origins; 2) a common existential status (members of a people of the Covenant); and 3) a common vision of the future redemption (and the role of the people of Israel in the "mending of the world" [*tikkun olam*]) can maintain the unity of the people under current conditions.

These three components of Jewish consciousness are included in the national-historical saga whose foundation is in the Bible and whose classical development is in rabbinic literature. The internalization of this saga is the crucial factor in the creation of a Jewish identity. The role of Jewish education is to foster this internalization by means of an educational program that emphasizes these three commonalities.

To foster among the Jews of Israel the recognition that they are brothers to the Jews of the Diaspora is no less important than to cultivate the consciousness among Diaspora Jews that they are brothers to the Jews of Israel. Each party has to cope with its own existential problems; as a result, they are in danger of progressive mutual alienation. The only means of maintaining unity among the scattered is to cultivate common sources of inspiration, as well as shared value-laden experiences (the study of Torah for its own sake, sanctity, moral values drawn from the fundamental books in an ongoing process of interpretation).

The attitude toward the "ingathering of the exiles," and, in its religious formulation, "the duty to settle the land of Israel," separates the inhabitants of the State of Israel from those of the Diaspora. It seems as though the Jewish people is divided between a party that is actualizing a value sacred in the past to the whole people, and a party that has abandoned that value and has thus broken away from the loyal core of those who are moving forward to "a complete redemption." Evidently, there was in the past a situation similar to our own – a vibrant Jewish settlement in the land of Israel contemporaneous with a large and creative Diaspora. It is not clear how the Jews in the "Babylonian exile" reconciled, for hundreds of years, the contradiction between their prayers for the ingathering of the exiles and their continued residence outside the land of Israel. Political and economic factors doubtless played a role. In the past, people attributed major changes in their status to divine initiative; in our time, human initiative is not only justified by the majority, it is glorified. Consequently, we are perplexed by the refusal of most Jews to join in the task of building the state. In the foreseeable future this perplexity will not be resolved, for authentic Jewish education will maintain the tension. On the other hand, the "portable" basis of Judaism is capable of supplying Jewish content and meaning even to the inhabitants of the Diaspora. Those who seek to close the gap between their deeds and their prayers will constitute, as in the past, a trickle of *aliyah* (immigration to Israel).

Jewish education will be able to connect the Jewish inhabitants of the State of Israel with the Jews of the Diaspora only insofar as it wins the hearts of those who live in the land of Israel to the idea that the state is merely a means to the higher end of "mending the world in the kingdom of God" (by whatever conception of the state as a means for realizing universal values); and the hearts of those who live in the Diaspora to the idea that "mending the world" must begin by a self-critique of "the people of the Covenant of God." To the extent that Jewish education succeeds with both parties, there will be a coming together of the two: Jews of Israel will move toward a way of life that seeks to embody Jewish values, while Diaspora Jews will be drawn, through their identification with Judaism, to participate in the fateful experiment now under way to find out whether Judaism is capable of sustaining a modern Jewish state.[8]

Although it is not my task to go into the means by which the product described here may be attained, I wish to touch on a matter that could be considered either a means or an end, namely, the Hebrew language. (What follows is relevant, of course, only to Jewish education in the Diaspora.) The uniquely Jewish store of concepts and values cannot be transmitted in translation. For Jews, translations of sacred texts were meant only as aids to mastering the originals. No translation could replace the original, but only accompany it as its explication. Custom even overruled law in this matter: By law one is permitted to recite the Shema prayer in any language one understands; in practice, however, throughout time the Shema (central prayer and declaration of faith) has been recited only in Hebrew. As a result, a rich store of untranslatable associations is contained in the Hebrew words. For example, the pronunciation of the final consonant of *eḥad* "one" – namely, *dalet* (whose numerical equivalent is four) – must be drawn out so as to enable contemplation of God's dominion over the four corners of the earth.

That it is possible to teach Hebrew in the Diaspora up to a level sufficient for understanding the sources in their original language has been proven by experience – given a curriculum that commits time, money, and skilled personnel to the task. All depends on the willingness of the community to recognize that Hebrew must be acquired in order for the Jewish heritage to be transmitted in all its force. But this willingness is in turn dependent on the weight the community assigns to a meaningful Jewish education.

A meaningful Jewish education will move those who enjoy and are edified by it to deepen their knowledge of Hebrew. The more students feel spiritual (moral, intellectual) fulfillment in their studies, the greater their readiness to invest effort in them, even at the expense of their full participation in the non-Jewish culture. But it is doubtful that such an identification with Judaism can develop without direct nourishment from its sources. On the other hand, a shallow Jewish education will not justify itself to the students, and will generate indifference and opposition until all of the teacher's attempts to pass it on will be defeated. The students will seek satisfaction from alien sources.

It must seem as if I have made my task easy by ignoring the grim realities of Jewish education, and that my portrait of an ideal product of Jewish education is visionary, not to say fantastic. Still, my hope is that the uninhibited musings of a lay educator may help stimulate professionals in the field to devise better solutions for the problems of Jewish education – even if, in the end, my ideas turn out to be useful only as a foil for debate.

NOTES

1 This English version – translated by Daniel Marom in consultation with the author – deviates at times from the Hebrew original for the sake of clarity.

2 The approach to Jewish sources adopted in this essay is not predicated on – but neither does it exclude – special revelation or any other a priori faith assumptions, or even the assumption of the uniqueness of Judaism. It is the approach of the study of religion, which appreciates religion as a phenomenon inherent in human nature. I do affirm that it is within the capacity of the foundational books of Judaism to meet the spiritual needs naturally ingrained in the learner's soul. Consequently, there is no need for dogmatic assumptions about these works in order to justify their being studied. See "*Al Zehut, Tevunah ve-Dat*," in the collection of my Hebrew essays, *Al ha-Mikra ve-al ha-Yahadut* (Tel Aviv: Am Oved, 1984), 247–74.

The study of Jewish history in the curriculum that I envisage serves the history of Jewish thought and literature. I distinguish between the spiritual history of the Jews (whose literary crystallizations define Judaism) and the material history of the Jews. The material history is the basis upon which the spiritual history was produced and, to a certain extent, the former determined the latter's characteristics (for example, its languages). To that extent, one must be familiar with the material history. However, the basic affirmation of Jewish spiritual creativity is that the spirit is superior to matter and cannot be subservient to it. This affirmation should guide the curriculum. The exemplary spiritual creations of Judaism crossed geographical boundaries and time periods and obstacles of language. Accordingly, they should be presented as works of enduring worth, which, though born in a temporal framework, transcend it as a result of internal developments and of ongoing encounters with surrounding cultures.

Material Jewish history and Jewish belles lettres are within the bounds of Jewish education as here defined to the extent to which they illuminate the fundamental texts, whether by depicting the conditions under which these texts arose and became widespread, or by providing an account of their development and impact. I do not regard the study of Jewish material history in and of itself nor the study of Jewish belles lettres in its formal and historical manifestations as belonging to Jewish education, but rather as subjects that an ideal Jewish education will motivate the student to pursue. These subjects intensify national consciousness, reinforce national identity, and add a measure of earthiness and aesthetic pleasure to the study of Jewish culture. However, when it comes to giving meaning to Jewish life, when we wish to transmit eternal values that bind one to the continuum of the generations, the fundamental books, shared by all the generations, are our primary educational resource.

3   In my article, "*Al Zehut, Tevunah ve-Dat*," I expanded on the need for religious symbols (see note 2). [See also Supplement that follows.]

4   The shelf of fundamental Jewish books does not stand in isolation. It is possible to derive fundamental values from books found on other shelves as well. The aim of this approach, as was stated, is to make it unnecessary for the Jewish student to turn to non-Jewish sources in order to draw from them fundamental existential values. In all periods, Jews entered into an ongoing negotiation with the cultural world in which they settled. In this negotiation, values originating in external sources were assimilated into Judaism, for Jews accepted them as necessary implications of Jewish tenets. For example, the value of democracy was created outside of Judaism, but Jewish thinkers sought and found a basis for it in Jewish sources (e.g., see the essay written by my father, Simon Greenberg, "Judaism and the Democratic Ideal," in his book *Foundations of a Faith* [New York: Burning Bush Press, 1967], 113–34). By adopting and Judaizing what is "good and fair" in gentile cultures, Judaism escaped petrification and obsolescence.

5   On the morality of the Bible and of Judaism and its problems, see the essay by Leon Roth, "*Ha-Tenudah ha-Mussarit be-Etikah ha-Yehudit*," in his book *Ha-Dat ve-Erkhei ha-Hayyim* (Jerusalem: Magnes, 1973), 89–106; also S. H. Bergman, "*Harhavah ve-Tzimtzum be-Etikah ha-Yehudit*," in his booklet *Ha-Shamayim ve-ha-Aretz: Hegyonot al Ahrayuto shel ha-Adam* (Tel Aviv: Shdemot, 1969), 29–38; and my essays, "'*Atem Keruyim Adam . . .*,'" in *Al ha-Mikra ve-al ha-Yahadut*, 55–67; and "*Keitzad Yesh Lidrosh et ha-Torah ba-Zman ha-Zeh*," in *Ha-Segulah ve-ha-Koah* (Tel Aviv: Oranim Sifriyat Poalim/HaKibbutz HaMe'uhad, 1986), 49–67.

6   Based on "Preliminaries to the Morning Service," *The Authorised Daily Prayer Book*, rev. ed., trans. J. H. Hertz (New York: Block Publishing Company, 1948), 17.

7   In a deliberation with Seymour Fox on this section, the following clarification emerged (I paraphrase): Whoever is devoted to Jewish values will want a "world" to support his values. This "world" [= a social context] could be an enclave – a community that intentionally develops a way of life different from that of its surroundings, a subculture, as it were. A difficult question is whether an ideal Jewish education is not contingent upon the development of a subculture. Perhaps graduates of all educational systems that cultivate defined ideas and values aspire to create an enclave or subculture in which they can attain a maximal degree of self-fulfillment.

8   I have enlarged upon the topic of the Jewish character of the State of Israel in the essay "The Task of Masorti Judaism," in *Deepening the Commitment: Zionism and the Conservative/Masorti Movement*, ed. J. S. Ruskay and D. M. Szonyi (New York: The Jewish Theological Seminary of America, 1990), 137–46.

Supplement: Moshe Greenberg

While religious in character, Moshe Greenberg's vision differs from traditional Jewish education in not asking that learners accept any prior faith assumptions about God, the universe, the Torah, or Jewish history.[1] Rather, Greenberg conceives of Jewish education as responding to learners' search for meaning.

The initial deliberations about Greenberg's essay focused on his assumptions about the nature and primacy of spirituality in human existence and the role of religion in answering spiritual needs. Greenberg suggested that religion be viewed as a storehouse of symbols and directed us to a theory of symbols as mediators between the here and now and the transcendent realm. For him, Judaism is a religion that has responded to the spiritual needs of Jews and has the capacity to do so now and in the future.[2]

What kind of Jewish education could activate Judaism's capacity to respond to the spiritual needs of contemporary Jews? At the center of Greenberg's approach, we learned in the deliberation, is the study of classical Jewish texts, which he saw as religious symbols that could help learners explore the spiritual realm. He proposed a way of interpreting these texts that would release them from the constraints of their antiquity and induct learners into the tradition of *parshanut,* commentary. As in generations past, Jews could then interpret these texts in light of contemporary realities.

Finally, Greenberg discussed the implications of his vision for the work of educators and Judaica scholars with learners as diverse as summer campers in America and secular university students in Israel. He demonstrated how his approach to the study of text could apply to such challenging topics as feminism, democracy, and fundamentalism. Discussions with the educators and others led him to clarify his position on such issues as the place of Jewish history in the curriculum and the boundaries of the interchange between Judaism and other cultures.

133

Part One: Greenberg's Theory of Religion and Its Implications for Jewish Education

Greenberg's vision of Jewish education is based on a view of religion not merely as the creation of the collective genius of a particular people, but as the expression of something inherent in human nature. All people are spiritual beings, whose need for meaning and purpose is instinctive. Religious education, according to Greenberg, must assume that spiritual needs are integral to personality, and that the learner should be educated to satisfy those needs through religious experience.

Religion as a System of Symbols

Greenberg has explained this theory of religion in a number of his writings, including an essay that links religion and education:

> Why is there a need for religious ceremonies, for holy scriptures, for a normative system of beliefs and practices? Why not simply follow what our eyes tell us, what our hearts discern, and what our instincts crave? Not only do children ask these questions. So do their forebears.
>
> An answer worthy of the questions and those who ask them must justify the existence of the elements of spiritual life as inherently valuable, not as a means to any other end, such as the pursuit of happiness, the improvement of society, or the unity of the nation (although such ends may result from these elements). Indeed, these elements are presented – and they present themselves – as absolute values and truths. The power of their influence on a person and on society derives from this characteristic. If they were perceived as relative or instrumental, they could never have such an impact. Holiness that depends only on an agreement for the sake of achieving happiness, improving society, or unifying the nation is not really holiness but only a social convention. To rephrase our question: What is the absolute value of religious ceremonies, of holy scriptures, of a system of beliefs and practices defined as normative? What is their truth?
>
> There is in human experience more than what is perceived by the eye. The person facing me is more than what I see; the chain of events that has brought us to this moment means more than what is apparent; the bearers of responsibility – a judge, a leader, or a mother – are enveloped by something beyond the visible; the relationship of one person to another is weighted with something greater than what is immediately evident. It is clear to us all that a surface view of the world cannot encompass its wholeness. In existence itself there is a dimension of depth, of the "transcendent," which is the meaningful element of reality.

How is it possible to portray or imagine the aspects of that hidden realm? How can one conceptualize these aspects in order to meditate upon them? How can they be expressed so that they can be shared with others? Only through the medium of symbols – objects, terms, stories, texts, or behaviors, whose only purpose is to point to a reality beyond them. Amorphous conceptions of the transcendent realm can be defined only through symbols; and only through them is it possible to develop our awareness of that transcendent realm, to meditate upon it, to communicate it with another, and to awaken it in his heart. Symbols of the transcendent realm are not only able to intimate and to represent, but also to move to action. The symbols incorporate passion, and through them it is possible as well to arouse passion.

The absolute value of a religion's appurtenances and behaviors is their symbolizing the transcendent realm and their infusion of the awareness of this realm into everyday life. This is no invention of a realm extraneous to a person's essence, but rather, an outer expression and manifestation of the hidden realm that every person recognizes. Thereby it is possible for a person to perceive, to be awakened, and to waken others to this realm. The truth of religious appurtenances lies in the extent to which they express and expand the transcendent realm. It is a truth that proves itself to the person who uses these appurtenances by the fact that through them his awareness of that realm continually grows, continually deepens. At the same time, it is crucial to recognize that the truth is not in the symbol, but in that which is symbolized by it. The system of religious symbols points not only to what is beyond and greater than humanity, but to what is beyond and greater than the system of religious symbols itself.[3]

Judaism as a Response to Spiritual Needs

Greenberg applies ideas from the scholarly study of religion to Judaism, but also finds supporting sources within Jewish tradition. One of his favorite references to support the characterization of Judaism as a system of symbols is the rabbinic adage that "the Commandments were not given other than for the refinement of God's creatures."[4]

We found Greenberg's descriptions of Jewish beliefs and practices as religious symbols to be most instructive for understanding his theory of religion and his conception of Judaism. Greenberg defines symbols as a means for attaining spiritual fulfillment. An intellectual understanding – however rich – of Jewish symbols that does not lead to this outcome would be insufficient. Jewish education is therefore not only teaching *about* Jewish religion; the character of its teaching *is* religious.

The scholars and educators pressed Greenberg to clarify his understanding of Jewish religious education. On the one hand, he had stated that Judaism is one particular path to a universal spiritual realm. Other cultures, both religious and nonreligious, offer legitimate alternative paths. Judaism, then, is not necessarily superior to other religions; it does, however, have the capacity to respond to the spiritual needs of Jews. Thus, he rejected apologetic approaches to Jewish education that try to demonstrate the preeminence of Judaism over other cultures and religions. On the other hand, he emphasized Judaism as the unique core of Jewish education, postponing encounters with other cultures and religions to later stages of learning.

What is Greenberg's larger conception of culture? How does it explain his emphasis on the exclusivity of Judaism in Jewish education in relation to other cultures?

What follows is an excerpt from his response to these questions in one of his meetings with the educators:

> Culture is an expanding and sifting treasure of spiritual possessions of a particular human group, a treasure that is shaped by the circumstances of this group's life and its unique confrontation with universal existential issues. All culture is the fruit of this confrontation, a singular rendition, a unique formulation of answers to universal questions.
>
> By spiritual possessions, I include all that the human spirit creates. The spirit creates a sculpture and a house. Even a scythe is the creation of a human spirit. Spiritual possessions include music, art, literature, dance, theater, sport.
>
> They are not all alike. Each scythe, sculpture, house is created within a specific culture; there are no cultural possessions that can be attributed to "general culture." Just as there is no universal language, so, too, is there no universal culture. Each language is a set of answers, the fruit of the creative spirit of one particular group, which provides a channel for communication and a coded expression for emotions. It is possible to transplant words from one language into another. However, these borrowed words are not to be seen as the fruit of a universal culture but of one particular culture that has been transplanted into another.
>
> What gives power and strength to a particular culture? My fundamental assumption is that each human being must sooner or later evaluate himself according to universal measures. Therefore, I also assume that the secret of a culture's strength is in the spiritual satisfaction it can provide its members. The question of a culture's power is similar to the question "What makes a book a classic?" I understand a classic to be a guess, an intuition, a description of a universal human predicament in local garb. The author has succeeded in clothing a universal dilemma

in a style that makes it understandable and satisfying for those among whom he lived and wrote.

When a particular culture is capable of providing its members with appropriate spiritual satisfaction, it will also persist over time. Of course, over time different issues are added and deleted from a specific group's agenda. Therefore, in my definition of culture, I regarded it as an "expanding and sifting treasure." The persistence of a culture also depends on the degree to which it is capable of maintaining both these activities simultaneously – to accumulate and to filter the spiritual possessions it creates in light of the shifting and ever-changing reality.

The power of a culture can be measured by its capacity to exert influence over other cultures through an invention that is indeed transferable. Biblical faith and its worldview responded to existential issues and the spiritual needs of the late Roman civilization, through the vehicle of Christianity, more so than did the indigenous pagan culture. Early Israelite culture is very powerful, since its impact extends until today.

There is also the capacity of a culture for absorption, according to its versatility and richness. One of the measures of a rich culture is its ability to assimilate and internalize as its own that which was created by another culture, to incorporate it into its own system harmoniously.

Jewish culture is the way Jews related to primary existential issues and matters: the purpose of life; the struggle with death; the relationship between the visible and the invisible, the invisible and the meaningful, the individual and his community, his community and other communities; relationships within the family, between man and woman, parents and children; the relationship to the trades and professions – how does one support oneself?; the relationship to success and failure, to hope and despair. The list is not all-inclusive but is representative.

The faith of the Jewish educator is in the sufficiency of Judaism to answer all spiritual needs. On what does the Jewish educator base this faith? On the historical capacity of Judaism to develop and change. Again, each human creature needs to assess himself, with reference to all matters I have just delineated and to others as well. He seeks a response that will restore harmony to his life, a harmony that is very difficult to attain; the faith of the Jewish educator is that Judaism can provide this response.

What about the tensions and contradictions between Jewish values and those of other cultures? The ideal of Jewish education I am proposing is that of creating a solid basis of identification with Jewish culture and with its historical development until today, along with a preparation for understanding the other, the foreign culture. I am convinced that any learner at any age wants first to know who he is, what his own identity is; this identity flows from the roots of his parents' culture. Therefore, it seems unnatural to me to take a Jewish child at an early age and educate him in a non-Jewish context. In such a situation, the non-Jews will not accept him as a member of their culture and the Jewish child will not know who he is; the result will be confusion. Since our culture is indeed *our* culture, it is only natural that the Jewish learner receive an explanation for his own Jewish identity as it has been transmitted to him through the spiritual creativity of his people.

At the same time, whether he wants to or not, the Jew comes into contact with his neighbors. He inevitably encounters neighbors of other cultures. My ambition is that such encounters indeed take place. I want Jewish education to prepare the learner for such encounters. My ideal is to create a Jew who can become familiar, in our ever-shrinking world, with various cultures and understand what they seek to express. The learner will not attain this ideal without being introduced to other cultures and trying to understand them on their own terms. How much better if this is undertaken in the language of the other cultures, and if not, then at least in translation.

True, in the encounter with other cultures, a Jewish learner is likely to discover aspects of these cultures of which he was previously unaware. However, if his identity has been established in advance, the learner will help shape a different Judaism – one designed by individuals who have absorbed those elements of other cultures that can be assimilated into their own Jewish culture. This process characterizes the history of Jewish culture in its totality and is one of the secrets of its persistence.

One prerequisite is the knowledge of a foreign language. It is impossible for us, bearers of a language spoken by scarcely six million people, to communicate with the contracting world without access to the lingua franca, which in our day is English. In addition, we in Israel must work to develop an understanding of the cultures of our immediate neighbors, no less than we exert ourselves to become familiar with the cultures of Europe and America.

I do not ignore the tensions between Jewish culture and others. As long as Jewish culture is firmly rooted, however, and provides a sufficient foundation for the satisfaction of the spiritual needs of the Jewish learner, the danger will be slight that these tensions will destroy his identity as a Jew.

Contemporary Israeli education is contending with a different ideal, one that can be termed "post-Zionist." Professor Joseph Dan described this ideal as follows: "Post-Zionism seeks out an Israeli nationalism that is based on territorial minimalism, without any unique cultural or moral aspirations, with no explicit religious dimension, no common foundation in a cultural tradition, no eschatological fantasies, no authentically rooted Hebrew language that draws from its sources throughout history – all with the aim of deepening the normalization of Israel as a nation among the nations and toward the spiritual integration that results from a position of being an equal among other cultures."[5]

There is a great self-contradiction here. Is there a normal people that does not have a language tied to its traditions, that does not have religion of its own, that does not have its visions of the future? How is it possible to integrate with other cultures if you do not have a culture of your own?

Post-Zionism is in essence the rejection of all claims of links among disparate phenomena. It assumes that there is no internal connection between the Jewish people of yesterday and the Jewish people of today, between the Jewish people in Israel and in the Diaspora, between Jewish culture and its sources, between the Hebrew language and its history. I see a contradiction in this rejection as well. If I defined culture as an expanding and sifting treasure of spiritual possessions, then post-Zionism as it has been described here is a nonculture. In this instance, one who has no unique culture aspires to integration without having anything substantial to contribute to that integration. This is a new historical phenomenon, the adoption of which undoubtedly demands a heavy price both materially and spiritually.[6]

Part Two: The Central Role of Jewish Text Study

Jewish Texts as Symbols

One of the characteristics of language is its metaphorical power – its capacity to transport the reader from the realm of the visible and the concrete to an abstract or transcendent world. Jewish texts have consistently demonstrated this power. Concerned with questions of existential significance, Jewish laws, parables, historical narratives, philosophical treatises, and other literary forms have been a major spiritual resource of the Jewish people. The extraordinary impact of the Hebrew Bible, beyond the Jewish world, is one potent example.

A passage from *Hovot ha-Levavot* (*Duties of the Heart*) by the medieval Jewish philosopher Rabbi Baḥya ibn Pakuda describes the metaphorical nature of biblical language and its relation to the transcendent:

> What we are all agreed upon is that necessity forced us to ascribe corporeal attributes to God, and to describe Him by attributes properly belonging to His creatures, so as to obtain some conception by which the thought of God's existence should be fixed in the minds of men.

The books of the Prophets expressed this in corporeal terms which were more easily understood by their contemporaries. Had they limited themselves to abstract terms and concepts appropriate to God, we would have understood neither the terms nor the concepts; and it would have been impossible for us to worship a Being whom we did not know, since the worship of that which is unknown is impossible. The words and ideas used had accordingly to be such as were adapted to the hearer's mental capacity, so that the subject would first sink into his mind in the corporeal sense in which the concrete terms are understood. We will then deal discreetly with him and strive to make him understand that this presentation is only approximate and metaphorical, and that the reality is too fine, too exalted and remote for us to comprehend its subtlety. . . .

Had Scripture, when expounding this theme, employed a terminology, appropriate in its exactness but only intelligible to the profound thinker, the majority of mankind, because of their intellectual deficiency and weak perception in things spiritual, would have been left without a religion. But the word which may be understood in a material sense will not hurt the intelligent person, since he recognizes its real meaning. And it will help the simple, as its use will result in fixing in his heart and mind the conception that he has a Creator whom he is bound to serve.

. . . So too, the Hebrew language as well as all the books of the Prophets and the writings of the pious, when referring to the attributes of the Creator, make liberal use of the concrete expressions (anthropomorphisms and anthropopathisms) we have mentioned, which are such as people easily understand and employ in their current vocabulary, when conversing with each other. In a similar connection, our Rabbis have said: "The Torah speaks in the language of men."[7]

Parshanut: *The Tradition of Jewish Text Study*

Why did Greenberg base his vision of Jewish education today on text study? One significant reason was its appeal to rational understanding, which he chose as a more effective path to religious experience than magical or mystical approaches, since it does not require a suspension of critical faculties.

"Religionists ought to have enough faith in the worth of biblical teaching," Greenberg writes, "to allow that if it be presented honestly and sympathetically it will work by its own authority – today it can have no other – on the soul of the student."[8] Greenberg also believed that Jewish text study has the power to open Jews' hearts to other Jewish symbols, such as Shabbat, the festivals, and prayer.

In Greenberg's view, each generation participated in the tradition of commentary, or *parshanut,* in order to maintain the spiritual relevance of Jewish texts to its particular time and place. The challenge of Jewish education is to continue the tradition in a way that enhances the spiritual lives of contemporary Jewish learners. He warned against the notion that Jewish learners could simply create commentary without their having first been inducted into *parshanut.* In particular, he was critical of programs that invited learners to develop their own Midrash, or commentary, without their having been systematically introduced to midrashic literature. Only when the corpus of traditional exegesis has been mastered is it appropriate for the learner to contribute his or her additions.

Greenberg's innovation is that he sees modern commentary on Jewish texts as an authentic continuation of *parshanut.* Rather than subverting the texts, modern exegesis has helped keep them alive.[9]

Parshanut *in Practice*

When we studied Greenberg's conception of *parshanut* with the educators, they challenged us to suggest an approach for its translation into classroom practice. We proposed five elements that can guide teachers and curriculum developers.[10] The first three prepare students for deeper engagement with the text by clarifying its basic meaning. The last two help them to interpret the meaning and apply the ideas of the text to their lives.

The first element is mastery of the original language and genre of the text. Since the language will be ancient Hebrew or Aramaic, this mastery is more than the capacity to answer the question "What do the words mean?" Rather, a learner must also understand something about the nature of biblical and rabbinic literature, its role in the life of the community, its uniqueness compared to other literatures, the rules that govern its proper interpretation, and other philological, hermeneutical, and exegetical aspects of the text.

The second element focuses on the text's historical and literary context. Such study is important, for it helps resolve the estrangement a learner might feel because of the differences between the time the ancient texts were written and contemporary life. For example, biblical laws of slavery may seem very archaic, but in their own time they were among the most enlightened in the world. When a learner knows the context in which these laws were developed, how they were appropriate for the world in which they were stipulated and yet responded to it uniquely, and how they compared with other cultures' responses, he or she can then perceive the values embedded in the laws.

The third element of *parshanut* makes possible the leap from the linguistic and historical understanding of the text to its spiritual intent. What higher principle is expressed through the text? Among the educational roles Greenberg envisions for scholars of Judaica is the articulation of such principles.

The fourth element relates to the ongoing interpretation of commentators over the generations. Within Jewish tradition are diverse efforts to direct the learner to the transcendent realm through consideration of the deeper meaning and spiritual message of the text. This element places rabbinic literature, medieval commentaries, and the literature of Jewish thought at the center of the curriculum.

The fifth element reveals how Jews throughout the centuries have applied the spiritual values suggested by the texts to everyday life. At this stage, a learner might study Jewish practices in halakhic texts but also reflect on his or her own experiences of these practices. This kind of study links the interpretive process to the learner's world. Ideally, the learner will pursue this advanced stage of study throughout his or her life. If successful, such a pedagogy should lead to the learner's participation in the tradition of commentary and to the application of Jewish texts to life.

Part Three: Jewish Text Today

The educators marveled at Greenberg's faith in the power of text, given the gap between the world of classical Jewish texts and the twenty-first century, and the decline in the status of text study in contemporary culture.

Greenberg was certainly not oblivious to this challenge. He recognized that in the past, "symbolic systems have ceased to serve their communities." Nevertheless, he believed that with a concerted effort, intellectual and educational leaders could preserve the capacity of Jewish symbols to be a resource for the spiritual lives of learners: "A community of Jews with a sufficient mass of knowledge and understanding, excitement, confidence, and courage will emerge from among these learners. And from its midst will arise fresh voices to revitalize our symbols according to the circumstances of the present."[11]

Ancient Texts and Contemporary Life

Although the revitalization of Jewish symbols is a large-scale communal activity, Greenberg thought that commentators on Jewish texts were especially qualified to preserve the texts' capacity to be spiritually illuminating. He predicted that they would come from among *anshei ruaḥ meḥunanim* ("gifted intellectuals," "scholars," or "spiritual leaders").

In the course of our deliberations, however, his view was tested in an unexpected, poignant way. Two acts of violence were committed in Israel by Jews who supported their deeds with Jewish sources. The first took place on the festival of Purim in February 1994, when Dr. Baruch Goldstein murdered twenty-nine Moslems who were praying at the Cave of Makhpelah in Hebron. He justified his act by citing various chapters in the Book of Esther. In 1995, Israeli Prime Minister Yitzhak Rabin was murdered by Yigal Amir, who based his crime on the halakhic injunction to eliminate a *rodef* (lit., "pursuant") who threatens the life of another Jew. (Jewish law allows the killing of a murderous pursuant in order to save the life of his targeted victim; some extremist rabbis and others in Israel saw Rabin's efforts in the Oslo peace accords as equivalent to those of a *rodef.*)

The educators asked Greenberg difficult questions about his faith in Jewish text study after these events, claiming that many verses in the classical canon were vulnerable to fundamentalist abuse. He invested considerable thought in responding to this critique. The challenge, as he saw it, was not to dissolve apparent contradictions among Jewish texts but to preserve their spiritual relevance by allowing them to critique one another.

In his essay "A Problematic Heritage: The Attitude Toward the Gentile in the Jewish Tradition – An Israel Perspective," Greenberg discusses the *ḥerem* (ban) in Deuteronomy 20:16 against the Canaanite nations, which calls for the total annihilation of all breathing beings among these nations, even their animals. Then he looks at the worldview within which the Bible discusses the relationship between Jew and gentile – one that sees the people of Israel as a means through which to restore the unity of humankind after it has disintegrated at Babel. Greenberg identifies this worldview as expressing a higher moral and spiritual principle:

> The Jewish heritage contains the deposits of very various ages and circumstances. The needs of the age determined which elements would be influential and which downgraded. Since warding off attacks by hostile surroundings was a constant preoccupation, it was important to cultivate a solid front of counter-aggressiveness against the gentile enemy. Today we are a nation of ingathered dispersions who seek to win acceptance among the family of nations as a constructive factor. The restoration of Israel to the family of nations challenges us to examine our tradition with respect to its image of gentiles to determine on what terms we can join them in a unified humanity. This is one area in which our Scripture was ahead of its time, in that both in its account of origins and its vision of the perfected future the unity of mankind was an essential element, as is the role of Israel in linking the two eras. Whatever elements in our heritage make for social cohesion by promoting within Israel kindness, justice and righteousness (God's moral attributes, Jer. 9:23 ...), thus rendering it a model for emulation and winning admiration for its Torah, are timeless and applicable today. Whatever elements promote human dignity, respecting the divine image in which all human beings are created, are timeless and applicable today.
>
> Those elements that raise barriers between our people and others must be recognized as in tension with Israel's universal purpose. The hostile and haughty attitude toward the gentiles is one such element whose elimination does not trench on any essential component

of Judaism, but on the contrary, is a necessary condition for an essential component to come to fruition. Other barrier-raising elements are less tractable, such as the definitional – e.g., who is a Jew, and the sacramental – acts and avoidances that symbolize a spiritual reality. Definitions go to essence and are much less contingent on circumstances than the attitude towards gentiles with which we are dealing. Changes in definition affect, indeed threaten the very fabric of the people, and require justification of a more fundamental order.

There is a tendency among rigorists to regard sacramental barriers between Jew and gentile as of the same essential nature as the definition. This is clearly an overevaluation. The rabbinic axiom is: "Though he be a sinner he is still a Jew" (Sanhedrin 44a – the comment is attached to a grave sacramental offense, violation of the *ḥerem*). . . . Now it cannot be denied that for observant Jews the Jewish sacraments are essential to establishing Jewish identity. But the rigorists' overevaluation of the sacraments that separate Jew from gentile causes them to undervalue those elements of the tradition that bind Jews to the rest of mankind. As a result they are insensitive to the imperative need to overhaul the body of received tradition on the subject.

The sacramental element in Judaism bears a certain resemblance to the linguistic. The Hebrew language gives expression to the uniquely Jewish perception of the world; just so do the sacraments of Judaism serve as vehicles for the uniquely Jewish experience of the transcendent realm. They establish a Jewish identity, as does the Hebrew language, but like language they are only one component of Judaism, a system of symbols that points to another reality. The sacraments point to a relation to God that from the beginning transcended the confines of Israel, in which Israel was to perfect itself so that humanity might be perfected. The biblical vision binds Israel morally to the rest of mankind. So while we express our relation to God in sacraments of language-like particularity, our identity is not determined solely by our particularity. It is determined no less by our distinctive moral vision which promotes values of universal scope.

The sacraments of Judaism originated in a world dominated by paganism, from which biblical Israel was bidden to separate itself in order to establish a frame within which a model society could be established. The world in which modern Israel is set gives at least lip-service to the cardinal biblical values. Its pressing need is not for a sect of xenophobic in-turned rigorists but for an imitable example of a society striving for justice and solidarity. The peculiar rites of Judaism serve constructively today as traditional vehicles of personal piety. They bond together those who practice them into a community seeking contact with holiness.

But they are not constitutors of a national agenda that grapples with the secular world, that seeks to redeem it.

In this world, how singular Israel would be were it to adopt as overall policy guidelines the Jeremianic trinity of divine attributes *hesed, tzedaqa umishpat* [acts of kindness, charity, and justice]. What a distinct identity it would have as a society devoted to working out within itself the ramifications of these attributes relevant to today, and exerting the pressure of emulatability on other societies. That would be an identity worthy of Israel's foundation document.

The Hebrew Scriptures have given us an ideal of a particular moral-political order, at the same time linking it to a universal ideal order. To this timeless vision, however, elements conditioned by time and circumstance have adhered. Those who cherish the vision are challenged to validate its lasting relevance by distinguishing the timeless from the temporary on the basis of criteria derived from the Scriptures themselves. The present effort to do so with regard to one topic has been predicated on the thesis that the Scriptural vision is basically coherent, and that discordance within it results from drawing excessive inferences from ideally compatible values. I offer it as a model for dealing with other cases of values in tension. Even the choicest vine needs seasonal pruning to ensure more fruitful growth.[12]

In meetings with the educators, Greenberg demonstrated the application of this method to other problems confronting Jewish life today, including gender equality, homosexuality, and the conflict between the Bible and science on the origins of the universe and the laws of nature.[13]

Jewish Education Within the Family

In a revealing interview, Greenberg spoke about the origins of his approach to Jewish texts.

My relation to our sacred texts is composed of at least two elements. The first is the way I was treated by my parents. I was raised in an atmosphere in which the texts were honored and regarded as holy. I saw my forebears learning and respecting and sanctifying the books in and of themselves: they did not place another book on top of the Torah and they kissed it when it fell to the ground. The other element appeared in my life as I grew up and studied these texts. Through contemplation and inquiry, I came to affirm for myself, out of my own understanding and appreciation, that which was practiced by my parents.

I believe that even without one's having received this inheritance from one's parents, it is possible to arrive at an appreciation of the uniqueness of the Bible and to regard it as sacred. In the heart of all human beings there is "in potentia" a dimension of sanctity, and even if it has not been actualized, it is never entirely locked away. The living encounter with people who embody this dimension of sanctity in their lives is the proven and shortest route to release the locks for those who did not receive it in the home in which they were raised. . . . And perhaps it is also possible to arrive at this feeling in solitude, from the study of the Bible itself, from the power that is embedded within its pages.[14]

Jewish Education at the University

Judaica scholars often reject attempts to impose extrascholarly goals on the academic study of Judaism. In Greenberg's view, however, a university may be a context for spiritual quest:

> On the face of it, one should not expect the university to address the deeper lives of its students. The purpose of a university is to develop and disseminate knowledge, not to respond to students' existential questions and to stir feelings. What is the purpose of developing and disseminating knowledge? It is to fulfill a human being's capacity to know. The university is the highest institution for the cultivation of the mind. Anything that will contribute to the development of a person's self-understanding (the humanities) and an understanding of the environment in which people live (the natural sciences) belongs in a university. Whatever use is made of this knowledge and the emotions it arouses – at the level of the individual and of society – relates to values and is beyond the scope of the university.
>
> But a second look renders this assertion less decisive. We said that the purpose of the humanities is the development of a person's self-understanding. Such an understanding is achieved through a consideration of human activity and of works of human creativity. . . . Certainly, the purpose of the humanities [lit., "the sciences of the spirit"] is to clarify, through description, values and answers to existential questions, answers that have shaped all human activity and creativity until now. The history of humanity and society is a continuity of ideas and feelings – and of actions that flow from them, actions that are anchored in conceptions of the purposes and aspirations of life, of what is above us and what is below, of the relationship between the individual and society, among members of the family, between nation and nation, between us and nature, between spirit and matter. These conceptions, as well as the feelings that accompany them, were all value-laden and existential in their times, and since it is impossible to understand an

action or creation without reference to them, it is incumbent upon the scholar of the humanities to expose the value-laden/emotional issues that are embedded in every subject he treats.

Given this assumption, the expectation that the university address the inner life of students is justified, on condition that they seek to understand the existential value embodied in any particular topic. In other words, what is significant about the topic that motivates the scholar or the university to treat it in the first place?[15]

Toward the Ideal

In an earlier version of his essay, Greenberg acknowledged the difficult realities that appear to impede the fulfillment of his vision, but he believed nevertheless in its prospects:

> When I conceived of the goals set forth herein, I did not tailor them to the capabilities of the existing system, but rather to what seems to me to be the inherently desirable and worthy outcomes of a Jewish education. The intent of this proposal, and the intent of the discussion of it, should be the elucidation of the direction in which we are headed – are we moving toward the right destination? – and not the elucidation of the ends it happens to be in our power to reach at the moment. He who concentrates on adapting his aims to the power he has to achieve them will find his power dwindling as his fear of failure grows; but he who sets for himself an aim that is beyond his power to achieve will, in the course of action, discover that his capability is greater than he had originally thought.
>
> While despair may arise out of the chasm between the attainment of the ultimate aim and the power required for its achievement, I offer the following counsel: Cover the distance to the aim one attainable segment at a time, and having reached that point, use it as a springboard toward the next.
>
> In any case, we need a far-off aim so that we can orient ourselves with reference to it – are we moving closer or not?

NOTES

1   Greenberg initially developed this approach for the teaching of Bible. It is so inter-twined with his life's work as a Bible scholar that his scholarly lectures and writings can be read as pedagogical illustrations of his educational ideas. A bibliography of his publications until 1997 appears in *Tehillah le-Moshe: Biblical and Judaic Studies in Honor of Moshe Greenberg*, ed. M. Cogan, B. Eichler, and J. Tigay (Winona Lake, IN: Eisenbrauns, 1997), xxiii–xxxviii. For an anthology of Greenberg's essays in English, see *Studies in the Bible and Jewish Thought* (Philadelphia: Jewish Publication Society,

1995). An anthology of his Hebrew essays, *Al ha-Mikra ve-al ha-Yahadut* (Tel Aviv: Am Oved, 1984), includes a section of essays on the teaching of Bible.

2   For a powerful example, see Greenberg's discussion of biblical prayer as a symbol in *Biblical Prose Prayer as a Window to the Popular Religion of Ancient Israel* (Berkeley: University of California Press, 1983), 47–52.

3   *"Zehut, Tevunah ve-Dat,"* in *Al ha-Mikra ve-al ha-Yahadut*, 247–52. All selections from this essay were translated by Daniel Marom in consultation with the author. For another articulation of this theory of religion, Greenberg referred to the works of Wilfred Cantwell Smith. See, for example, *The Faith of Other Men* (New York: New American Library, 1963); *The Meaning and End of Religion: A New Approach to the Religious Traditions of Mankind* (New York: Macmillan, 1963); and "Religion and Symbolism," in the *Encyclopedia Britannica*.

4   *Bereishit Rabbah* 44. Greenberg did not base his vision on a particular Jewish philosopher or school of thought. He claimed that every attempt to formulate contemporary ideals for Jewish education on the basis of Jewish sources or the writings of a Jewish thinker in the past was necessarily an act of interpretation. He preferred to present his educational ideas as his own and to select from the wealth of Jewish and general sources those that explained his vision.

5   Joseph Dan, *"Al Post-Tzionut, al Ivrit shel Ozen ve-al Meshiḥiut shel Shav,"* *Haaretz*, March 25, 1994. Translated by Daniel Marom.

6   Protocols of Moshe Greenberg's meetings with the educators at the Mandel School for Educational Leadership, May 4, 1994. Translated by Daniel Marom.

7   R. Baḥya ibn Pakuda, *Duties of the Heart*, trans. Jehuda Ibn Tibbon and Moses Hyamson, vol. 1 (Jerusalem: Feldheim, 1970), 105, 107.

8   "On Teaching the Bible in Religious Schools," *Jewish Education* 29:3 (1959): 46.

9   See "Exegesis" in *Studies in the Bible and Jewish Thought*, 361, 366–67.

10 This section is based on notes from meetings with the educators about the translation of Greenberg's ideas into practice. For more on the implications for teaching of Greenberg's approach, see Seymour Fox's Chapter 10. Greenberg has written several articles on the teaching of Bible and the training of Bible teachers. See "On Teaching the Bible in Religious Schools," 27–34. For articles in Hebrew, see *Al ha-Mikra ve-al ha-Yahadut*, 245–349. Greenberg was also involved in the development of various curricula in Bible, both at The Jewish Theological Seminary of America and Israel's Ministry of Education. See, for example, *Understanding Exodus* (New York: Behrman House, 1969).

11 *"Zehut, Tevunah ve-Dat,"* 259–61.

12 *Conservative Judaism* 48:2 (1996): 33–35.

13 On the latter, see "On Teaching the Bible in Religious Schools," 46–51.

14 *Al ha-Mikra ve-al ha-Yahadut*, 279. Passage translated by Daniel Marom.

15 From Greenberg's address to students of Ben-Gurion University, December 1991. Translated by Daniel Marom. Greenberg also discusses the State of Israel as a primary setting for his vision of Jewish education. See "The Task of Masorti Judaism," in *Deepening the Commitment: Zionism and the Conservative/Masorti Movement*, ed. J. S. Ruskay and D. M. Szonyi (New York: The Jewish Theological Seminary of America, 1990), 139–42.

7

Reflections on the Educated Jew from the Perspective of Reform Judaism

MICHAEL A. MEYER

In the Eternal, in the depths of life and on its heights, teacher and student, maturity and youth, can come together. Of the Eternal alone can they speak with one another; on all else they can only converse. It is religion that creates the connection.

Leo Baeck, "Religion und Erziehung" (1926)

Introduction

A dominant theme in the writings of Leo Baeck, the theologian and leader of German Jewry during its darkest hours, is the presence of polarities within Judaism.[1] God, he insisted, is for religious Jews both unfathomable mystery and the source of inescapable commandment. My own worldview has been greatly influenced by his: negotiating the religious path of Judaism, I believe, necessarily involves passing between opposing poles, living in the tensions that they create. If, as Baeck suggests in the excerpt cited above, all true Jewish education is religious education on the highest level, then such an education must confront the tensions without evasion.

These tensions do not begin with modernity, nor are they limited to the liberal currents in Judaism. Prophets and priests in ancient Israel expressed truths about God's nature that did not contradict one another but existed in a state of opposition: prophets spoke of God's insistent moral judgment; priests brought God's presence near through sacrifice on the altar. Millennia later, within the traditional Jewish society of Eastern Europe, Hasidim and Mitnagdim struggled over the conflicting demands of prayer and study. Which of the two brings one more closely into God's presence? Which represents the principal religious occupation of the Jew?

We who live in modernity (or postmodernity) are beset by new tensions. We experience not only those inherent within the Jewish tradition, but also

149

those that lie between it and the outside world that we also – and, in most cases more completely – inhabit. We have integrated values external to Judaism into our lives and we seek to transmit these, along with the ones we have inherited from Judaism, to the next Jewish generations. Taken as whole, these external values constitute one pole on the principal axis of our religious lives; the Jewish heritage is the other. We face the risk of being drawn dangerously far from the pole of our Jewish existence in subtle as well as blatant ways. Yet, much as we seek to preserve Judaism, we cannot deny such values as have become a deeply internalized and cherished part of our selves.

My conception of Jewish education flows from an idea of Judaism that recognizes and affirms the value of modernity, represented especially by personal autonomy, while insisting upon the priority of Jewish religious faith. It is critical of the excesses of modern life: the self-absorption and the arrogant certainties. But it also casts a critical eye upon Judaism, recognizing its texts to be imperfect and sometimes totally wrong expressions of our ancestors' sincere desire to understand the obligations that flow from the divine mystery. Hence my conception is, in the last analysis, focused upon the individual who stands within the multiple tensions of autonomy and obligation, integration and separation, peoplehood and religion, dispassionate knowledge and life-determining commitment.

My reflections on the meaning and implications of the concept "educated Jew" are based on this understanding of Judaism. They are influenced by my own perspective as a historian of the Jews and Judaism as well as by my personal commitment to a liberal interpretation of the Jewish faith. Although they reach, I believe, beyond any denomination within Judaism and apply in different ways both to Diaspora and to Israeli Jews, they focus in particular on my experience as a Reform Jew in the United States.

Within the sphere of Jewish education, Reform Judaism sets for itself a task that is both unique and exceedingly difficult. Committed to liberalism, it holds personal autonomy in the highest regard. Its educational work is therefore not the inculcation of a revealed and normative body of Jewish law that requires obedience, as is that of Orthodoxy, but the incorporation of personally configured elements of Jewish tradition into individual lives. At the same time it seeks not merely to present alternatives with cold objectivity, but to influence choice by educating toward core Jewish values and aiming at the creation of Jewish religious lives that stand under the authority of an obligating God.

Committed to universalism, Reform Judaism recognizes truth – even religious truth – as emanating from multiple traditions. It is critical of chauvinism wherever and however manifest. Its ultimate aim is recognition of divine sovereignty by all peoples of the earth, as envisaged by Israel's prophets. Yet at the same time it recognizes that an untrammeled universalism, as teaching for the present age, loosens or destroys the bonds that unite Jews with one another.

It is the strength of Reform Judaism that it is more open to the intellectual and social challenges presented by the contemporary age than any other major religious form of Judaism. At the same time it recognizes that secular forms of Jewish expression, at least in the present, lack the power to gain centrality in individual lives or in the collective life of the Jewish people whether in its diasporas or in the State of Israel.

Definitions, Dilemmas, Goals

A. From Education to Commitment

Since the term "educated Jew" is equivocal in meaning, it requires some preliminary semantic analysis. Two hundred years ago in Germany, for example, for a Jew to become educated meant acquiring a *secular* education, becoming *gebildet*. Education, in the sense of *Bildung,* was not conceived as inherent within Judaism but involved a cultivation of intellect, taste, and manners that were seen to emanate from outside of it. A Jew *qua* Jew might be "learned" (a תלמיד חכם), but not educated. An "educated Jew" in Central or Eastern Europe (a משכיל) was one who had broadened his perspective beyond the confines of Judaism through the acquisition of non-Jewish culture and values.

Our vocabulary is very different. We have appropriated a term of Latin origin that applies to the entire process of rearing a child into cultural adulthood and used it to describe a level of Jewish literacy. In one sense the term is too broad for the purpose; in another too narrow. It is too broad because "educated Jew" can still refer – as it has in the past – to the non-Jewish as well as to the Jewish components of education, when today only the Jewish part is our concern: We seek to create a *Jewishly* educated Jew. It is too narrow because creating an educated Jew is, to my mind, not yet the ultimate goal of our educational effort. An educated Jew may still be an uncommitted Jew. There are abundant examples of Jews whom we would have to call highly educated in Jewish texts and traditions, but who have withdrawn themselves from the implications of their childhood studies, whose life decisions are motivated by factors unrelated to the rich and extensive Jewish education they once enjoyed but at some stage of life put out of mind and heart. Thus "educated Jew" is problematic because it implies the end of a process. In fact, Jewish education is the indispensable instrument for the ongoing task of creating the fully conscious Jew. By that I mean to suggest that Jewish identity may begin with birth into a Jewish family, but it does not approach completion until it has become Jewish identity in a sense other than the biological. Jewish education is the tool for making ascribed identity into chosen identity. Choice for Judaism out of ignorance is clearly faulty because it is shallow and counter to the value placed upon learning within the tradition to which the commitment is made. Yet it is precisely that choice, deepened through knowledge and ever and again reaffirmed, to which Jewish education in our time must be dedicated. In short, education in Judaism, itself of high intrinsic value, must also be seen in its role as a prerequisite for commitment, and it is ongoing commitment, understood as identification with Jewish tradition and Jewish peoplehood, that is the ultimate goal. We must create educated Jews in order to create committed Jews. Or, put even more baldly, especially in the contemporary Diaspora historical context – but also in Israel – the task is to create, *tout court:* Jews.

Thus the goal of Jewish education must, from the first, be existential, with the cognitive taken as means to the existential end. Jewish knowledge deepens Jewish commitment, but it does not create it. Indispensable as it is, it is also insufficient. Jewish experiences, especially those gained in early childhood, create the emotional matrix within which cognitive learning can be lodged. Without the former, absorption of the latter will remain unsuccessful. The emotional matrix is first created and then principally sustained in the home. Only with great difficulty, and usually without lasting success, can it be created *ex nihilo* in the school. What the school can do is to expand upon it by adding collective Jewish experiences of the peer community (often most successfully conveyed in the camp setting) to those of the family.

B. Concentrating on Jewish Uniqueness

If at the beginning of the period of Jewish acculturation the *maskilim* set themselves the task of expanding the non-Jewish sphere in the thought and conduct of Jews, today's objective is clearly the opposite: to expand the Jewish sphere. That requires careful consideration of the boundary lines between the Jewish and the non-Jewish realms. If the boundary remains undefined or vague, then the content of Judaism will lack clear differentiation from its milieu and Judaism will appear simply as a historical tradition that validates the values of the dominant culture. As such, it becomes merely ornamental, if not superfluous.

The determination of boundaries is an anxiety-filled and difficult task for it involves nays as well as yeas, the need to maintain openness while yet establishing and upholding a clear sense of self. American society has never been more accepting of Jews nor American religion of Judaism than they are today. However, in each case the result has been potentially devastating for Jewish survival. The acceptability of mixed marriage with Jews by Christians and the acceptability of Jewish traditions (but not a separate, distinct, and fully self-conscious Judaism) within the American multicultural fabric have resulted in a Jewish identity that is no longer hidden out of shame or fear, but whose borders have been rubbed away. As Judaism has burst its own boundaries and entered American society and culture, the assumption has become widespread that these boundaries should become more permeable, allowing an influx not only of American or

Western, but also of Christian elements. Under these circumstances the dominant thrust of Jewish education must be inward. Once it seemed important to show how Jews were similar to Christians and how Jewish traditions anticipated American values enshrined in the Constitution. Judaism was taught via the catechism as a species subordinated to the genus "religion," which also included Christianity. That integrationist perspective did not harm Jewish continuity as long as Jews lived in social separation. Today it is clear that an educated Jew must know Judaism and Jewish values not only in their relation to Christianity and American culture, but as distinguishable from them. The requisite goal of Jewish education today is the creation not of Jewishly educated Americans but Jewishly educated Jews. The former would be persons who have enriched their fundamental identity as Americans by selected elements drawn from Judaism; the latter are those whose principal identity lies in being Jews.

On the other hand, a cultural (as opposed to a religious) boundary between the Jewish and the non-Jewish spheres cannot but create an isolationism, which, except in a ghetto setting, forces a decision for one against the other. In the open society of the Diaspora, placing students in the position of having to choose will almost invariably result in choice of the non-Jewish culture, which enjoys all the advantages of media exposure and peer-group pressure. Only a total education, which relates the Jewish heritage to the non-Jewish, can create an awareness of both points of contact and points of dissonance – or even antagonism – between Jewish and non-Jewish values. (That the practical implication of this is the indispensability of a day-school education that integrates Jewish with non-Jewish cultural elements should be obvious.)

It is therefore an important task of Jewish education to determine where the points of contact and dissonance lie, to make clear to students what Judaism shares with the Western traditions and where it differs from them. They could, for example, be asked to read passages from Jewish texts together with parallel texts from other literatures. In this way they would discover for themselves how certain core values of Judaism – פיקוח נפש or תיקון עולם ["saving a life" or "repairing the world," meaning social justice] for example – are expressed in Jewish literature; at the same time they would learn how other traditions – especially the Greco-Roman and the Christian, but also Eastern religions and documents that reflect American civic and popular culture – regard human life and social improvement. Such study would enable students gradually to develop an internal sense of where the boundaries between Judaism and other faiths and philosophies lie. They would be in a better position to argue for the intrinsic value of a Jewish life-orientation that is worth preserving within the organism of the Jewish people, and could reject the seductive notion that Judaism offers only historical and ethnic forms which give particular expression to universally accepted values.

C. Education as Drawing into the Circle

Jewish education for Jewish commitment within a liberal religious context is beset by its own unique problematics. *Secular* Jewish education, especially within an Israeli context, can unambiguously view the child as the judge and critic of the Jewish traditions that he or she is studying. Such education cannot limit the child's freedom of determination, for it regards individual freedom (whether or not itself a Jewish value) as superior to the imperatives embodied in the tradition. Hence the tradition can never override the child's power to choose, and the educator can and should expose the child to various Jewish options, which have been historically and contemporaneously taken, as possible but not necessary models. On the other hand, most *religious* Jewish education does insist that the tradition be viewed as offering norms. It asserts that atheism is not a valid Jewish option, and neither is conduct that conflicts with the *halakhah,* even if Jewish law is understood to be interactive with its environment, historically developmental, and modulated by midrashic interpretation. There is a sense in which liberal (implying autonomy) and religious (implying the "binding" force of tradition) are תרתי דסתרי [a contradiction].

The conflict between the liberal and the religious, as it exists within Reform Judaism, is not one that can be entirely resolved, and in practical terms it presents a major obstacle in the area of education. The goal of a liberal religious Jewish education is neither to make the child master over the tradition nor to make the child its servant. The common failure to articulate clearly an in-between position often leaves the learner unclear as to whether Judaism is a treasure trove of beliefs and customs from which to choose at will or a body of obligations that has a claim upon her or him. "Informed choice" as an educational goal is clearly not a resolution of the dilemma but a decision in favor of autonomy, which reduces the educational enterprise to providing resources for individual decision. On the other hand, the teacher's preselection of particular imperatives or particular models over others not only eviscerates the corpus of tradition but limits the child's freedom no less than presenting the entire received tradition as normative.

The way out of this dilemma lies, I believe, in the initial assumption that the child is being educated into a tradition that is religious and not merely cultural, which aims to direct life, not merely enhance it. These claims must be taken seriously in their totality. The task of the parent and teacher is to expound and analyze them from within the circle of their own commitment. (Jewish education is not "objective.") The goal is to draw the child into the circle, not so much to educate (in the sense of "drawing out") as to "instill" a sense of what it is like to live within the circle. Choice then follows after commitment, after "binding." It operates in response to challenges thrown up by contradictions inherent within the tradition (which is itself composed of multiple and sometimes conflicting components) as well as by values internalized from outside the Jewish realm and, through reinterpretation, brought into harmony with Judaism.

D. Bringing Liberalism into the Jewish Religious Sphere

A second dilemma for a liberal Jewish education, besides the conflict between choice and obligation, arises from the apparent externality of liberalism to Judaism. Liberalism, though variously defined in different historical epochs, today implies tentativeness, toleration, and compromise. It inclines toward the universal rather than the particular. Judaism in the past – and, according to some of its most vocal exponents, also in the present – rests upon the certainty that it is transcendent in origin and particularly revealed to Israel. As a result, liberalism (especially in the State of Israel) is for this reason – as well as on account of the above-mentioned issue of personal freedom – generally associated with secularism.

The task of the liberal Jewish educator is difficult because of the need to argue that liberalism is not foreign to Judaism (at least not potentially), let alone its inevitable antagonist. From this difficulty arises the temptation to read liberalism (or universalism) into texts that clearly will not bear such interpretation. The teacher resorts immediately to Midrash, the interpretive technique that has enabled its masters to read personal meanings into sacred scripture. The teacher declares that here is a text that we can read in our own fashion, in accordance with our own cognitive, moral, or aesthetic predilections. (This is made the easier in today's intellectual context where readers, not authors, are thought to determine textual meanings.) But this strategy, if it stands alone, requires abandonment of the historical perspective, which has been fundamental to liberal forms of Judaism since the origins of חכמת ישראל [lit., wisdom of Israel; *Wissenschaft,* academic Jewish studies] at the beginning of the nineteenth century. Historical honesty would require the recognition that, by and large, liberal values have emerged from outside of religious traditions (despite the occasional text to the contrary), that they are a product of modernity, not religiosity. A liberal Jewish education must at some point recognize the conflict, embracing the exposition of text in context (history). Only then can it move on to the clear discernment of those Jewish vessels (rituals, for example) that can age new wine without shattering. The alternative would be to leave fundamental values of liberal Jews outside Judaism, reducing it through the exclusion of basic existential commitments and perhaps ultimately relegating it to the status of "beautiful traditions."

E. From Memory to Mitzvah, from History to Halakhah

In the process of Jewish education, the creation of Jewish memory plays a vital role. But as important as memory is in Judaism (זכור!) [the biblical injunction: "Remember!"], a Jewish education that places too much emphasis upon it runs the serious risk of creating a vicarious rather than an actual Jewish identity. Museums are places where Judaism (and what has been done to Jews) are enshrined; they create and nourish memory. To view them is itself surely a Jewish experience, but it is a secondary one. The experience is historical, not actual; the past is viewed, not personally reenacted. A Jewish education that aims to reach the core of self must focus on the regular (the מצוה) [commandment], not on just the episodic (the חויה) [experience]; it must lead to Halakhah, whether that term is understood literally or metaphorically. It cannot rely on visits to Jewish museums or motion pictures or other sporadic Jewish acts (even on trips to Israel for Diaspora Jews). A successful Jewish education is one that has achieved two aims: the inclusion of recurrent specifically Jewish acts within the routine of personal and family life (Halakhah in a broad sense), and the application of values drawn from Jewish sources (both textual and nontextual) to life decisions within both the private and the public spheres. In short, the Jewishly educated Jew will speak and act regularly both within Judaism and from within Judaism outward toward the larger world.

The Community of Jewish Learning

A. The Home

Given the powerful centrifugal forces that act to fragment and diminish Jewish identity in the Diaspora, Jewish education requires a supportive environment that is characterized by shared belief in the intrinsic value of belonging to a Jewishly knowledgeable Jewish people. The fundamental task for Jewish educators is therefore to create multiple communities of Jewish learning characterized by the common conviction that a Jewish education is, for Jews, the primary source of ultimate meanings. Unlike professional training, such an education has no point of completion. Hence even the most educated Jews remain students: never fully learned, always still learning.

Parents and children must see themselves as engaged in a common, necessarily incomplete, venture. It is not the task of children simply to reach the level of their parents' knowledge, nor even to exceed it, but to join them upon their journey. For parents and children the first community of Jewish learning is the home. Only when bonds of common commitment to Jewish study are strongly forged and continuously reinforced in the home is it possible for the school to function properly as the second community of learning. When the home fails to educate by word and by example, then Jewish education is removed from the principal nexus of character formation and peripheralized. The study of Judaism becomes a project undertaken and accomplished alongside other disciplines, but not intrinsically different from them. It then has a point of beginning and a point of conclusion (often taken to be the age of thirteen).

The home that is empty of Jewish learning and observance in one generation is only with great difficulty reconstituted as a Jewish home in the next. Where it has already become Jewishly arid, the best solution seems to be educating entire families together in the basics of Judaism under the auspices of the synagogue with the intention of eventually transplanting the process back into its proper soil, where it can provide a bond of continuity between generations.

B. Schools and Teachers

The school, too, should be understood as a community of learning, the teacher a fellow learner, not alone one who imparts learning. Teachers need to convey to students that they themselves are not yet "educated Jews" but have traveled farther along that path than have their students. Their task is to help the beginners get started, the advanced move ahead more rapidly, and all to appreciate the experience. Teachers will influence their students only if they personally serve as exemplars of Jewish study.

In addition to being for their students models of Jewish learning, teachers are also, more broadly, model Jews. Given the religious divisions into which the Jewish people is riven, the teacher will necessarily be the representative of a particular Jewish orientation. Hence, within the Jewish schools of the Reform movement, for example, teachers of Judaism will dominantly or exclusively be Reform Jews, not alone in name but by conviction. The Reform approach of the teacher will color his or her understanding of Jewish history, doctrine, and obligation. As communities exist within territories, those created in Reform Jewish schools lie appropriately within the landscape of their movement.

C. Curriculum

The curriculum that the Jewish school requires rests upon twin pillars: ethnic awareness and religious knowledge, Jewishness and Judaism. Fundamental for both is the Hebrew language. For the first, it is the chief cultural attribute of the Jewish people, both its historical channel of expression and the locus for values that do not transfer fully to other languages. For the second, it is the sacred bridge between God and Israel. It is the vehicle for Torah and for prayer. There can be no claim to being Jewishly educated without classical and modern Hebrew. Even in the absence of fully developed linguistic capacity, individual Hebrew words can express ideas and values that define the community and which cannot always be rendered adequately by equivalents in other languages. The most minimal Jewish education should at least teach the meaning of key words, mostly in Hebrew but partly also in other Jewish languages, that constitute a vocabulary of Jewish discourse. Obvious examples are: תורה [Torah], תפילה [prayer] and מענשליכקייט [*Mentschlichkeit*].

The ethnic pillar will be further strengthened when the history of the Jews in all periods is studied and Jewish historical experience in its variety compared with that of the learners. Knowledge of contemporary Jewish life everywhere is especially important, for it helps to create a sense of Jewish solidarity and mutual responsibility. For Diaspora Jews, learning about Jewish life in Israel plays a central role; for Israelis to become educated Jews requires their having accurate information about the Diaspora. Familiarity with Jewish tragedy, especially the Holocaust, and with modern Jewish and Israeli literature likewise plays a role in instilling the sense of common fate and common culture that constitutes the ethnic component of a Jewish education.

Yet as a Reform Jew I am persuaded that a Judaism that rests upon the ethnic pillar alone is not viable beyond a few generations. In the Diaspora, ethnic Judaism is speedily being devoured by an absorbent American culture; in Israel it is being transformed from Jewish to Israeli. Only a Jewish education that nurtures religious belief and religious practice can sustain Jewish identity in the long run. That means Jewish education must speak a loud nay to secularism even when that secularism is combined with Jewish cultural elements. This is so, however, not only because secularism represents a threat to Jewish survival, but because, from the standpoint of Reform Judaism, the Jewish people is fundamentally defined by its religion. As Leo Baeck noted, the community of Jewish learning is qualitatively different from secular learning communities because it addresses the ultimate questions of human existence. For the Jew, Jewish education guides the religious quest.

Thus the religious texts of Judaism assume great importance. For Reform Jews they represent documents neither of literal revelation nor of secular composition. Torah, broadly understood, is from the Reform viewpoint the product of the relationship between God and the Jewish people, in which both are involved. The Reform learning community views the texts neither as merely historical documents nor as inherently authoritative dicta. Rather, it sees them as vehicles conveying religious and ethical messages that the individual, out of his or her religious commitment and personal autonomy, can choose to accept as binding for belief or practice.

The community begins with commitment to the tradition as a source of truth and values. Even when the texts contain elements that the community, or some of its members, find it necessary to reject on intellectual or moral grounds, such dissent does not vitiate commitment to the tradition as a whole. The subjectivism of teacher and students is balanced by the objectivity of the tradition in its totality. Moreover, frequently the tradition itself provides options, and the teacher does well to stress its internal variegation.

The educated Jew should be familiar with the broadest range of Jewish religious creativity. Yet it is natural that Reform Jewish education will stress those texts which Reform Judaism regards as being of contemporary relevance.

These may be drawn from Bible, Talmud, Midrash, or later religious literature (including especially the prayer book), although the Bible will have pride of place both because it is the fountainhead and because of its use in worship.

D. Midrash and Memory, History and Critique

The learning community's relation to the texts of Judaism will vary according to age and cultural location. Younger children come to Judaism unreflectively and uncritically, before exposure to a critical general culture. Parents and teachers immerse them in Jewish experiences and tell them value-laden stories of their people with the intention of creating early positive memories that will shape a Jewish identity. The stories, which are to become part of their own personal story, are in traditional Jewish parlance אגדות; when they are stimulated by biblical and rabbinic texts they are מדרשים. Like classical midrash, these stories are "naive," prereflective, and precritical.

As Jewish children mature and their horizons broaden through expanding general education, Jewish texts become embedded in historical contexts. The children begin to understand Judaism in relation to the changing historical experience of the Jewish people. Comparative study now yields not only awareness of how Judaism has differed, but also – certainly in a Reform educational context – how it has developed and progressed. In addition, critique is brought to bear upon traditional notions that conflict with modernity, such as literal revelation of the Written and Oral Law. Yet story is not cast aside in favor of history. Instead, a dialectical relationship emerges between midrash and history, between collective memory and its critique.

The process that for the child begins with midrash and moves toward history for the adult often begins with history and moves toward midrash. In many instances parents who join the learning community lack Jewish memories, possessing neither the collective memories of the Jewish people nor the personal memories of Jewish experiences gained in childhood. This is clearly the case for Jews-by-choice, but is increasingly true also for Jews-by-birth. They enter the community with the relativistic and perhaps also critical perspectives implanted by general education on the university level. Within the community their trajectory runs from history to midrash and memory, to finding their own personal story within the collective story of Israel and to locating Jewish values they can internalize from within the textual treasury of Judaism.

Thus within a multigenerational community of learners a double dialectic prevails. The trajectories of child and adult approach each other from different directions, creating an interpersonal dialectic. At the same time the goal for each is a fruitful ongoing dialectic between story and history, intimacy and distance, commitment and critique.

Let us take only a single example: the Exodus story. For small children it is a tale of heroes and villains that arouses their amazement at the course of events and instills identification with the enslaved ancestors seeking physical and religious freedom. For adults seeking to enter or reenter Judaism it is initially a tale – perhaps a myth – set in the context of the ancient Near East, to be understood within Jewish and general history, no differently than the redemptive accounts preserved by other peoples. But even as the children, in the process of advanced learning, gradually lose their historical naïveté and broaden their understanding, Jewish study for the adults leads from context back to text. Although the historical perspective is not abandoned, it is brought into relationship with a newly developed and internalized Exodus story, a story of redemption that is shaped from all the studied texts that bear upon it: the biblical account, the midrashim, and whatever sources external to Judaism can shed light upon it. The discovery of new inscriptions or archeological evidence on the one side and deeper and more extensive reading of the Jewish sources on the other carry forward this dialectic between the inner and the outer perspectives. When the Exodus story is then ceremonially reenacted at the Passover seder, midrash and history, in concert, produce mitzvah.

In general, the community that studies texts together (rabbis, teachers, parents, children, single adults, and so forth) should also be a community that practices Judaism together. Thus the educated Jew becomes the observant Jew; personal identification and intellectual cognition lead to religious expression. Within a liberal setting individual practice will vary, but persons who have adopted similar configurations of norms from the tradition can nonetheless function together as a community of religious deed (a חבורה). When they take upon themselves the practice of mitzvot, the participants will likely differ with regard to the theological rationale for their commitment. Some will have come to accept them as divine imperatives, others as sacred traditions of the Jewish people. But differences with regard to origin and authority need not inhibit collective observance and celebration.

E. Completion

Although the first objective of Jewish religious education – a strong sense of the Jewish self securely grounded within the Jewish community and within the Jewish religious tradition – requires emphasis on particularity and separation, it does not therein find completion. Judaism itself, in its messianism, turns toward the world. The Jewishly educated Jew is anchored in Judaism, but that very anchorage enables her or him, without loss of Jewish selfhood, to reach outward to the human community and forward to the universal goal. What sets such outreach apart from Jewish self-dissolution is that it is undertaken from a position within Judaism across a boundary that Jewish education has clearly marked. Jewishly educated Jews, knowledgeable in the past and present of the Jewish people and immersed in its spiritual life, need not fear assimilation. They can participate fully in the open society, confidently as Jews.

NOTE

1 Essay newly revised and expanded, August 1996. I wish to thank those who helpfully commented on one of the two earlier versions: Seymour Fox, the late Isadore Twersky, Israel Scheffler, Mordecai Nisan, Samuel Joseph, Jonathan Cohen, Marc Rosenstein, Ruth Calderon, Howard Deitcher, Lesley Litman, and Zeev Mankowitz. I am especially grateful to Daniel Marom, who entered into an extended written and oral dialogue with me, stimulating a number of the ideas present in the essay.

Supplement: Michael Meyer

The task of Jewish education, in Michael Meyer's view, is to help Jews find their way through complex contemporary realities while maintaining a vibrant Jewish identity. Meyer bases his vision of Jewish education on tenets of "classical" liberal Jewish thought even as he advocates significant change. His scholarship on the history of modern Jewish identity, religion, and education illuminates the accepted approach to Jewish education in the Reform movement while highlighting the innovative elements in his vision.[1] For example, whereas Reform Jewish education has stressed freedom in decision making, Meyer believes that children should be inducted into Judaism from the earliest age in order to establish a basis for their crafting of Jewish beliefs and practices as adults. In contrast to the traditional Reform emphasis on the universal aspects of Jewish religious and social ideals, Meyer argues for a focus on "where Judaism differs." Furthermore, while most Reform education takes place in the synagogue and afternoon school, Meyer makes a case for a greater emphasis on the home, day school, and summer camp. In addition to the study of Jewish holidays and the Bible, Meyer insists on instruction in ritual practice and the study of *halakhah* (Jewish law) and Jewish history.

Meyer's views articulate an emerging voice within the Reform movement, but one that has not become mainstream. Convinced that these educational ideas were critical for the future of the Reform movement he pressed for an opportunity to convene Reform educators so that they might consider his proposals. In November 1996, leading educators, scholars, rabbis, and others from the Rhea Hirsch School of Education (RHS) of Hebrew Union College and Reform educational institutions across North America met in Los Angeles with Meyer and members of our project's staff to deliberate over a draft of his essay. The timing of this meeting was fortuitous, because the Reform movement's congregational and day schools were engaged in a process of reconceptualizing their educational programs. Subsequently, Meyer's essay and the responses to it were published in the journal of the movement's rabbinical body, the Central Conference of American Rabbis.

In the introduction to the proceedings, Sara Lee, Director of the RHS, reported discussions of Meyer's essay during meetings of the movement's *Day Schools for the 21st Century* project and at a colloquium for RHS students. "All these conversations have generated new questions and issues," Lee wrote, "and thus the discussion must continue."[2]

The deliberations on Meyer's essay and the issues it raises for Reform educators demonstrate what can happen when a denomination explores new ideas for revitalizing its educational vision. Meyer's ideas are also valuable to a broader audience of modern liberal Jews.

This supplement to Meyer's essay begins with excerpts from his scholarly writing on modern Jewish identity and the history of Reform Judaism. It continues with his comments on the future of the Reform movement's educational system, including the role of the rabbi.

Part One: The History of Reform Judaism

Modernization and Jewish Identity

In premodern times the congruity between family and society prevented Jewish identity from becoming a problem. Parents implanted in children the same values that they had absorbed in growing up, values sanctioned by a spiritually self-sufficient Jewish society. Continuity prevailed across the generations. This is not to say that the transition from childhood to adulthood among premodern Jews was entirely smooth in each instance. Surely the psychodynamics of maturation created family crises even then, but they were contained within the framework of limited options available upon reaching adulthood. These might indeed include alternative ways of being Jewish, pietist or rationalist, for example. But they were all within well-understood boundaries. The parentally implanted superego regularly made a "maximum of collective sense in terms of the ideals of the day."[3]

It is modernization that breaks down the barriers to the world outside the Jewish community and creates the choices that threaten continuity. From the perspective of Jewish identity, modernization is best understood as the historical process whereby increased exposure to non-Jewish ideas and symbols progressively erodes the given generational continuities, first in one location, then another, first among certain classes of Jews, then among others. Its product is Jewish modernity: the ongoing situation where internal continuity stands in potential or actual conflict with forces exterior to Jewish tradition. Put somewhat differently, a premodern, encompassing Jewish identity contracted to make room for other identity components, sometimes simply persisting alongside them, sometimes mingling with them freely. The relative influence of the Jewish component became subject to fluctuation, waxing or waning in relation to the new elements drawn from outside the Jewish sphere.[4]

... For the Jew in the modern world Jewishness forms only a portion of his total identity. By calling himself a Jew he expresses only one of multiple loyalties. And yet external pressures and internal attachments combine to make him often more aware of this identification than of any other. Conscious of an influence which Jewishness has upon his character and mode of life, he tries to define its sphere and harmonize it with the other components of self. Such Jewish self-consciousness – while not entirely without precedent in Jewish history – has been especially characteristic of the last two centuries.[5]

The Development of Reform Judaism

Meyer's scholarship focuses on the pioneering attempts of German Jews to negotiate the conflict between Jewish and non-Jewish elements in their identity. Their efforts encompassed the study of philosophy, theology, and Jewish history, as well as their application to areas related to society and culture, such as education, synagogue life, Jewish law, and the arts. While these pioneers may not have entirely succeeded in reconciling the conflict, their efforts established the foundation for "progressive" Judaism, both in and beyond Germany.

Meyer sees the development of progressive Judaism as a major factor in Jewish continuity in the modern period, for it offered a way for the majority of Jews who could no longer live by or identify with Orthodoxy to remain within Judaism. Without this option, he argues, a great many more Jews might have assimilated.

He traces Reform Judaism's evolution from Germany to America, from inspiration to institution, and from a few spiritual leaders to a substantial movement in world Jewry:

> The origins of today's American Reform Judaism lie in the social, political, and intellectual transformation undergone by Central European Jewry when it began the process of acculturation and emancipation. A segment of the Jewish community during the first decades of the nineteenth century sought to reform Judaism in such a way as to adapt it to the new situation of an entity no longer physically and intellectually isolated from its environment. The early reformers did not seek to establish a separate denomination; they were concerned rather to

influence the religious life of all Jews. They wanted to make worship services aesthetically satisfying; they sought to render theology and ritual more compatible with philosophical principles, moral sensibilities, and political loyalties. However, only a portion of European Jewry, mainly in Germany, was won over to the ideas of the reformers, so that by mid-century the larger German communities were split into traditional and liberal factions.

During the 1840s congregations subscribing to the European modifications in theory and practice were established in the United States. By 1873, Rabbi Isaac Mayer Wise was able to bring together a nucleus of liberally oriented synagogues in a Union of American Hebrew Congregations (UAHC). Both the UAHC and the Hebrew Union College (HUC), the rabbinical seminary established by Wise in Cincinnati two years later, were intended to encompass and serve the broadest spectrum of American Jewry. But the influx into the United States of traditionally inclined East European Jews, on the one hand, and the pressure of more radical reformers, on the other, soon drove both of these institutions into a more separatist and more narrowly defined position. By the end of the century, the UAHC, the HUC, and the Central Conference of American Rabbis (CCAR, established in 1889) had become the institutions of but a single branch of American Jewry, the Reform Jews.

Until the 1930s, and to some extent thereafter, Reform Judaism, as expressed in the Pittsburgh Platform of 1885, focused upon "ethical monotheism." Positively, it stressed the universal ideals of Judaism and the mission of Israel to bring these tenets and values to all mankind. Negatively, it sought to dissociate itself from what it regarded as no longer viable theological doctrines, from excessive ritualism, and from any expression of Jewish nationalism. Its social composition consisted almost exclusively of Jews from Germany whose economic standing was well above the mean of American Jewry.

With the cessation of massive Jewish immigration to the United States after World War I, resulting in a greater amalgamation of American Jewry, and with the rise of Hitler in Germany, the character of Reform Judaism began to change. The Columbus Platform of 1937 reflected a considerably more positive attitude to ritual and Sabbath and festival celebration, and it affirmed the obligation of all Jewry to aid in building a Jewish homeland in the Land of Israel.

The destruction of the major part of European Jewry in the Nazi Holocaust left American Reform Judaism in the position of undisputed leadership of liberal Jewry. During succeeding years it would increasingly dominate the World Union for Progressive Judaism, the international body of liberal Jewry that had been established in 1926. However, as it emerged into the postwar world, American Reform Judaism was modest, at best, in size and influence. The UAHC consisted of slightly more than 300 congregations with which about 75,000 families were affiliated. The Hebrew Union College was ordaining about a dozen Reform rabbis per year, and the CCAR had a total membership of little more than 500.[6]

Reform Judaism continued to develop in the United States as well as in countries such as Germany, England, and France, especially in the period preceding World War I.

In 1926, an international conference in London for leaders of Reform communities resulted in the formation of the World Union for Progressive Judaism (WUPJ), which has since served as the movement's international administrative body. The WUPJ headquarters are now in Jerusalem, guiding the development of Reform communities beyond Western Europe and America, including Israel, the former Soviet Union, Australia, South Africa, and South America.[7]

American Reform Judaism since World War II

In the twentieth century, America became the major Reform Jewish community in the world. Meyer discusses the developments that shaped Reform Judaism after the mass immigration of Eastern European Jews to America: the growth of the Conservative and Modern Orthodox movements in America, the advance of Zionism in its cultural and political modes, the tragedy of the Holocaust, and the establishment of the State of Israel.[8]

Growth. By the mid-1970s, the Reform movement had more than tripled its membership. Reform Judaism represented one-third of all affiliated Jews, about one million people. There were twice as many synagogues in the UAHC and rabbis in the CCAR as there had been before the war, and HUC was ordaining fifty rabbis a year. Meyer attributes this growth to a number of factors: general postwar expansion of American institutions, Jewish wealth, the movement to the suburbs, the impact of Christian revivalism, and strong Reform leadership. Today Reform Judaism has the greatest number of affiliated American Jews, including a high percentage of Jews who have left other movements.

Another factor is the influx of Jews by choice. Encouraged by the experience of converts who choose to be Jewish without the motivation of an impending marriage, some groups within the Reform movement have advocated active proselytization of non-Jews.

Grassroots Social Action. Social action had always been on the agenda of American Reform rabbis, both as individuals and through the CCAR. Reform Jews were reluctant to adopt this agenda, however, until "a new, vigorous staff encouraged formation of social-action committees in Reform temples and published books attempting to relate Jewish moral values to major political, economic and social problems afflicting American society." The movement adopted clear stances on such issues as racial desegregation, which it supported, and the war in Vietnam, which it opposed. Reform movement leaders participated in public protests and expanded interfaith dialogue and programs. Finally, "the abiding commitment of the movement to presenting its moral and religious perspective on public issues was institutionalized in 1961 when the UAHC established its Religious Action Center in Washington, DC."

Theological Debate. As the Pittsburgh Platform of 1885 illustrates, early Reform theology favored a universalist, rationalist understanding of Jewish religion. In response to the Holocaust and the racial and international conflicts of the postwar period, however, Reform Jews' fervent faith in moral progress and the mission of Israel among the nations began to weaken. Humanist, nontheistic and non-supernaturalist positions emerged, although they remained distinct from purely secular definitions of Jewish identity by the commitment "to participate in the life of a synagogue and to give ceremonial expression to moral aspirations."

Alongside these two positions was a third within the movement that, while influenced by religious existentialism in modern Europe, propounded a far more traditional and particularist theology than Reform Judaism had known. "Covenant theology" tried to preserve religious authority without compromising liberal principles by defining the *brit* (covenant) at Mount Sinai as the basis for the historical but open-ended dialogue between God and Israel.[9] "Though allowing for biblical criticism, this approach is frankly supernaturalistic, affirming a personal God who can and does speak to the modern Jew even as He spoke to his biblical ancestors – provided only that he will listen and study the texts."

Traditional Practice and Religious Choice. As the rejection of Orthodoxy is no longer the defining principle of Reform Judaism, there has been a renewed interest in *halakhah:*

> A generation no longer in revolt against the *halachah* and no longer satisfied with determining practice on the basis of personal preference alone was seeking to establish a new relationship to the vast corpus of Jewish law. It would not allow the *halachah* to be determinative – and therefore Reform Judaism could not be considered halachic – but it listened respectfully to what the legal decisors had to say and weighed carefully their arguments and conclusions.

At the turn of the twenty-first century, the question of a unified code of practice for Reform Jews continues to be debated. While proponents stress the need for guidelines and boundaries among Reform Jews, others continue to argue for individual freedom. Among the compromises resulting are official "guides" to Reform Jewish practice (as opposed to "codes") that suggest the observance of various *mitzvot* not necessarily as "divine commandments" but as "options and opportunities" for the enrichment of celebration and observance.

Reform Judaism is also experiencing an increase in traditional practice among its congregations. Many of the Jewish life-cycle ceremonies that were almost universally abandoned in Reform practice are being reintroduced today:

> Half a century ago, most Reform synagogues prided themselves on the decorum of their religious services, their abandonment of rituals that originated in folk superstitions, and the ethereal atmosphere of a worshipful, largely passive congregation stirred by the preachments of its rabbi and exalted by the contrapuntal singing of its professional choir. Today this situation has changed, at least somewhat, for nearly all Reform congregations. A majority of Reform rabbis now favor incorporating more traditions; some even advocate merger with Conservative Judaism. Services today are likely to include a generous quantity of Hebrew and have the musical portion conducted by a cantor with or without the assistance of a choir. Rather than the "cathedrals" of an earlier period, congregations have built more intimate sanctuaries (expandable for the High Holy Days) out of a desire to stress intimacy rather than awe in worship.

Meyer concludes that "while Reform services continue generally to be more formal than those of the Orthodox, a definite trend toward freer self-expression by the congregation and a more favorable attitude to ritual seems apparent."

Reversal on Zionism. According to Meyer, "no transformation within Reform Judaism has been as dramatic and complete as its sharp reversal on Zionism." At the turn of the twentieth century, the UAHC declared that "America is our Zion. . . . The mission of Judaism is spiritual, not political. Its aim is not to establish a state, but to spread the truths of religion and humanity throughout the world." Over the next half century, with the entry of more ethnically oriented Eastern European Jews into the movement and the persecution of German Jewry by the Nazis, the need for a secure refuge for the Jewish people became evident to the majority of Reform Jews. Anti-Zionism declined among Reform leadership and lost its impact on the movement. By 1937, the UAHC had declared the need for all Jews, regardless of their ideological differences, to unite in furthering the establishment of a Jewish homeland and spiritual center in Palestine; and in 1942, the CCAR passed a resolution in favor of the creation of a Jewish army. In 1948, the establishment of the State of Israel "was welcomed by virtually all Reform Jews."

This influence of Israel affected Reform practice and education. Israeli Independence Day was introduced into the Reform calendar of religious festivals. The CCAR began to hold some of its conferences in Israel. As of 1970, HUC's rabbinical program was requiring that its students spend their first year at the Jerusalem campus. The World Union for Progressive Judaism moved its headquarters to Israel and joined the World Zionist Organization. The UAHC established two Reform kibbutzim and supported *aliyah* (immigration to Israel).

Decline in Consensus. Differences over theology and ritual practice were accompanied by a growing emphasis on free and autonomous choice. This trend undermined the movement's authority; in 1978, Meyer claimed that such differences resulted in "deeply splitting Reform Judaism to the point that it appears today a more loosely knit 'organization' than a 'movement' in the proper sense." Reform Judaism has updated its original platform with the 1937 Columbus Platform, "Guiding Principles of Reform Judaism"; the 1976 San Francisco Platform, "Reform Judaism – A Centenary Perspective"; and the Pittsburgh Platform of 1999. In the quest to preserve a minimal consensus, however, even these documents might be seen as reflecting the growing diversity within the movement.

This diversity is especially apparent in the debates over rabbinic officiation at interfaith marriages. Acceptance of intermarriage grew until Reform rabbis were under considerable pressure from their congregants to sanctify such unions. Many Reform rabbis justified officiation at intermarriage "by the hope or the promise that in specific instances the non-Jewish partner will gradually be brought into Judaism or at least the children will be raised as Jews." By the mid-1970s, almost half of all Reform rabbis were, under special conditions, performing mixed marriages. Even an explicit resolution – formulated after "lengthy and rancorous debate" – declaring the CCAR's "opposition to participation by its members in any ceremony which solemnized a mixed marriage" did not resolve this debate. A few dissenting members remained within the CCAR but formed the Association for a Progressive Reform Judaism, which opposed the CCAR's declaration. Their criticism went beyond the debate over intermarriage to protest "the tendency to make concessions to Orthodoxy for the sake of Jewish unity, the trend toward regarding the State of Israel as the center of Jewish life, and the pronounced shift in emphasis from universalistic human aspirations to particular Jewish concerns."

There was growing agreement, however, on gender equality. From its founding, Reform Judaism was relatively more dedicated to this value, although the commitment did not initially lead to egalitarian congregational practice. Meyer describes the rise of women's status in Reform Judaism, in principle and in practice, as a slow process. During the twentieth century, however, the Reform movement took pioneering steps to enhance women's status and, consequently, had a large impact on modern Judaism. The most evident of these changes occurred in 1972, when HUC became the first seminary to ordain a woman rabbi.

Meyer summarizes some of the other changes:

> Between 1956 and 1970 the percentage of congregations that had
> elected women to their boards rose from 72 to 96 percent. By the
> 1950s, there were already a few Reform congregations with women
> presidents; in 1973, when such presidencies were no longer unusual,
> the UAHC elected its first woman vice chairman. Under the influence
> of the feminist movement, Reform Judaism supported the Equal Rights
> Amendment and women's freedom to obtain abortions. Its textbooks
> began to present female role models other than mothers and teachers
> and its Sisterhoods adapted their programs to the rising percentage of
> working women. *Gates of Prayer,* in its English portions, removed male
> language in reference to the worshipers: "all men" became "all"; "fel-
> lowship" became "friendship." One English version of the *avot* prayer
> made reference to the "God of our mothers" as well as of our fathers.[10]

Reform Judaism Today. The expansion and diversification of Reform Judaism since
World War II altered its identity both internally and with respect to the larger
Jewish community. "Present-day Reform Judaism no longer seeks to reform
Judaism for all Jews," writes Meyer. "Reluctantly it has made its peace with a
Jewish world where it occupies one position on the spectrum between a persisting Orthodoxy and a secularism that replaces religion with Jewish national or ethnic identity."[11] Yet as the trend toward individual choice and diversity continues,
the preservation of this "one position" becomes more difficult. While Reform
leadership emphasizes those elements that are essential for making autonomous
choices responsibly, it must also seek consensus on the boundaries of choice:

> What binds today's Reform Jews to the founders and to one another
> is neither a common theology nor a wholly common regimen of re-
> ligious life. Some Reform Jews are selectively moving toward more
> traditional concepts and practices, others are on a personal odyssey
> away from them, yet others remain indifferent. Some retain an over-
> riding commitment to universalism, others enthusiastically endorse the
> new particularism. There is less a sense of moving along together than
> a shared feeling of tension that cannot be fully resolved, even as the
> contradictory forces and divisive issues which produce it themselves
> remain beyond final resolution.
>
> The movement today represents that current within religious Judaism
> that flows precariously in a channel close to its edge. Unlike Conser-
> vative Judaism, it does not possess the comfort of being in the center;
> unlike Orthodoxy, it lacks the security of unshaken faith. . . .
>
> To be a Reform Jew today means to live in a community whose
> shared affirmations of tenet and intent, formulated and reformulated

in books, sermons, and platforms, remain ever in flux, even when the individual seeks to give them permanence through persistent application to daily life. That is a situation common to all religious liberalisms. What endures and binds, however, is not merely the "condition" of being a Reform Jew. There is also an ongoing task. The German Reformers spoke repeatedly of integrating two elements: *Lehre und Leben*, the teaching (Torah) and the life led in the modern world. Individual Reformers and Reform communities have differed – and continue to differ – on the relative weight to be assigned each of these elements. Those closest to tradition have stressed the teaching, those furthest from it have argued for the decisive impact of modern life. Yet the reestablishment of the scale's fulcrum in every generation, in every individual religious conscience, and in the collective life, has been an enduring characteristic of Reform. Perhaps it is the ongoing and common task of creating ever anew that shifting and delicate balance between Torah and modernity – and of relating the two to each other – that in the broadest sense best defines the Reform movement.[12]

The risk, in Meyer's view, is that liberal Judaism is in danger of reducing itself to a peripheral sect in Jewish history:

We find ourselves on the "slippery slope" toward syncretism and sectarianism, propelled by the desire always to embrace and never to exclude. Ahead lies the prospect of a Reform Judaism clearly definable only by its units of affiliation, not by any principles that may not be bent when the situation seems to require it. It is a Reform Judaism in which conversion has become superfluous or meaningless since it has no clearly defined goal and since non-converts feel no estrangement whatsoever within a Reform temple that welcomes them not only as individuals who are not yet Jewish, but also as continuing adherents of a sister faith that is gaining increased status within Judaism itself.[13]

Part Two: Traditions and Trends in Reform Jewish Education[14]

Postwar Reform Jewish Education

Until the postwar period, Reform Jewish educators understood that Reform parents regarded the religious education of their children as "a minimal project." There was a consensus among congregants and rabbis that Jewish children should receive their secular education in public schools and their religious education in synagogue programs for a few hours each week.

These programs sought to familiarize learners with the tenets of monotheism and morality. Reform schools conveyed "little more than a sense of Jewishness, some knowledge of Bible stories and holidays, and a cursory familiarity with Jewish beliefs." Some Hebrew was taught, but not intensively, and there was no informal education, with the exception of programs for adult learning.

In early Reform education, commitment to individual choice was expressed by the replacement of the Bar Mitzvah with a confirmation ceremony at which teenage Jews affirmed their acceptance of Jewish identity. According to Meyer, the confirmation was often treated as a perfunctory and externalized ritual – at times less significant than the social celebration that accompanied it – and did not appear to have a lasting impact on an individual's Jewish development.

During the interwar years, significant change took place in Reform Jewish education, much of it driven by the movement's leading educator, Emanuel Gamoran. The increased emphasis on education found expression in the policies of the Commission on Jewish Education and the programs of the Department of Jewish Education. The National Association of Temple Educators (NATE) was also founded to support the professional development of teachers.

Meyer notes several changes. Many Reform schools offered weekday as well as weekend classes. Beginning in 1970, Reform day schools began to be established. The Reform movement also invested more heavily in summer camps and youth groups, which offered rituals such as *havdalah* (marking the passing of the Sabbath), the concentrated study of Jewish sources, and social-action projects. Furthermore, with changes in the demographics and character of American Jewry, new formats were developed for adult education, ranging from outreach programs for Jews by choice to *havurot* (study groups) for Jews who sought "meaningful communities" within or outside the synagogue.

In the mid-1970s, the Reform movement faced a great educational challenge: "The period of rapid growth in membership had come to an end; religious school enrollments dropped with the demographic decline of appropriately aged Jewish children." Furthermore, a turn from a solely religious definition of Jewish identity toward one that emphasized ethnicity and transdenominational community undermined the idea of a distinct Reform ideology and, with it, the desire to be associated with and involved in the movement.

Writing in the mid-1970s, Meyer discusses what he sees as the most severe problem:

> From its very beginnings the Reform movement had drawn a great many Jews for whom religion, and in some cases Jewishness, was distinctly peripheral to their lives. They attended synagogue rarely, having joined for reasons of respectability and their children's Jewish

identity. Many, especially in the larger cities, were not desirous of deeper involvement. They were content to come to the temple for the High Holy Days or for the celebration of life-cycle events. At present this segment tends to see the rabbi as more of a priest who officiates on special occasions than a spiritual or moral guide, while, for their part, the rabbinical and lay leaders are now rarely imbued with that effervescent self-confidence which had done battle with apathy in an earlier age. A few have become discouraged or themselves indifferent.[15]

More recent research on the development of Reform Jewish education shows that while there has been significant growth in Reform day schools and informal education, basic trends remain the same. Since only 3 percent of Reform families send their children to day schools, the afternoon or Sunday school program continues to be the chief framework for Reform Jewish education. The diversity of these programs makes it difficult to identify a specifically "Reform" approach to education. Their curricula continue to center on Jewish holidays and *Tanakh* (the Hebrew Bible), with some study of Jewish history and life-cycle events. Older students might study rabbinics or issues in contemporary Jewish life. Hebrew language instruction is oriented to participation in the prayer service although prayer services themselves are often not included in the curriculum.[16]

Despite these realities, Reform educators are making great efforts to train teachers and introduce new models of formal and informal education. They seek to reimagine Reform Jewish education and produce ideas and practices that will facilitate much-needed change.[17]

To See the World Through Jewish Eyes

Meyer maintains that by steering a path between "authoritarian religion" and "idolatrous secularism," Reform Judaism remains "an indispensable sanctifying element in the ceaseless flux of human life." In his view, Reform Judaism is unique in its capacity to offer a religious expression of Judaism that is "both intellectually attractive and emotionally satisfying." For Reform Judaism to be compelling, however, its educational approach must now be strengthened:

> A philosophy of Jewish education whose goal is to create separation through dissonance (a technique among some recruiters for Orthodox institutions) will only create disaffection. To be successful, Jewish education must begin with harmonization, interrelating the Jewish values that are taught with those that have equivalents in the contemporary world outside Judaism. Examples would be the moral values underlying environmentalism, nondiscrimination, or reverence for all life. But

not to go beyond this approach means to depict Judaism simply as a yea-sayer to the Zeitgeist and hence as entirely dispensable. Pointing out how much Judaism shares with contemporary culture, except as an opening gambit, is a luxury we may have been able to afford earlier in our social history but cannot any longer.

Our contemporary social and demographic situation demands that the ultimate stress be on disjunction and difference, not on similarity. The task is to delineate more clearly the boundary between the Jewish self and the non-Jewish one and to show how the two spheres, while they may in some respects be similar or complementary, contain elements that cannot be reconciled. . . .

Of course, the intellectual component is only part of the educational enterprise, and when one is educating for identity perhaps less consequential than nurturing emotional attachment. The latter, however, depends on experiences, not knowledge. Ideally, such experiences are recurrent, in the nature of ritual acts rather than in one-time life-cycle events or personal confrontations with Holocaust sites or with the State of Israel. But the common element in these is their particularity. Jews and only Jews observe the Sabbath in this manner, have undergone an unparalleled disaster, and have re-created a national culture in a land that for millennia was not theirs.

It is time also to emphasize the negative: "To be a Jew is not to be . . ." – especially not a Christian, but also not a pagan and not a syncretist. The lines of incompatibility need to be redrawn for our own time and conveyed to our children. I fully realize how difficult this is in an age of families that are multiply diverse. But there can be no effective yea without an unabashed nay.

Obviously, Jewish education should not end in negation. The positive task is to increase the territory lying within the segmented sphere of personal identity that is recognized as Jewish and to make it fundamental for identity as a whole, both in its separation and uniqueness and as the integrator of a larger totality. Within the specifically Jewish realm, Jewish education needs to shape patterns of thought and action in ways that render them most impervious to dissolution. Beyond the Jewish sphere, its goal is well expressed in a phrase already employed by Judah Leon Magnes that has recently gained popularity: to enable Jewish children to see their entire world "through Jewish eyes." The two spheres together – the enhanced and sharply differentiated specifically Jewish one along with its non-Jewish counterpart penetrated by Jewish vision and purpose – can constitute a viable Jewish identity, even today.[18]

Meyer's emphasis on Jewish particularity would change the way Judaism is taught, with greater prominence given to Jewish ethnicity, peoplehood, and Zionism in Reform education:

> Jewish identity today continues to lie within the fields of force represented by enlightenment, antisemitism, and Zion. Only a minute portion of world Jewry lives in a situation of such complete self-segregation as to remain impervious to the influences that induce broader identifications. Nearly all contemporary Jews feel they are Jews and at the same time something not specifically Jewish as well. For some, Jewishness remains their principal orientation in life, the center of their being. These are mostly the serious religious Jews, of whatever specific denomination, who continue to believe in some sense of Jewish chosenness and special destiny. For others, enlightenment has drawn them almost entirely outside their Jewish identity. Reason and universalism have worn away their particular loyalty to Jews and Judaism. Some are basically universalists; others have substituted new particularisms for old. Most actively identifying modern Jews, however, have in one fashion or another absorbed the influence of enlightenment. They argue that their Jewishness has nothing to fear from new discoveries of science or widening cultural horizons and that their universal commitments do not interfere with their Jewish ones. . . .
>
> Although antisemitism has declined since World War II, it continues to play a major role in determining Jewish identity. Even in countries where antisemitism is least severe, such as the United States, Jews nonetheless believe they are potentially endangered. Jewish defense organizations flourish and expand their activities. Supporting them serves as a means of Jewish identification in the present as it has in the past. Since Jews in Israel see their protection of Diaspora Jews as a basic component of the relations between them, the presence of discrimination or persecution in the Soviet Union, Ethiopia, or Syria has also served to energize the Israeli sense of ethnic responsibility. . . .
>
> It is, however, the sense of Jewish peoplehood that represents the strongest component of Jewish identity today. Although, as noted earlier, Jews by Choice tend to understand Jewishness principally as denominational, most religious Jews link Judaism closely to Jewishness. Their synagogue activities are ways of expressing ethnicity. Attending religious services is something Jews do as members of the Jewish people. Because the ties of peoplehood remain strong, tensions between Diaspora Jews and Israeli Jews will not quickly dissolve their shared sense of solidarity. . . .

Whatever the outcome, whatever forms Jewish identity may take in the near or long term, to be a Jew vigorously in the modern world will continue to mean confronting new external enticements, sorting them out, and seeking to integrate those that do not contradict the fundamental principles of the Jewish tradition. It will also continue to mean coping with hostility in such a way as to prevent it from misshaping Jewishness either through the internalization of negative stereotypes or through allowing memory of persecutions past and fear of persecutions in the future to become the exclusive, cheerless content of Judaism. Mostly, I trust, Jewishness will focus in the future, as in the past, on Zion. For Zion not only represents Jewish origins and Jewish unity. It is also the symbol of that Redemption which orients Jewish identity to its highest goal and gives it intrinsic meaning.[19]

The Educational Role of the Rabbi

In the 1996 symposium in Los Angeles, Reform educators asked Meyer about the role of the rabbi in an education based on liberal Judaism. Meyer responded by stating unequivocally that "the real authority within Reform Judaism is God," although Reform Judaism respects each person's capacity to determine what God commands. He described the Reform movement's position as, "Rabbis must have authority, but not absolute authority."

The educational implication of this stance is that the Reform rabbi "must empower the congregation to gain the knowledge to have its own authority." The rabbi plays a critical role in "liberating" Jews to make their own decisions about Judaism by steeping them in the teachings of Jewish religion. As one of the educators put it, "the more educated Jews become, the more they take over the role of rabbi."

Although in many contemporary communities rabbis have been asked to serve as ritual guides, charismatic pulpit masters, and official community leaders, Meyer's rabbi might also be a congregational "headmaster," whose task is to transform the institutional culture of the synagogue so that all its activities are forms of Jewish education.[20]

NOTES

1 See *Response to Modernity: A History of the Reform Movement in Judaism* (New York: Oxford University Press, 1988).

2 Sara Lee, "Introduction: Perspective on the Educated Reform Jew," *CCAR Journal* 46:2 (Spring 1999): 5.

3 Erik H. Erikson, *Childhood and Society* (New York: W. W. Norton, 1950), 270.

4 Michael Meyer, *Jewish Identity in the Modern World* (Seattle: University of Washington Press, 1990), 6–7.

5   Michael Meyer, *The Origins of the Modern Jew: Jewish Identity and European Culture in Germany 1749–1824* (Detroit: Wayne State University Press, 1967), 8.

6   Michael A. Meyer, "Reform Judaism," in *Movements and Issues in American Judaism,* ed. Bernard Martin (Westport, CT: Greenwood Press, 1978), 158–59.

7   See *Response to Modernity,* 335–52.

8   The following summary is based primarily on "Reform Judaism," 158–70. At various points, other sources that update that article are quoted and noted.

9   *Response to Modernity,* 360–64.

10 Ibid., 380.

11 Ibid., 385.

12 Ibid., 385–86.

13 Meyer, "On the Slope Toward Syncretism and Sectarianism," *CCAR Journal* 40 (Summer 1993): 44.

14 The following section summarizes Meyer's discussion of education in *Response to Modernity,* 39–40, 286, 298–303, 373–74, and 377–79; and "Reform Judaism," 162–69.

15 "Reform Judaism," 169.

16 Samuel K. Joseph, *Portraits of Schooling: A Survey and an Analysis of Supplementary Schooling in Congregations* (New York: UAHC Press, 1997); Jack Wertheimer, "Jewish Education in the United States: Recent Trends and Issues," *American Jewish Year Book 1999*: 21–22, 50–57, 61–77, 79.

17 See, for example, *A Congregation of Learners: Transforming the Synagogue into a Learning Community,* ed. Isa Aron, Sara Lee, and Seymour Rossel (New York: UAHC Press, 1995).

18 "Being Jewish and . . ." in *National Variations in Jewish Identity: Implications for Jewish Education,* ed. Steven M. Cohen and Gabriel Horencyzk (New York: State University of New York Press, 1999), 32–33.

19 *Jewish Identity in the Modern World,* 83–85.

20 Meyer referred us to a case study written by Rabbi Richard Block, "A Pilgrim's Progress: Educational Reform and Institutional Transformation at Congregation Beth Am," in *A Congregation of Learners: Transforming the Synagogue into a Learning Community,* 228–41.

8

Educated Jews: Common Elements

MICHAEL ROSENAK

As we explore options for educating Jews in our era, two kinds of concerns must inevitably preoccupy us.

On the one hand, we are looking for discrete visions of what is worthy; and we wish to have these visions clearly spelled out. More specifically, we want knowledgeable and scholarly writers to tell us what kinds of Jewish human beings they see as success stories of Jewish education. Who do they think adequately and nobly express the religious, national, and ethical traditions of the Jewish people in this age? Furthermore, we want each of them to suggest, in some curricular detail, what it might mean to nurture such human beings, both as individuals in the world and within meaningful communities and associations.

On the other hand, the very specificity of the visions and their often competing characters require that we ask ourselves whether these visions have commonalities that will permit dialogue and fraternity among Jews of differing orientations and convictions.

Three Educational Dimensions

In answer to the first concern, this volume presents us with distinct models of "the educated Jew" that respond to the question: How do you, the scholar, envision success in Jewish education? The second concern suggests the question: How shall different visions, such as those before us, nourish and not demoralize the wider Jewish community? To spell out the answers to the first question in educational terms and to look toward a solution to the second one, which is my main concern here, we may fruitfully address three fundamental queries to each writer. These questions deal respectively with what we shall call the philosophical, the cultural, and the existential dimensions of education.

178

(a) Our first question may be formulated as follows: *What is the philosophical basis of the education you are proposing?* That is, what are the basic principles and beliefs that inform your conception?[1] Do you, for example, base your conception of reality, knowledge, and value on a divine–human relationship ("revelation") or, conversely, on exclusively human responsibility for all validity, value, and meaning in a universe that seems empty of extrahuman purpose and sense? In your conception, is there something unique about the Jewish people and Judaism, or do you consider beliefs about uniqueness to reflect pernicious conceit? On the basis of your principles, which knowledge is most valuable – and why? Is sense bought in the coin of absolute values, or should we look for value primarily in the needs and preferences of groups and individuals? Are people fundamentally different, ordered by God or nature in some hierarchy, or are they, in least in some significant ways, equal?

On the basis of the principles you affirm, which individual and collective ideals are plausible or even directly called for? What kind of Jewish society would you see as ideal, and who, if anyone in particular, will most appropriately speak for it? Learners of Torah? Courageous soldiers? Researchers who address themselves to the problems of humankind? Creative spirits? Compassionate ones? Those most loyal to the particulars of *halakhah* (Jewish law)? Those who seek godliness by way of a religious humanism? Those who labor to secure a place for the Jewish people among the nations and cultures of the world? Those who labor without illusion for small improvements in an absurd world?

In times past, so the records indicate, all Jews shared beliefs and differed only in nuance about Jewish ideals. Then people "knew" when it was time to burn *hametz* (leavened bread, forbidden on Passover) or fast or pray. These acts embodied principles about reality and value, and pointed unambiguously toward ideal situations: a society in which all observed Pesah (Passover), fasted on Tishah b'Av (the ninth day of the month of Av, commemorating the destruction of the Temple), and organized their daily routine according to the set times of prescribed prayer, as demanded by God of His covenanted people, Israel.

Today, it is clear that each conception of the educated Jew is based on diverse and chosen beliefs about God, humankind, the nature of Jewish existence, and even, to an extent, the meaning of nature and the world; and correspondingly, that there are different and even conflicting ideals of Jewish communal and personal life. These conceptions and ideals, in their rich diversity, are reflected and articulated in this volume.

(b) The second question to be addressed to each of our scholars is: *What is the cultural vision behind your conception of the educated Jew?* How do you envision ideal ways to draw young people into Jewish culture (however defined)?

How do you want them to *inherit* it, to *participate* in it, and perhaps to *contribute* to it? How does your vision permit negotiating the tensions between inheritance and contribution: between absorption and innovation? Where is the line to be drawn between loyal creativity and iconoclastic change?

Elsewhere I have suggested that the concepts of "language" and "literature" may help us to make and maintain such distinctions.[2]

By "language" I referred to the canons, the ways of thinking and imagining, the basic assumptions and procedures of a culture (or a field of study or realm of experience) that give it a specific identity. The text of the Torah and its "reading," never altered and always reapproached for meaning, is a prime example of language.

"Literature" I understand to refer to what people (can) do within the specific language into which they have been initiated, thereby demonstrating the language's vitality and its ability to provide a cultural home for different people, in diverse times and circumstances. The vast literature of biblical commentary and interpretation is a foremost example of what we mean by literature.

The concepts of language and literature are helpful in describing what we should like to see happen in education: namely, to initiate the young into the language of a culture by way of its most cherished literatures, including and perhaps particularly those formative literatures called sacred or "classic." When it succeeds, education provides learners with the tools to select literature for use by abundantly exposing them to the forms and substance of diverse literatures. Optimally, education also prepares them to take part in the enterprise of making new literature.

Again, we must imagine the situation of two or three centuries ago when almost all Jews shared a language and were in agreement as to what constituted literature. Then, it appears, almost all Jews considered the halakhic principle to be fundamental to Jewish language (that is, there could be no Judaism without it) and looked upon the minutiae of Jewish law as sacred literature, in practice indistinguishable from the language itself. Then, everyone knew what initiating children into *Yiddishkeit* (Yiddish for "Judaism") entailed. Although there were diverse literatures (philosophy, mysticism, poetry, *minhag ha-makom* [local custom], different emphases and styles of commentary), there was only one universally acknowledged language.

Jews in those times could not have understood Jews who differed about whether the *halakhah* was language (Judaism itself) or literature (one way among others for Jews to articulate their Judaism). Secular Zionist Jews for whom the elements of language focused on the land and Hebrew, with Zionism itself and Hebrew letters pointing to the possibilities of new literature within the language, would have been incomprehensible to them. They would, for the most part, not have understood classic Reform Jews who largely equated the canon of Judaism, its language, with prophetic ethics and theology. Even modern Orthodox

Jews, who argue about whether systems of theology and belief are just a kind of vintage literature while *halakhah* is the soul of Jewish language, might have looked strange to them.

In the contemporary absence of a consensus about language (Judaism) and literature (Jewish cultural articulation), we lack a common conception of Jewish education as cultural initiation, participation, and contribution. And we ask each presenter of a Jewish educational model: Which conception do you propose?

(c) Now the final question: *What is the basic existential vision of the Jew as human being that characterizes your conception?* How do you envision Jewish education as helping the learner become a whole person? The assumption behind this question is that the enterprise of education can and should be clearly distinguished from more limited ones, such as training or even instructing; that while one teaches subjects, skills, or competences, one educates persons. The whole "educated" person has not merely been helped to become highly knowledgeable, or imbued with strong feelings, or possessed of a firm will, but has largely achieved the ability to integrate action, emotion, intelligence, and will. As Thomas Green put it, educated persons are not merely well behaved but capable of acting well.[3] They can explain why they do what they do, they can reflect upon their actions, and they bring appropriate feelings to chosen actions. They have a way in the world. They can identify with the motivational forces that make up their personalities.

In a well-known essay, Gershom Scholem described three traditional models of piety – actually, three types of educated Jews: the *talmid ḥakham,* the *tzaddik,* and the Hasid.[4] The first is a scholar of the Torah, a leader of his normative community; the second, an individual who strives to live faithfully and punctiliously by these very norms; and the third is one who concentrates, even idiosyncratically, on those actions and virtues that speak most strongly to his inner being.

Most contemporary Jews would express reservations about all three types, or would deny their monopoly on educated virtue. What about the *ḥalutz* (pioneer) who contributed mightily to the Zionist enterprise and who, while now in eclipse, may someday recapture the limelight? What about the rational and committed scholar ·or expert who is qualified to address problems facing our people? What about the professional and lay leadership of our communities?

Once again, it appears that just as we do not embrace the same principles or "speak the same language," so do we not share a vision of the whole Jewish human being. While all medieval Jews thought that scholars, punctiliously observant Jews, and saintly Jews were part of the same community and ambiance, most contemporary Jews who admire *ḥalutzim* are not in that field of vision, nor are irreligious thinkers and doers. What is the challenge this situation presents to us?

"What If They Are *All* Right?"

The portraits of the educated Jew that our project sets before us address a reality and a need. We can no longer assume that "everyone knows" what "good Jews" are like and what elements we should look for in their education. The diversity we find is, indeed, what we are looking for. The underlying message is that there are various ways of envisioning ideals for Jewish life and that no one need feel excluded.

In this sense, then, the assumption underlying "models of the educated Jew" is liberating. It is a pluralistic assumption; it invites us to consider how to cultivate different types of teachers, competent to write and teach different and perhaps competing curricula, opening complementary or competing vistas of understanding and commitment. By this underlying assumption we are also invited to locate exemplary educational institutions that respectively embody each vision of the educated Jew and to follow them, their teachers and pupils and communities through specific school careers and beyond.

Yet there is another way of looking at this diversity. For the assumption behind the idyllic view that there are a multiplicity of options from which one can freely choose on the basis of deliberative examination reflects not only an objective insight but, alas, an academic bias as well. In fact, the presentation of each model is not simply an intellectual exercise, even when put forward by outstanding intellectuals. Rather, it is also and almost always an attempt to solve a problem of vital concern to the writer.

This problem is what is seen to be the sorry state of the Jewish people, and each prognosis of that state points to proposed and desirable solutions. Each model claims, or wagers, that it contains the key to making Jewish life meaningful again. Each hopes that it has the power to make more Jews immune to the omnipresent danger of the disappearance of the Jews.

Hence, even biblical researchers such as Moshe Greenberg, learned literary scholars such as Menachem Brinker, astute historians of men and ideas such as Isadore Twersky and Michael Meyer, and philosophical savants such as Israel Scheffler present their models not as detached researchers but as concerned persons who see their conceptions competing with other, less worthy, ones.

I recall the American Jewish theologian and educator Irving (Yitz) Greenberg once remarking on the way spokespersons for various Jewish movements vigorously defended their diverse positions. Each enthusiastically rehearsed the alleged inadequacies of the others; each proclaimed that the adherents of all the other positions would cease to be significant to anyone, and that none of them would survive. His dour conclusion: "What if they are *all* right?"

We need not carry that dire anticipation to its ultimate conclusion: that each group within the Jewish people will be convinced by the inadequacies of its competitors-in-vision to relinquish Jewish commitments and identity altogether.

Another perhaps more realistic scenario, already massively in evidence, is that each group will foster alienation from all the others. Orthodox Jews and non-Orthodox ones in Israel will read each other out of the fold, ceasing to see the other as partners in fate and in the project of creating a Jewish commonwealth. *Ḥaredi* (ultra-Orthodox) Jews will live increasingly segregated lives, shutting out everyone else, with the others reciprocating the distrust and hostility, disclaiming any commonalities with "primitive fundamentalists." Caught on the horns of the dilemma of universalism and particularism, some will become particularistic at the expense of moral sensibility, and others will be universalist at the expense of all genuine fraternity. Each, thinking that the others will eventually accept his or her convictions, will approach the others with a battery of negative judgments about them and about the fatal flaws in their so-called Jewish allegiance and activity.

Here, we wish to address the question of whether, despite real polarities among the positions elucidated in this book, it is possible to locate a language common to all of them; and, if so, whether one can conceive of community-wide goals for Jewish living.

Before embarking on that exploration, a word about my own position, lest the reader conclude that I alone among the writers here am the genuine academic who stands above the fray, devoid of specific Jewish commitments. Like the scholars presenting their paradigms here, I believe that academic identity does not free any individual from deciding upon paths to an authentic and responsible life. Elsewhere I have outlined a position about the educated Jew that, in my case, aims to cultivate the modern Orthodox one, who lives by the motto *Torah im derekh eretz,* Torah and worldly culture.[5] This allegiance of mine "threatens" to preoccupy me even in some of my professional life as a Jewish educator, although as a teacher and writer on educational theory I am expected to be somewhat detached from my inquiries.

Living with Diversity

Aiming for some "objective" detachment, I look at the various conceptions before us and ask myself whether any of the models of the educated Jew, those represented in our project and those absent from it, looks to become the way-of-Jewishness for all Jews. My conclusion is that unless Jews are defined as those who think and act as we do, the answer is "no." We shall continue to be different from one another. We shall continue to have differing ideals based on at least partially different principles. We shall not define language and literature in the same ways, and we shall have sometimes incompatible visions of the ideal Jew.

At the same time, most of us will wish, or feel obliged, to live in some spiritual proximity to the others. This requires of us to examine whether we can find any language, any standards and expectations that we can hold in common in order to do Jewish things, however circumscribed, together, in trust and some shared allegiance.

If the answer is that there are ways of creating spiritual and cultural proximity among text-centered religious humanists like Moshe Greenberg, halakhic-philosophical classicists like Isadore Twersky, liberal religionists like Michael Meyer, liberal cultural humanists like Menachem Brinker, and analytic philosophers of education like Israel Scheffler, then we may have to rethink basic categories of what nearness and distance are for contemporary Jews in order to overcome conceptual conflict without loss of specific commitments and without the reductionism that makes them look like our own commitments. This is a difficult task, theoretically and practically. Theoretically, the difficulty arises because concepts that are meant to solve the problem of how to conceive of the entire Jewish people *(Klal Yisrael)* are themselves heavy with predispositions and specific, potentially exclusionist, agendas.

Everyman's "Educated Jew": A Theoretical Exploration

What may be said, then, to characterize the educated Jew, no matter of which philosophical, cultural, and existential orientation, as a partner in a covenant of destiny, culture, values, and conviction? On the basis of the paradigms before us, let us venture to suggest some potential commonalities.

1. Having a Language and Doing Literature

To begin with, the educated Jew may be defined as one who has a "language" of Jewishness and uses it to make Jewish "literature." Stated most simply, there are factors that function for this Jewish person as staples of Jewish life, that demand attention no matter how interpreted (by diverse literatures). For all the conceptions of the educated Jew in this book, there is a foundational literature that establishes Jewish culture or Judaism in the world, although there is disagreement over whether this foundational literature is sacred or only classic. But all the scholars will agree that medieval commentaries, modern *midrashim* and poems, recognizably Jewish memories, actions, and aspirations can be categorized as literature, serving the purpose of saving the language from archaic insignificance, or, as some might more "reverently" state this, assuring its accessibility.

It is reasonable to assume that all the conceptions of educated Jews will agree with the statement of Walter Rathenau, one-time foreign minister of the Weimar Republic who was assassinated in 1922, that "if a Jew tells you that he enjoys hunting, he is lying." Rathenau was hardly a traditional Jew, but he assumed a given attitude that one could expect from Jews about the imposition of pain upon sentient creatures in the name of sport. Here, then, there is an assumption that Jews share not only a fate (who would know that better than the Germanized

Rathenau, killed as a Jew) but also a core universe of value that allows the recognition of something akin to permanencies in what some call "Judaism" and others "Jewish civilization" or the ongoing historical experience of the Jews.

2. Learning Literature

Since the educated Jew has an interest in learning the language, despite disagreements with other Jews about its delineation, s/he is committed to learning considerable parts of its historical literature, for that is how the language is contextualized and brought down to earth. The literature is all that has been said and done in the language throughout its millennia. The primacy of literature is especially prominent wherever the concept of language as something primordially sacred, hewn in stone, is perceived as mythical or otherwise reactionary; where language is understood more as a quality that takes shape through the plentitude of literature created in its name. Previous literature may or may not obligate the educated Jew, depending on what of the past s/he considers sacred, but it does provide paradigms and precedents for present cultural activity.

Not all Jews, then, will share similar attachments to previous literature. Some will consciously and uninhibitedly select from it. There will be differences of opinion whether the "language-presenting" literature of the hoary past is normative or simply formative. Those who do not believe in the authority of the past but only in its background presence are likely to have greater respect for and to place greater curricular emphases on contemporary literature. It is the latter that they consider the sharpest lens for seeing what may be called the language (i.e., the historical identity of the Jews as a cultural entity), albeit through a glass, sometimes intriguingly dark.

3. Competence and Comprehensiveness

The way all educated Jews use the language and its literatures suggests that being educated means having some competence and striving for a degree of comprehensiveness. Consequently, the educated Jew, of whatever variety, will not wish to be represented by proxies or "professionals" who speak for him or her as a Jew. A halakhically observant Jew will not expect "the rabbi" to do *mitzvot* for him; the Zionist will do Zionism in some fashion, rather than simply "take pride in (the way others do) it." Similarly, a synagogue-going Jew ideally need not be told that "we begin our service on page 13"; and educated Jews may be expected to refer to Rosh Hashanah and Shavuot as "the holidays" (or the ḥagim or "yomtovim"), rather than as "the Jewish holidays."

4. Unity Amidst Diversity

We may assume that educated Jews of all types, with the likely exception of ultratraditionalist ones, have at least formal respect for the communities that claim to speak the language.[6] This manifests itself, externally, by the readiness of all to defend the entire Jewish community against its ill-wishers. Internally, the matter is more problematic, especially for the modern Orthodox.[7] But to the extent that sincere convictions and commitments are thought to glimmer in the sky of every Jewish association, then the relationships among different ones may be seen as characterized by controversy, *mahloket*.

On this point, my comments are openly prescriptive. I am positing that those educated to specific visions and commitment to them must be taught to be comfortable with *mahloket* as well, that controversy among committed Jews should not appear threatening. If it does, it is attributable to lack of awareness of what unites them: minimally, what Rabbi Joseph B. Soloveitchik termed "the covenant of fate";[8] optimally, shared Jewish tasks, insights, and ideals that transcend their differences.[9]

5. "Nothing Human Is Foreign"

All educated Jews have the desire, need, and ability to link Jewish matters to wide vistas of reality and experience, those generally termed "universal."[10] That is, the language of Jewishness spoken by the educated Jew plugs into all human concerns and can be partially translated into other cultural ("particular") languages. The educated Jew must, of course, know other significant languages, both because much of what he does takes place in the context of these languages, and because these languages challenge (philosophically, morally, humanistically) aspects of previous Jewish literature and spur the creation of new theological, social, and imaginative literature.

The ability of all educated Jews to translate Jewish concerns, concepts, and creativity into the languages of the non-Jewish civilization in which they live, and thus to communicate meaningfully with others, is tempered by their cultural autonomy and reflectiveness. This means that educated Jews carefully consider both commonalities and differences among languages, cultural groups, and human experience. While they are attuned to understanding the lives and realms of significance that others bring with them to a common public sphere, they strive to remain situated in Judaism.

6. Judaism and Ultimate Concerns

Universalism, then, suggests to the educated Jew discrete types of interaction with non-Jewish society and culture. But the notion of "the universal" extends beyond social interactions. It has an internal existential dimension, connecting Jewish matters to ultimate concerns. The educated Jew wishes or knows him/herself to be commanded to express what is most important, engaging, and "deep," primarily and *specifically* in the idiom (or within the norms) of Judaism. Judaism appears to the educated Jew to be a holy or a valuable or an adequate vehicle for obligation and meaning, as both source and medium.

This articulates what the religious Jew, of whatever denomination, may view as the service and the love of God; in secular varieties of Judaism, it is more likely to be grasped in terms of cultural and historical situatedness. The secular-minded educated Jew takes for granted that the treasures of human existence are best discovered where one finds oneself, culturally and historically.

For both the religious and secular-minded conceptions spelled out in this book, these ultimate matters are intensely personal as well as national and cultural. For all of them, it is important that the Jewish expressions of the ultimate meet criteria of sense, morality, and decency in conversation with others as well. This desire to be comprehensible to others in moral and philosophical and humanistic discourse is not to be identified with insecurity or lack of self-respect, but with the principle that all languages have some divine, or universal-human, source in common. Expressed in the classic language of Judaism: All humans are created in God's image, and all who abide by Noahide commandments (or standards) deserve moral dignity, appreciation, and reciprocity.

7. The Individual and the Community

The educated Jew, in all our models, has learned to value a dialectical relationship between his or her individuality and the community. The community is not viewed as threatening identity. Rather, it is the locus where identity is worked out and primarily articulated. Being community minded, either through the *ha-lakhah* or the moral-religious tradition that they explore together or through the commonwealth of Jews that gives them a particular identity, educated Jews wish their Jewish identity to be their public face whenever and wherever appropriate. They represent the community, always and everywhere, and hope to do so in an exemplary fashion. Religious models will view this feature of the educated Jew as bound up with the commandment of *Kiddush Hashem,* sanctifying God's name, while secularly oriented ones may speak here of pride.[11] At the same time, all can agree that there is not always a need, or even the urge, to articulate this representation. The educated Jew is secure enough to take for granted that love of his or her own language does not entail the constant need to say something on its behalf or to "put down" other languages.

8. Teaching Diligently

The educated Jew, loving the language, however understood, and swimming in a sea of Jewish literatures, feels the need to educate Jewishly. This is perceived not as an individual preference but as an obligation. The obligation may be a religious one, or it may flow from the sense that a Jewish presence in the world enriches human experience, or simply that Jewish existence is experienced as significant. The educated Jew may call this significance "mission" or "election" or historical treasure. S/he may simply be concerned that the civilization that Judaism represents not be erased from the mosaic of human spiritual options. In any case, s/he feels obliged to pass it on to children. They, in turn, will be invited to choose it and perhaps will gain the perspective that they "have no choice" but to themselves continue an historical chain of (Jewish) being.

9. Loyal Critique

The educated Jew does not see criticism of aspects of Jewish life as disloyal; rather, s/he may consider critique a kind of innovative or restorative literature that protects the language from abuse or restores its pristine value. The ideal image of Jewish life that the critic expresses may often conflict with the real situation. The educated Jew will wish to articulate criticism to others who are significant to him or her; and these, in turn, if educated Jews, will be expected not to interpret critique as disloyalty. If the prophetic model of critique is adopted, and indeed it appears appropriate to all our models, then only a blatant lack of identity and attachment reflected in the critique will be suspect, especially if the critique is directed at and addressed to those outside the family. That kind of criticism may be termed a *ḥillul Hashem* (profanation of God's name) or "spreading evil reports" (*hotza'at dibah*) among religious educated Jews, or, among secular-humanistic ones, undignified behavior that testifies to lack of self-respect.

10. Solving Jewish Problems

Finally, we may expect all educated Jews to have been given the desire to solve problems facing the Jewish people and to have learned appropriate competences. We will, of course, not expect ultra-Orthodox and secular Jews to have the same list of urgent problems and to adopt the same means of solution, but all can see in problem-solving deliberation an important aspect of Jewish literature. For some, it will be the most crucial aspect. Secular-minded models of the educated Jew will perhaps be most articulate about this aspect of teaching, but no model but the most quietistic can posit a conflict between locating and resolving the practical issues of the age and speaking Jewish language. Where such a conflict is implied, the comprehensiveness of Jewish language and literature is diminished or denied.

The most conservative elements of the Jewish community may well prefer to leave many problems (and their solutions) in the hands of "the others," and there is logic in that. For in the encounter with many problems and issues (including moral ones), there emerges a literature common to various languages. On this plane more obviously than on any other, languages are recognized to overlap. This is hardly an insight that *ḥaredi* education wishes to foster.

Yet there are theological options for understanding this phenomenon of overlapping languages that even ultra-Orthodoxy may beneficially explore — for example, those features of our tradition that speak of revealed language that is universal in principle and "invitations" to the Gentile world to seek an anchor in the Torah itself.[12] As for secular models, we may expect them to attribute a universally common literature of problem solving to common human needs and vulnerabilities.

The educated Jew throughout the various paradigms knows, of course, that there are issues and problems agitating Jews no less than other humans that do not, in principle, require Jewish literature, that do not depend on Jewish culture, and that suggest modes of action and standards of excellence learned from universal experience. Whether you know how to change a tire, for example, does not depend on your language. Barring ill health or other infirmity, one should know how to do it. Our children already think of the word "enter" to refer less to rooms than to computers, and most of us have had to learn how to use a "mouse" and how to look at "windows."

Nevertheless, those who champion the comprehensiveness of Jewish language may point to frames that are part and parcel of Jewish deliberation. For example, a halakhic Jew will note that one is commanded to help the weak and infirm to change tires and that, like "entering" on a computer, this action may not be done on Shabbat. A Zionist, perhaps more secular, paradigm will point to the national value of the return to normal physical concerns and consciousness that involves doing things that were formerly assigned to "the hands of Esau."

If we agree that among the greatest problems for which education should prepare us is the problem of ourselves — how we manage the time, including the leisure time, at our disposal; how we distinguish between the problems we can solve and those we have "to live with"; how we learn to love others and yet leave room for the love of self — then it becomes clear that problem solving has a great deal to do with what you adopt as your language and the literature that flows from it. And yet, all educated persons, speaking different though sometimes overlapping languages, should know how to spend a leisurely evening. Not all Jews will do this the same way — and certainly not all "civilized" people. This variety does not perturb the educated Jew. As a humanist s/he respects individuality; as a religionist s/he blesses God for having "diversified His creatures."

On the Plane of Practice: Is Community Feasible?

Up to this point, we have been searching for a common language for our various schools of educated Jews. In doing so, we have been skirting the borders between the mostly acknowledged common covenant of fate that R. Soloveitchik defined as binding Jews in their "aloneness" and the "covenant of destiny," of religious and cultural Jewish meanings and obligations.[13] We have found that in broadening the scope of the covenant of destiny to include those outside of our particular paradigm, we have had to embark on a search for a common core universe of intrinsic Jewish value. Have we uncovered one that makes a difference, or will the various educated Jews shun one another and move toward self-segregation?

It is a truism that within the often ethereal sphere of philosophy and theory, conflicts and dichotomies may be resolved simply by moving them to high levels of abstraction. When this is done, *commandments* more plausibly resemble *insights*; "election" looks like historical situatedness; and *Kiddush Hashem* translates facilely into (national) pride. The testing ground of such theoretical abstraction is, of course, in the realm of practice. Can the smooth resolutions of conflicts and dilemmas worked out on the plane of philosophy and theory actually be applied? What new and perhaps incorrigible problems become visible at the moment of application?

The practical problem, it must be admitted, begins with the very conception of community. We have found in our paradigms that all educated Jews live in communities and are dependent on them for cultural transmission. We have seen that even the secular model in our group of options is so community minded that it arrives at pessimistic conclusions about the viability of Jewish education – and life – in the Diaspora where there is no majority Jewish society, no public domain to carry and confirm significant Jewish cultural presence.

And yet, in fact, do most Jews today live in communities that can confirm Jewish culture and education, and that can bring people to conform to standards and obligations? Actually, no.

Traditionally, when people spoke of "the community," they meant a normative cultural and religious agenda. The agenda meant common practices and purposes. It carried with it the assumption that there are right and wrong ways to do things. It was self-understood that qualified authorities guided the communities. These authorities made the rules, interpreted them, enforced them. They spelled out what an educated person and an educated public[14] had to know and had to do.

Although for a small section of the Jewish people community remains the blatant social and existential reality, today that blatancy is exactly what alienates others. The concepts of identity, authority, and "agenda" seem to be so authoritarian in these traditional communities that they can be taken to demonstrate why *kehilot kodesh* – "holy communities" with agendas, authorities, and standards – are unacceptable to all who see themselves as living consciously in the modern world.

For most of the Jews, then, community can no longer be a coerced agenda. If they think of congenial community, they are most likely to think of it as a voluntary association that does not normally involve absolutely clear and

permanent commitments[15] because such commitments are associated by contemporary people with public coercion. Communal coercion is acceptable only
if it can be demonstrated to protect the broadest range of choice and the highest
degree of security for the individual.[16] Under most circumstances, however, it is
the individual who has to decide when and how to be associated with others.
The community of voluntary association has no self-understood authority and
thus no self-understood right to impose duties on individuals. If, then, duties
are nevertheless accepted by individuals in voluntary communities, they have a
different status than the kind of rules that used to be imposed by authorities.
They bespeak the integrity and good intentions of the one who abides by the
rules, not the sublime wisdom of external authority.

And so, the self-understood ideal for every educated Jew, that s/he live in the
community – whether halakhic, national, cultural or liberal-religious – becomes
a minefield as soon as we move the ideal from the realm of theory to that of
practical reality. And on the practical level, the possibility that Jews can share
a core covenant of destiny seems to recede; covenants are public, social, and
binding! What, then, do we have that may allow for some implementation of
the philosophical ideas we have been discussing?

Association and Agenda

What we still have, I believe, is a manifest desire on the part of most
educated Jews for community of association and for some agenda that those
associated will have in common. Those who "select themselves in" recognize (or
believe) that they don't *have* to belong, yet they wish to and see such association
as appropriate, as reflecting also the success of their Jewish education. They do
not wish to deny themselves participation in modern culture, but neither do
they wish to lose their Judaism. They are "in the middle" between what they
perceive as premodern Judaism and the postmodern consciousness of limitless
and rootless choice.

These Jews wish to be together and to do certain things together with other
Jews of their persuasion and paradigm. Yet they know that the common purpose
they have discovered for themselves, together with congenial others, cannot
be totally alienated from what other committed Jews do, and, conversely, that
their sense of community cannot be adequately defended and honestly cherished
without first moving it through the prism of pluralism. For they know about
themselves (and others) that they cherish the right to be themselves, even while
they work toward and within a community that has some common agenda. The
agenda they have in mind must somehow take into account such differences as
we have found among our paradigms of the educated Jew.

On a theoretical level, we have already discussed the drawbacks of basing
this pluralism only on the covenant of fate. We have warned that it made real

dialogue impossible, that it fostered well-intentioned paternalism on the one hand and alienation on the other hand. Now, on the practical level, we may add that a pluralism of fate is incorrigibly issue oriented: It imagines those who are spiritually outsiders to one another interacting (only) to find solutions to common problems. What shall they do when the problems are solved or seem simply to disappear?

And so we return to the question that previously engaged us theoretically: Are there still things that Jews "in the middle" take for granted Jewishly, that they hold dear, that they will defend at all costs, matters that distinguish, yet without pretension or pomposity, between "Israel and the nations"? Is there still a realm in which we engage in collective activity and controversy "for the sake of Heaven," that is, within a Jewish universe of discourse? Are we enough of an educated public that we know what we are arguing about and how an education we can all recognize as legitimate moves us toward it? Is there anything toward which we can still educate together?

(It should be clear that the practical difficulties we have now encountered have circumscribed our working concept of community. We have limited it to "those in the middle" whose philosophical reservations and orientation we have had to take into account. We shall, however, come back to the significance of this for the relationships between the ultra-Orthodox [*haredi*] and the non-*haredi* sectors of the Jewish people.)

I am suggesting that no matter how fragile it often appears to be, there is still a common cultural language, a kind of "plausibility structure" among Jews. Here I will briefly note four features of it that can create common ground for educated Jews along the continuum: from the halakhic-philosophical to the liberal humanist models.[17]

The first is a possible communal approach to the study of the sacred literature of Judaism. This literature may be defined as exposing to view our language of Jewish culture and spirit in a primary and foundational way. For this reason, sacred or classic literature has traditionally been believed to deal with the most important things, to delve profoundly into origins and ends – in short, to treat of ultimate matters. It was studied in depth and was believed to be "deep." Although one of our models of the educated Jew recommends somewhat limiting instruction in this material to make room for later literatures, it remains valued within this model, too.

It is true that contemporary Jews no longer agree how it should be studied, what it demands, and by what authority it can demand anything at all. But educated Jews throughout our models still find it legitimate and enriching to open these books, and to discover points of contact among themselves that come to light when they learn together. They still view these books as singularly theirs. The sociologist Charles Liebman once noted that there is no Jewish community on record that ceased studying Torah yet survived. On a theoretical level, it might be maintained that one cannot learn Torah together without sharing a belief about what it includes, how one shall understand it, and what courses of action it prescribes. And yet here practical wisdom and experience may be kinder than theory. Those who have studied together without demanding too much in advance, of themselves or their fellows, have discovered great teachers, surprisingly engaging texts, and conversations and complexities never anticipated that changed them.

The second avenue for a common agenda is in the articulation of a common vocabulary of Jewish life. The publicist and thinker of cultural Zionism, Ahad Ha-Am, spelled this out lucidly. In a short and concise essay entitled "*Bein Kodesh ve-Hol*" ("Between the Sacred and the Profane"), he argued that sacred matters are to be identified with these cultural artifacts that do not shed their shell (or framework) even when their contents change. For example, the term "Shabbat" remains sacred even when its particular historical content as a day of rest changes. Likewise, the Torah remains forever within its shell of parchment and handwritten verses, although the "Oral Torah" reflects its changing contents, its evolving ideals and norms.

In the spirit of Ahad Ha-Am's conception: A common sacred vocabulary may delineate what we share and what we may then explore together. It will make a lot of difference, I believe, whether Jews refer to the Bible as *Tanakh* or as the Old Testament. It is significant whether they refer to *Motzei Shabbat* or to Saturday night. This is so mainly because language, even as lexicon, invites so many associations that it determines how we see the artifacts to which it refers. After all, the Old Testament must be followed by a New; and if we look for an Old Testament in the library rather than a *Tanakh*, we shall find an un-tanakhic arrangement of the books that conveys a Christian message.[18] Similarly, one cannot possibly say, without being quite ridiculous, that Saturday night begins this week at 7:42, although it makes eminently good sense to refer to *Motzei Shabbat* in this way. And as our Yiddish- and Ladino-speaking forebears well knew, the lexicon does not even have to be in Hebrew. Imagine a Jew being told that "Shabbat comes in at 6:24"; accordingly, at that precise moment, he looks to the door to observe Shabbat coming in. There is obvious cultural illiteracy here, not because the individual is uncultured but because he or she lives in a different vocabulary. Those who live in diverse vocabularies will find it difficult to build a common community. Different kinds of educated Jews do, at least, understand what the others are saying.

An interesting and significant project for community educators is to determine what the basic vocabulary of community is and to explore some of the ramifications and spin-offs of its various terms. If we were to write down 100 value-concepts couched in specific words or phrases, what would we learn from them? What further explorations would become accessible to us?[19]

A third possibility for creating and possessing a core universe for a pluralistic yet common agenda is in the realm of carefully considered community practice. Here we may expect matters to become far more complicated than with regard to vocabulary or even study. In fact, however, practice may itself be viewed, certainly by the less normative types of educated Jews, as a kind of vocabulary and even a kind of learning. It is a conversation involving such terms as Shabbat, *tzedakah* (charity), and kashrut. It raises such questions as: What kinds of activities are or are not conducted by the community on Shabbat? Is shrimp ever allowed on the premises of our community center? Does the community maintain a kosher kitchen?

When I say that matters here invariably become more sticky, it is because common practice readily appears to be a string of concessions to the more traditional members of the community. In operative terms, we may say that some of these practices are unlikely to be adopted unless or until the traditionalists suggest or even demand them as a condition for their association. Yet there is another side to the coin: namely, that the community is unlikely to adopt these practices unless the traditionalists agree to throw in their lot with the less normative members and sectors of the community. The traditionalists must also make a concession: to be less "denominational" and more communal. In a sense, everybody has to do so, for everyone has to pay a price for community. A common language of practice, too, emerges when people study together and use a common vocabulary. A continual negotiation goes on because members of the community wish to say certain things to their comembers, who indeed wish to be heard by them. And one who wishes to be heard has to take the capacity and willingness of others to listen into account.

The fourth feature of common community practice is one in which the theoretical and the practical are unlikely to clash, namely, the joint goal of identifying problems and dealing with them. For this feature of the agenda speaks to all educated Jews anchored in the covenant of fate. Yet it quickly grows beyond it in practice, because the ability and willingness to deal with Jewish problems arises not only out of anxiety but also caring. Caring is a fundamental feature of all that educated Jews of different persuasions can do together.

In this aspect of the agenda, we find that the community that learns, speaks, and acts together is one that cares about Jews and their problems. Today, for better or for worse, the problems of Jews are manifold. There is the problem of expressing "particularistic" Jewish concerns in the face of an alleged universalism (often, someone else's particularism) and, conversely, the problem of defending universal concerns in the (particularistic) Jewish contexts of Israel and Jewish communities. There are problems of ecology in Israel, where it has, happily, become a specifically Jewish problem, and elsewhere, where Jews, together with others, have the duty to protect environments and the right to breathe freely.

Two Stories About Concern

We have said that the key to moving beyond the covenant of fate, even with regard to the "fate-oriented" community activity of problem solving, revolves around active empathy and concern, around *ahavah* (love) and *ḥesed* (kindness). For communities struggling to identify a common language, although they operate with different ideal types of the educated Jew, such concern refers not only to the community, to the protection of its members and to its own survival, but to relations between individuals and groups within and without, who seem adamantly different yet wish to find themselves in some cultural proximity and some existential kinship to one another.

Here I shall elucidate with two examples. Both are about concern, and both happen to deal with religious Jews who are very sure about their communities, and their relationship to "the others." And they are very different.

In 1959, there was a heated debate in the Knesset about an educational program proposed by the minister of education, Zalman Aranne. Entitled "Jewish Consciousness," it was meant to impart love and appreciation for the Jewish tradition among pupils whose homes were largely nontraditional and who studied at nonreligious (i.e., non-Orthodox) state schools. Some Knesset members belonging to religious parties declared in that debate that there was actually no problem, or rather that they had the solution. They suggested that instead of instituting a "pathetic" program of Jewish Consciousness in the state schools, the minister should change the secular school system by instituting the curriculum of the state religious (i.e., Orthodox) schools in all of them. Then, happily, all Jewish Consciousness programs would become superfluous.

It sounded like caring but, of course, it was merely polemic and triumphalist one-upmanship, not a genuine community conversation. After all, the families of the pupils for whom the Jewish Consciousness program was devised were not going to change their lifestyles, their convictions, or their search for Jewish meanings in their own way. The religious Knesset members who refused to see that were refusing to engage in a conversation of concern and community. They could not put themselves in the place of the other, which allowed them to bask in judgmental bliss.

My second and reverse example has at its center a Jew who, at the time of the episode, represented the ultra-Orthodox *Poalai Agudat Yisrael* (*Agudat Yisrael* workers) party on the Israel Broadcasting Authority. This is the way it was told to me by Dr. Hanoch Rinott, the first director of the Hebrew University's Melton Centre for Jewish Education:

When television was first introduced into the country, a fierce debate ensued in the Authority as to whether there should be television broadcasts on Friday evening on the one existing (state-sponsored) channel. And, of course, the view of the religious parties represented on the Authority was that such a desecration of the Sabbath should not be permitted. The secular members were naturally annoyed and incensed. They turned to the religious representatives and said, "It's all very well for you to oppose television broadcasting on Shabbat, but we live in a culture that naturally associates recreation with electronics. Now you religious people have this quaint notion that the use of electricity is taboo on the Sabbath and yet you think that by virtue of activating a timer ["Shabbat clock"] you can have your electric cake and eat it, too. But we are not party to such notions and we want to spend our day of rest as we wish."

At that point, the *Poalai Agudat Yisrael* member indicated that he understood. "I realize," he said, "that some of my fellow citizens are bored on Friday nights and television may change that. I cannot, as an observant Orthodox Jew, vote for television, because its use on Shabbat certainly is proscribed by the *halakhah*. But if I abstain from the vote, can you guarantee – or at least promise – that the programs offered on Friday nights will have a spiritual content that differs from weekday fare?"[20]

This man had a sense of community. He could not vote with the secular parties, but the problems of other Jews were in some way his problems; he asked himself how his view and that of the others might be bridged. He thought that even the secular members wanted to have a different atmosphere prevailing in Israel on Shabbat. He cared about what he perceived as the dilemma of the secular people, who, though not perturbed by halakhic problems associated with electricity, also "wanted to have their Jewish cake and eat it."

Our discussion of the practical aspects of Jewish commonality in the face of diverse paradigms of the educated Jew led us to the conclusion that, realistically, the ultra-Orthodox would not be able to participate in the consciousness of communities "in the middle." How, then, is even the covenant of fate to be preserved? How is care to be expressed across the divide? It seems plausible to suggest that while "the middle" and the (religiously) right cannot ever generally function as one community in the realm of destiny, they can remain in close and concerned touch.

Here, additional aspects and attributes of the educated Jew must come to light and be spelled out: that, for example, no one, wherever located on the continuum of the educated Jew, will agree to stereotype the others, and that everyone will cherish Jewish caring, undoubtedly most widespread in the *haredi* community,[21] wherever it is called for.

When unable to learn Torah together, they will yet wish to know what the other is doing that can further their own sense of community and their own education. (It would be interesting to examine how much *haredi* Torah study has been affected by the hermeneutics of the modern Orthodox scholar Nechama Leibowitz, or how pietistic and mystical approaches within the *haredi* community have affected existential explorations into the tradition in postmodern Jewish thinking.)

The concept of concern as a key concept for the translation of scholarly portraits of the educated Jew into educational endeavors that go beyond each one of them may be variously grounded. It may be a theological concept; or a halakhic one of *kol Yisrael arevim zeh la-zeh* ("All Israelites are responsible for one another"); or a humanistic one that allows the strong to recognize himself in the weak; or a religious–moral one that places the Jewish person in God's Presence, demanding that s/he assume responsibility for "the other" because of the text and sometimes, subtly, beyond it.

S. Y. Agnon, perhaps the greatest Israeli writer of the century just ended, seems to have put all of these together in his "*Kaddish* for those who have fallen in the land of Israel." Here is an appreciation for all encompassed in the notion of fate, but it includes God, Who, too, as it were, requires our care. Here is a sense of community that transcends specific ideologies but is linked to the Land of Israel. Here is "religiosity," but also a secularized irony. We can expect the text, "Before the *Kaddish*: At the Funeral of Those Who Were Killed in the Land of Israel," to appear in the *beit midrash* of every type of educated Jew, perhaps as one that they can study together:

> When a king of flesh and blood goes forth to war against his enemies, he leads out his soldiers to slay and to be slain. It is hard to say, does he love his soldiers, doesn't he love his soldiers, do they matter to him, don't they matter to him. But even if they do matter to him, they are as good as dead, for the Angel of Death is close upon the heels of everyone who goes off to war, and accompanies him only to slay him. When the soldier is hit ... and slain, they put another man in his place, and the king hardly knows that someone is missing – for the population of the nations of the world is big and their troops are many. If one man is slain, the king has many others to make up for him.
>
> But our king, the King of kings of kings, the Holy One, blessed be He, is a king who delights in life, who loves peace and pursues peace, and loves His people Israel, and He chose us from among all the nations: not because we are a numerous folk did He set His love upon us, for we are the fewest of all people. But because of the love He loves us with and we are so few, each and every one of us matters as much before Him as a whole legion, for He hasn't many to put in our place. When from Israel one is missing, God forbid, a diminishing takes place in the King's legions, and in His kingdom, blessed be He, there is a decline of strength, as it were, for His kingdom now lacks one of its legions, and His grandeur, blessed be He, has been diminished, God forbid.
>
> That is why for every dead person in Israel we recite the prayer "Magnified and sanctified be His great Name." ... May He establish His sovereignty so that His kingdom be perfectly revealed and visible,

and may it suffer no diminishing, God forbid. In our lifetime and in your days and in the lifetime of the whole house of Israel speedily and soon – for if His sovereignty is manifest in the world, there is peace in the world and blessing in the world and song in the world . . . and the holy ones, Israel, are beloved in the world and His grandeur continues to grow and increase and never diminishes.

If this is what we recite in prayer over any who die, how much the more over our beloved and sweet brothers and sisters, the dear children of Zion, those killed in the Land of Israel, whose blood was shed for the glory of His blessed Name and for His people and His land and His heritage. And what is more, everyone who dwells in the Land of Israel belongs to the legion of the King of kings of kings, the Holy One, blessed be He, whom the King appointed watchmen of His palace. When one of His legion is slain, He has no others, as it were, to put in his place.

Therefore, brethren of the whole house of Israel, all you who mourn in this mourning, let us fix our hearts on our Father in heaven, Israel's king and redeemer, and let us pray for ourselves and for Him too, as it were: Magnified and sanctified be His great Name in the world which He created as He willed. . . .[22]

How each educated Jew will study Agnon's reflection and prayer may tell us how each paradigm differs – and perhaps, too, what they have in common.

NOTES

1 This category of questions was, to my knowledge, first proposed by Seymour Fox, "*Prolegomenon le-Filosofiyah shel Ḥinukh Yehudi*," in *Kivunim Rabim: Kavanah Aḥat* (Jerusalem: School of Education of the Hebrew University and Ministry of Education, 1968), 145–54.

2 Michael Rosenak, *Roads to the Palace: Jewish Texts and Teaching* (Providence and Oxford: Berghan Books, 1995), Chapter 2.

3 Thomas F. Green, "A Topology of the Teaching Concept," *Studies in Philosophy and Education* 3:4 (1964–65): 308–12.

4 Gershom G. Scholem, "Three Types of Jewish Piety," *Ariel, Review of Arts and Letters in Israel* 32 (1973): 5–24. In Hebrew: "*Sheloshah Tippusim shel Yir'at Shamayim Yehudit*," *Devarim Bego,* Vol. 2 (Tel Aviv: Am Oved, 1975), 541–56.

5 Michael Rosenak, "Towards a Curriculum for the Modern Orthodox School," in *Orthodoxy Confronts Modernity*, ed. Rabbi Jonathan Sacks (Hoboken, NJ: Ktav Publishing House, 1991), 62–80.

6 This is not likely to be true with regard to the ultra-Orthodox community, since it is not comfortable with the possibility of diverse "literatures" of Judaism. We shall return to this problem.

7 See Samuel C. Heilman and Steven M. Cohen, *Cosmopolitans and Parochials: Modern Orthodox Jews in America* (Chicago and London: The University of Chicago

Press, 1989), Chapter 4. In Israel, the reservations of the Orthodox community are tempered by the common Jewish civic attachments and security needs.

8   On these two covenants, see Rabbi Joseph B. Soloveitchik, *"Kol Dodi Dofek,"* in *Ish haEmunah* (Jerusalem: Tal Orot, 5743), especially, 43–47. The book was published in English as *Fate and Destiny: From Holocaust to the State of Israel* (Hoboken, NJ: Ktav Publishing House, 2000).

9   For example, Zionism, as a spiritual as well as political program.

10 These "universal" concerns include, of course, moral, philosophical, and humanistic issues.

11 Both will claim, from their varying perspectives, that *Kiddush Hashem* and "pride" are not identical, and they may resent what they view as reductionist attempts to equate them. Here we note that the problem of "translation," from concepts situated in one universe of discourse to those in another one, is a live issue even within the (total) Jewish community itself.

12 On this, see Menachem Hirshman, *Torah le-Kol Ba'ei Olam* (Tel Aviv: HaKibbutz HaMeuḥad, 1999).

13 *"Kol Dodi Dofek,"* 43–47.

14 For an enlightening description of an "educated public" as one that can actively participate in cultural interchange and inquiry and that shares texts and assumptions, see Alasdair C. MacIntyre, "The Idea of an Educated Public," in *Education and Values,* the Richard Peters Lectures, Institute of Education (London: University of London, 1985), 15–36.

15 Modern Orthodoxy is different, considering community to be part and parcel of the halakhic commitment. Yet even the Modern Orthodox are conscious of having chosen their absolute commitments.

16 So far at least, the public Jewish education in Israel, required by law, is understood in this way, as is compulsory service in the Israeli Defense Forces.

17 This does not mean that all Jews, of differing convictions, will necessarily study or act together in the ways discussed here. Rather, that within their own communities, they cultivate the activities important to all of them, and even, *because* they are important to all of them. It also implies a willingness, where this is feasible, to do things together.

18 A fascinating if somewhat unnerving pinpointing of the difference between the *Tanakh* and the "Old Testament," even with regard to the arrangement of its books, is Jack Miles, *God: A Biography* (New York: Vintage Books, 1996), "Prelude," 8–24.

19 In this connection, I am fond of the classic joke of the Jewish gentleman who walks into a restaurant that, unknown to him, has passed from Jewish to Gentile proprietorship. As he sits down, a waiter appears to take his order. The customer says, "Well, this week is the nine days, so I can't have meat and will have to have something 'milky.' So would you bring me a nice piece of fish?" The waiter rushes into the kitchen to report on a madman in the restaurant: "He says there are nine days this week so he can't eat meat but only milk and that I should bring him fish!" This joke, based on an incommunicability between different "language speakers," opens many interesting opportunities for vocabulary learning. What are "the nine days"? What is Tishah b'Av? What can it mean to contemporary Jews? And so on, through kashrut to the difficulty of sharing ideas across "language barriers."

20 I am told that the promise was given, but not kept.
21 Results of a journalistic study in 2000 indicated that while 15% of the secular public in Israel are engaged in volunteeristic charitable work, 45% of the *ḥaredi* public engage in such enterprises. This includes charitable activities that benefit the entire community, such as hospital meals (*glatt* kosher, of course) served indiscriminately to Jews and Arabs of all religious or nonreligious orientations. *The Jerusalem Report,* February 14, 2000, Vol. X, No. 21, p. 22.
22 S. Y. Agnon, "Before the *Kaddish*: At the Funeral of Those Who Were Killed in the Land of Israel," in *The Jewish Expression,* ed. Judah Goldin (New Haven and London: Yale University Press, 1976), 469–70.

Supplement: Michael Rosenak

Michael Rosenak's writing, teaching, and curricula have influenced Jewish education in the Modern Orthodox community and beyond.[1] Rosenak has persistently searched for a language and approach that would make it possible for Jews of different ideologies to recognize that they are one community.

In our project, he asked the other scholars to consider these questions: How do conceptions of Jewish education prepare learners to respect and cooperate with Jews whose education differs from theirs? What are the characteristics that any vision of Jewish education must seek to cultivate in students that will enable them to live with Jews who have different ideological commitments? Can there be a vision for Jewish education that is acceptable to various groups within the community? Are there elements common to all conceptions of Jewish education? How could educators, community leaders, and rabbis of different denominations be guided by these common elements in such areas as curriculum and pedagogy?

For some of the educators, these questions were profoundly troubling, highlighting their fear that the commitment of all Jews to the value of Jewish peoplehood was dwindling. For others, the opportunity to explore pluralism in Jewish life was inspiring. Often the discourse among Jewish groups becomes politicized or devolves into a "conversation among the deaf." Rosenak's contribution offered a fresh perspective. In response, many participants were more willing to try harder to accommodate one another than they would have thought.

Some educators focused on the prospect of a shared "Jewish civics" curriculum for all Jewish schools. Rosenak's work on common elements encouraged others to consider developing educational "indicators" through which programs in Jewish educational institutions could be assessed and compared. The indicators would consist of common topics (e.g., the Jewish past, the Hebrew language) and areas (e.g., early childhood education, adult education).

The educators also studied Rosenak's argument that the Modern Orthodox community should, in its educational program, demonstrate a concern for non-Orthodox Jews. Rosenak develops this approach in his discussion of the "realms" of Modern Orthodox education, particularly that of *da'at*, understanding.

From "Towards a Curriculum for the Modern Orthodox School"[2]

> We suggest that the realms which lay foundations for a comprehensive religious Jewish education are the following:
>
> > *Knesset Yisrael,* the community of Israel
> > *Adam,* or "existence"
> > *Bnai Noach,* or humanity
> > Problem-solving, or what Rabbi Soloveitchik has called *hod*
> > Beauty, or *chochmat lev* and *hiddur*
> > *Da'at,* or understanding
>
> Let us briefly outline several foci of each "realm."

1. The realm of *Knesset Yisrael* has to do with the initiation of the young person into the Jewish people, his/her socialization into the religious-national fellowship of Israel. In this context or realm we teach "the language of the *halakhah*"; we attempt to make this language a self-understood medium of cultural and spiritual life. The goods of *Knesset Yisrael* include the Hebrew language, habits of learning Torah, and a readiness to both respond to it and to represent it; as well as "at-homeness" in the text-cycle, in the life-cycle of the Jewish people, and in its land, Eretz Yisrael. In the framework of this realm of meaning, young people learn to signal "naturally" in the language of Judaism. They understand what is meant by such questions as "Have you *davened* [prayed] yet?" "Can you have coffee (with milk)?" "What does Rashi say?" and they respond to them with what we may call "cultural reliability," i.e., they answer within the limits set by halakhic Judaism (e.g., either they have *already* or *not yet* davened. For they are truly members of the covenant community, under the aegis of what I have elsewhere called "explicit religion,"[3] that corpus of religious norm and cultural reality that preceded them into the world and that imposes itself upon them. As for the educating community, it sees itself as the agent whereby God links the young person to the covenant of Torah.

2. The realm of *adam,* or existence, is concerned with the *individual,* who, like every human being, was created singly. For him or her was the world created, but the young person does not yet know what that means and what to *do* with it and what to *make* of it. So the young person must find him/herself. Here, therefore, we are concerned with the questions children ask more than with the answers they are taught: the curriculum of *adam* is geared to arouse these questions. In this realm, the "existential" aspects of Torah are emphasized: first, stories of interesting heroes who will later be seen as complex; eventually *Tehillim* [Psalms], Job, and *Kohelet* [Ecclesiastes]. In the realm of *Knesset Yisrael,* we teach *halakhah,* but in the realm of *adam,* we speak the language of *aggadah* [nonlegal rabbinic literature], teaching "readiness" for mature religious thought.

Poetry, from everywhere, releases powers of reflection and unlocks stores of empathy; children are permitted to think, dream, and express themselves in sundry ways. The school provides for music listening at leisure, for making things to coax forth what has been called "the fun of handling materials." In this realm, the guiding principles are those of what I have called "implicit religion"[4] – i.e., the search of the person for God, addressing Him in his/her life in ways that are connected to the realm of *Knesset Yisrael,* or so we anticipate if we have adequately utilized this realm to intimate a Jewish theology of human existence, but which are irreducible to the norms of the community. For each person is a unique individual.

3. The realm of *bnai Noach,* of humanity, is designed to make children see themselves as members of the human family, sharing a planet, a physical and psychic structure, a common fate, common createdness in God's image. In the realm of *bnai Noach* we teach ethics, but also ecology. We reach toward an understanding of mankind through social studies, but also teach foreign languages and world literature, hoping to expand horizons and to make it clear that while there are times when our differences are of cardinal importance, there are also moments where the loving, the suffering, and the striving of people create human kinships that make these differences insignificant. And so, if the realm of *Knesset Yisrael* gives the child bases and understanding of commandment, the realm of *bnai Noach* intimates redemption. Introduced to the condition of mankind within the framework of Torah, the child will not be able to feel that he or she "has nothing to do with it" and that this is "the best of all possible worlds." Rather, it will appear to be waiting for *yimot Hamashiach* [the Messianic era], for which one must pray and work, of which one may not despair lest the moral sense be eroded by cynicism. Thus, on the ethical level this realm presents the child with the tension reflected in the controversy between Rabbi Akiva and Ben Azzai as to "the great principle of the Torah." The realm of *Knesset Yisrael* suggests R. Akiva's "Love thy neighbor [fellow Jew] as thyself"; Ben Azzai's principle is both more universal and more theological: "These are the generations of man [*all* men!] . . . for in the image of God He created him."[5]

4. The realm of problem-solving is, of course, the realm of science in both its theoretical and practical aspects. Since activities in this realm are guided by and based upon scientific modes of thinking (e.g., creation of hypotheses on the basis of the inadequacy of previous ways of understanding, experimentation, and other problem-appropriate forms of inquiry, as well as proposing tentative solutions), they raise serious questions for religious educational philosophy. A crucial one is: can young people be educated to a normative allegiance, of the kind characterizing the realm of *Knesset Yisrael,* and at the same time be initiated into a culture of authentic inquiry and deliberation? For the former posits *a priori* truths and the latter insists on testing and keeping an open mind. This difficulty tempts religious educators to either minimize the teaching of science, reducing it to its mechanical and technological aspects (thereby "hiding" the philosophical problems), or to compartmentalize religion and science as "Jewish" and "general." Yet the theology of either approach raises more problems than it solves; the former undermines wholeness *in the name of wholeness,* and the latter creates precisely the differentiation which leads to a secular orientation, which assumes that all "real" problems have scientific solutions. The key to a solution would seem to lie in a conception of the religious Jew's relationship to the created world and humanity's place both in and, via understanding, in a sense also "above" it. The conception of the "community of majesty" proposed by Rabbi Joseph B. Soloveitchik, seems like a large step in the right direction.[6]

5. The realm of *chochmat lev* and *hiddur,* of beauty, introduces in the curriculum the dimension of aesthetics, both appreciated and made. In this realm children learn to listen carefully to music and to look competently at art. They learn to admire the structure of mathematical formulae and to "see" how a literary work or a *suggya* [lit., topic] is "constructed." In this part of the curriculum children learn to enjoy playing, not as something childish to be outgrown but as an important dimension of life, where one tests and expands one's powers within "the rules of the game." In the realm of *chochmat lev* one gets the "sense" of how things "out in the world" connect to the inner life and light of individuals who then *give back into the world* by good performance. In this context, Bezalel "saw," even better than Moshe Rabbainu, what God had shown regarding the *mishkan* [Tabernacle] (Brachot 55a). Even more ordinary mortals learn, through prayer, that God, who gives us the power of speech, is asked to "open our lips" so that we may praise Him. We take the sights and sounds and forms of the world which are given to us, we cultivate and distill, reaching an understanding of why we must bless God for what is beautiful and why we must perform mitzvot with *hiddur.* And as God has given us a world for which we bless Him, He has given us bodies which we can learn to use gracefully and powerfully, and for this health and beauty we are grateful.

This is a realm which requires careful development in Jewish educational thought. (One possible approach to its most problematic dimension, art, is suggested by Rabbi Abraham I. Kook, in his letter upon the opening of the Bezalel School in Jerusalem [1907].)[7] In any case, even though aspects of this realm appear to be situated on the edge of "Greek wisdom" and therefore were often restricted and neglected, they cannot on that account be shunted aside in the Modern Orthodox school. Beauty and a sensitivity which "sees" and creatively responds to God's creation has surely been given to "every person," and we "find" them readily in the Torah.[8]

6. The realm of *da'at*, of understanding, is, like [Philip] Phenix's "synoptics," concerned with large and comprehensive ways of "seeing the whole picture." In his conception, it is related to the study of history, religion, and philosophy. In our scheme, too, this realm is meant "to put things together," to enable students to see and make connections between *halakhah* and *aggadah*; to "see the point" of diverse activities like scientific inquiry and literature; to build structures of insight and concepts regarding the relationship between Judaism and other faiths, between Israel and the nations. In the realm of *da'at*, the sense of meaning and relationship is fostered by study, reflection, and discussion. Clearly, activities stimulating children to "see the point" are also designed for "seeing the problems." Before one can put "realms of meaning" together, one must, to avoid apologetics and pseudo-philosophizing, discover the tensions within and between them. For example, who in our generation can ignore the dilemma, within the realm of *Knesset Yisrael,* between the demand for loyalty to Torah and the imperative to maintain the unity of *Am Yisrael* [the Jewish people] and to foster kinship and a sense of community with every Jew? And, that there are tensions *between* realms is obvious. What about the *adam, within* us, or amongst our pupils, who is uncomfortable with a given norm of *Knesset Yisrael*? Or, how much are we *Knesset Yisrael* and how much *bnai Noach* – and how much contact with "the others" is too much?

If the educational process is successful, there will be, as a result of it, a degree of integration. Through the realm of *da'at*, represented in the curriculum by subjects such as *Machshevet Yisrael* [Jewish philosophy], *parshanut* [commentary], study of *ta'amai hamitzvot* [rationales of the commandments] and philosophy (including issues in scientific thought!), students may learn not only to "see the point" of diverse activities, but to build into their personalities points of contact between them. They may discover not only the possibilities inherent in each realm, but how each enriches the other and how each sets limits to the others. (For example, there is "non-kosher" art; there are unaesthetic – therefore unpleasant and wrong – ways to perform *mitzvot*.) Learning about the interrelationship between realms even while comprehending what constitutes the integrity of each is learning to be one person who can do many things.[9] *Da'at* has to do with becoming a whole person!

But from the realm of *da'at* we also learn that, ultimately, wholeness is not a matter of knowing *about* the world, or being able to explain why something is beautiful or even knowing reasons for the *mitzvot*. It is *being in the world* in a certain way, *having* beauty in the soul, *being a Torah person. Da'at,* Rashi tells us, is *ruaḥ hakodesh* [divine inspiration].[10] It is not what schools teach but what they prepare us for. It cannot be explained to the end, and the explanations are not what count.

Peter Winch has said something important about this, in his description of the "limits" of philosophy.

> If one looks at a certain style of life and asks what there is in it which makes it worthwhile, one will find nothing there. One may indeed describe it in terms which bring out "what one sees in it," but the use of these terms already presupposes that one does see it from a perspective from which it matters. The words will fall flat on the ears of someone who does not occupy such a perspective even though he is struggling to attain it. . . .
>
> . . . what a man makes of the possibilities he can comprehend is a matter of what man he is. This is revealed in the way he lives; it is revealed *to him* in his understanding of what he can and what he cannot attach importance to. But philosophy can no more show a man what he should attach importance to than geometry can show a man where he should stand.[11]

Haredim [the ultra-Orthodox] would applaud Winch's words. Haven't they always said that the Modern Orthodox, going back to Hirsch, "explain too much"? What is needed, they say, is a community, without which schools cannot educate, because certain kinds of people are only "made" in certain kinds of communities, which have leaders, *gedolim,* who *are* Torah people and not only *know* a lot of Torah. A *da'at Torah* requires no *asmachta* [verse cited as support of an argument, but not as a prooftext]. I think they are right about that.

Yet on the road to understanding there are no short-cuts, and those who are modern have a better sense of how much ground there is to cover than those who are not. Can we and our schools walk that road together, as a modern religious community that values both wisdom and *yirat Shamayim* [fear of heaven], that holds fast to Torah more than all because there is no real *da'at* or *yir'ah* [fear] for us without it? That, it seems, is the underlying educational question.

The educators believed that Rosenak's application of his ideas to the realities of a particular movement could be illuminating for the broader Jewish community. It is often assumed that Jewish tradition and pluralistic values are largely antithetical – that those who want to teach pluralistic values must either reject significant portions of the tradition or use outside sources as a basis for these values. One result has been a compartmentalized curriculum in settings such as Jewish day schools, where pluralistic values are taught in the general curriculum without application to the Jewish community, and Jewish values are taught through Judaic studies, without any application to matters of pluralism.

Rosenak, in contrast, suggests that respect for diversity within the community is a Jewish value, and that a Jewish pluralist education can be based on traditional sources. He also demonstrates how a dialogue between traditional and other Jewish groups might allow Orthodox Jews to preserve their identity within the Jewish community while advocating the importance of the tradition to other Jews.[12]

In the following essay, originally delivered in 1996 at a conference on Jewish education, Rosenak draws on sociological categories and insights to look at the challenges posed by open societies to religious education. He bypasses the defensive or apologetic strategies that religious educators sometimes adopt, suggesting instead a response that permits members of religious communities to participate actively in those societies without a threat to their religious values. In Rosenak's view, such encounters allow religious people to learn and grow in their religious lives, to discover allies for their causes from beyond their inner circle, and to contribute the best of their worlds for the good of all.

From "Religious Education in an Open Society"[13]

The "open" or "neutral" society that characterizes modern liberal states constitutes a dual challenge for religious people and for the religious education they wish to impart to their children. The challenge is dual, first, because the open society insists on viewing religious conviction as one choice among many available to its members, and second, because the neutral society has its own subtle norms and expectations. These are based on the assumption that significance and commitment are intrinsically variegated and "open," an assumption that is itself often identified with a secular ethos.

The religious person is therefore called upon to live a religious life in a secularized environment that insists that such a life is no more than one option, chosen not for its self-evident truth but, rather, for the inherent meaning believers hope to discover in its patterns of obligation and its promise of redemption. The open society therefore transforms what was once a social and self-understood normative demand (for obedience, discipline and loyalty) into an existential decision, a personal choice. This is a radically new situation for religious persons, and it affects the ways in which religion functions.[14]

Before we discuss how religion "functions" and educates in an open society, we may ask: What actually makes a society "open"? Is it, as its enemies claim, the datum that "everything goes," that people may do whatever they wish? Most of its adherents will consider that a libel, and will insist that social and moral chaos is not representative of free societies at their best but a corruption of their essence.

What then characterizes the open society? Let us leave aside its outstanding political manifestation, which is democratic, and dwell briefly on two of its central social and moral features.

Honor and Dignity. The first feature may well be described in terms suggested by the sociological theory of Peter Berger, Brigitte Berger and Hansfried Kellner.

These scholars distinguish between honor and dignity, as categories of existence.[15] Honor, as they explain the term, refers to the sense one has of oneself as a member of society and what is "expected" of one, what "the honorable thing to do" is. . . . Honor is concerned with "acting properly" and the shame associated with not doing so. . . .

The authors posit that when honor was debunked, the modern sense of dignity was born: When the disguises behind which we hide our common humanity were removed, we discovered our freedom and our rights "irrespective of race, creed and color" or of sex and social status. . . . Whereas honor "implies that identity is essentially and importantly linked to institutional roles, the modern concept of dignity implies that identity is essentially independent of them." Where dignity reigns, honor is decried as unauthentic. . . .

Needless to say, the open society is both the product and the protector of dignity, and it cultivates a distrust of honor. But this (at times veiled) animosity to honor makes the social fabric of the free society fragile and threatens not only social but even individual identity. As Berger, Berger and Kellner point out, the loss of honor means that institutions become unstable and ultimately "unreal." Consequently, "the individual is thrown back on himself, on his own subjectivity, from which he must dredge up the meaning and the stability that he requires to exist." Since we are social beings, this is a problematic state of affairs. A life of undiluted dignity often leads to Erich Fromm's celebrated "Escape from Freedom."[16] That is, having given up the institutions of society and the "honorable" patterns that maintain them, people are likely to run away from their solitude, to seek release from the solitary "search for meaning" by embracing totalitarian movements and states. These frameworks only too gladly impose honor. They ride roughshod over their enemies, namely, their own citizens, who have found dignity without honor to be "too much for them."

The paradox, therefore, is that one must be liberated from honor in order to have the inner freedom of a dignified individual existence, and at the same time, a life without honor makes stable social existence untenable. The open society, which is proud of its members' dignity, is confronted by this paradox, but it cannot easily relinquish its distrust of those who point this out. There always lurks a suspicion that the yearning for honor is romantic and reactionary, that honor cannot be restored without artificiality and without the surrender of inner freedom.

Religious individuals and communities are often the objects of this fear. Because they appear as the custodians of honor, they are suspected of being enemies of dignity. This goes far towards explaining why the open society, which in principle is hospitable to many existential options, may yet look upon "organized religion" and religious people as subtly or even blatantly subversive.[17]

Absolute, Instrumental and Personal-Aesthetic Values. The second, yet closely related feature of "the open society" arises out of the differentiation in moral value theory and educational theory between different kinds of valuative judgement. If we define values as "rationales for certain courses of action that are chosen over or against others," we can distinguish among absolute, instrumental and personal rationales for actions or values.[18]

The dominant characteristic of absolute values is that they create commitments that are both intrinsic and universal in their demands. The intrinsic feature means that the rationale for a specific course of action can be justified only by something internal to the course of action itself. Thus, the reason to "obey God" is because "that is His will." For those who consider themselves obligated to give their children religious education, the reason is that they will hopefully become religious personalities thereby, which, once again, is the will of God. To say that absolute values are universal in their demands means that they obligate everyone, under the circumstances in which they become operative.... The importance of absolute values is not only in what they demand but also in what they bestow. For they give no less than a common human identity: They confer upon their adherents a particular conception of human existence. Thus, the sanctity of life, which dictates the imperative not to kill, "teaches" something about what it means to be human and to belong to the human family.

The imposition of education on the young can also be seen as based on an absolute value; one may be seen as "not fully human" until educated. The absolute value underlying the biblical commandment "and you shall diligently teach your children" (Deut. 6,7) is said, therefore, to bestow an actualized humanity on those who live by it.

Specific religions, while obliging only their adherents, also look upon their norms as dictated by absolute values, and they "look towards" a universalization of their ethos. For example, the specific absolute values that relate only to Jews are universal with regard to all who live within the covenant. Thus, commandments given within the specific framework of the covenant between God and Israel are based on God's sovereignty over Israel. These commandments, most specifically, define what a Jew is, or "must be." But they also declare what potential status of human–divine encounter is available to humankind, through what has been "given" to Israel and will become the lot of all in Messianic times.

Being so important, absolute values are protected by "fences." These are the instrumental values. They make the achievement of absolute values feasible. For example, the value of order in schools, leading to such rules as "everyone must come on time," is designed to enable teachers to educate, which is itself based on an absolute and intrinsic value.

Instrumental values are given to a certain self-aggrandizement. It is therefore advisable to frequently examine which (absolute) value they serve. Where this is not done, instrumental values often pass themselves off as absolute ones, to gain independent (absolute!) standing and status. If, for example, order in school begins to look like an absolute value and school uniforms take on an aura of "holiness," the path is being paved to authoritarianism and, in theological terms, idolatry.[19]

Personal or "aesthetic" values, while also perceived by their adherents as supremely important and identity-bestowing, do not make universal claims. Rather, they serve to define the individual. For example, persons who decide that they want to be Torah-learning individuals will clear time for it. They will make the requisite efforts to learn well, and may proclaim that they intend to make Torah study a feature of who they are, "till the day of death." A more trivial aesthetic value may lead certain people to always wear brown suits or green dresses, because that's the way they "see themselves." Obviously, such a value-act as on-going Torah study can be based on an absolute value as well. In that case, the learners may be acting as they do because God commanded knowledge and study of Torah, and that is what good Jews must do. In other words, it is possible to study Torah because of an (absolute) value that confers (collective) identity. But the person who is guided by the aesthetic value of learning has chosen to "see him/herself" that way. His or her learning makes no demands of others. Moreover, s/he is quite comfortable with the fact that while he or she studies Torah, the neighbors play Mozart, read medieval literature or devote every spare moment to gardening – or football. . . .

The world of absolute values is not necessarily antithetical to that of aesthetic-personal values. One may be both absolutely committed to the one and yet find one's own unique way in the other without collision. One may be a pious person who diligently obeys the commandments of his or her religion while seeking self-realization in a given "way in the world," whether personal and/or professional. Yet, one who sees "everything" as contained within the world of absolute values, or of instrumental values (often) posing as absolutes, will have no understanding or patience for aesthetic values. Nor will the person who lives only by personal-aesthetic values understand the intention of "respectable" people who make demands on others in the name of absolute values. These two types of people will not only disagree about values, but they will misunderstand valuative statements or claims made by the other. The former will say about the latter that s/he has no values; the latter will say about the former that s/he lacks autonomy and authenticity. . . .

The Ethos of the Open Society. We may now state more clearly what distinguishes the open society and its educational ethos.

(a) The open society is one in which dignity is given prominent moral status, and made synonymous with freedom and the potential of the individual for autonomy and "authenticity." Hence, it is more concerned with the rights of its members than with their duties. However, since rights make demands on those who must enable other individuals to enjoy them, the dichotomy between rights and duties is not as clear-cut and comprehensive as is sometimes polemically claimed.

(b) The open society is one that places great emphasis on aesthetic values, and plays down absolute ones, especially those that are not deduced from what experience finds to be "the common human condition." That is, since all people are vulnerable and susceptible to pain, torture is generally forbidden in a comprehensive and universal fashion, and this is considered eminently reasonable even in an open society. But absolutes that arise out of religious or metaphysical principles are shunned as irrational, arbitrary and divisive.

Not surprisingly, then, the open society favors liberal religions, for these are most inclined towards dignity and to aesthetic values. Conversely, it views traditional religion and religious education as potentially threatening, corrosive of personal (aesthetic) values and personal ("dignified") freedom. Adherents of the morally "open society" will point out that classic religions are extremely honor-oriented and make comprehensive and universal value judgements.

We may take traditional Judaism as a clear-cut example of both: It is an honor-oriented faith, and it rests on absolute values. Where is the dignity in a religion that makes clear status differentiations between Gentiles and Jews, between men and women, between priests and "plain" Israelites? That tells you how to dress, and when? That informs worshippers what to feel, when, and how (be sad on Tishah B'Av, happy on Simchat Torah, repentant on Yom Kippur)? In the comprehensive process of collective self-definition, is there room for the individual to try out identities (as most Western teen-agers do continually, with ear-rings, zany clothing, weird hair-dos, etc.) so that they can finally "find" themselves? Are the multitude of absolute values and the regulations that derive from them concerned with anything but socialization? Are distinctions clearly drawn between instrumental and absolute values? Are the absolute values derived from religious faith not arbitrary? Though perhaps legitimate when freely (aesthetically) chosen, are they not aggressive and tyrannical when imposed on others?

Dimensions and Concerns of Religious Education. Clearly there is tension between "the open society" and traditional religion, but is it as clear-cut as our distinctions above indicate? Let us look at the issue through the prism of one of religion's central pursuits and institutions: Education.

Religious education, we may safely say, has two primary, seemingly contradictory, functions. On the one hand, religious education initiates young people into what [R.] Stark and [C.Y.] Glock have called "the dimensions of religious commitment,"[20] and, on the other hand, it offers direction to the young person in his or her search for ultimacy. The first is a socializing enterprise; the second concerns itself with the individuation of the religious person. What is involved in each of these?

Stark and Glock list five "dimensions of religious commitment."

1. First, there is "the dimension of belief." The community has a view of how one should correctly understand reality, knowledge and goodness, and this should be transmitted to the coming generation.[21]

2. On the basis of the belief dimension, there is erected "the dimension of knowledge." In the world as it is believed to be, certain things are considered worth knowing and important. Others appear to be trivial, worthless or even dangerous. For example, if a particular community believes in the divine revelation of a given corpus of moral truth, the knowledge of that corpus is considered to have supreme worth. And learning many other things may even be deemed a waste of time, or a frittering away of the soul. . . .

3. Then there is "the dimension of practice." Given what the community believes and what it considers worth knowing, certain practices are normative; they correspond to true belief and knowledge. Without practice, knowledge is not actualized, and belief too remains "a dead letter." Young people must be taught these practices and socialized into them.

4. Fourth, children are introduced into "the dimension of (socially anticipated and approved) experience." This means that the cultural frameworks of the community provide opportunities for profound experience and invite them. For example, a Jewishly educated child who shares the practice, knowledge and belief dimension of his or her community (of Judaism) is likely to (frequently or occasionally) have "deep" experiences on Yom Kippur or Passover, or while praying or otherwise carrying out a religious precept. . . .

5. Finally, each religious (or other cohesive) community has a "dimension of consequences." This dimension is concerned with the question: What is the character of a person who lives within a community of this particular belief, practice, knowledge and experience? What is he or she like? How does the person whose life has been shaped by these dimensions of commitment reflect them? . . .

Initiating the young into "dimensions of religious (community) commitment" is one facet of religious education. The other is what Phenix, following [Paul] Tillich,[22] has called the cultivation of an ever-growing and developing concern with "ultimacy" and its "ultimate" source, God.

Phenix describes five characteristics of what is ultimate and the focus of "ultimate concern" in the lives of people.

1. The ultimate is "most important" in the lives of the particular human being. It occasions "complete seriousness," and invites awe and reverence.

2. It is considered to be of supreme worth. In addition to being most important, it is also most valuable. While the "most important" may be morally neutral, the most valuable makes a judgement with regard to good and evil. . . .

3. The ultimate is concerned with depth, with the deeper significance of things. Religious education for "ultimate concern" teaches children not to take life experiences at face value but to discern the profound meanings and purposes to which they point. . . .

4. Ultimacy involves totality and comprehensiveness. It has to do with "what one makes of one's life as a whole." Being concerned with all of one's existence, it naturally raises questions about origins and destinies. . . .

5. Finally, ultimacy raises questions about right conduct. Given what is important, most valuable, "deepest" and most total, what is the good way of life? . . .

Though traditional religious frameworks sometimes emphasize socialization into "the dimensions of religious commitment" at the expense of inner religiosity ("ultimate concern"), experience teaches that education that does so inculcates conformism and "milieu *frumkeit*." Children will learn to do and even to mechanically "experience" the way they are taught to, but they may be left with deficient religious personalities. Conversely, "ultimate concern" in isolation from religious "dimensions of commitment" is vague and even vacuous.

One engaged in "doing his or her own thing" may be imbued with "ultimate concern" yet confuse the ultimate with his or her own ego. . . .

Yet, one can never be completely reduced to the other. In the instance of Judaism, the "dimensions of commitment" will inevitably gravitate towards the "commandment (*mitzvah*) pole" and to the social side of religious life, while the orientation of "ultimate concern" will tend to stress the personal, the "reward of the *mitzvot*," i.e., the redemptive meaning of the life lived by them.

Now, in the open society of modernity, with its predilection to dignity and to aesthetic values, "good" religion is almost naturally identified with that pole of religious life that is rich in individuality, choice and self-making, namely, that of "ultimate concern." The spiritual ideal of the modern and open society, while generally secular, does not shirk from a general religiosity. . . . On the other hand, the open society, while generally professing tolerance of religious life that is centered on the social "dimensions of religious commitment," is also suspicious of it. This type of religious life seems honor-bound and absolutist, for it always intimates the threat of loss of identity, hence, existence, for those who defy its norms.

As a result, there is a problem for traditional religious education in the open society. Traditional religion must insist on the inter-locking character of "dimensions of commitment" and "ultimate concern." It envisions that the educator will initiate the child into these dimensions so that, in the course of the child's life, s/he will come to live with ultimate concern....

Defence and Dialogue. Contemporary religiously educated children, if they belong to non-fundamentalistic communities, are generally part and parcel of the open society, sensitive to its sentiments. How, then, can religious educators and leaders mount a defence against society's reservations and anti-religious slurs?

The aforementioned sociologist, Peter L. Berger, suggests three possible strategies available to religious people in their encounter with a larger secular society: Defiance and cognitive segregation, surrender, and cognitive negotiation.[23]

Defiance and segregation are intellectual and social strategies designed to make the larger "open" society invisible and inaccessible by conscious social closure. The "others," as it were, inhabit a different planet and are made accessible only for limited, generally technical, purposes, such as earning a livelihood or other commercial contact....

Yet defiance and segregation have serious drawbacks. One cannot consciously fight the open society of modernity without developing a modern ideology of anti-modernity. Yet, any modern ideology, even an anti-modern one, generates a modern consciousness. Consequently, the segregated community tends to become sectarian even in its own eyes. Those who are against "them" not only think about them all the time but wonder constantly what "they" are thinking! In addition, segregation engenders alienation, even with regard to one's own existential needs....

The opposing option, cognitive surrender, ultimately agrees that the liberal open society is right about everything that is important. Where there is cognitive surrender, the religious person tries to persuade everyone that his or her religious life is just a variation on secular life, or that the civil religion of secularized Christianity is no different in principle from the life-style of secularized Judaism....

The strategy of "cognitive negotiation" takes into account that one is involved in the surrounding culture but wishes to maintain a distinct identity even when it is at loggerheads with that culture. Cognitive negotiation requires distinguishing between what may be considered "open to discussion" in a given situation, and what is essential and non-negotiable to what Berger calls the "cognitive minority."[24] In a situation of negotiation, traditionally religious people will find themselves seeking religious legitimation for a large degree of "dignity" in their lives and may find themselves locating and emphasizing their traditions' positive orientation to it. Likewise, they will look with favor upon aesthetic values that do no violence to their traditions, and they will find precedents for such values within them. But at the same time, they will vigorously defend the basic tenets of their traditions with regard to the legitimacy and intrinsic worth of absolute values and of "honor.". . . .

Where there is cognitive negotiation there will be dialogue between the religious community and the open society. In this dialogue, religious communities will themselves be open – and will learn. . . . Religious people will seek and hopefully discover moral and spiritual assumptions that they share with their allies: Namely, all those who recognize mercy, justice and a basic humility to be values.

The discussion will not be complete, however, unless religious communities impress upon the open society what it may learn from people of faith: That no commonwealth can endure without honor, that discipline is a necessary counterpart to freedom, and that it is natural and good for people to associate their most fundamental commitments and significances with commanded deeds and absolutes. Religion must teach not only the sublime value of faith and piety, but warn, in a modern and comprehensible idiom, against the dangers of idolatry. In the open and larger secular society this must be translated into the teaching that certainties and absolutes become dangerous precisely when they are not linked to moral Transcendence. Modern people in open societies grown weary have all too often proposed (and implemented!) alternatives to such moral Transcendence, of idolatry (*avodah zarah*) and cynicism (*k'firah*). In our century, both have been experienced in extreme and horrendous forms within once liberal and "open" societies.

Alongside socialization into dimensions of commitment and careful nurture of the young towards "ultimate concern," religious education should conduct a dialogue with the surrounding culture. Religious education that does so will of course reject segregation but it will defend the uniqueness of the religious community. In rejecting segregation, it earns its right to play an educational role in the larger society that is a common home for all who live within it and, in contemporary times especially, a veritable life support system for all its members.

If they recognize that fact, even while "defiantly" insisting that ultimate sovereignty is God's, religious educators can be both sharp critics of their society and yet responsible and loyal participants in it.

NOTES

1 See, for example, *Commandments and Concerns: Jewish Religious Education in Secular Society* (Philadelphia: Jewish Publication Society, 1987); *Roads to the Palace: Jewish Texts and Teaching* (Providence, RI: Berghahn Books, 1995); and *Tree of Life, Tree of Knowledge: Conversations with the Torah* (Boulder, CO: Westview Press, 2001).

2 "Towards a Curriculum for the Modern Orthodox School," in *Orthodoxy Confronts Modernity*, ed. J. Sacks (London: Ktav/Jews College, 1991), 72–77.

3 See *Commandments and Concerns*, Chaps. 6, 7.

4 Ibid., Chaps. 6, 8

5 *Sifra, Kedoshim.* See discussion on this *mahloket* in Yehuda Moriel, *Ba-Derekh Tovim: Mitzvot she-bein Adam le-Haveiro le-Or ha-Mekorot ba-Mikra u-ve-Halakhah* (Jerusalem: World Zionist Organization, 5736), 15–16. For a survey showing that "neighbor" has been most often interpreted as referring to fellow-Jews, see Ernst Simon, "The Neighbor (*Re'a*) Whom We Shall Love," in *Modern Jewish Ethics: Theory and Practice*, ed. Marvin Fox (Columbus: Ohio State University Press, 1975), 29–56.

6 Joseph B. Soloveitchik, "The Lonely Man of Faith," *Tradition* 7:2 (Summer 1965): 7–8.

7 *Rav A. Y. Kook: Selected Letters*, trans. and annotated by Tzvi Feldman (Ma'aleh Adumim: Ma'aliot Publications, 1986), 190–98. R. Kook praises the renaissance of Jewish art but also warns against "idolatry" in art.

8 See, for example, Nechama Leibowitz, *Studies in Shemot, Pekudei* (2), "Finishing the Tabernacle," where she points to the analogies of God's *making* the world and Israel's *making* the *mishkan*.

9 It is crucial that interrelationships and integration not precede competence and care to do the specific thing being done *the way it is done* by those who are acknowledged masters of it. How corruptions of scientific study may take place in the name of the theological conceptions being furthered is well illustrated (for Catholic Schools) by George R. La Noue, "Religious Schools and 'Secular' Subjects," *Harvard Educational Review* 32:3 (Summer 1962): 225–91.

10 Commentary on Exodus 31:3.

11 Peter Winch, "Moral Integrity," in *Ethics and Action* (London: Routledge & Kegan Paul, 1972), 190–91.

12 See *Tree of Life, Tree of Knowledge*, particularly Chap. 9, "Learning and Leadership: Hillel and Menahem," 155–75.

13 "Religious Education in an Open Society," in *"Wie ein Einheimischer soll der Fremdling bei euch sein – und bringe ihm Liebe entgegen wie dir selbst ..."* ed. Miriam Gillis-Carlebach and Barbara Vogel (Hamburg: Dölling und Galitz Verlag, 1997), 129–40.

14 Nevertheless, it has certain partial historical parallels, such as "standing up for Jewish faith" against conversionary pressure in dark ages of seeming divine "eclipse."

15 Peter L. Berger, Brigitte Berger, and Hansfried Kellner, *The Homeless Mind* (Harmondsworth, Middlesex, Eng.: Penguin Books, 1973), 78–89. Citations are from pp. 83–85.

16 Erich Fromm, *Escape From Freedom* (New York: Farrar and Rinehart, 1941).

17 Radically liberal parties or movements, like *Meretz* in Israel, seem to move readily from a platform of individual rights and dignity to an antireligious position, featuring

the claim that religious groupings and individuals are obsessed with honor, hence, irrational and freedom threatening.

18   See Nicholas Rescher, *Introduction to Value Theory* (Englewood Cliffs, NJ: Prentice Hall, 1969), 8–10; James P. Shaver and William Strong, *Facing Value Decisions: Rationale Building for Teachers* (New York: Teachers College Press, 1982), 20–30.

19   In Maimonidean terms, we may say that, in such a case, God's "servants" will be worshipped rather than He Himself. See *Mishneh Torah: Hilkhot Avodat Kokhavim u-Mazalot* I:1–2.

20   R. Stark and C. Y. Glock, "Dimensions of Religious Commitment," *Sociology of Religion*, ed. Roland Robertson (Middlesex, Eng.: Penguin Books, 1969), 253–61.

21   This, of course, will be true in non-religious communities as well. The effort of the poor swimmer to save a drowning person is evoked by the belief, whether religiously grounded or not, that human life is precious.

22   Philip H. Phenix, *Religious Concerns in Contemporary Education* (New York: Teachers College, Columbia University, 1959), 9–11.

23   Peter L. Berger, *A Rumour of Angels* (Garden City, NY: Doubleday-Anchor, 1970), 18–22.

24   Ibid., 18. "By a cognitive minority I mean a group of people whose view of the world differs significantly from the one generally taken for granted in their society."

9

The Concept of the Educated Person: With Some Applications to Jewish Education

ISRAEL SCHEFFLER

Introduction

I want, in the following paper,[1] to outline a normative concept of the educated person that has been prominent in the Anglo-American philosophy of education of the last several decades, and then to consider some of its applications to Jewish education.

Education and Teaching

Let me begin by contrasting the concept of *education* with that of the related but quite different concept of *teaching*. The concept of education is, first of all, wider or more amorphous than that of teaching. "Teaching" is more activity-directed or descriptive of role, whereas "education" less typically describes an activity or role. It is, rather, an umbrella term covering a variety of activities or processes including, for example, those associated with child rearing and, more generally, human development. To describe someone as a teacher gives a more precise account than to describe him as an educator.

Teaching is, secondly, more circumscribed in its manner than is educating. Teaching is thus more often contrasted with indoctrination, and affiliated with respect for the pupil's judgment, with the offering of explanations and demonstrations and with openness to the pupil's questions. Education is less typically thus restricted in manner.[2]

On the other hand – and this is a third point of contrast – teaching is less constrained than education with respect to the value of the outcome sought. I have no qualms in describing you as teaching someone safecracking, but I do have reservations in describing you as educating someone in safecracking.

To be sure, if you live in a society where schools teach safecracking, I may then after all describe your school system as educating safecrackers. I am not myself then expressing a positive evaluation of your system's goals but, at best, describing your system as valuing such goals.[3] However, when I describe myself as educating, I am typically making a claim of value with respect to my goals; I am then speaking normatively rather than descriptively.

In this normative vein, "education" typically implies a certain breadth in the intended outcome. It is thus implicitly contrasted with "training," construed as concerned with skills having a narrow scope, or with information lacking an interpretive base of understanding. Here is a fourth and final contrast of "teaching" with "education," since "teaching" itself does not carry with it a comparable implication of breadth of outcome, as does "education." Even narrow skills can be, and are, taught.

Now it is the expressions "an educated man," "an educated woman," and "an educated person" that in particular carry an implication of breadth of outcome, along with other value implications. Indeed, these expressions are perhaps typically used to convey the normative educational conceptions of the speakers in question. When we speak of the educated person, we are expressing our own ideas as to what an education should be.

The Concept of the Educated Person

On the normative notion of the educated man, R. S. Peters has written much over a period of many years.[4] He has analyzed this notion as incorporating both value conditions and cognitive conditions. The value conditions imply the worthwhileness of the content learned by the educated man and its significance as against trivial forms of achievement.

The cognitive conditions imply an acquisition of understanding as against mere information, and the attainment of cognitive perspective as contrasted with narrow skill learning, associated with training. Training is here contrasted with education not simply, as before, because it is narrower in scope, but because it does not convey an understanding of the bases of the skills acquired.

Education, by contrast, is presumed to imply a grasp of underlying principles or theoretical explanations of the skills learned, of their effectiveness, their limitations, and their relations to other forms of educational content. Furthermore, the idea of cognitive perspective imports the requirement that the understanding be not limited to explanation of just the particular skills learned, but that it afford a framework capable of ranging over various sorts of skill, departments of knowledge and forms of practice.

The contrast of education with information is, parenthetically, a very important point to make, especially in the present period in which the computer model of education has become so prevalent. The notion of education as consisting in a treasury of information – that is, in a so-called database, which can be called up at will by the computer operator or metaphorically by the mind of the student – is detrimental to any likely view of education as requiring understanding. An item of information is hardly understood unless you know to what it relates and can apply it intelligently when relevant to the question at hand or the problem you are trying to solve. The notion of education as information moreover leaves out of account the ability to raise a question, which is distinct from the ability to supply an informative answer.

The normative conception of education implies that you must not merely be able to formulate a question to which an item of known information might be relevant but that you must also know how such item works, be able to retrieve it appropriately, use it aptly, see why it has whatever credibility it may have, grasp what might be said for it and what against it, how it fits with and how it contravenes other items. A whole panoply of competences surrounds any bit of information, and its omission trivializes the normative notion of education. In forming a concept of the educated person, you need to include these competences if you are not to distort the concept beyond recognition.[5]

Cognitive Perspective

The notion of cognitive perspective is related to the idea of wholeness. A man who is a highly trained scientist might not be considered an educated person because his science is intellectually isolated. Such a man could, as Peters says, "have a very limited conception of what he is doing. He could work away at science without seeing its connection with much else, its place in a coherent pattern of life. For him it is an activity which is cognitively adrift."

The idea of training is compatible with specialization in a way that "education" is not. In Peters' words,

> We talk about a person being trained as a philosopher, scientist, or cook when we wish to draw attention to his acquired competence in some sphere; we do not use the phrase, "educated as a philosopher, cook, or scientist." For "education" cannot be tied down in this way to a specialized competence. We can, however, ask the further question whether such people are educated men. To ask this question is at least to probe the limitations of their professional vision.[6]

Cognitive perspective not only requires breadth; it demands also that the knowledge of the educated person be active. It must not simply be stored as information, but should enter into the educated person's perception and commerce with the environment. It is possible, says Peters,

> for a man to know a lot of history in the sense that he can give correct answers to questions in classrooms and examinations; yet this might never affect the way in which he looks at the buildings and institutions around him. We might describe such a man as "knowledgeable" but

we would not describe him as "educated"; for "education" implies that a man's outlook is transformed by what he knows.[7]

A familiar tradition has defined science as organized information, but a telephone directory is not science. You want science not merely to incorporate what is known but to point outward and forward, to be fertile in guiding explorations of the unknown, to offer conceptual schemes relating facts through principles unexhausted by the particular items already available to us. The idea of cognitive perspective, in short, embodies an emphasis on breadth of knowledge, on the possession of principles, on the activity of the mind, and on the transformation of perception. An additional word about these points will bring out further aspects of their meaning.

The search for breadth in the form of explanatory principles overcomes the tendency to exalt our beliefs just because they are familiar or our habitual forms of conduct simply because they are ours. To locate our beliefs and actions within a framework of general principle implies that we cannot give them special advantages of consideration, or make exceptions for ourselves in holding to them; they require justification by reasons impartially and generally applicable. A code of conduct, for example, is a necessary part of moral education, but is by no means sufficient. For moral education, as distinct from moral training, requires the disposition to probe into the principles underlying the code of conduct to which one is attached by training. To provide a student with a moral education means promoting his power to rethink the very code we are inculcating in him. We are risking our own code in the process of teaching it.

My predecessor at Harvard, Robert Ulich, used to say that all education is a dangerous business. You had better be prepared for risks if you enter into education. John Dewey expressed the same point more generally when he remarked that every time you think, you place a piece of the world in jeopardy. A system of schooling that does not place the world in jeopardy in the process of teaching its students is, accordingly, not providing them with an education.

Not only does the educated mind possess principles; the educated mind, as we have seen, is active; its knowledge is not inert. The notion of inert ideas is A. N. Whitehead's; and he views education as developing toward an ideal stage in which the student grasps both generalizations and particulars, deploying them actively in discovering new patterns, inventing novel configurations.

Whitehead, in his celebrated essay "The Rhythm of Education," discusses education in terms of stages. The first stage is the stage of romance, where the point of education is to charm, to enchant, to give an entry into some field by sketching its large structure. The second stage, that of precision, leads into detail, offering a view of the fine-grained articulation of the area. It is paradigmatic of the secondary school by contrast with the elementary school's preoccupation with romance. The third stage is what Whitehead calls the stage of generalization, where learning rises again to the broad stage of romance but now fortified by the detailed knowledge acquired earlier. The stage of generalization, peculiarly appropriate to the university, is one of active combination and recombination of ideas rather than acquisition of new information. New structures are sought, new conceptual forms brought forth, new comprehensive patterns shaped through a dynamic juxtaposition of ideas.[8]

Finally, as we have seen, cognitive perspective connotes a transformation of perception. The knowledge of an educated person enters into and characterizes his or her way of looking at things. Such knowledge is not segregated as a potential set of verbal responses but transforms perception, sensitivity, alertness, discrimination and disposition. B. F. Skinner in fact tried to analyze knowledge and education in terms of verbal responses, but historical knowledge presented him with a special problem, since it does not appear to be mirrored in any kind of contemporary verbal response. Skinner suggested that such knowledge be interpreted as a set of potential responses to questions on history examinations. Now there is a world of difference between Skinner's conception and the notion of cognitive perspective. For the latter notion denies that historical knowledge is merely a set of potential answers to the grilling of a hypothetical history professor. Such knowledge, as a component of education at least, transforms the way you look at the persons, the land, the buildings, the arts and institutions around you now. History is active rather than inert in the degree your contemporary landscape is informed by what you know about it.

A museum invites us to see, but in order to see what it contains, you need to come well-stocked with the historical knowledge that opens your eyes. Actually, you see not only with your eyes but with your education. Your knowledge is a visual instrument; it is not optical but it is visual because it modifies what you see. The mark of an education is indeed the measure in which what one has learned is not stored away for examinations but enters actively into one's perceptual engagement with the world.

Care

We come now to an additional element of the normative concept of education, and this is care. In science, for example, the educated person must not only know what counts as evidence but also care that it should be found. "In forms of thought where proof is possible," writes Peters,

> cogency, simplicity, and elegance must be felt to matter. And what would historical or philosophical thought amount to if there was no concern about relevance, consistency, or coherence? All forms of thought and awareness have their own internal standards of appraisal. To be on the inside of them is both to understand and to care. Without

such commitment they lose their point. I do not think that we would call a person "educated" whose knowledge was purely external and inert in this way.[9]

Peters is evidently not clear whether caring is prerequisite to understanding or whether it is supplementary. On the one hand, he says, "A man cannot really understand what it is to think scientifically unless he ... knows ... what counts as evidence and cares that it should be found." On the other hand, he says that "to be on the inside of [a form of thought and awareness] is both to understand and to care."[10] Now it seems to me clearer to take caring as supplementary. The requirement of caring then comes to this: that an educated person must care about at least some forms of knowledge and understanding that he possesses. He has to be on the "inside" of such forms; he cannot be dispassionate about all or indifferent to the fate of each. Passion is part of your equipment as an educated person. A nihilist – if you can conceive of someone who cares about nothing – might be extremely knowledgeable but would not be educated.

Caring involves active participation in at least some of the forms of thought into which the person has been inducted, and such participation is the basis of critical modification of these forms themselves. John Passmore writes that the educated man must

> be able to participate in the great human traditions of imaginative thought – science, history, literature, philosophy, technology – and to participate in these traditions, one must first be instructed, must learn a discipline, must be initiated, to use Richard Peters' language. The critical spirit ... is a capacity to be a critical participant within a tradition, even if the effect of his criticism is profoundly to modify the operations of that tradition.[11]

Initiation into a tradition of thought implies the ability to participate within it and presupposes the acquisition of discipline. Becoming initiated into science is not a matter of simply acquiring the information that a given branch of science has to offer, but learning to participate in a way of thinking, absorbing its methods and modes of thought, its history, ethos and aims. Nor can you learn a science just by learning such matters in the abstract. You need to learn the corpus as it stands but come to see it as an embodiment of method and style. You can't learn a tradition without learning its details. The tradition lives and breathes in the details.

In speaking of critical thought, Passmore emphasizes the acquisition of discipline via instruction. It is worth noting the connection of the concept of the educated person with the concept of teaching in particular, which we have seen to be associated with respect for the pupil's judgment, with the offering of explanations and demonstrations, and with openness to the pupil's questions. The educated person is one who has been initiated into appropriate disciplines through teaching, not merely drilled or indoctrinated. The path to becoming an educated person is the process of having been taught – that is, having been treated after the manner associated with teaching, as an agent in a rational exchange. It is such exchange in the process of teaching that constitutes the vehicle of the critical spirit.

Conversation

The rational exchange invites questions, and probes into explanations, exposing to the pupil's judgment the cogency of the explanations offered. In this respect, teaching resembles conversation; it is to a considerable extent unpredictable in its course, following where the exchange leads. Unlike mere conversation, teaching indeed operates under the constraints of relevance, regard for evidence and respect for truth, but in its openness to variant perspectives and its unpredictable course it resembles – in fact is a specialized form of – conversation. This is the dialectic aspect of teaching, in which it merges with learning, opening paths to originality of statement, and to manifestations of the critical attitude.

A corollary of this attitude is that teacher and pupil are alike in respect of their judgmental position as intellectual and moral agents. As in conversation, participants in the teaching and learning process are presumed to have their own capacities for judging what they hear from others and their own resources for generating statements and raising questions. Implicit in the exchange is a hospitality to individual perception and a respect for each participant's struggle to understand. What teaching ought ideally to instill in the educated person is a certain freedom from cliché, an effort to transcend the trite opinion and the tired response, a willingness to formulate one's own point of view and the courage to represent it in discussion.

The educated person is characterized by self-respect as well as respect for others, capable of responding to his individual situation and articulating his own thought and feelings as they arise. The educated person is in this respect someone whose attitudes and responses cannot be prejudged; they have the potential to teach him and us something new. Capable of self-teaching, the educated person learns as well from what others have to teach. He or she is not so opinionated as to be incapable of responding constructively to what others have to say. He has acquired, through having been taught, the sense of himself as member of a critical community, responsible to general canons of evaluation to which his own beliefs and actions are subject, canons that allow him no special exceptions in his own favor. He has in effect acquired an intellectual and a moral character.

In joining such community, he incurs the risk of surprise, incapable of ensuring that his own critical canons may not rule against him. The outcomes of an education are thus, and ought to be, unpredictable. As a teacher, you don't know in advance what creative visions your students may produce, stimulated by your teaching. You need to prepare to be surprised by what your students tell you – if indeed you succeed in nurturing an educated man or woman.

To sum up our discussion of the concept of the educated person, we have described the learning such person acquires as worthwhile and significant, as broad rather than narrow, as involving understanding rather than mere information or trained skill. We have emphasized the cognitive perspective afforded by such learning, incorporating knowledge that is active, principled and transformative of perception. We have further required that the knowledge acquired be supplemented by care, producing some form of passion or engagement. We have stressed the development of an individual point of view free of cliché and the ability to articulate it in exchange with others. Finally, we have emphasized membership in a critical community and participation within various traditions of imaginative thought.

Jewish Education and Schooling

Having reviewed certain features of the general philosophical discussion in recent years concerning the educated person, I want now to introduce some considerations pertinent to Jewish education.

A preliminary remark on education and schooling: It is of paramount importance to distinguish these two concepts. We must not confuse the question of what a Jewish education requires with the question of what Jewish schools or their curricula should be like. To suppose that an acceptable answer to the former question would guide us unerringly to the resolution of issues of school practice would be a serious mistake, for three major reasons.

First of all, education is the province not only of the school but of other agencies as well. The family, the institutions of religion, agencies of the state, political groupings, informal as well as formal media of communication, and the general quality of human associations and cultural traditions – all have a part in education. When we think of designing or evaluating school practices, we typically take for granted certain constellations of these other channels of educational influence. With the current deterioration of traditional family patterns in the United States, for example, schools have had to expand their roles in day care, counseling, and health services. With the decline of church influences, schools have had to rethink their functions in moral education.

Traditional Jewish schooling could count on a home life permeated with Jewish religious sentiments, concepts, and practices; it could therefore concentrate its attention on the formal teaching of sacred texts. Current Jewish schools cannot rely on such home life as a given in the lives of their pupils. They need therefore to contemplate anew the role they might play in affective education, in adult education, in the teaching of Hebrew, and so on. In brief, what schools take it upon themselves to do is a function not only of what an ideally educated pupil should learn but also of how the components of such learning should properly be apportioned among the various agencies of education at a given time and place.

Secondly, education is lifelong in its scope, whereas schools are limited institutional agencies. An ideal conception of the outcome of an education need not be translated wholly into a person's school experience, even waiving for a moment the question of what other social agencies might contribute. After a certain point, school pupils ought to take the initiative and responsibility for directing their own learning. Traditional Jewish education, in particular, requires each person to continue to study and to learn throughout life. It does not therefore require the total content of an ideal education, thus conceived, to be incorporated into school practice. The curriculum of an ideal education is in good part a product of continued self-education and is to be distinguished from the particular curriculum of a given school.

Thirdly, granted that the first two points have already been adequately addressed, we must note that any design for school practice depends on a number of assumptions independent of our conception of an ideal educational outcome. For example, what resources for schooling are available? Who are our teachers, and what is their preparation? What is the structure of the community upon which the school depends? What scheme of school management is in place, or contemplated, and so forth?

To sum up the implications of these points for Jewish education, we need, beyond developing conceptions of an ideal educational outcome, to think through the role of the Jewish school in current actual circumstances, and to develop the relation between the school's functions and the learning to be promoted during a person's entire life span. For example, it could be argued that Jewish schools in North America need to consider a substantially expanded role for themselves, to include informal, affective, adult, and family education, and to address the hugely expanded philosophical, ideological, and cultural environment within which Jewish learning must sustain itself in the lives of our pupils. Such schools need, further, to prepare the ground for continuing Jewish learning by pupils after they leave the environment of the school and to promote supports for such learning through the forging of relationships with other agencies.

Value and Cognitive Perspective

The normative concept of education discussed implies the worthwhileness of the content to be learned. It imposes the constant need to exercise selection, to acknowledge that not every choice of materials from the corpus of Jewish cultural achievement is sufficient to promote a genuine education. Rote learning of certain elements, training in certain forms of behavior, and mastery of various details are certainly important as components of what needs to be learned in a Jewish education, but they cannot comprise the whole, which must be seen as broadly meaningful, as making a fundamental demand on the heart and mind. For example, the teaching of textual materials cannot be restricted to concern with their philological, grammatical, or literal aspects, important – indeed indispensable – as these may be, but must encompass an entry into their historical, cultural, and moral significance.

Moreover, the emphasis on cognitive perspective requires understanding rather than mere information, skill, or response. Information, skill, and response are certainly necessary, but they need to be grasped intelligently so as to sustain themselves under changed conditions and unforeseen challenges in the future. Without understanding they remain inert, foreign objects in the mind, segregated from the insight and motivation that guide adult belief.

Cognitive perspective is a mature achievement. It is a goal of education but not realistically to be thought of as a product of schools. Schools can promote its growth but not guarantee it. On the other hand, schools can stunt its growth by downgrading the natural questioning of the pupil, by squelching sincere doubts, by cutting off the linkages between Jewish contents and other materials. To attain cognitive perspective in any area is a difficult development; to achieve it in relation to Jewish identity and the profound and subtle legacy of Jewish religion and culture is an especially daunting matter that is the work of a lifetime, not of school curriculum alone.

But the Jewish educator in the Diaspora faces the difficulty of a very small number of years given over to Jewish schooling. Whatever can be achieved during these years can provide only an immature grasp at best, a juvenile conception of complex subject matter. As the pupil continues to achieve advances in cognitive perspective in non-Jewish areas of education, his Jewish understandings, truncated at a juvenile level, cannot hope to compete. If they are preserved at all, they are preserved in a separate mental compartment, not to be taken seriously in the same realistic way that characterizes other learned subjects. Dissatisfaction with this state of affairs is the beginning of wisdom for the Jewish educator. In gaining a full sense of what cognitive perspective means in other areas, he can realize how far Jewish schooling falls short.

A Jewish education, if it is not to be "cognitively adrift," in Peters' phrase, ought to be seen as having a connection with other aspects of education, as possessing a place within a coherent pattern of life. To confine such education to rudimentary synagogue skills, activated at pitifully few occasions in the year and associated with conceptual material that cannot be taken seriously as relating to the real world, is to guarantee its triviality.

Cognitive perspective requires not only breadth of content and understanding by reference to explanatory principles; it requires also the transformation of perception. This means, for example, that the learning acquired is not simply verbal, but has a purchase in the learner's experience. The concepts ingredient in religious narratives and rabbinic writings, for example, are not simply words on a page but are to be seen as having reference to living circumstances in the contemporary world. The challenge to the Jewish educator is to use what might be thought of as "case methods" to make the semantic power of traditional concepts evident – that is, to encourage pupils to see how to use such concepts descriptively in categorizing their experience.

Caring

Education, as we have seen, implies caring, but caring cannot be coerced or brought about by formula. We can, however, at least make it possible for caring to emerge by providing favorable conditions, respecting all the while the independent student's autonomy in directing his or her own life's path.

To provide favorable circumstances for caring to emerge is to enable the subject matter to become the *property* of the pupil. By this I mean that it is no longer to be seen as the alien possession of the teacher or other adults or authorities. When a pupil can say "It's mine," he has acquired ownership.

In the context of Jewish education, an example already discussed is the semantic ability the student acquires in wielding traditional concepts to describe his or her experience. More generally, such power releases creative opportunities to make "literature" out of the inherited "language." The language is no longer viewed as a static structure; the received corpus is no longer seen as a fixed body of completed texts. Rather, the language is now grasped as an instrument with limitless possibilities for application, as a perennial challenge to describe, express, articulate, discover, and create. If the challenge is accepted, care may begin to emerge. With its issuance into action, participation ensues. The received battery of concepts has now become a natural vehicle with which the student's mind can converse with itself, think things through, and share its insights and feelings with others.

Conversation Again

The semantic power of traditional concepts does not, however, stand alone. The traditional language grew out of a rich texture of religious belief, which has been heavily disrupted by postmedieval intellectual and cultural life. The belief matrix of the traditional concepts needs to be repaired if the language itself is to find a secure foothold.

To put this point in other words, the concepts of the tradition are theory laden, and the theory is no longer coherent with the major frameworks of current belief. To make the concepts live as preferred semantic instruments, the old theoretical presuppositions have to be subjected to the challenge of modern belief and the outcome of such challenge employed to repair the foundations.

To take but one example, the concept of *"mitzvah"* (proper action) has enormous power as a descriptive notion applicable to current as well as historical actions. But it comes with the accretion of ancient theory. In using it, does the pupil need to accept such theory, to subscribe to the belief in a personal Deity who literally commanded us to behave in certain ways authorized by tradition? Does the inherited notion of prayer need to be adopted in toto if the language of prayer is to be encouraged as a basic feature of current religious education?

Lack of clarity or candor about these questions poses a risk for the Jewish educator. The questions will arise naturally in the mind of the modern pupil, either now or later. If they are met with silence, defensiveness, or authoritarian fiat, the language to be learned is not fully incorporated into the cognitive apparatus of the pupil but segregated in a separate compartment of the mind. Religious language is then reserved for ceremonial occasions or restricted to the classroom; it does not fully enter into the serious thought of the pupil. The challenge to the educator is to engage in a serious conversation with the pupil on these matters. This implies taking his questions as honest probings, respecting his doubts, and – most important – making the effort to come to grips with such questions oneself.

The natural defensiveness of teachers is powered by the fear of not having the answer to questions the pupil might pose. But even without an answer, the teacher's willingness to recognize the problem and admit his or her involvement in the search for a solution gives the pupil the basis for assimilating the learned material into his general stock of serious belief. Such willingness is the basis of a conversation with the pupil, in which the pupil is taken into the teacher's confidence and treated as an equal, with the right to seek an understanding of what he is expected to learn.

Traditions of Thought

We have noted Passmore's emphasis on participation in "the great human traditions of imaginative thought – science, history, literature, philosophy, technology." This is a corollary of the requirement of breadth, the need to strive to place one's learning within a coherent pattern, so that it does not become isolated from other concerns. To apply this notion to Jewish education is to place Jewish learning within the stream of general history, to allow it to interact freely with intellectual and literary endeavors, to put it into contact with modern scientific and technological thinking.

Developing such free interactive contact does not mean surrender or dissolution of what is peculiar to Jewish learning. The special insights and values growing out of the unique Jewish historical experience are not to be presumed overridden by the "traditions of imaginative thought." They are to be allowed to enter into dialogue with these traditions, to contribute their part to interpretations of life that emerge from such dialogue. If the dialogue is truly free, the outcome is not foreordained or predictable; no lines are to be drawn in advance. The supposition is that Jewish learning will have an essential role to play both in transforming what comes from other sources and in giving rise to new interpretations of its own received content. The educated Jew will, at any rate, be someone whose Jewish identity is not compartmentalized or "cognitively adrift," but rather set into a dynamic pattern of thought, feeling, and action, characterizing the whole context of modern life.

Knowledge of One's Own Past

It is such reflections as these that indeed prompt a criticism of Passmore's conception of the educated person. For in emphasizing the "great human traditions of imaginative thought," he omits reference to the special role to be played by a person's knowledge of his own heritage of thought, culture, and experience. The particular educated person is not simply interchangeable with every other such person. He or she is situated historically and culturally; and it is, I would argue, essential that knowledge of this situation enter into the educational learning of such a person, having a peculiar claim on his educational energies. One who had no knowledge of his own past, had no contact with the history that formed him, no understanding of the philosophical, religious, psychological, and sociological trends that had shaped his contemporary situation, could hardly be accounted an educated person. In these reflections, Jewish education has an important form of justification based on the very concept of education.

NOTES

1 Portions of this chapter, from Introduction through Conversation, originally appeared in V. A. Howard and Israel Scheffler, *Work, Education and Leadership* (New York: Peter Lang, 1995), 81–90, and are reprinted here with permission of the publisher.

2 R. S. Peters suggests that the descriptive content of "education" does not rule out indoctrination, even if it rules out conditioning and other devices that bypass the pupil's awareness of what is going on – what Peters calls "wittingness." See Peters, *Ethics and Education* (London: Allen and Unwin, 1966, 1970), 41–42.

3 Ibid., 25.

4 See, in addition to the work earlier cited, his "What Is an Educational Process?" in *The Concept of Education,* ed. R. S. Peters (London: Routledge, 1967), 1–23; and P. H. Hirst and R. S. Peters, *The Logic of Education* (London: Routledge, 1970), Chap. 2.

5 See I. Scheffler, "Computers at School?" in Scheffler, *In Praise of the Cognitive Emotions* (New York: Routledge, 1991), Chap. 8.

6 *Ethics and Education,* 31–32.

7   Ibid., 31.

8   A. N. Whitehead, *The Aims of Education* (New York: Macmillan, 1929), Chap. 2.

9   *Ethics and Education,* 31.

10 Ibid.

11 John Passmore, *The Philosophy of Teaching* (Cambridge, MA: Harvard University Press, 1980), 173.

Supplement: Israel Scheffler

Part One: Autobiographical Reflections

In his memoir *Teachers of My Youth: An American Jewish Experience*,[1] Israel Scheffler describes his early experience of Jewish education, from traditional *ḥeder* [lit., room; setting of traditional Torah education for Eastern European youngsters] and *yeshivah* settings to rabbinical training at the Jewish Theological Seminary, and his complementary experiences in settings of general education, ranging from public school to Brooklyn College. One of his motivations in writing these reminiscences is to understand how he was able to maintain a positive and interactive relation with both religious and secular life.

"Jewish secular intellectuals have often been uneven in their secularism," he explains. "Appreciative of other religions they did not accept, they have been obtuse about the religion of their parents. Understanding the cultures and nationalisms of others, they have frequently been particularly unsympathetic to the Jewish variants. Universalism and secularism have, in their hands, been applied unfairly." Scheffler feels a "special responsibility" to explore his continuing commitment to Judaism despite a career in philosophy, "the most universal of universal subjects, the most vigorous claimant to rationality in judgment and belief."[2]

Scheffler attributes his avoidance of this double standard to a rigorous and positive experience of Jewish education: "Because I am one of the very small number of my generation who did in fact receive a strong Jewish religious education, I have felt a special responsibility to reflect, and reflect on, this aspect of my life which, received from my parents and teachers, has formed my character and existence in quite fundamental ways."[3]

In the last chapter of the memoir, entitled "Beyond," he argues for a "rethinking of the bases of Jewish life and learning in our times":

> The work of the teachers I have recounted here could never have been effective without the supporting religious culture of Jewish families

233

and the pervasive presence of Jewish communities and institutions for which Jewish learning had the highest metaphysical status, intrinsic value, the character of religious worship, as well as the reliability to serve as practical guide in all spheres of life.

Jewish teachers of today cannot, by and large, rely on a religious family culture, nor on an authoritative Jewish community. Neither, since they are unlike public school teachers, can they depend on political or civic incentives for education, or on those of self-interest or career advancement. It is commonly said that education is a reflection of its society. Contemporary Jewish education has the task of creating the very society of which it should be the reflection. Not only must it interpret the received texts, it needs to reinterpret the very conditions of its role, assess the new situation and invent unprecedented methods for meeting it. A repetitive application of traditional approaches will not suffice. There is no substitute for philosophy in this context – a rethinking of the bases of Jewish life and learning in our times.

... It is the questions posed by the contemporary intellectual and historical situation that need to be faced by current Jewish education if it is to have a chance of succeeding in the modern world. Old answers mindlessly repeated breed confusion, encourage intellectual dishonesty, and preclude effective action. To question such answers frees us at least to search for suitable replacements.

... No philosophy means bad philosophy. Sacred texts taught without a philosophical attitude are in danger of being received either as literal but incredible dogma, or as mere fairy tale, or as nonsense to be repeated with a pious incomprehension that will not survive adult reflection. Certainly there are degrees of sophistication that must be apportioned suitably to the levels of maturity of the pupils. But adult teachers need to be philosophically prepared to provide at least tentative explanations upon demand, to respond to serious questions as to how this or that text is to be taken, even if such response consists only in further questions. Philosophy is in this sense no luxury but a vital necessity for cultural survival.

If philosophy thrives on questions, it also lives with diversity. The questions to be met will not likely receive uniform answers. I do not suppose Jewish education to require some single philosophical underpinning if it is to be carried forward successfully. Pluralism is the prospect I foresee and welcome, a pluralism of doctrines compatible with a common seriousness of reflection and search, a pluralism of ideological approaches to Jewish life, consistent as well with common efforts to preserve common values, memories, institutions and practices. ...
For those of us who are committed to the continued growth of Jewish

culture, religion, and learning, there is an obligation to seek suitable ways of fostering such growth under present circumstances. But we will find many ways rather than one, longer as well as shorter routes, detours and mazes as well as paths that lie straight and smooth. . . .

I have said that I would not here elaborate on my own philosophy of religion, nor is this the place to spell out my views on Jewish education in systematic fashion. But I have already intimated my own sympathy for a historical and naturalistic approach, which eschews apologetics and builds on the firmest views available in general scholarship, rational philosophy, and scientific research. This implies . . . that our independent conceptions of truth, morals, logic and evidence must take precedence over the inherited text as it stands. We not only may, but are bound to reassess the epistemic and moral authority of the traditional text and its associated practices as received, differentiating clearly between our current interpretations and the beliefs of our ancestors. I reject the view that religious authority derives from some occult source, obliging us to deny our ordinary powers of observation, logical judgment, funded scientific information or moral intuition. On the contrary, I hold that religion, insofar as worthwhile, is harmonious with all of these and provides a commentary on our human life rather than a report of never never lands beyond.

But to say that our independent conceptions of truth and morals take precedence over received texts does not mean that the texts can be wholly dispensed with. Critical reflection on method takes precedence over received views in science, but scientific method cannot dispense with an inherited corpus of scientific beliefs. Critical reflection on practice from a legal or ethical standpoint takes precedence over received social practice, but neither law nor ethics can operate in airy abstraction from actual life. Nor does critical reflection precede the subject matter which is the object of its attention. Though superior in authority, such reflection grows out of the very subject matter which it transforms, selecting from it key insights and values to be suitably modified and declared authoritative. The process is interactive or dialectical throughout. . . .

Why preserve any religious tradition whatever, given a historical and naturalistic interpretation such as I favor? If religion does not report on an occult world, if it does not break the continuity of nature or extend mortal life, what is its point? If ordinary powers of observation, logical judgment and funded scientific information are to be granted authority over received doctrines in any case, why not relinquish these doctrines altogether? One can of course do so. But it is a fact that these doctrines embody categories not prevalent otherwise, providing a commentary on life not abstractly available in the mere functioning of observation or judgment, in the mere concept of scientific method or information. All these are compatible with, but do not themselves provide categories, classifications, properties and relations by which to represent experience.

The categories available in the separate sciences, in politics, in technology and the professions do not exhaust those that are possible to us, and in particular do not take the place of those available in the rich symbolic traditions of religion, literature and the arts. These traditions are important not because they report on another world but because, and to the extent that, they give us a new purchase on this, not because they illuminate the afterlife but because they reveal the hidden depths of this. To live in the presence of ultimate questions, whether of religion or philosophy, is to live a different life, here and now. To live with constant symbolic reminders that sensitize one to the categories of justice, compassion, holiness, truth, duty, conscience is to acquire a particular character.[4]

Part Two: "Jewish Education: Purposes, Problems and Possibilities"[5]

Purposes

... The purposes of Jewish education differ wholly from those of public education. These purposes are neither civic, nor individualistic, nor utilitarian. Viewed in relation to the pupil, they are: to initiate the Jewish child into the culture, history, and spiritual heritage of the Jewish people, to help the child to learn and face the truth about Jewish history, identity, and existence, to enhance his or her dignity as a Jewish person, and to enable the child to accept, and to be creative in, the Jewish dimension of its life.

Viewed rather in its relation to the Jewish people, the purposes of Jewish education are: to promote Jewish survival and welfare, to interpret and communicate authentic Jewish experience, to sustain and defend Jewish honor and loyalties, to create living links with the Jewish past, preserving and extending its heritage for future generations. Ideally, Jewish education should be a natural reflection of the inner dignity of the Jewish people, and of its ethical, spiritual and cultural resources, as well as a response to current social and intellectual realities. This means: it should not be merely defensive, or apologetic, or imitative, or archaic, or nostalgic for a past that is no more. Rather, from its own position of inner strength and historical self-awareness, it should have the courage not only to reevaluate its directions, but also to adapt whatever is worthwhile in the environment to its own purposes, thus promoting the creative continuity of its civilization.

Problems

The problems facing Jewish education in modern industrial society stand out sharply by contrast with the pre-modern period, for which education in the Jewish school, home, and community was one continuous entity, embodied concretely in all spheres of life. Insofar as formal Jewish schooling or study was differentiated in the earlier period, it was accorded the highest religious and metaphysical status, regarded as an intrinsic value, a form of worship, but also a practical guide in all spheres of life. . . .

The Jew lived a precarious existence, but the philosophical framework of Jew and non-Jew alike was largely the same. The world revealed by faith was created by a personal and omnipotent God, who put mankind at the center of his creation, endowed human beings with free will and made absolute moral and devotional demands of them. Human actions were freighted with significance, supervised by Providence, consequential in the last degree. History, an interplay of God's will and men's wills, was to be read partly as natural, partly as miraculous, but in any case as inviting interpretation by personal, moral, and religious categories, such as loyalty, gratitude, reciprocity, covenant, punishment and reward, reverence, sin, stubbornness, and repentance.

The holiness of the Jewish Scriptures, central to this philosophical worldview, was virtually unquestioned. Although Jews suffered for refusing to accept Christianity or Islam as the higher fulfillment of these Scriptures, the Scriptures themselves were regarded by all as sacred. Jewish education was thus based on systematic beliefs, of which the basic philosophical features were recognized and shared by all. Such education offered a genuine reflection of historical Jewish existence, offering an authentic response to that existence in the doctrines and practices of Judaism.

Now every feature of the pre-modern context has been destroyed or rendered problematic in the modern period. The emancipation and entry of the Jew into the mainstream of Western life broke the tightly knit harmony of home, school and community. The general breakdown of the medieval worldview shattered the inherited conception of nature and history shared by Jew and non-Jew alike, undermined traditional attitudes to their religious Scriptures, and destroyed the uniform traditional response to Jewish existence which constituted the task of education in the past.

The Jewish genius for religious creativity, already severely threatened by these changes, has now, further, been profoundly shocked by the incalculable trauma of the Holocaust. Jewish predilections for intellectual and otherworldly thought have, concomitantly, been secularized, largely diverted into scientific, commercial, and academic channels – thus reinforcing universalistic ideologies corrosive of Jewish loyalties. . . .

There is no use bemoaning these facts, or looking back fondly to the memory of circumstances more favorable to Jewish education. If such education is to succeed, it must do so here and now. If it fails, fond memories will afford no consolation. To grasp the possibility of success, educators need to realize the magnitude of the problem and then to mobilize their efforts to address it. Concerted action on several fronts is needed. I shall here offer some suggestions, divided into two rough categories: organizational and philosophical.

Possibilities

Organizational Suggestions. The problems of Jewish education, arising from a shared commitment to Jewish survival, nevertheless vary qualitatively with the communities into which the Jewish people is divided. Seen in the worldwide perspective of its overriding purpose, Jewish education must, however, take as a primary task to strengthen the bonds among these communities, to build and reinforce lines of communication among them, developing morale, understanding, and mutual support. . . . Each must . . . foster an awareness of all, seeing itself not merely in local and current terms, but as part of a continuous people, stewards-in-common of a precious heritage of culture.

. . . Jewish education . . . must take into account the rich content of Jewish experience throughout the centuries, reckon with the diverse characteristics and needs of diaspora Jewish communities, and take as its fundamental goal the strengthening of informed Jewish loyalties in diverse spheres of life. It must educate each Jewish community to take a role in the worldwide deliberations of the Jewish people, for each such community has a role to play and a point of view to represent. . . .

Jewish education ought, in every one of its realizations, to promote an inclusive sense of time – an awareness of, and affiliation with, the history of the Jewish people; a comprehensive sense of space – an awareness of, and association with, the Jewish communities scattered across the globe; and a cultivated sense of self – a knowledge of the Hebrew language and other languages of Jews, and an acquaintance with the treasured achievements and literatures of Jewish thought, feeling, striving, and expression throughout the ages. . . .

Philosophical Suggestions. The problems of Jewish education are not, in any event, primarily organizational. Nor are they wholly soluble by exhortation, inspiration, funding, or research. All of these have their place, but none can substitute for a philosophical rethinking of the bases of Jewish life in our times.

By philosophy, I intend nothing technical or abstruse, but an engagement with such basic questions as: How can the purposes of Jewish education best be realized in the present? What is the justification for such education? What is our positive vision of an ideal Jewish life in this century? What ought we to expect of Jewish youth under the actual constraints of their life conditions? How help them, and ourselves, to an authentic appreciation of Jewish values? How enable them to go beyond us to develop the latent intimations of Jewish traditions and insights? How shall we introduce them to Jewish materials so that these materials may germinate and grow in their minds and hearts and flourish in the world they will inhabit rather than the worlds we can remember? . . .

Texts. Jewish education is said to be traditionally text-centered. The attribution is misleading, for the study of sacred texts in classical Judaism was not self-sufficient, but supported by constant educative influences flowing from the life of the family and the practice of the community. Nevertheless, these texts and their interpretive literatures did constitute the basic focus of formal study.

. . . If these texts seem so obviously meaningful to us − that is, to adult educators − it is only because we have already gone through the processes of learning to hear them. The obviousness of their meaning is an artifact of our early training, and cannot be generated in our youth by mere exposure. They need themselves to learn how to hear the message, to grasp it in a way that will be effective for them, whether or not it was our way in the past.

A reflective or philosophical approach to this task requires us to rethink the texts ourselves; unlearning our habitual perceptions, we need to look at the texts again with fresh eyes and from new angles. The teaching of the young ought to be an occasion for the re-teaching of ourselves − their teachers. . . .

Religious Rituals. Religion is a closed book to large numbers of Jews and non-Jews alike. To open this book, at least partially, through reinterpretation in contemporary intellectual terms is a philosophical task of the first importance. . . .

To begin with, it is worth emphasizing the fact that religion has a history, despite common denials by religionists themselves. Every doctrine and rite preserves echoes of earlier beliefs no longer accepted reflectively today. The continuity of religion is in substantial part a product of reinterpretation, acknowledged or not. Thus, the effort at contemporary reinterpretation has ample precedent.

Attitudes toward ritual have clearly undergone enormous changes, the details of which can here be left to the scholars. But a brief sketch, following Yehezkel Kaufmann, will make the point.[6] Primitive pre-Biblical culture conceived of ritual as magic, a technique for manipulating nature. . . .

A more humanistic but still primitive view which overlay the magical conception was that of ritual as propitiation of the gods or spirits in control of some natural resource. Pleasing the god in control of rainfall would, it was hoped, guarantee rainfall – not automatically – but through the mediation of the will of the god, who could be dealt with on the basis of pleas and gifts, but not coerced through a mechanical technique. . . .

Biblical religion wrought a radical transformation in these beliefs, propounding the doctrine of a transcendent, single God, who was not part of nature but who stood wholly beyond it, having created it and all that it contains, and whose will was the source of absolute moral commands laid upon human beings generally and the children of Israel in particular. Such a being had no need of magical devices to attain his goals. He could not be manipulated by the techniques of men nor bargained with like a local landowner or petty politician. The Bible contains the record of this transformation in its rejection of all mythology and its strong polemic against magic, idolatry, and divination. . . .

Prophetic attitudes toward the rites as conditional and subordinate to the moral commands prevailed in later, Rabbinic Judaism. What, however, was the purpose of rites for which no rational meaning could be found? Kaufmann says, "The ultimate sanction of the rite became the divine will. Judaism thus created a noble symbol for its basic idea that everything is a divine command: fulfilling the command is an acknowledgement of the supremacy of God's will. . . . To laws for which no rational explanation could be found, the Rabbis applied the general principle, 'The commandments were given only for the purpose of purifying human beings'" (Gen. *Rabbah* 44.1).[7]

This humanistic attitude of the Rabbis views the rites as, in effect, educative through their symbolic value. Ritual "purifies human beings" not through magical force or propitiatory effect but through its reflexive symbolic impact which helps to relate its participants to higher values and more exalted purposes.

This historical attitude is available to reinterpretive efforts today, and can indeed be considerably extended. . . .

The symbol system of Jewish ritual can, I suggest, be treated in these terms in contemporary education. This system is not a piece of magic, superstition, rational theory, cosmic technology or outmoded theology. It constitutes a language which organizes a world, structuring time and space, orienting us in history, binding us in community and sensitizing us to those features of life in which our forebears have found the highest value and deepest meanings – freedom, responsibility, sincerity, humility, care, loyalty, righteousness, compassion. The specific interpretations given to this symbolic system have changed throughout our history more frequently than the system itself. It is the system itself we need, however, to treat seriously again, recovering it as a potent resource for Jewish education.

Part Three: "Moral Education and the Democratic Ideal"

In his essay "Moral Education and the Democratic Ideal," Scheffler explores the tension between tradition and progress from the perspective of general education.[8] He argues that the habits of reasonableness unifying moral, scientific, and democratic realms are attainable only by acquiring appropriate traditions of thought and practice.

Education in a Democracy

Commitment to the ideal of democracy as an organizing principle of society has radical and far-reaching consequences, not only for basic political and legal institutions, but also for the educational conceptions that guide the development of our children. All institutions, indeed, operate through the instrumentality of persons; social arrangements are "mechanisms" only in a misleading metaphorical sense. In so far as education is considered broadly, as embracing all those processes through which a society's persons are developed, it is thus of fundamental import for all the institutions of society, without exception. A society committed to the democratic ideal is one that makes peculiarly difficult and challenging demands of its members; it accordingly also makes stringent demands of those processes through which its members are educated.

What is the democratic ideal, then, as a principle of social organization? It aims so to structure the arrangements of society as to rest them ultimately upon the freely given consent of its members. Such an aim requires the institutionalization of reasoned procedures for the critical and public review of policy; it demands that judgments of policy be viewed not as the fixed privilege of any class or elite but as the common task of all, and it requires the supplanting of arbitrary and violent alteration of policy with institutionally channeled change ordered by reasoned persuasion and informed consent.

The democratic ideal is that of an open and dynamic society: open, in that there is no antecedent social blueprint which is itself to be taken as a dogma immune to critical evaluation in the public forum; dynamic, in that its fundamental institutions are not designed to arrest change but to order and channel it by exposing it to public scrutiny and resting it ultimately upon the choices of its members. The democratic ideal is antithetical to the notion of a fixed class of rulers, with privileges resting upon social myths which it is forbidden to question. It envisions rather a society that sustains itself not by the indoctrination of myth, but by the reasoned choices of its citizens, who continue to favor it in the light of a critical scrutiny both of it and its alternatives. Choice of the democratic ideal rests upon the hope that this ideal will be sustained and strengthened by critical and responsible inquiry into the truth about social matters. The democratic faith consists not in a dogma, but in a reasonable trust that unfettered inquiry and free choice will themselves be chosen, and chosen again, by free and informed men.

The demands made upon education in accord with the democratic ideal are stringent indeed; yet these demands are not ancillary but essential to it. As Ralph Barton Perry has said:[9]

> ... Democratic education is ... a peculiarly ambitious education. It does not educate men for prescribed places in life, shaping them to fit the requirements of a preexisting and rigid division of labor. Its idea is that the social system itself, which determines what places there are to fill, shall be created by the men who fill them. It is true that in order to live and to live effectively men must be adapted to their social environment, but only in order that they may in the long run adapt that environment to themselves. ...

To see how radical such a vision is in human history, we have only to reflect how differently education has been conceived. In traditional authoritarian societies, education has typically been thought to be a process of perpetuating the received lore, considered to embody the central doctrines upon which human arrangements were based. These doctrines were to be inculcated through education; they were not to be questioned. Since, however, a division between the rulers and the ruled was fundamental in such societies, the education of governing elites was sharply differentiated from the training and opinion-formation reserved for the masses. Plato's *Republic,* the chief work of educational philosophy in our ancient literature, outlines an education for the rulers in a hierarchical utopia in which the rest of the members are to be deliberately nourished on myths. . . . In nondemocratic societies, education is two-faced: it is a weapon or an instrument for shaping the minds of the ruled in accord with the favored and dogmatic myth of the rulers; it is, however, for the latter, an induction into the prerogatives and arts of rule, including the arts of manipulating the opinions of the masses.

To choose the democratic ideal for society is wholly to reject the conception of education as an *instrument* of rule; it is to surrender the idea of shaping or molding the mind of the pupil. The function of education in a democracy is rather to liberate the mind, strengthen its critical powers, inform it with knowledge and the capacity for independent inquiry, engage its human sympathies, and illuminate its moral and practical choices. This function is, further, not to be limited to any given subclass of members, but to be extended, in so far as possible, to all citizens, since all are called upon to take part in processes of debate, criticism, choice, and co-operative effort upon which the common social structure depends. "A democracy which educates for democracy is bound to regard all of its members as heirs who must so far as possible be qualified to enter into their birthright."[10]

Implications for Schooling

Education, in its broad sense, is more comprehensive than schooling, since it encompasses all those processes through which a society's members are developed. Indeed, all institutions influence the development of persons working within, or affected by, them. Institutions are complex structures of actions and expectations, and to live within their scope is to order one's own actions and expectations in a manner that is modified, directly or subtly, by that fact. Democratic institutions, in particular, requiring as they do the engagement and active concern of all citizens, constitute profoundly educative resources. It is important to note this fact in connection with our theme, for it suggests that formal agencies of schooling do not, and cannot, carry the whole burden of education in a democratic society, in particular, moral and character education. All institutions have an educational side, no matter what their primary functions may be. The question of moral education in a democracy must accordingly be raised not only within the scope of the classroom but also within the several realms of institutional conduct. Are political policies and arrangements genuinely open to rational scrutiny and public control? Do the courts and agencies of government operate fairly? What standards of service and integrity are prevalent in public offices? Does the level of political debate meet appropriate requirements of candor and logical argument? Do journalism and the mass media expose facts and alternatives, or appeal to fads and emotionalism? These and many other allied questions pertain to the status of moral education within a democratic society. To take them seriously is to recognize that moral education presents a challenge not only to the schools, but also to every other institution of society.

Yet the issue must certainly be raised specifically in connection with schools and schooling. What is the province of morality in the school, particularly the democratic school? Can morality conceivably be construed as a subject, consisting in a set of maxims of conduct, or an account of current mores, or a list of rules derived from some authoritative source? Is the function of moral education rather to ensure conformity to a certain code of behavior regulating the school? Is it, perhaps, to involve pupils in the activities of student organizations or in discussion of "the problems of democracy"? Or, since morality pertains to the whole of what transpires in school, is the very notion of specific moral schooling altogether misguided?

These questions are very difficult, not only as matters of implementation, but also in theory. For it can hardly be said that there is firm agreement among moralists and educators as to the content and scope of morality. Yet the tradition of moral philosophy reveals a sense of morality as a comprehensive institution over and beyond particular moral codes, which seems to me especially consonant with the democratic ideal, and can, at least in outline, be profitably explored in the context of schooling. What is this sense?

It may perhaps be initially perceived by attention to the language of moral judgment. To say that an action is "right," or that some course "ought" to be followed, is not simply to express one's taste or preference: it is also to make a claim. It is to convey that the judgment is backed by reasons, and it is further to invite discussions of such reasons. It is, finally, to suggest that these reasons will be found compelling when looked at impartially and objectively, that is to say, taking all relevant facts and interests into account and judging the matter as fairly as possible. To make a moral claim is, typically, to rule out the simple expression of feelings, the mere giving of commands, or the mere citation of authorities. It is to commit oneself, at least in principle, to the "moral point of view," that is, to the claim that one's recommended course has a point which can be clearly seen if one takes the trouble to survey the situation comprehensively, with impartial and sympathetic consideration of the interests at stake, and with respect for the persons involved in the issue. The details vary in different philosophical accounts, but the broad outlines are generally acknowledged by contemporary moral theorists.[11]

If morality can be thus described, as an institution, then it is clear that we err if we confuse our allegiance to any particular code with our commitment to this institution; we err in mistaking our prevalent code for the *moral point of view* itself. Of course, we typically hold our code to be justifiable from the moral point of view. However, if we are truly committed to the latter, we must allow the possibility that further consideration or new information or emergent human conditions may require revision in our code. The situation is perfectly analogous to the case of science education; we err if we confuse our allegiance to the current corpus of scientific doctrines with our commitment to scientific method. Of course we hold our current science to be justifiable by scientific method, but that very method itself commits us to hold contemporary doctrines fallible and revisable in the light of new arguments or new evidence that the future may bring to light. For scientific doctrines are not held simply as a matter of arbitrary preference; they are held for reasons. To affirm them is to invite all who are competent to survey these reasons and to judge the issues comprehensively and fairly on their merits.

Neither in the case of morality nor in that of science is it possible to convey the underlying *point of view* in the abstract. It would make no sense to say, "Since our presently held science is likely to be revised for cause in the future, let us just teach scientific method and give up the teaching of content." The content is important in and of itself, and as a basis for further development in the future. Moreover, one who knew nothing about specific materials of science in the concrete could have no conception of the import of an abstract and second-order scientific method. Nevertheless, it certainly does not follow that the method is of no consequence. On the contrary, to teach current science without any sense of the reasons that underlie it, and of the logical criteria by which it may itself be altered in the future, is to prevent its further intelligent development. Analogously, it makes no sense to say that we ought to teach the moral point of view in the abstract since our given practices are likely to call for change in the future. Given practices are indispensable, not only in organizing present energies, but in making future refinements and revisions possible. Moreover, one who had no concrete awareness of a given tradition of practice, who had no conception of what rule-governed conduct is, could hardly be expected to comprehend what the moral point of view might be, as a second-order vantage point on practice. Nevertheless, it does not follow that the latter vantage point is insignificant. Indeed, it is fundamental in so far as we hold our given practices to be reasonable, that is, justifiable in principle upon fair and comprehensive survey of the facts and interests involved.

There is, then, a strong analogy between the moral and the scientific points of view, and it is no accident that we speak of reasons in both cases. We can be reasonable in matters of practice as well as in matters of theory. We can make a fair assessment of the evidence bearing on a hypothesis of fact, as we can make a fair disposition of interests in conflict. In either case, we are called upon to overcome our initial tendencies to self-assertiveness and partiality by a more fundamental allegiance to standards of reasonable judgment comprehensible to all who are competent to investigate the issues. In forming such an allegiance, we commit ourselves to the theoretical possibility that we may need to revise our current beliefs and practices as a consequence of "listening to reason." We reject arbitrariness in principle, and accept the responsibility of critical justification of our current doctrines and rules of conduct.

It is evident, moreover, that there is a close connection between the general concept of *reasonableness,* underlying the moral and the scientific points of view, and the democratic ideal. For the latter demands the institutionalization of "appeals to reason" in the sphere of social conduct. In requiring that social policy be subject to open and public review, and institutionally revisable in the light of such review, the democratic ideal rejects the rule of dogma and of arbitrary authority as the ultimate arbiter of social conduct. In fundamental allegiance to channels of open debate, public review, rational persuasion and orderly change, a democratic society in effect holds its own current practices open to revision in the future. For it considers these practices to be not self-evident, or guaranteed by some fixed and higher authority, or decidable exclusively by some privileged elite, but subject to rational criticism, that is, purporting to sustain themselves in the process of free exchange of reasons in an attempt to reach a fair and comprehensive judgment.

Here, it seems to me, is the central connection between moral, scientific, and democratic education, and it is this central connection that provides, in my opinion, the basic clue for school practice. For what it suggests is that the fundamental trait to be encouraged is that of reasonableness. To cultivate this trait is to liberate the mind from dogmatic adherence to prevalent ideological fashions, as well as from the dictates of authority. For the rational mind is encouraged to go behind such fashions and dictates and to ask for their justifications, whether the issue be factual or practical. In training our students to reason we train them to be critical. We encourage them to ask questions, to look for evidence, to seek and scrutinize alternatives, to be critical of their own ideas as well as those of others. This educational course precludes taking schooling as an instrument for shaping their minds to a preconceived idea. For if they seek reasons, it is their evaluation of such reasons that will determine what ideas they eventually accept.

Such a direction in schooling is fraught with risk, for it means entrusting our current conceptions to the judgment of our pupils. In exposing these conceptions to their rational evaluation we are inviting them to see for themselves whether our conceptions are adequate, proper, fair. Such a risk is central to scientific education, where we deliberately subject our current theories to the test of continuous evaluation by future generations of our student-scientists. It is central also to our moral code, *in so far as* we ourselves take the moral point of view toward this code. And, finally, it is central to the democratic commitment, which holds social policies to be continually open to free and public review. In sum, rationality liberates, but there is no liberty without risk.

Let no one, however, suppose that the liberating of minds is equivalent to freeing them from discipline. *Laissez-faire* is not the opposite of dogma. To be reasonable is a difficult achievement. The habit of reasonableness is not an airy abstract entity that can be skimmed off the concrete body of thought and practice. Consider again the case of science: scientific method can be learned only in and through its corpus of current materials. Reasonableness in science is an aspect or dimension of scientific tradition, and the body of the tradition is indispensable as a base for grasping this dimension. Science needs to be taught in such a way as to bring out this dimension as a consequence, but the consequence cannot be taken neat. Analogously for the art of moral choice: the moral point of view is attained, if at all, by acquiring a tradition of practice, embodied in rules and habits of conduct. Without a preliminary immersion in such a tradition – an appreciation of the import of its rules, obligations, rights, and demands – the concept of choice of actions and rules for oneself can hardly be achieved. Yet the prevalent tradition of practice can itself be taught in such a way as to encourage the ultimate attainment of a superordinate and comprehensive moral point of view.

The challenge of moral education is the challenge to develop critical thought in the sphere of practice and it is continuous with the challenge to develop critical thought in all aspects and phases of schooling. Moral schooling is not, therefore, a thing apart, something to be embodied in a list of maxims, something to be reckoned as simply another subject, or another activity, curricular or extracurricular. It does, indeed, have to pervade the *whole* of the school experience.

... The critical questions concern the *quality* of the environment: what is the *nature* of the particular school experience, comprising content as well as structure? Does it liberate the child in the long run, as he grows to adulthood? Does it encourage respect for persons, and for the arguments and reasons offered in personal exchanges? Does it open itself to questioning and discussion? Does it provide the child with fundamental schooling in the traditions of reason, and the arts that are embodied therein? Does it, for example, encourage the development of linguistic and mathematical abilities, the capacity to read a page and follow an argument? Does it provide an exposure to the range of historical experience and the realms of personal and social life embodied in literature, the law, and the social sciences? Does it also provide an exposure to particular domains of scientific work in which the canons of logical reasoning and evidential deliberation may begin to be appreciated? Does it afford opportunity for individual initiative in reflective inquiry and practical projects? Does it provide a stable personal milieu in which the dignity of others and the variation of opinion may be appreciated, but in which a common and overriding love for truth and fairness may begin to be seen as binding oneself and one's fellows in a universal human community?

If the answer is negative, it matters not how effective the environment is in shaping concrete results in conduct. For the point of moral education in a democracy is antithetical to mere shaping. It is rather to liberate.

NOTES

1 Israel Scheffler, *Teachers of My Youth: An American Jewish Experience* (Dordrecht: Kluwer Academic Publishers, 1995). For a bibliography of Scheffler's writings until 1992, see "Writings of Israel Scheffler," *Synthese* 94 (1993): 139–44.

2 Ibid., 13.

3 Ibid.

4 Ibid., 173–78.

5 "Jewish Education: Purposes, Problems and Possibilities" was originally given at a commencement of the Jerusalem Fellows, in June 1985, and excerpts are reprinted from D. J. Margolis and E. S. Schoenberg, *Curriculum, Community, Commitment* (West Orange, NJ: Behrman House, 1992), 20–28.

6 Yehezkel Kaufmann, *The Religion of Israel* [translated and abridged by Moshe Greenberg], (Chicago: The University of Chicago Press, 1960), esp. 53–59, 101–03.

7 Ibid., 102.

8 Originally prepared at the invitation of Rep. John Brademas, Chairman, Select
   Subcommittee on Education, Committee on Education and Labor of the House
   of Representatives, it was offered as a background paper for the subcommittee's
   hearings on the proposed National Institute of Education. A version also appears
   in *Educational Research Prospects and Priorities,* Appendix to Hearings on H.R.
   3606, Committee Print, 92d Congress, 2d Session, Washington: U.S. Government
   Printing Office, 1972. Written in response to a growing interest in moral education
   as a special area or aspect of schooling, the paper stresses the connections between
   moral, scientific, and democratic education and the centrality, in all three, of the
   habits of critical thought. (Extracts from R. B. Perry, *Realms of Value,* 1954, by
   permission of Harvard University Press.) Reprinted in Scheffler, *Reason and Teaching*
   (Indianapolis: Hackett, 1973), 136–45.
9 *Realms of Value,* 431–32.
10 *Realms of Value,* 432.
11 See, for example, Kurt Baier, *The Moral Point of View* (Ithaca, NY: Cornell
   University Press, 1958); William K. Frankena, *Ethics* (Englewood Cliffs, NJ:
   Prentice Hall, 1963); and R. S. Peters, *Ethics and Education* (Glenview, IL: Scott
   Foresman, 1967). Additional articles of interest may be found in Sect. V, "Moral
   Education" and Sect. VI, "Education, Religion, and Politics," in I. Scheffler, ed.,
   Philosophy and Education, 2d ed. (Boston: Allyn and Bacon, 1966).

Part III

Visions in Context

10

The Art of Translation

SEYMOUR FOX

The Translation of Theory into Educational Practice

The essays in this volume offer distinctive visions of an ideal Jewish education. They address thoughtfully – and variously – such questions as What should successfully educated Jews know and feel? How should they behave? What is their responsibility to the Jewish community and to humankind?

This chapter makes three assumptions that are foundational to our project. The first is that vision makes a difference, and that differing visions result in different kinds of Jewish education. But visions incorporate more than theoretical propositions; they embody as well the translation of these propositions into practice.[1]

Although the visions developed in our project have elements in common – some surprising – their differences are consequential. A visitor to an early childhood program based on Isadore Twersky's vision would not mistake it for a program based on Moshe Greenberg's vision. The mission of a teacher, according to Menachem Brinker, conflicts with the mission of a teacher in Michael Meyer's view.

The second assumption is that for these visions, or any others, to be implemented, they need to include an understanding of the real-life settings – schools, community centers, adult education programs, and summer camps – where education takes place. Vision cannot be separated from implementation. The act of incorporating vision in a complex reality releases its power and reveals its limits. In the process of concretizing a dream – inspiring a community, choosing a principal, recruiting educators, identifying students, developing a curriculum, or designing a community center building – we discover how real-life conditions can both challenge our vision and contribute to its fulfillment.

Finally, a thoughtful, compelling vision can not only improve existing institutions; it can lead to the invention of new ones. Such a vision can galvanize the will of the community and its leaders, ignite the creativity of teachers, hearten parents, and motivate gifted people to invest their talent and passion in the revitalization of Jewish life.

What does translation mean in the context of education?

Visions are often formulated in the language of theory. They make claims about the nature of the human beings to be educated and about the purposes of education. Thus, Greenberg believes that human beings are born with a spiritual instinct, an innate need to find answers to profound questions that must not be thwarted.[2] Twersky, on the other hand, contends that the spiritual curiosity of human beings will be distorted rather than cultivated unless they are initiated from the earliest age into a life of religious practice (*mitzvot* and *halakhah*).

Visions are, however, more comprehensive than theories. They make a variety of factual assumptions about the relevant educational environment – that is, they assume what powerful learning can achieve. They invite us to speculate about how enduring the educational experiences of early childhood, adolescence, or adulthood can be. They suggest educational goals, lead us to choose particular approaches to teaching and learning, and specify the content of a curriculum. Visions emphasize the importance of some educational settings over others. They may suggest how schooling and informal education can be connected or even integrated.

As specifically theoretical statements, visions draw on the conceptual vo-cabularies of academic disciplines – philosophy, psychology, sociology, polit-ical science, and others – as well as on the subjects taught in schools, such as physics, chemistry, social studies, philosophy, and Jewish philosophy. Their rhetoric can be appealing intellectually and emotionally, but the experience of those who participate in education – learners, teachers, and policy makers – cannot be encompassed by any one theory or even a combination of theories, however ingenious. An analysis of the life of students or teachers in a school will disclose that they are bombarded by scores of influences, affected every day by many different people, by the rules of the institution, and by the society beyond the school doors.[3] The richest theoretical formulation inevitably falls short of explaining the impact of education in its intricate and unpredictable reality.

The history of education is replete with examples of promising ideas that failed because their proponents assumed that the power of the idea was sufficient in itself to reform educational practice. A perennial example is the claim that to be successful, all a teacher needs to know is the subject matter. According to this view, if a teacher really knows history, for example, he or she is bound to teach it well. It is therefore assumed that courses in departments of education and mentored experience in classroom teaching are unnecessary, even a waste of time.

Teachers and students continue to pay for such simplistic thinking. So many of us have suffered from boring classes taught by great scholars, or from elementary and high school teachers who knew their subject but were unable to make contact with their students.

The translation of a theory into practice is an art, one that requires us to consider the necessary elements of education, one by one and together as they influence each other. It is only such translation that can turn theory into vision, a comprehensive guide to education in the actual circumstances that confront us.

For over fifty years, scholars of education have discussed which elements must be taken into account in deliberations about education and in efforts to improve it. Ralph Tyler has proposed key elements in curriculum, Joseph Schwab in scientific enquiry and curriculum, Lee Shulman in professional education, Seymour Fox in personality theory, and, most recently, David Cohen in teaching and learning.[4]

Schwab, the philosopher of education, calls these elements "commonplaces."[5] He suggests four: the student, the teacher, the milieu (the society in which education is enacted), and the subject matter being taught. Further, Schwab claims that any educational problem requires their concurrent consideration. If one of the commonplaces is excluded in educational deliberations, the decisions that result will be skewed and the programs based on those decisions are very likely to fail.[6]

To move from theory to implementation, then, all the elements considered indispensable must be taken into account. Otherwise, a new method of teaching Bible, for example, may captivate students and excite parents, but can nevertheless be sabotaged by teachers who do not believe in it or by a culture of materialism so pervasive that it undermines the values advocated in the classroom.[7]

Our project encouraged us, and sometimes forced us, to undertake the difficult, invigorating activity of translation. The interaction between the scholars who proposed the visions and the educators invited to consider them in practice raised challenging questions. Do we know how to educate teachers so that they can help students become adults committed to Judaism while intensely involved in the modern world, as Meyer's vision proposes? Or, since mastery of the Hebrew language is essential for a successful Jewish education in Greenberg's view, are there enough teachers to teach Jewish texts in Hebrew? If not, how long would it take to recruit and train them – and how expensive would it be?

In their contributions to the deliberations, the educators challenged the scholars about both the meaning and the feasibility of their visions in the everyday world. Sometimes the scholars elaborated on their initial formulations; at other times, they adapted the visions to respond to the educators' practical knowledge.

There were also times when the educators' objections to a vision's apparent impracticality were reversed by the experience of the scholar himself. For example, the educators believed that Michael Rosenak's vision was overly optimistic in its conviction that a Jewish community could agree on common elements to be emphasized in the curricula of all its schools, whether Orthodox, Conservative, Reform, Reconstructionist, communal, or secular. They were surprised and moved to learn about the enthusiastic response of lay leaders in New York to Rosenak's presentation of his essay. That these leaders had been inspired by Rosenak's ideas and felt such a vision had a "fighting chance" led the educators to reconsider their initial skepticism.

Our work with the educators persuaded us that the process of translation is equally effective when it moves from practice to theory. What takes place in a camp or classroom can reveal the implicit vision of education, provide its most persuasive critique, or even amplify its scope.[8]

To make words on a page come alive in a community means to experiment, to learn from mistakes, to try a new approach, sometimes to fail, and inevitably to reformulate the initial idea in light of experience. No one can write a step-by-step manual for success. Rather, success is the consequence of the ability both to justify an idea and demonstrate its implementation.

Focusing on some of the current critical topics in Jewish education, this chapter discusses the implications of the scholars' visions for practice – and the improvement or even transformation of the field that could result.

Lifelong Learning

All the scholars were committed to visions that require lifelong learning, since "graduation" from Jewish education is an oxymoron.

The human beings Twersky hopes to educate are halakhic Jews, challenged throughout their lives by day-to-day dilemmas they may not have previously encountered. If Jews are leading their lives according to *halakhah,* they do not expect to have a rabbi or scholar at their side to help them make every decision in family life, business ethics, or politics. Rather, to resolve their problems they need to make decisions about which principles of Jewish law and thought (or *halakhah*) should be applied and how to apply them. Although they may need to consult a rabbi from time to time about a difficulty they cannot resolve, as educated Jews they are continually refreshing and replenishing their knowledge of the tradition, striving to broaden and deepen their *bikiut* (erudition) so that they have a sufficiently rich set of principles from which to choose the appropriate action.

The ongoing and never-ending process of learning and of choosing the halakhic course of action links them to their fellow Jews around the world who are engaged in the same process and also to Jews across past centuries. This point is beautifully illustrated by Rabbi Joseph B. Soloveitchik's portrayal of the living engagement of students with the great sages of the tradition:

> Suddenly, the door opens and an old man, much older than the Rebbe [R. Soloveitchik], enters. He is the grandfather of the Rebbe, Reb Chaim Brisker (1853–1918). It would be most difficult to study Talmud with students who are trained in the sciences and mathematics, were it not for his method. . . .
>
> The door opens again and another old man comes in. He is older than Reb Chaim, for he lived in the seventeenth century. His name is Reb Sabbatai Cohen (1622–1663), known as the *Shakh,* who must be present when civil law, *dinei mamonot,* is discussed. Many more visitors arrive, some from the eleventh, twelfth, and thirteenth centuries, and others harking back to antiquity – Rabbenu Tam (1090–1171), Rashi (1040–1105), Rambam (1135–1204), Rabad (1125–1198), Rashba (1245–1310), Rabbi Akiba (40–135), and others. These scholarly giants of the past are bidden to take their seats.
>
> The Rebbe introduces the guests to his pupils, and the dialogue commences. The Rambam states a halakhah; the Rabad disagrees sharply, as is his wont. Some students interrupt to defend the Rambam, and they express themselves harshly against the Rabad, as young people are apt to do. The Rebbe softly corrects the students and suggests more restrained tones. . . . Rabbenu Tam is called upon to express his opinion, and, suddenly, a symposium of generations comes into existence. Young students debate earlier generations with an air of daring familiarity, and a crescendo of discussion ensues.
>
> All speak one language; all pursue one goal; all are committed to a common vision; and all operate with the same categories. A *Mesorah* collegiality is achieved, a friendship, a comradeship of old and young, spanning antiquity, the Middle Ages, and modern times.[9]

Brinker's worldview is very different. His vision of Jewish education is based on the principle of freedom. Educated Jews are people steeped in the sources of Jewish culture and civilization, active members of their Jewish communities and the Jewish community worldwide, but free and able to choose those aspects of Jewish life, as well as those of other cultures, that will guide them.

According to this view, a successful Jewish and general education should offer learners the tools and strength to be able to make such decisions. Brinker emphasizes this point by calling the learner a *mithanekh* – someone who is continually educating himself throughout his life.[10] A *mithanekh* is prepared and motivated to contend with the moral and cultural issues facing humankind. There is no effective way for a person to do so, however, without his being deeply rooted in a particular culture. On this critical matter, Brinker agrees with Israel Scheffler, who at the close of his essay states:

> The particular educated person is not simply interchangeable with every other such person. He or she is situated historically and culturally; and it is, I would argue, essential that knowledge of this situation enter into the educational learning of such a person, having a peculiar claim on his educational energies. One who had no knowledge of his own past, had no contact with the history that formed him, no understanding of the philosophical, religious, psychological, and sociological trends that had shaped his contemporary situation, could hardly be accounted an educated person. In these reflections, Jewish education has an important form of justification based on the very concept of education.[11]

Although lifelong learning was an ideal for all the scholars, they knew they were vulnerable to the charge of elitism, given that many Jews have not been exposed to Jewish learning either through their families or through education. Nevertheless, every one of them believed that the ideas in his vision, carefully analyzed and skillfully translated into practice, could address the needs of people with very limited Jewish backgrounds as well.

In fact, the scholars were eager to engage with adults who had not had the opportunity to study or were not previously interested in Jewish learning. In his essay, Greenberg articulates his belief that "the soul knows no rest until it gains some comprehension of . . . the realm of value": A human being is always searching for spiritual meaning. Thus, adults who have attained prosperity and status but feel unfulfilled may be intrigued by the study of such texts as Ecclesiastes, which speaks of the limits of affluence. Greenberg has taught biblical texts to adults in secular kibbutzim and in adult education programs throughout North America; he has seen the exhilaration of questing adults who first encounter the power of Jewish sacred literature.

One of the educators in our project, Ruth Calderon, founded in the heart of Tel Aviv a college called Alma Hebrew College that has drawn some of Israel's most prominent — and secular — intellectuals, artists, television celebrities, and politicians to the study of Jewish texts from a cultural perspective.

So remote is such study from the experience of many Israelis that a well-known novelist told her, "My children, who have never seen a page of Talmud, are unable to understand my decision to devote time to studying Talmud on a daily basis. They made one request: '*Abba*, please don't tell anybody about your unusual habit!' "

At Alma, Calderon held a *Tikkun Leil Shavuot*, the traditional all-night study session on the holiday of Shavuot to commemorate the Jewish people's receiving of the Torah. Together, students studied such texts as the Book of Ruth and discussed topics such as the influence of talmudic texts on contemporary Hebrew literature.

After the first year, the crowd was so large and the experiment so successful that the study sessions were televised live to thousands of viewers throughout Israel, confirming Greenberg's faith that classical texts and their interpretations can speak to adults who have not been immersed in them all their lives.

Michael Meyer recognizes the inability of many families to transmit Jewish learning to their children. In his essay, Meyer urges synagogues to help foster communities of adult learners who can discover the vitality of Jewish study:

> In many instances parents who join the learning community lack Jewish memories, possessing neither the collective memories of the Jewish people nor the personal memories of Jewish experiences gained in childhood. This is clearly the case for Jews-by-choice, but is increasingly true also for Jews-by-birth. . . . Within the community their trajectory runs from history to midrash [commentary] and memory, to finding their own personal story within the collective story of Israel and to locating Jewish values they can internalize from within the textual treasury of Judaism.

Although for the scholars the ideal Jewish education begins in childhood, all feel strongly that learners can join the process of becoming educated Jews at any point in life.

Early Childhood Education

The Jewish education of young children is essential to the visions of all the scholars. For Meyer, early childhood education is extremely significant because of his belief that a deep emotional attachment to Judaism is a precondition for commitment. Since today only a minority of Jewish homes in the Diaspora can create an environment likely to lead to commitment, early childhood education must concentrate on cultivating in a child powerful memories and lasting ties. The lingering melodies of Jewish songs, the awe of candlelighting, the joy of giving thanks in ancient words of blessing can have a strong emotional impact that are central to Meyer's vision of early childhood education.

Brinker is influenced by the critical role of early childhood education in nurturing a "new Jew" – the Israeli. It was in early childhood programs that the children of immigrants mastered the Hebrew language; celebrated as a community the Jewish holidays; and came to understand the significance of holidays such as Tu bi-Shevat, which Zionist educators directly connected to the cultivation of the land. Through their children's education, parents born in Israel, as well as those who recently arrived, were introduced to the latest approaches to child care.

Despite the shoestring budget of the young state, the Ministry of Education, the *Histadrut ha-Morim* (Teachers Union), and the kibbutzim invested significant resources in the education of talented and committed early childhood teachers, who were sent abroad to study with the students of Froebel, Pestalozzi, and Montessori.[12]

When Jewish children are educated in an environment where all the holidays are Jewish (compared to the Western Diaspora, where the holidays and their symbols are primarily Christian), they are likely to develop a natural sense of belonging that is a cornerstone of identity in Brinker's vision.

For Twersky, a child should be introduced to Jewish practice by loving parents, whose character and conduct the child will want to imitate. This mimetic process is further developed in early childhood programs led by teachers who also serve as role models. Imitation begins at the earliest possible age, which is the first stage of *hergel,* religious habituation. This stage is subsequently enriched by the intellectual and emotional understanding acquired through study in school.[13]

Greenberg sees early childhood experiences, particularly those that nurture curiosity, as precious resources. The questions a child asks about God, or about why there is evil in the world, must be encouraged and taken very seriously as reflections of humankind's spiritual quest. They are pristine forms of questions Jews have asked and addressed in their sacred texts throughout their history. When adults respond to such questions, they are introducing the child to educational antecedents of the skills required to enter the tradition of *parshanut,* commentary.[14]

Even more momentous than the content of the adults' answers are the feelings and body language that accompany them. Children must sense that their questions matter tremendously to the adults they love and respect. Greenberg would say to parents and early childhood educators: "You know how excited you get when a child utters his first words or takes her first step? Isn't that how you should feel when a child asks a spiritual question?"

To respond well to children's questions such as "Why does the sun rise?" or "Why are there seasons?" parents and educators have turned to the natural sciences for their answers and to the social sciences – especially child psychology – for how best to express those answers so that children will understand them. Greenberg joins researchers, such as Robert Coles, J. W. Fowler, and R. G. Goldman, who have studied the importance of spiritual questions in young children, but he emphasizes spiritual development as a goal of early childhood education.[15] The curriculum in a Greenberg program of early childhood education would become the joint effort of talented teachers; perceptive rabbis and scholars who can suggest appropriate responses to children's questions; and psychologists who are committed to the belief that spirituality is a basic element of personality.

A critical objective of a Greenberg early childhood program in the Diaspora would be the acquisition of Hebrew as a second language. Since, according to Greenberg, "the uniquely Jewish store of concepts and values cannot be transmitted in translation," the study of sacred texts and their commentaries, in their original language, is of the highest importance.

Early childhood schooling is the period in a child's development when a second language is most easily acquired, fortified in this case by the child's motivation to understand how the Jewish tradition has responded to his or her central concerns. For both reasons, an intensive program of Hebrew study in early childhood is eminently feasible. Such programs have been introduced in schools such as the Tarbut School in Mexico City; the Herzl Bialik School in Montreal, Canada; and as early as the 1940s, the Beit Hayeled School in New York City.

What is the practical result of these differing approaches to early childhood? Greenberg, for example, would disagree with the special emphasis Meyer places on the emotional realm, because he is convinced that intellectual and spiritual discovery is itself a profound emotional experience. In distinction from Twersky, Greenberg would insist that the spiritual dimension must be given primacy over the behavioral, for in his view religious habituation without explicit attention to its spiritual dimension runs the risk of sterility. And unlike Brinker, Greenberg hopes that in their early childhood education, even very young children will begin to find the answers to their existential questions within Judaism.

Notwithstanding the differences among them, the scholars agree that effective early childhood education is necessary for their visions of a successful Jewish education. The reality of current practice, however, belies the vanguard role the scholars assign to this period of a child's development. Although the number of Jewish early childhood programs in the United States has grown rapidly, the teachers and directors are the most underpaid professionals in the field. In the United States, their training in general education is often advanced, because of state accreditation requirements, but they have minimal training in Jewish studies and have received the least Jewish education of all teachers in Jewish schools.

Indeed, with 10 percent of teachers in Jewish early childhood settings not Jewish (and in one community, as many as 21 percent), imagine the limitations for a program like Greenberg's, with its demands that teachers both respond to their young students' theological questions from a Jewish perspective and immerse them in a Hebrew-language environment![16] Even in Israel, the emphasis on and investment in early childhood education, once the envy of the world, is declining.

Paradoxically, early childhood education provides the Jewish community with an extraordinary opportunity. Many parents, when they start out, secretly believe that with the right education their child could change the world. The Jewish tradition supports this notion. Maimonides claims that any human being may grow up to become as great as Moshe Rabbenu (Moses).[17] During these years parents are willing to invest incredible energy, hope, and money in the future of their children, and, consequently, in their education. While children are in nursery and kindergarten, their parents' initial faith in education is a priceless resource for the education of the entire family.

What do parents want above all? That their child turn out to be a decent human being, a *mensch*. Imagine if parents could hear the message of Jewish education as "What does it mean to be a *mensch*? Come see an early childhood program where the process is well under way."

Lee Shulman brought to my attention the power of such programs. He calls them existence proofs, or "visions of the possible." An existence proof is a demonstration that an important educational idea can be translated into practice.[18] When educators, parents, and other policy makers can visit a site where they see and experience a vision as it lives, the impact is enormous. Encouraged by the evidence before them to replicate such programs, they are then motivated to invest greater effort and resources in Jewish education.

The creation of existence proofs in early childhood education is a unique opportunity for Jewish education both in Israel and the Diaspora. Throughout our project, we discussed how a school or community could join forces with a foundation or, in Israel, with the Ministry of Education to demonstrate that if an early childhood program is saturated with a compelling vision, the children and their parents would be deeply affected. If the educators were well prepared and the curriculum sensitive to the particular interests and abilities of the children and their families, parents might also be convinced to set aside serious time for their own Jewish education.

Education Formal and Informal

Jewish schooling cannot be equated with Jewish education. In our discussion on vision and schooling, we emphasized that Jewish education must include the application of ideas to life. The scholars concur that, for Jews, learning cannot be separated from doing. Jewish education is character education.

Brinker's educated Jews must be knowledgeable, sophisticated, fully participating members of their Jewish communities. Only when they are committed to "their family" – the Jewish people – will they be able to make a significant contribution to contemporary life.

For Twersky, halakhic Jews must live righteously, as they resolve the complex issues they encounter every day through a talmudic dialectic illuminated by nuanced philosophic concerns.

According to Meyer, Jews need to learn how to live ethically as they face the conflict between tradition and modernity. However, their Jewish identity demands a bias in favor of a commitment to a Jewish approach to existential concerns. Such a bias must be buttressed and justified by a profound knowledge of the Jewish tradition.

From Greenberg's perspective, successfully educated Jews will, throughout their lives, use the classical Jewish sources and their commentaries – in the original Hebrew – to "serve as a moral guide in our day and age."

In the project's deliberations, we considered how the scholars' visions could influence and even transform the essential elements of formal education – schools, their curriculum, and their personnel. We looked at the way these visions might shape education and educators in informal settings, and at the possibilities of integrating the two realms, since we know of no way that a serious vision of Jewish education can neglect thinking, feeling, or doing.

For the most part, contemporary Jewish education in Israel and throughout the Jewish world reflects the notion that schooling and the learning that takes place in classrooms are mostly cognitive activities, minimizing and sometimes neglecting the role of emotions and behavior. Pressed for time, educators consider themselves fortunate if students understand and appreciate Judaism's basic ideas. To act on these ideas, to behave according to the moral principles taught in classrooms, is a key goal of Jewish education but is often seen as beyond the influence of Jewish schools, nurtured instead in the family or in informal educational settings.

The power of youth movements in Israel from the 1930s to the 1960s is cited to demonstrate the impact of education outside the classroom:

> The story of the settling of the land of Israel, of the laying of the foundations of a new society and its culture, and finally of the establishment of national sovereignty is, to a very large degree, the story of these youth groups.... It is hard to imagine that in a period of twenty-eight years all these accomplishments took place: the inspiring of generations of youth in the Diaspora; their training for labor in the land of Israel; their *aliyah*; their settling the country, which was the chief accomplishment of the Zionist endeavor; the transformation of Jewish lifestyle and culture; and the readiness to defend what had been established in the land of Israel through organized military activity that later became the army, without which the establishment of the State of Israel would have been impossible.[19]

Although youth movements are no longer as significant as they were in the 1950s and early 1960s, they continue to be a factor in Israeli education and identity building. Today, the Israel Association of Community Centers is making a significant contribution to informal Jewish education. *Matnasim* (Israeli community centers, or ICCs) are not only critical in the absorption of hundreds of thousands of Russian immigrants but have also developed religious services for secular Israelis, with thousands participating each year in Yom Kippur services.

In the Diaspora, Jewish summer camps have long been recognized as a powerful means for forging Jewish commitment. In the United States, denominational camps are a significant part of the religious education of both campers and staff members. Jewish community centers (JCCs) have 100,000 Jewish children in their camping programs. Denominational and Zionist youth movements, and such campus organizations as Hillel, create contexts for young people to "behave Jewishly." Sports, art and drama, field trips, family weekend retreats, and travel to Israel provide rich educational opportunities for Diaspora students, particularly in the moral domain.

For Israeli students, trips to study the Holocaust and visits to Diaspora Jewish communities are influential. In France, the Jewish scouting movement continues to play a very important role in the education of young people, as do Zionist youth movements throughout Europe.

Whereas in the past, the family, the neighborhood, and even "the street" were living demonstrations of Jewish ideas as they were interpreted and practiced, today it is informal education that can offer settings for the implementation of ideas that have been studied in the classroom but must shape life beyond its walls.[20] Such activities as camping and educational travel can potentially foster a learning community that engages adolescents, teachers, counselors, and parents in an ongoing attempt to live by the insights of the Jewish tradition: No matter how eloquent a teacher may be about how to behave to a fellow human being, when a teenager at a summer camp is setting up a tent with his or her study partner during a downpour, an abstract principle is put to the test!

Programs of informal education also offer enough time, which is not to be minimized in contemporary life, and a unique environment in which the body and soul can speak to each other, rather than being compartmentalized.

The distinction between formal and informal education may be useful for the organization of Jewish education, but it can be an impediment to the attainment of its goals. To encompass both the learning and the doing that Judaism demands, great schools must incorporate *tzedakah* and community service into their curriculum, just as outstanding summer camps have also offered programs of text study and Hebrew literacy. The relationship of formal to informal education is not one of mutual exclusion. Schooling focuses more on thinking and understanding, whereas informal education addresses itself more to feeling and acting – but they do, and should, interrelate and overlap.

There have been many attempts to link the work of Israeli youth movements, both religious and secular, to the programs of schools, particularly in the area of citizenship education, but with little success. The Community School movement in Israel was established in 1977, with the specific goal of enriching what was taught in the classroom through programs held after school hours. Despite the nobility of its intention, this movement has not yet achieved its aspirations.

In the worldwide Jewish community, there have been sporadic attempts to create camping programs that are year-round or designed for entire families. There have even been efforts to coordinate education in schools with the education that takes place in informal settings, most prominently with educational experiences in Israel. However, there are almost no examples of sustained efforts to develop a comprehensive plan – a curriculum – to coordinate the way concern for your fellow human being, for example, is taught in the classroom *and* acted upon on a sports field.

Despite its avowed importance, informal education is not yet viewed as a serious profession, grounded in a theoretical basis, with the components that formal education has in place. For example, there are very few programs – in the United States, Israel, or anywhere else – where people can be prepared specifically for a career in Jewish informal education. Nor are there yet enough opportunities for their ongoing professional education.

Certain institutions in a community have come to be equated with either formal education (schools) or informal education (JCCs and ICCs). Often sponsored by different organizations and sometimes competitive with one another, they suffer from a lack of integration, which is a loss for everyone.

For fifty years, both literature in education and speeches about Jewish identity have been arguing that neither formal nor informal education alone can create Jews who are excited about their tradition, want to participate in it, and know how to do so. Imagine a community in which the JCC says to schools: Our centers are open to you. Tell us what texts you are teaching pre-Bar and pre-Bat Mitzvah students about how the Jewish tradition defines a responsible person, and then let us suggest experiences, extrapolated from those texts, that will allow them to act on those values. Today, JCCs see their role as introducing Jewish values through the activities that take place under their sponsorship – working with the elderly or preparing for Jewish holidays. In the future they could also ask: How will members of our swimming staff begin to see themselves as Jewish educators?

A challenge for Jewish education in our day is to find contexts where formal and informal education are permeable to each other, where the intellectual, emotional, and behavioral are cultivated together, deliberately and educationally.[21]

Text

In considering the role of schooling in Jewish education, the scholars' visions highlight the centrality of text. Whether you are a halakhist or staunchly secular, you will have to refer to books. A well-known rabbinic formulation sums it up: *Neitei sefer v'nehze,* "Let us open the book and see." If you and I are having an argument, let us turn to the text to see whose position it substantiates.

Judaism is text rooted. All the scholars – specialists in Jewish thought, comparative literature, Bible, Talmud, modern Jewish history, philosophy of Jewish education, or general philosophy – center their visions of Jewish education on the written word.

Text, not textbooks, is at the heart of Jewish schooling. It must be at the core of the curriculum and influence pedagogy as well. The scholars believe in text and insist upon it, even as they disagree about which texts are essential and what role they should play. By text they mean original sources – not summaries or descriptions.

The scholars are equally committed to close analysis of the sources and their commentaries (also texts). They want the student to learn to ask: What question is the author answering? What dilemma is being addressed? For example, what distinction is being drawn between Jewish law and the Greek or Roman law of the surrounding societies?

What is a text meant to do? First, to arouse and respond to intellectual desire. All the scholars think that human beings are guided and energized by an appeal to the intellect. Second, to stir and satisfy emotional yearning. Read the text properly, and it will inspire profound feeling. Even a text that has no apparent connection to emotional issues can be, if you are prepared, intensely engaging as you decode it and understand its intent.

A teacher who is extremely responsive to his or her students can serve as a *shadchan* – a matchmaker, in Greenberg's term – between the text and the students' sensibilities. Of course, all caring teachers ask the question: How can I make contact between this text and that learner?

In 1975, the Melton Centre for Jewish Education in the Diaspora of the Hebrew University developed a curriculum on Jewish values, created by Michael Rosenak. The curriculum was eventually adopted by schools in Israel and in Jewish communities throughout the world. Accompanying the curriculum was a seminar on how to introduce the material and approach to the participating teachers and students.

One of the first experimental sites was a Jewish school in Melbourne, Australia. The curriculum expert sent by the Melton Centre to work with the teachers in that school returned to the seminar in despair. The unit, on the Book of Ruth, focused on the value of loyalty – which the curriculum developers thought would be very moving to adolescents, who are preoccupied by the meaning of loyalty and friendship.[22]

Instead, the teacher reported, some of the students burst out laughing, making fun of the text and declaring, "Who cares about loyalty? All we care about is making money."

How might she respond to these students? The teacher's colleagues at the seminar proposed that she begin by saying, "All right, you believe the Book of Ruth is composed of ridiculous and naive values. What are your values?

Let's put them under a magnifying glass and imagine a world guided by your values."

The students would respond that their values are getting rich and "making it." Then the question becomes: How do you conduct a society built on those values? As the students sketch for themselves a portrait of a society based on "survival of the financially fittest," whose members are interested only in protecting their gains, they will realize that such a society is bound to implode.

The teacher can point to a biblical narrative that corresponds to the students' realization. In the Book of Genesis, as Nahum Sarna and others have explained it, the flood happened after *va-timaleh ha-aretz ḥamas,* the world was filled with lawlessness. Based on his philological expertise, Sarna interprets *ḥamas* as moral violence. When the moral order has been destroyed, the physical order cannot survive. A flood is the result of the breakdown.[23] When the teacher has helped students encounter the consequences of their expressed values, when they see that a world based on their values cannot work, then he or she can return to the original question of what values *can* guide humankind, and perhaps ask at this point, "What is loyalty and why is it important? Here is a text called the Book of Ruth, a text about building a world rather than destroying one. Let us read it together, understand what problems the text is grappling with and how they are addressed."

Clearly, we are not talking about text in isolation from the student, the teacher, and the world in which they live. We soon find ourselves considering Schwab's four commonplaces and their interrelationship – the nature of the student, the understanding of the teacher, the influence of society, and a penetrating analysis of the subject matter – in this case, the text.

Although all of the scholars have faith in the power of text, Greenberg has the most extreme faith, since he has confidence in the capacity of a text, rendered authentically, to touch even an adult alienated from Judaism.

The scholars also agree that one of the major purposes of a Jewish text is to guide behavior.[24] For some learners, their ability to understand the full meaning of a text is enhanced when informal education accompanies formal study. If, as Greenberg teaches us, biblical prayer was revolutionary in inviting people to pray personally and spontaneously,[25] how can we reconcile that idea with the fixed liturgy of the Siddur and its three-times-a-day mandatory ritual? The student can study the words of the prayer, but may need music and an aesthetic setting to release the emotions that motivated the religious writers whose words the Siddur preserves.

In Jewish schools, the activity of *tefillah,* prayer, can be educationally troubling, often lacking fervor or meaning for the student. The customary approach of formal education is much more appropriate for the analysis of a prayer text than for the experience of prayer. A continuum between formal and informal education would allow students to explore fruitfully the tension between predetermined, traditional texts and the need for spontaneity that is central to both Greenberg's and Twersky's conception of prayer.

To animate inert words, Greenberg cautions, Jewish education must transmit a significant amount of sacred texts – significant in being persuasive choices for contemporary students and significant in quantity. In other writings, Greenberg has addressed the most difficult challenges faced by the teacher who tries to match ancient texts to contemporary learners: feminism, democracy, and, as mentioned, fundamentalism.

Invited to give a lecture to an audience of senior Jewish educators in 1983, Joseph Schwab asked the question, "Can a book change your life?" The answer he offered was, "It depends. If you are ready, it can."

What is readiness? A person can read an essay and forget it the minute she has turned the last page. Ten years later she may come upon the essay accidentally – and suddenly it seems to have been written solely for her.

It is the task of Jewish education to make such contact likely rather than accidental. Once in a while, a unique individual may read a text that transforms his way of thinking. But we must not build an educational system on the exceptional person, because exceptional people are likely to find their own way, even if they have to go outside the system. Greenberg's point is that text can change your life, but you need to be prepared – by education – for the encounter.

How would a Greenberg teacher differ from a Twersky teacher in their approach to teaching Jewish text, since both would immerse the student in sacred sources?

An important aim of a Twersky teacher would be to deepen the student's practice of *mitzvot* through study. Uninformed practice can become rote behavior, whereas study dissociated from practice can be detached from life. The teacher's assignment is to maintain a living link between text and practice.

In a Twersky school, a teacher would have to believe in *Torah min-ha-shamayim* (that the text was divinely written and transmitted) in order to convey the text authentically to her students. Twersky's teacher must be a religious role model, a *shomeret mitzvot* (observer of the commandments). If she were capable of illuminating the beauty of such a life but did not herself practice it, she would not be the role model Twersky requires.

In a Greenberg school, however, the beliefs and religious practice of the teacher are not as significant as the ability to reveal the text's profundity and its capacity to speak to the spiritual yearning of students. As Greenberg says, "The basic requirement of a Bible teacher is not faith, but understanding; not assent, but recognition of the profound issues of which he treats. It is not necessary to subscribe to Islam, or Christianity, or Buddhism in order to teach them well. It is necessary to recognize in them a significant possible position on ultimate religious problems."[26] The teacher will have succeeded in transmitting the message of the text when the student understands that the text, in its discussion of ultimate theological issues, is also a symbol of the transcendent realm beyond the self.

For Brinker, text is the agent of liberation, not merely induction. The task of text in a Brinker school is to introduce the student to his history, to the thought and literature created by Jews, especially in the modern era, so that he can establish his relationship to his people on a deeper and more independent basis. Brinker wants a student whose active involvement in the world is grounded in the values and commitments of his family – which means the Jewish people and its ideas.

If the student is alive only to the message of his own culture, he is not free but provincial, which Brinker considers a failure. On the other hand, if the student immerses himself in Jewish texts and ideas and then rejects aspects of Judaism while still participating in the Jewish community and the world as a responsible citizen, Brinker would claim that the study of Judaism has nevertheless made an important contribution to the student's development. Defending the student's freedom to choose what to retain and what to discard, Brinker nevertheless believes that the student is likely to find some aspects of Jewish life meaningful.

Brinker, too, is committed to original sources, and to Hebrew, but for different reasons than Greenberg. Greenberg's vision is addressed to Jews all over the world, whereas Brinker is focused mainly on Jews in Israel, whose mother tongue is Hebrew. His attention is on the texts of the Jewish people in the last 200 years – because for Brinker, civil emancipation was more determining of the Jewish condition than anything that preceded it. The Enlightenment was as influencial an event for Jews as Sinai; the Enlightenment is when Jews began to move into the modern world, to became a nation like other nations, with a dream of shaping their own destiny and building their own society.

The Brinker teacher would ask such questions as, What values should characterize our Jewish society? How should we treat the Arabs in our midst? What is the value and risk of nationalism? The texts as they are conveyed in a Brinker school would reveal not only the nobility of the Jewish past but its conflicts. In such a school, Brinker's students would be in the process of becoming *mithankhim*, people for whom the goal of schooling is to become self-educating throughout their lives.

The induction into the Jewish tradition of students in a Meyer school, as in a Twersky school, would be deepened through text. In both institutions the text would be viewed as conveying not only values but belief. Theology is important to Meyer, as it is to Twersky: We are commanded to live in God's image and to express Jewish theological commitments in our dialogue with the world. Meyer's critique of Reform Jewish education in the past is that it taught what we as Jews have in common with the rest of the world without sufficiently emphasizing how we are different.

In Meyer's approach, text contributes to the student's initiation into religious practice. Greenberg's approach to text includes no such requirement. But Meyer also differs from Twersky, because his school would prepare the student to choose only those practices that seem most meaningful. Unlike Twersky, Meyer focuses on texts from Jewish history that show how Judaism has changed over time. His teachers would not subscribe to Twersky's view of Judaism as a conversation all participants would recognize as continuous from the biblical era through the Talmud through Maimonides until our day.

The Principal

Both research and experience demonstrate that visions can be mere pronouncements or can have the most intense impact on a school.[27] As we worked on our project, the scholars and educators continually returned to the observation that the principal has to be not only an effective administrator but, above all, an educational leader.

If the principal is not encouraging, supporting and leading the school in the translation of the vision's ideas into day-to-day practice, the school will drift, its teachers will lose their focus, and students and parents will be denied the excitement of an education whose details are designed to offer them both discernment and meaning.[28]

Equally, if management is relegated to second-class status, if those responsible for administering a school are not partners to the vision and full participants in actualizing its aspirations, then the vision is likely to deteriorate into slogans, rather than being rooted in the real life of the school. The means of education are not neutral, whether they involve student discipline, a school's policy on scholarships, or the job description of a new secretary.

Thus, in schools where vision matters, there cannot be a situation in which management means dealing with the mundane and educational leadership means dealing with the elevated and spiritual. The environment of a school – its "oxygen" – is determined by the commitment of the entire staff.

The leaders of the school – principal, administrators and board members – have to ask not only "What do we hope to achieve?" but "How are we doing?" They are the ones who must insist that evaluation and self-assessment be built into institutional life. Despite the unrelenting pressures of the day, they must refuse to separate the vision from its ongoing implementation and review.

If vision is to be taken seriously in Jewish education, then communities in Israel and the Diaspora will have to view the recruitment, training, and placement of outstanding people in the role of principal as essential.

James Coleman's groundbreaking research on school desegregation in the United States was interpreted by some to mean that the socioeconomic status of parents was more influential than the school on the parity of educational achievement between black and white students.[29]

Thirteen years later, Ronald Edmonds cited follow-up studies that found schools had definitely improved the achievement of students of lower socio-economic status.[30] A determining factor in the success of these schools was the principal.

Those interested in improving American public education understand the power and impact of principals.[31] Principal centers have been created in the United States to offer the kind of ongoing in-service education that increases principals' effectiveness.

Neither in Israel nor in Jewish education in the Diaspora has there yet been a sufficient investment in the pre- and in-service education of principals. Only recently have parents and lay leaders recognized the critical shortage of principals for day schools, both elementary and high school. With the growth of day school education, there has been simultaneously a significant reduction in the number of full-time supplementary school principals. How can the result be improved Jewish education for the approximately two-thirds of children in the system whose Jewish learning takes place in supplementary schools? Someone has to be in charge of a school, devoting not only the time and energy to running it as it deserves but also to introducing, guiding, and goading all the "shareholders" to shape the school's vision of the kind of Jew they want to develop and nurture there.

At a Scheffler school, for example, students' thoughts and feelings would be given the utmost respect, whatever the starting point of their educational journey. The way the office staff greets a parent, the atmosphere when a student comes in with a problem, how teachers are treated by the administration – these factors either enhance or undermine the school's commitment to regard each person in the building as a unique human being. The principal is the key person responsible for creating a school culture that expresses and cultivates this value.

A Brinker school, which places a premium on the capacity of its students to make independent decisions based on their critical analysis of profound ideas, has to make students' experimentation and mistakes essential aspects of their learning. The principal has to support such experimentation – which is not easy to do and sometimes even less easy to justify.

In a Greenberg school, the principal not only studies during the school day but is seen by his students as applying the fruits of his study to his work life. Students have to pass him in the library, or see him poring over a classical text. Although there are never enough hours in the day, the Greenberg principal has set aside a fixed time for learning. We must remember, too, that Greenberg described his third goal as intense involvement in the community. The principal, then, is working with students during school hours as they raise funds and prepare food packages (*ma'ot ḥitim*) to be distributed to the poor before Passover.

It may seem from these descriptions that very few people qualify for such a role. One response is ongoing professional education, since principals, like teachers, can and do grow through in-service education. If the role of the principal requires fifteen areas of expertise, a principal may, at the beginning, be very strong in five and very weak in five. Someone, perhaps a coach or a group of consultants, has to work with the principal to assess which of the areas need to be strengthened immediately, which can be developed over time, and which ones can be delegated to members of the faculty or a lay member of the board.[32] A principal's abilities also need to be deepened and refined, because every professional has to grow, a leader all the more so. And yet in Jewish education there are even fewer opportunities for serious in-service development for principals than there are for teachers.[33]

No matter how much we strengthen those who hold current jobs, however, and even surround them with others to complement their talents, there are not nearly enough qualified people to do the work, particularly since many new Jewish schools are opening every year.

Let us look at one current response to this crisis. A new community high school is opening in your city, and you, the chair of the search committee, need a principal who not only understands the mission of the forthcoming school but can create the kind of school whose students will be accepted (preferably by early decision) into top American colleges. You have interviewed candidates with wonderful Jewish studies backgrounds who have never run a high school, as well as talented candidates from general education who are not Jewish.

Suddenly the following resumé appears on your desk: The headmaster of one of the most elite high schools in the United States – the equivalent of Andover or Exeter – who happens to be Jewish is interested in a career change and has applied for the position. Everyone is excited. The anxiety about admissions to college is moot – and the headmaster is even Jewish! Of course, you recognize that this candidate lacks a background in Jewish studies, but you are prepared to invest in a director of Jewish studies to fill the gap.

This appears to be an acceptable solution to the problem of too few qualified candidates. However, such an approach ignores the fact that no matter how outstanding your candidate, he will not be able to build a Jewish school steeped in vision. If the principal of your new school is going to be the one who articulates the vision, fights for it, and embeds it in the culture of the school, how can he inspire faculty, parents, students, and the community to be his partners when he has so little familiarity with Jewish thought, Jewish behavior, and Jewish life?

Judaism is a language, both literally, as transmitted by Hebrew text, and metaphorically. If you are trying to create a vision-suffused school, how can the principal not be someone deeply knowledgeable and committed to the chief rationale for your school's existence? If Jewish education is character education, then the goal of your school is to produce a person of both Jewish learning and the life meant to result from it. The head of the school should represent the kind of Jewish person to be fostered there.

How can our hypothetical candidate become such a person? The number of impressive people in Israel and the Diaspora who are willing to change their professions in midcareer is indeed encouraging.[34] Even exceptional people, however, are not yet qualified to lead Jewish educational institutions without an extended training program to introduce them to the intensive study of Jewish texts in the Hebrew language, to alternative visions of Jewish education, and to experiences in the implementation of key aspects of those visions.

There are people in related careers who might find work in Jewish education fascinating and meaningful – for example, M.A.s and Ph.D.s in Jewish studies who may not want to be academics or rabbis who may not want to serve in pulpits. Members of either group would need intensive training in education and administration, but the challenge is not an impossible one. Even so, their recruitment, training, and apprenticeship would demand a heavy investment of time – and money.

Businesses often send their top leaders to executive training centers. In the United States, in Israel, and around the world, there are now regional principal centers in general education that work with a school's professional leader throughout his or her career. It would be very exciting for a foundation, in partnership with a community, to take on the establishment of such a center for Jewish educational leaders.

In fact, this is a time for Jewish communities and Jewish foundations all over the world to think together about how we might meet the great challenge of training enough people to lead our educational institutions. There is no instant solution to the shortage of principals. However, it is important to begin a serious conversation, to consider alternatives, to inspire committed people to recognize the problem – and to get to work.

The Teacher

In discussing the primacy of text in all the visions of Jewish education conceptualized by our scholars, we offered sketches of the different teachers each vision specifies. A comparison of the teacher in Twersky's vision with the teacher in Greenberg's illustrates how two visions require different kinds of teachers.

As mentioned, Twersky's vision of Jewish education leads him to introduce the idea of *hergel,* or religious habituation, because he will not separate the practice of Judaism from its philosophical understanding. His educated Jew needs both and is engaged in both, modeling *avodat Hashem,* worship of God, and *ahavat Hashem,* love of God.

In our deliberations, Twersky emphasized that teachers also demonstrate their love of God through love of their students. Love should permeate the classroom as it does, ideally, the family, since children should begin Jewish life by watching caring parents model the first words they have been taught to say: *Torah tzivah lanu Moshe.* The meaning of the phrase is "Moses commanded us to live according to the Torah" (Deut. 33:4). Parents in such a family interpret its meaning to their children as "This is how God wants us to live."

In a Twersky school, teachers would not only live according to the commandments but be committed to and trained in a philosophical way of thinking so that they can induct their students into that mode of thought, which for Twersky is an essential aspect of *hergel*.[35]

Like Twersky, Greenberg asks that teachers be role models, but he has such faith in the power of the text that he has room for teachers who may not themselves observe many of the *mitzvot*. What Greenberg requires is a commitment by teachers to a contemplative life, so that they can, with understanding, candor, and sympathy, demonstrate in their behavior and express in the classroom the profundity of the texts they are studying with their students.

Greenberg recognizes that he is asking a great deal more of teachers in a religious school than of university professors, who can "content themselves with the Bible as literature or as archaeology without responsibility for its religious teaching." Greenberg teachers must "convey the religious significance of the Bible," which they can do only after "having gotten hold of the great spiritual issues that animate it."[36]

Such teachers must be sensitive to the psychological needs of their students, their religious growth, and their Jewish lives beyond the classroom so that they can match the learners with the texts that will continually awaken and satisfy their spiritual curiosity. In a Greenberg school, teachers are responsible for cultivating their students as "commentators in training." From the start, students would learn to recognize the questions that the classical commentators disclose in the sacred texts and join that tradition so that they might invent powerful questions and responses of their own.[37]

Curriculum specialists have learned in their work with teachers that a vision of Jewish education can succeed only when teachers understand it, are capable of teaching it in their classrooms, and are committed enough to want to do so:

First, to bring a vision to life, teachers need to recognize that it can make a vital difference in the lives of their students – and in their own lives.

Second, teachers have to be able to teach it. Almost all innovations in curriculum involve a change in both the subject matter being taught and the way it will be taught, its pedagogy. Just because teachers understand a new approach does not mean they can easily change their method of teaching.

Consider the following example. Beginning with the curricular reforms in the United States in the late 1950s and 1960s, scholars in the natural sciences and later in the social sciences, humanities, and Jewish studies urged teachers to change their teaching methods from the "lecture method" to "teaching by inquiry." In science, teachers would help students understand a scientific concept through their own experiments in a laboratory, replicating the way scientists developed or discovered the concept. In history or Bible studies, teachers would help students understand an idea through their own analysis of an original historical source or of a biblical text and its commentaries.

In evaluating the impact of these reforms, researchers discovered that there were teachers who either could not easily master the "teaching by inquiry" approach or who took a long time to do so; the same people were much more capable teachers when they used methods that were a better match for their style and skills.

Third, teachers have to want to teach the material and must believe in the assumptions underlying the approach. In 1963, when the Melton Research Center for Jewish Education at the Jewish Theological Seminary in New York introduced the new Melton curriculum for the teaching of Bible to Conservative supplementary schools in North America, its approach was very much influenced by the question: How do you teach the Bible to young people who come from families not committed to *Torah mi-Sinai,* to the idea – axiomatic in Orthodox Judaism – that the Torah was given by God to the Jewish people at Mount Sinai?

As it turned out, a considerable number of teachers in Conservative supplementary schools either identified as Orthodox Jews or had a nostalgic attachment to its ideology. They could not base their teaching on a version of Judaism whose assumption was that the Torah might not have been divinely given.

When the curricular materials were prepared, no one was aware of that possibility. The Melton method was being introduced to schools where many of the teachers understood the proposed curriculum and were capable of teaching it – but could not support one of its chief assumptions.

Teachers' own commitments must be taken into account because when the classroom doors close, it is teachers who are in charge. They are the ones in direct contact with students; they will interpret and apply the key ideas of the curriculum in such a way that students will weigh its meaning for their lives.

What kind of education nurtures teachers who are capable of contributing to the realization of these or other visions?

Twersky's teachers will have to master the curricular units of *Mikra, Mishnah,* and Talmud. They will have been habituated into the life of *halakhah* that is practiced with *kavanah* – in a manner that is earnest, purposeful, and from the heart – and have been trained in the systematic study of philosophy. These teachers will then be able to help students take the preliminary steps that can lead them to *avodat Hashem* and *ahavat Hashem.*

Greenberg stipulates that his teachers "must study Hebrew and become acquainted with the civilizations of the Near East. . . . They must also familiarize themselves with the history of ideas, with religious thought in general, with philosophy, especially in its religious garb – theology."[38] Finally, they must be willing to address contemporary existential issues forthrightly.

In our project, we recognized that the preparation of teachers requires an ongoing program of professional education. Just as doctors are expected to continue their studies throughout their professional careers, so the pre-service education of teachers has to be supplemented by in-service education – ideally, planned together. There are Israeli universities and teacher training colleges that have already combined their departments of pre-service and in-service education for this purpose.

There are also Jewish schools that have instituted in-service education programs for teachers that take place during the school day. For twenty-five years, the Tarbut School in Mexico City has organized an ongoing curricular seminar for all its teachers every Tuesday afternoon. The teachers report that the in-service training program has not only made it possible for them to master both new subject matter and new methods of instruction, but also encourages them to be more receptive to innovative projects in the future.

In the Israeli education system, biology teachers meet every Tuesday to continue their studies, a practice established thirty years ago. These meetings, which take place at Israel's universities, include the teachers in both the Jewish and Arab school systems.

When teachers have taken advantage of all that their local community offers to further their professional education, where might they go to extend their learning?

In general education in the United States, regional labs have been established that specialize in key areas to meet the evident needs of the field. For example, WestEd, a regional laboratory in San Francisco, has developed a program in which teachers are trained to develop case studies of problems they encounter in their teaching and how they have negotiated them.

In Jewish education, a community could sponsor a lab that, drawing on local expertise as well as consultants in the region, might serve as a center of knowledge. Thus, regional laboratories could be established for the teaching of Bible or Jewish history.[39]

If the Jewish community hopes to develop teachers who are willing to invest the time and energy required to translate the ideas of a vision into their classrooms, we need to take a hard look at the realities of Jewish education:

Today, principals of Jewish day schools can earn very respectable salaries with appropriate benefits. The status of principals is also considerably higher than it ever was.

In the case of teachers, however, salary and benefits remain low, and status correspondingly so. The recruitment of teachers is a severe problem. A solution to the chronic shortage of qualified teachers will be found not by avoiding the issue but by asking the question: What might make a difference?

Although the shortage of teachers, like the shortage of principals, cannot be solved locally, a sophisticated community with committed federation leadership could join one or more local foundations to address the question: What plan could improve our teaching force?

Some key elements for teachers already in the field might be:

- An intensive, mandatory in-service training program for current staff, which could improve teaching and may contribute to the retention of good teachers who become excited about their ongoing professional growth.
- The development of a career ladder of advancement that does not force good teachers to abandon teaching in order to "move up" to administrative positions. Newly created positions might include "lead teachers," whose job is to model powerful teaching and to serve as mentors to other teachers in the school, or even among several schools; or "specialists," experts in specific subjects, such as Bible, Hebrew, Jewish history, Talmud, or Jewish thought, who can work closely with teachers who may not know the material as deeply. Later in their professional careers, these expert teachers might become department heads in day schools who would work to improve classroom instruction.

Communities could also target underutilized sources for the recruitment of teachers and offer these candidates a customized training program:

- People who have accumulated sufficient financial resources and are now interested in second careers that will make a difference in the lives of the next generation;
- Highly motivated retirees with an understanding of children, who, with early retirement and longer, healthier lifespans, have time to devote to this meaningful profession.

What other resources can we deploy in addressing this problem? In the Diaspora, there are many Jews who have excelled in the field of general education and are interested in making a contribution to Jewish life. As leaders in American education, they are an enormous resource for helping us think about how to meet the challenge of recruiting, training, and retaining outstanding people for the field of Jewish education. Some of them already have profound Jewish commitments; others are interested in exploring their own Jewishness. In our project, we have benefited from the generosity of eminent academics in general education who willingly lent their expertise to the particular challenge of increasing the pool of qualified teachers for Jewish education.

There are also some experiments that could be attempted by an intrepid community or funder. For example, what would happen if an affluent Jewish community in the Diaspora decided to pay all of its very capable full-time teachers a substantial salary? No one knows whether salary is the determining issue for the recruitment of superb teachers – or for their retention. But it is certainly worth finding out. Surely a necessary condition of excellent Jewish education is that teachers must be able support their families – and go to the theater, too.

What would such an experiment entail? First, a group of wise and experienced people would need to sit together to think about the idea seriously. They would ask such questions as: What is the state-of-the-art wisdom in this area? What do we know about teacher recruitment and retention in general education, since the shortage of committed and qualified teachers is a problem all over the world? They might also ask: What are the minimal salary and benefits that would attract exceptional people to this profession?

They could develop a plan to test the idea and conduct well-considered tryouts with rigorous follow-up. And then they would ask additional questions: Is this approach working? Does it need minor changes or a major overhaul? Can it be replicated in other schools or communities?

To those who respond to an experiment in raising teachers' salaries by asking "How do you know it will make a difference?" the answer has to be "We do not know – yet." But we do know that thinking, planning, monitoring, rethinking, reporting to the Jewish community, generating spin-offs and competing ideas, and engaging foundations and community leadership on specific issues appear to be among the necessary components of any effort to augment the ranks of teachers who can inspire and challenge us.

The problem of recruiting and retaining appropriate teachers is similar in Israel. The low salary and status of teachers, as well as the very large number of students in the Israeli classroom, have discouraged many of the most committed and talented teachers from remaining in the field. The difficulties have been complicated by the insistence of the Teachers Union on a unified salary scale that does not distinguish between the more successful teacher and the less so. (This is true of teachers unions in many other countries as well.)

If a school or a community could develop a strategy for the recruitment and retention of talented teachers for Jewish education, it would be a powerful existence proof for a dramatic improvement of Jewish education.

The Team

Given the complexity of influences that shape an educational experience, what is a realistic plan for infusing the institutions of Jewish education with compelling visions that bridge theory and practice?

As we have said, even the most wonderful principal cannot conceive, coordinate, and fulfill such an intricate assignment. No single teacher, nor a group of teachers, can be responsible for the translation of a vision's ideas into a school's practice. In order to move back and forth along the continuum of theory to real-life conditions, an educational institution needs a team.

In a day school, a team might be composed of the principal, the head of Jewish studies, the head of general studies, a curriculum specialist (whether full time or a consultant), and whoever is charged with the continuing education of teachers, without which even the most sophisticated plan will remain on the drawing board. A scholar who is both committed to education and familiar with it is indispensable to the process. Such a scholar would need to be sensitive to the role that her discipline can play in the intellectual, emotional, and spiritual development of the students. Furthermore, she would have to be aware of the background, abilities, and problems of the teachers. If a school is preparing a new Bible program or adopting Greenberg's vision, such a Bible scholar would have to be a member of the team. If a school were changing its curriculum to integrate medieval history and Jewish history using primary sources, as Brinker advocates, it would need the help of a historian to compile an anthology of sources from both Jewish and Muslim history and philosophy. If a Meyer curriculum identifies the issues treated by contemporary Israeli literature in relation to Philip Roth's fiction, a school might want a specialist in American or even American Jewish literature.

An expert in informal education would also be a key member of the team. Because, as we have claimed, Jewish education involves not only thinking but feeling and doing, an informal educator could help a school conceptualize opportunities for its students to act on the ideas being taught. In informal contexts, students can try out the ideas and report what was resonant and what was problematic when they return to the classroom.

The head of administration would be as invested in the vision as the principal. She is the person in charge of finances, janitorial services, and timely communication of vital information for parents. But she would also have become a very knowledgeable, involved member of the team, not only developing the budget but interpreting its priorities and engaged in realizing them. She would continually educate her staff members, too, so that they care not only about efficiency and keeping the premises clean but also how these matters and others contribute to the learning environment of the school.

As the head of the team, the principal may decide to take leadership in dealing with the community and ask a local rabbi to serve as a consultant. Or the principal may say, "I am going to invite a key lay leader at the outset to contribute to formulating a vision, be an advocate for it, interpret it to the community, be a voice for the community at our table, and, not incidentally, run interference when the inevitable objections arise."

For example, the board chair of a Greenberg school would have to participate in the deliberations about why an intensive Hebrew study program in early childhood is indispensable in educating children who are capable of being touched by sacred texts. Then, when a group of board members proposes the underwriting of a feasibility study for a capital campaign to build a new wing of the school, rather than continuing to spend large sums of money on curriculum efforts such as Hebrew-language study, the board chair would remind them of their agreement that mastery of the Hebrew language is essential to the school's vision of Jewish education.

Schwab's commonplaces can function as a checklist so that no critical elements are being omitted in any consideration of how to translate a vision's ideas into practice: Who is going to infuse the conversation with an understanding of the community's concerns? Who will guarantee the scholarly authenticity of the new material being taught? Who will have insight into what might engage the students? And who will make sure that teachers can master the material and the approach in a reasonable amount of time?

In Israel, or in any national education system, the notion of the team expands to mean that there are experts who need to be consulted in the appropriate departments of the Ministry of Education, such as the chief supervisor of the Department of Bible Instruction or the head of the Department of Teacher Education. These professionals decide on key policy issues for the ministry and all its schools.

At the start of a new project, only an unusual school would be able to compose its team entirely of its own staff members. Realistically, most institutions would have to bring in consultants to fill particular roles. Not only does the school or program benefit from all the talent around the table, but the various specialists also have a unique opportunity to learn from one another.

Finally, if teachers are offered ongoing opportunities for professional education over the course of their careers, a school may be able to build part of the team by using members of its own teaching staff, who have been trained over time to become experts in specific areas.

One reality is not negotiable: A spectacular educator can be the leader of a team that develops a school's vision, but not a soloist. The range of diverse competencies and the time involved in implementation require the development of a team.

The Policy Maker

In his book *Of Human Potential*, Israel Scheffler devotes a chapter to the education of policy makers. He describes them as "educational decision-makers, . . . all those whose attitudes and ideas affect the making of policy."[40]

In this chapter, I use the term "policy maker" to refer to those people whose decisions – whether about vision, personnel, curriculum, or budget – influence Jewish education. They may be professional Jewish educators, but also Israeli ministers of education and their deputies, heads of organizations whose mission includes Jewish education, foundations and their leadership, and especially lay leaders. This is the era in which lay leaders – in partnership with educators and others – are becoming essential to any version of a vibrant future for the field.

In the past, Jewish educators have been, for the most part, the dominant policy makers, their vision and energy responsible for important innovations and improvement. Today, we can see the extraordinary impact on the field when educators join forces with other policy makers – with lay leaders, rabbis, scholars, parents, and intellectuals.

Jewish educators have tended to minimize the role of these policy makers in the improvement of education. Even in Israel, where it is clear that the policy makers – that is, the minister of education and the staff of the ministry – are responsible by law for determining educational policy and practice, their influence is often underestimated by professional educators and their potential contribution unrealized. Because ministers are frequently lay people, in the sense that they have not been trained professionally for the field to which they have been appointed, educators tend to think of them as politicians rather than partners, obstacles to be overcome in securing approval – and funding – for new ideas and programs. In Israel, parents' groups and committed educators have even established semiprivate schools to minimize the ministry's control.

In the Diaspora, too, policy makers who are not trained educators have seldom been involved in determining the goals, curriculum, and pedagogy of Jewish education, matters that are largely decided at the local level by the principal, the staff, and consultants and at the national level by the professional heads of educational organizations and their staffs.

Nevertheless, in the past there were rabbis and scholars in the Diaspora and in Israel who, by making Jewish education a priority and a passion, had a profound impact. In 1937, Rabbi Soloveitchik founded the Maimonides School in Boston. Later, his daughter, Atara Twersky, and son-in-law, Isadore Twersky, joined him to build a leading institution of Orthodox education in North America. At Bar Ilan University, Nechama Leibowitz, a biblical scholar and scholar of literary theory, revolutionized the teaching of Bible throughout the Jewish world.

Organizations led by visionary professionals have also been instrumental in setting the course of Jewish education. In the 1950s, Ezra Milgrom, director of the United Synagogue Commission on Jewish Education, a policy-setting group composed of rabbis, educators, and lay leaders, was the force behind the commission's decision that Conservative congregational schools had to hold classes for a minimum of three times a week. If a child did not attend, he would not be permitted to have his Bar Mitzvah at a Conservative synagogue. This decision, which affected the content and achievements of Jewish education in the Conservative movement, was adopted despite the fact that many congregational schools in the Reform movement at that time met one or, at most, two days a week.

Milgrom encountered great resistance from members of the Conservative rabbinate and lay leaders who were concerned that they would lose many congregants. Despite the opposition, he prevailed, a classic example of how the leader of an organization was consequential in setting policy for a movement.

In his book *Response to Modernity,* Michael Meyer describes the influence of Emanuel Gamoran on the education program of the Reform movement through the Commission on Jewish Education,[41] which Gamoran led: "Gamoran was tireless. He commissioned and edited new textbooks, worked out a religious school curriculum, and was co-author of a series of primers in modern Hebrew. . . . In the interwar period, the UAHC was the only national organization printing such texts. By 1930 they were finding their way into Conservative, Orthodox as well as Reform schools."[42]

Not all heads of educational organizations are as strong or as skillful. Job role alone does not ensure the impact of a policy maker. Vision, determination, and effective implementation do.

Foundations, too, have played a significant part in the improvement of Jewish education in the past. Today, as a result of their stunning growth and influence, Jewish foundations have the potential to make a huge contribution. Their support in the form of ideas, funding, and advocacy is energizing the community and beginning to change the way Jewish education is conducted throughout the Jewish world and in Israel.

Although a volume could be written on how Jewish education is benefiting increasingly from the commitment and expertise of diverse policy makers, I want to focus my discussion of Jewish education in the Diaspora on lay leaders because of the pivotal role they can play in the translation of a vision's ideas into practice.[43]

We have already looked at lay leaders as policy makers when they are members of the educational team in a school. As we noted, lay leaders must be full participants in any serious attempt to infuse the field with visions. If they are deeply immersed in the discussion from the start, they can become eloquent negotiators for change and improvement, as they have the ability and credibility to make the case on behalf of a vision to their peers. They can help guide the planning team on how to persuade parents and the community that what appears impossible is really only difficult, and that the ideal can indeed become real. And they know how to navigate in "the real world" – to move an idea into action.

These policy makers can also remind the rest of the team that in the adoption of a vision, there are indispensable elements – but also inevitable sacrifices of what cannot be included because it is either not essential or not practical. Then, when the principal is pressured by constituents to make a school all things to all people, the policy maker can help protect the vision by saying: "This is what our school stands for – and this is what we cannot do. This is the kind of person we are trying to nurture here; but if you want another kind of person, we are not the right place."[44]

Although institutions of higher Jewish learning, congregations, JCCs, and Jewish foundations have made significant progress in introducing lay leaders to Jewish study, there is not yet a program designed to illuminate, in all its complexity, decision making within Jewish education.[45] If a single community decided to take on this challenge – a project to cultivate lay leaders as a cohort qualified to improve decision making in local and national Jewish education – the project could be emulated and adapted by many other communities. Such a project would also constitute an existence proof. Policy makers are very adept at using successful examples in practice to marshal support and broader communal involvement.

To learn how to foster such a cohort, to explore and develop a curriculum that inducts policy makers into the complexity of decision making and examines its effectiveness, and to understand how to transmit a vision such as Twersky's or Meyer's to leaders who are not educators is an increasingly necessary project. The implementation of the ideas that are basic to the various visions proposed in this volume, or any other visions, will require an immense investment by the worldwide Jewish community. It is unreasonable to expect such a commitment by policy makers unless they understand what is at stake and what can make a difference.

Having been initiated into the difficulty – and exhilaration – of making consequential decisions in Jewish education, such policy makers would understand that in a Twersky school the teachers must be Orthodox and in a Meyer school they must be Reform, but in a Brinker or Scheffler school the teachers' diversity is an asset. Policy makers involved in a Twersky school would want to know if philosophy is being taught, how it is being taught, and how early. Policy makers in a Greenberg school would ask: If we put all this effort into an intensive program for the study of the Hebrew language, what happens if we fail? And they would understand that a heavy investment in Hebrew acquisition and in students' mastery of text would necessarily come at the expense of other subjects, such as the intensive study of Jewish history. These policy makers would recognize the importance of evaluation and participate in it because of their thorough understanding of the relationship of a vision's goals to an institution's practice.

As policy makers, lay leaders are seldom experts in the content of Jewish education. Rather, they are intelligent, engaged citizens who need to be informed by experts in order to make critical decisions. If an expert cannot explain his ideas to an interested and committed lay leader, it is the responsibility of that expert to learn how to frame the issues in a more comprehensible fashion. A school principal, for example, needs to know how to articulate and justify to her board chair what she wants to accomplish and why.

Rather than being a burden, an educator's work with policy makers – whether board members or parents – offers a priceless opportunity to expand the range of questions they can and should ask.

Today, unaware of alternative visions and possibilities for Jewish education, many lay leaders are limited to posing such questions as, Are the children happy? Are they learning anything? Are parents complaining? Do teenagers enjoy the sports program at our JCC? What is the attendance at our adult education lectures?

But they might be invited – indeed, encouraged – to ask:

- Why is this proposed program a good idea? Are there alternatives? Can we defend why we should choose this idea over other possibilities?

To address such questions, policy makers would learn that research is indispensable, both to check the assumptions underlying an idea and to find out if it has been attempted previously – and if it worked. If they are indeed inclined to the idea and want it to succeed, they could join educators to ask intelligent critics of the idea to take an active part in the deliberation. Then, by the time they decide to go ahead, they have already heard and learned from the most cogent criticism available.

- Even if it is a brilliant idea, is it one that our staff and our institution can carry out?

Understanding what is required for success, policy makers could ask: Do we have the resources of personnel, commitment, funding, and patience? In a school setting, with which teachers will we work? What is the board's or foundation's responsibility? Which elements can be undertaken simultaneously and which must wait?

- If we conclude that we can do it, how long will it take to implement the idea, and how will we keep our constituency both informed and engaged until we succeed?

Policy makers would ask themselves: How can we foster a community of people who care about this idea and will persist in its support rather than give up along the way? Who will nurture them? Are we being honest with ourselves and our constituents about how long it will take, and have we allowed enough time for the inevitable mistakes and unanticipated consequences? If the program takes five years, can we identify the results that might be expected after six months, a year, or two?

- What will we do when the professionals charged with turning vision into practice lose heart?

At the School of Education of the Hebrew University, my colleagues and I found that, in the development of a curriculum for a vision, there are always serious obstacles in the first few months of its introduction into a school. The burden is particularly heavy for teachers, who find it difficult to change their style and habits as they encounter new content and innovative pedagogy. Policy makers can include in their planning the training of qualified people to work directly with teachers and be available to them to resolve their dilemmas.

- As members of a team, how can we, together, be able to evaluate what we have done? How do we know we are succeeding? Are we doing what we set out to do – or are we inadvertently accomplishing something else? How much time will we give ourselves if we fear we may be failing?

It is essential to monitor the project and to evaluate it at appropriate times throughout.

Policy makers who learn to ask these questions and others – whether through their participation in the nuts and bolts of implementing a program or, more rarely, their being educated to concern themselves with such questions – can transform the depth and impact of an idea and become ever more sophisticated in assessing the merits and hazards of future ideas.

What is the justification for allowing nonexperts – lay leaders and others – to be so intimately involved in making decisions?

First, there are moral reasons. In the case of lay leaders who are involved in a school, it is often their children and grandchildren who are the focus of the education being designed. Their commitment represents a great act of faith.

Second, there are legal reasons. As mentioned, in Israel the law mandates that the minister of education make such decisions for the nation's education system.

Third, policy makers have power in education – and they will use it. It is important, then, for them to be thoughtful in its exercise.

Fourth, the field needs the resources of policy makers – government officials, opinion makers, funders, and others – to maximize the impact of Jewish education.

Finally, policy makers bring wisdom and expertise that educators do not have.

To return to Schwab's commonplaces, policy makers as we have defined them are the experts on the milieu or the community environment in which education will be shaped and which it hopes to influence.[46]

For all these reasons, the relationship between Jewish educators and lay leaders is at long last being renegotiated. Certainly, the sorry state of some aspects of Jewish education reveals what happens when policy makers are not sufficiently involved. For Jewish educators to dismiss lay leaders as uninformed Jewishly or simplistic in their thinking is a luxury no one can afford.[47] All of us need a new conception of this partnership.

For their part, these policy makers have to join educators as partners in understanding what is being proposed, in all its daunting complexity. Schwab claims that there are seldom successful revolutions in education; change is necessarily incremental.[48] If policy makers involved in trying to improve education have the illusion that a simple solution is possible, they will be disabused of that notion as they become involved in the nitty-gritty of making it work.

Policy makers deserve to be initiated by learned, sophisticated, and persuasive educators into an understanding that the value of an important idea may not be obvious from the start. Otherwise, they will be attracted to solutions whose impact may be more immediate and evident but which will not result in real, measurable, and lasting improvement.

Like communal leaders in the Diaspora, elected officials and senior civil servants in Israel are not trained educators but make determining decisions. For example, Zalman Aranne, minister of education from 1955 to 1960 and 1963 to 1969, was committed to help close the gap between the haves and have-nots in education. The wonderful Hebrew term for the disadvantaged, *te'unei tipuaḥ,* means "requiring nurturing," which is how Aranne saw Israel's responsibility. There was a compelling body of research that showed how these children were likely to fail in school by the time they reached the fourth grade.[49] Aranne used to say: When you plant a tree in the shade and it dies, whose problem is it – the planter's or the tree's? These children have been brought up their entire lives in a context that has denied them the chance to develop.

Aranne decided to do nothing less than integrate the Israeli education system. He studied James Coleman's report on American public education, *Equality of Educational Opportunity,*[50] and accepted Abraham Minkowich's interpretation of the report – that if you join in a classroom 60 percent advantaged students to 40 percent disadvantaged, the advantaged do not lose but the disadvantaged make significant gains. Aranne then claimed that the seventh and eighth grades of the Israeli school system were not effective, and so he created junior high schools in Israel. Because they were a new institution on the educational landscape, he was able, in his ministerial role, to legislate the makeup of their population: He concluded that these new junior high schools must be integrated.

Today there is much disagreement about whether this experiment was successful. But for the purpose of our understanding the impact of a policy maker who oversaw the implementation of a vision, Aranne is an outstanding example.

Nor did he do it alone. Aranne worked closely with Joshua Prawer of the Hebrew University and Moshe Smilansky of Tel Aviv University, as well as with members of the faculty of the Hebrew University's School of Education. He consulted James Coleman and invited Ralph Tyler, the world-renowned expert in evaluation and dean of the faculty of the Division of the Social Sciences at the University of Chicago, to appear before the Knesset Committee on Education to discuss the successes and failures of junior high schools in the United States.

A great policy maker will involve thinkers of stature to guide, justify, interpret, and criticize an idea before it is adopted and to accompany and evaluate its implementation.

In the translation of his vision into the Israeli education system, Aranne recruited not only scholars but also lay people as his partners. He encouraged the National Council of Jewish Women to establish The Research Institute for Innovation in Education at the Hebrew University. The institute created more than twenty programs whose purpose was to improve the prospect for the disadvantaged child to succeed in school.

Other ministers of education translated their ideas into new institutions and programs. Yigal Alon, minister of education from 1969 to 1974, studied higher education in the United Kingdom and then intensified the work of the Council for Higher Education in Israel. As a result, the Council governs the policy and has great influence over the budget of Israel's universities and colleges.

Zvulun Hammer, Israel's first minister of education from a religious party, created the Tali school programs out of his concern for the 70 percent of Israeli students in secular schools who were receiving a minimal Jewish education. Tali schools offer an alternative to the choice between Orthodox Jewish education and very little Jewish education by enlarging and intensifying the time a school devotes to Jewish studies, taught from a more pluralist perspective. Hammer prevailed despite the opposition of his own party, the National Religious Party.

Like Aranne, Alon and Hammer were guided in their work by academics and other consultants from Israel and elsewhere.

Ministers are not the only example of government officials who have made important contributions to educational policy. Mayors are another. For example, formal and informal education are different departments in the ministry and in city government as well. When Teddy Kollek was mayor of Jerusalem from 1965 to 1993, he realized the importance of integrating formal and informal education at the local level. In 1985, working with the city's director general, Michael Gal, Kollek combined the two departments into one unit, the Municipal Education Department (*Manḥi*). It was now possible to integrate important aspects of formal and informal education in Jerusalem.

Although any government has its share of cynical bureaucrats, there are always policy makers who hold their positions for the noblest of reasons. They are operating within severe constraints – usually in office for a period too brief to effect the profound change required in education, tired and overwhelmed by the complexity of the challenge and yet committed to improving their societies. They need not only inspiring ideas but ideas that can be implemented while they are still in office. Their time line for showing initial results may be as brief as six months to a year, and their perspective is often limited by that reality. Even more than the policy maker in Jewish education in the Diaspora, ministers of education and their deputies have to offer rewards that are evident to the public very soon after an idea is approved.

The cost of these constraints is best illustrated by superb ideas that were abandoned prematurely. In 1969, Lawrence Cremin, the distinguished historian of education and later president of Teachers College, Columbia University, delivered a lecture at the Hebrew University in which he described ideas that were abandoned "ten minutes before midnight." He urged Aranne and the ministry leadership, as well as some of Israel's leading academics in the social sciences and education, not to give up too early on promising ideas.

Michael Rosenak's essay poses the question: What might Jews of very different beliefs nevertheless share in their visions of Jewish education? When presented with drafts of this essay, communal leaders in several American cities responded with optimism to Rosenak's articulation of common elements. They saw a justification for their faith in developing a community-wide commitment to Jewish education and possibly even cooperation among diverse groups, based on respect and a true understanding of pluralism.

All of our scholars, devoted as they are to their particular visions of Jewish education, recognized and emphasized the importance of creating strong community support for Jewish education despite disagreements about goals, content, and methods. They were deeply committed to pluralism as a central value for educated Jews. Twersky became so involved in this particular discussion that he wanted to write a book on the concept of *ahavat Yisrael* – love of one's fellow Jew – to provide a grounding in the tradition for why Jews have to find a way to respect one another and work together, particularly in Jewish education.

As recently as twenty-five years ago, the major priorities of Jewish organizations worldwide were the welfare and social services of their communities and the rescue of Jewish communities in distress. Today, Jewish education has risen to be among the highest communal priorities. In Israel, too, within the last decade, the government has recognized that no matter how difficult the economic situation, the budget must continue to reflect the great importance of education to the electorate. The unrelenting advocacy of policy makers in the Diaspora and Israel is largely responsible for that transformation.

Conclusion: The Practicality of Great Ideas

These are encouraging times for Jewish education. Day schools are growing at an impressive rate. Increasing numbers of very talented people are entering the field in the Diaspora and Israel.

The Jewish community's faith in the potential of Jewish education is also bolstered by changing attitudes in the culture of the West, where there is a consensus about the power of education to advance society's goals and redress some of its inequities. If Jewish survival over millennia is owed in large measure to a remarkably consistent and unwavering emphasis on learning, today that value is reflected in the front-page coverage of educational issues and in national press conferences that highlight their importance to policy makers in government and philanthropy.

At the same time, there are fascinating problems in the Jewish world that demand new thinking and approaches. To cite a glaring example, there are approximately 650,000 Jewish students studying in day schools and supplementary schools in the Diaspora and approximately 30,000 educators who work in these schools. Yet there are fewer than 50 full-time professors of Jewish education in the entire Diaspora. If great ideas are essential for education, who is going to do the requisite thinking?

It is inconceivable that so small a number of specialists and academics can meet such challenges as preparing the missing cadre of teachers and principals; developing compelling curricula to address the changing circumstances of young people; conceptualizing strategies to address the condition of the Jewish family in its strengths and shortcomings; adapting for Jewish education the state-of-the-art knowledge available on early childhood; training educators to specialize in informal education; and conducting the research to undergird all such efforts and inform us about what works and what does not.

Because there is almost no research being commissioned for the field of Jewish education in the Diaspora, we are creating programs, establishing institutions, and investing increasingly substantial resources without sufficient data. We know almost nothing about the economics of Jewish education. How much is the world Jewish community currently spending on Jewish education? And how much more must it spend for our institutions to embody a range of compelling visions?

Throughout our project we encountered key research issues to be addressed: How do we educate for commitment? How can the curriculum of a school contribute to moral development? How can we integrate general education and Jewish education? Jewish history and general history? Jewish thought and contemporary philosophy? But almost no one is at work on these issues.

There was a time when pundits claimed that even if there were people who were interested in becoming professors of Jewish education, there would be no positions for them. Today, institutions of higher Jewish learning and universities in the United States are creating those positions – but they cannot find qualified candidates to fill them.

In the United States, more than 60 percent of Jewish children who participate in Jewish education are enrolled not in day schools but in supplementary schools. And yet almost no attention is being devoted to this population. Available thinking and planning is focused on the day school, with scant energy remaining for the improvement – or reinvention – of the supplementary school. How can we justify to ourselves the neglect of those children, who deserve the same thoughtfulness and creativity as their peers in day schools? What are alternatives to the current system? How could informal education contribute to the education of supplementary school students? What thoughtful experiments might be tried that are worthwhile and feasible?

Since the establishment of the State of Israel, ministers of education, intellectuals, and academics have been concerned about the difficulties – some contend the failure – of Jewish education for students in the secular education system. In recent years, the impact of the religious education system on its students has also been a source of concern. Yet there has been very little systematic study of the kind of education that might lead young people and their families to grapple with the issues that will determine the Jewish character of the State of Israel:

How should the Bible be studied? How has Jewish thought developed throughout the ages and what are the themes that should be emphasized today? How can informal education make its full contribution and how can the youth movements be rejuvenated? What ideas might be examined both in the general and the religious systems of education in the hope that they could contribute to communication between the religious and secular communities in Israel?

We have contended that some of the most urgent problems require not immediate action but profound thought, and that outstanding people who are advocates for visionary ideas can make the most practical difference. Our great challenge today is not only financial resources but intellectual wealth. Now is the time to capture the Jewish mind, the disproportionate number of Jewish thinkers in the fields of education, social sciences, and humanities.

In working on this project, we were surprised and encouraged to find that such people were eager to join us in the thinking and experimenting that might help meet the many challenges of a renewed Jewish future. Some were attracted to Jewish education because of their search for their own Jewish identity. Others became involved because they were intrigued by basic issues, such as character education, alternative ways to integrate formal and informal education, and the challenge of interpreting complex ideas to the public and its policy makers. They were excited about making a contribution to Jewish life in innovative ways.

What might happen if we could recruit enough of these gifted people? What would Jewish education look like if we could harness their knowledge, imagination, and energy?

Above all, how might we launch and sustain a range of conversations among scholars, intellectuals, and policy makers – those in the field and those enticed to join us – in order to generate ideas for translation into the current settings of Jewish education, or into newly invented ones?

In a session devoted to considering the future of Jewish education in Israel and worldwide, David Cohen, of the University of Michigan, responded to the skepticism of Israeli academics by saying, "My friends, we dare not forget that education is a profession of hope."

There is no greater evidence for optimism than the history of the Jews, who have regarded learning as both the object of their aspirations and the most important means of fulfilling them.

NOTES

1 See description of vision in Chapter 1.
2 Instinct is used here to mean a first cause or a principle that is irreducible; or, in Freud's language, a "basic concept." See Seymour Fox, *Freud and Education* (Springfield, IL: C. C. Thomas, 1975), 29, 30, 54.
3 See Joseph J. Schwab, "The Practical: A Language for Curriculum," in *Science, Curriculum, and Liberal Education: Selected Essays*, ed. I. Westbury and N. J. Wilkof (Chicago: University of Chicago Press, 1978), 287–321. See also Seymour Fox, "Theory into Practice (in Education)," in *Philosophy for Education*, ed. S. Fox (Jerusalem: The Van Leer Jerusalem Foundation, 1983), 96–98.
4 Ralph W. Tyler, *Basic Principles of Curriculum and Instruction* (Chicago: University of Chicago Press, 1950); Joseph J. Schwab, "What Do Scientists Do?" in *Science, Curriculum and Liberal Education: Selected Essays*, 184–228; Schwab, "The Practical: Arts of Eclectic," in *Science, Curriculum and Liberal Education: Selected Essays*, 322–64; Schwab, "The Practical: Translation into Curriculum," in *Science, Curriculum and Liberal Education: Selected Essays*, 365–83; Lee Shulman, "Theory, Practice, and the Education of Professionals," *The Elementary School Journal* 98:5 (1998): 511–26; Seymour Fox, *Freud and Education*, 26–28; D. K. Cohen, S. Raudenbush, and D. L. Ball, "Resources, Instruction, and Research," in *Education Evaluation and Policy Analysis* (in press).
5 Schwab, "The Practical: Arts of Eclectic." Schwab says he "pilfered" the term from Aristotle and Bacon.
6 Schwab, "The Practical: Translation into Curriculum." I am greatly indebted to my teacher, Joseph J. Schwab, for my understanding of the challenge of translating theory into practice. The decision to undertake this project, *Visions of Jewish Education*, was largely inspired by him. In recent years there have been a series of critical essays on Schwab's work, particularly in the area of curriculum. Some of these essays have influenced current thinking about the importance of Schwab's contribution to educational thought and particularly to the field of curriculum. In my view, these essays failed to understand the depth and importance of Schwab's thinking for the field of education. One important example is Philip Jackson's essay in *The Handbook of Research on Curriculum* (New York: Macmillan Publishing Company, 1992), 28–37. A penetrating critique that points to the misunderstanding of Schwab by Jackson will be found in Nehama Mosheiff's article, "The Curriculum Specialist: Deliberation, the Quasi-Practical, and Policy," in preparation.
7 See the example about teaching Jewish values in the "Text" section of this chapter.
8 In Chapter 11, Daniel Marom demonstrates how he helped disclose the implicit vision of the Magnes School by eliciting inquiry and discourse about the curriculum, teaching methods, and culture of the school.
9 Joseph B. Soloveitchik, *Man of Faith in the Modern World: Reflections of the Rav*, vol. 2 (Hoboken, NJ: Ktav Publishing House, 1989), 22–23.
10 In Chapter 5, Brinker delineates the characteristics of such an education.
11 All quotations by the scholars are from their essays in this volume, unless otherwise indicated.

12 The contribution of early childhood programs to the building of Israel as a new nation has been well documented. See, for example, Z. Scharfstein, *Toldot ha-Ḥinukh bi-Eretz Yisrael* (Jerusalem: Reuven Mass, 1965), 64–67, and Shlomo Haramati, "*Trumat Gan ha-Yeladim le Haḥayyat ha-Dibbur ha-Ivri*," in *Reishit ha-Ḥinukh ha-Ivri ba-Aretz ve-Terumato le-Haḥiyyat ha-Lashon* (Jerusalem: Reuven Mass, 1979), 206–34. For many years, Israel's early childhood education was esteemed as a model throughout the world.

13 I want to thank my colleague Mordecai Nisan, who drew my attention to the renewed philosophical and educational interest in the concept of habituation in Aristotle and its importance for character education. See Nancy Sherman, *Making a Necessity of Virtue: Aristotle and Kant on Virtue* (Cambridge: Cambridge University Press, 1997), 241–48. Maimonides' and Aristotle's concepts of habituation are closely related. See Chapter 3.

14 See Greenberg Supplement, Parshanut *in Practice*.

15 Robert Coles, *The Spiritual Life of Children* (Boston: Houghton Mifflin, 1990); J. W. Fowler, *Stages of Faith: The Psychology of Human Development and the Quest for Meaning* (San Francisco: Harper and Row, 1981); R. G. Goldman, *Religious Thinking from Childhood to Adolescence* (London: Routledge and Kegan Paul, 1964).

16 In the policy brief *Background and Professional Training of Teachers in Jewish Schools* (New York: Council for Initiatives in Jewish Education, 1994), Adam Gamoran, Ellen Goldring, and their field researchers found that 55% of preschool teachers received no Jewish education after the age of thirteen. See also Shira Ackerman, who claims that 30 percent of early childhood teachers are not Jewish, in *Untapped Potential: The Status of Jewish Early Childhood Education in America* (Baltimore: Jewish Early Childhood Education Partnership, 2002).

17 Maimonides, *Laws of Repentance* 5:2.

18 Lee Shulman has discussed this idea with me on several occasions and has taught it to the Fellows at the Mandel School for Educational Leadership in Jerusalem.

19 Zvi Lamm, *Tnu'at ha-No'ar ha-Tzionit be-Mabat le-'Aḥor.* (Tel Aviv: HaKibbutz HaMeuḥad, 1991), 8. This passage was translated by Daniel Marom.

20 Israel Scheffler reminds us in his essay: "Traditional Jewish schooling could count on a home life permeated with Jewish religious sentiments, concepts, and practices; it could therefore concentrate its attention on the formal teaching of sacred texts. Current Jewish schools cannot rely on such home life as a given in the lives of their pupils." Scheffler then discusses the need to expand Jewish education to include informal, affective, adult, and family education.

21 Israel Scheffler, in *In Praise of the Cognitive Emotions* (New York and London: Routledge, Chapman & Hall, 1991), argues against the tendency of philosophers, psychologists, and educators to distinguish between cognitive and affective experience, between thinking and feeling. Schwab makes a similar point in his description of the power of discussion for education, in "Eros and Education," *Journal of General Education* 8 (1954): 54–71. See also Seymour Fox with William Novak, *Vision at the Heart: Lessons from Camp Ramah on the Power of Ideas in Shaping Educational Institutions* (New York and Jerusalem: Mandel Foundation, 1997, 2000).

22 The curriculum was influenced by the work of Erik Erikson, who emphasizes the importance of loyalty for adolescents. He describes adolescence as the period when the young person is struggling to live according to the virtue of fidelity. See Erik H. Erikson, *The Challenge of Youth* [originally published as *Youth: Change and Challenge*] (Garden City, NY: Anchor Books, 1965), 1–23.

23 See Nahum M. Sarna, *The Heritage of Biblical Israel* (New York: Melton Research Center of The Jewish Theological Seminary of America, 1964), 49–50.

24 Greenberg was so distraught over the twisted interpretation of sacred texts used by Baruch Goldstein to sanction his murder of 29 Arabs on Purim 1994 while they prayed at the Tomb of the Patriarchs in Hebron that he wrote an essay to express his horror at the shocking distortion of texts by fundamentalists. See, "A Problematic Heritage: The Attitude Toward the Gentile in the Jewish Tradition – An Israeli Perspective," *Conservative Judaism* 48:2 (1996): 23–35.

25 See Greenberg, *Biblical Prose Prayer as a Window to the Popular Religion of Ancient Israel* (Berkeley: Univesity of California Press, 1983), 47–52.

26 Greenberg, "On Teaching the Bible in Religious Schools," *Jewish Education* 29:3 (1959): 45.

27 In *The Good High School: Portraits of Character and Culture* (New York: Basic Books, 1983), Sarah Lawrence Lightfoot describes six successful schools, each characterized by a principal who has a clear vision and has successfully communicated this vision to the teachers and administrative staff.

28 Bruno Bettelheim, when training the staff of his Orthogenic School at the University of Chicago, described the important role that a sensitive custodian can play in the education of students. For a description of the school, see Bruno Bettelheim, *Love is Not Enough* (Glencoe, IL: Free Press, 1950).

29 James S. Coleman et al., *Equality of Educational Opportunity* (Washington, DC: U.S. Office of Education, National Center for Educational Statistics, 1966).

30 Ronald Edmonds, "Effective Schools for the Urban Poor," *Educational Leadership* 37 (1979): 15–24.

31 The importance of the principal to the actualization of vision is also discussed in M. D. Usdan, "The School Administrator: Modern Renaissance Man," *The Teachers College Record* 69 (1968): 641–48; Thomas J. Sergiovanni, *The Principalship: A Reflective Practice Perspective* (Boston: Allyn and Bacon, 1987), 177–92; Seymour Sarason, "The Principal," in *Revisiting "The Culture of The School and The Problem of Change"* (New York: Teachers College Press, 1996), 139–62; and Michael Fullan, *The New Meaning of Educational Change*, 3d ed. (New York: Teachers College Press, 2001), 137–50.

32 There are communities, such as Johannesburg and Capetown in South Africa or Melbourne, Australia, where lay leaders are often responsible for budgets and fundraising for the school. In "The Team," we discuss the importance of a team for introducing and implementing a school's vision. A team is equally essential for supplementing the abilities and capacity of a principal.

33 Goldring and Gamoran describe the very limited opportunities for pre- and in-service education in North America. See E. B. Goldring, A. Gamoran, and B. Robinson, *The Leaders Report: A Portrait of Educational Leaders in Jewish Schools,* an unpublished 1999 report by the Mandel Foundation, New York, 9–13. In

recent years, Israel's Ministry of Education has invested substantial resources in the in-service education of principals. Programs have been established at the schools of education at Israeli universities and teachers colleges.

34   For the past 10 years, the Mandel School in Jerusalem, in partnership with Israel's Ministry of Education, has trained leaders for Israel's education system through its Mandel School for Educational Leadership (MSEL). Lawyers, scientists, and other academics, men and women in business, and high-ranking officers in the Israeli army have attended MSEL; and rabbis, young Jewish scholars, journalists, and artists have attended the Mandel Jerusalem Fellows program, a department of the Mandel School that trains Jewish educational leaders for the Diaspora. Both MSEL and the Mandel Jerusalem Fellows, however, are very expensive to run, require of their students a two-year, full-time commitment, and are only the "tip of the iceberg" in relation to what is needed. In the Diaspora, the Avi Chai Foundation has supported programs for the preparation of day school principals at the Davidson School of Jewish Education at The Jewish Theological Seminary of America, at the Azrieli Graduate School at Yeshiva University, and, in Israel, at Bar-Ilan University. For fifteen years, the senior educators program of the Melton Centre for Jewish Education in the Diaspora at the Hebrew University, with the support of the Jewish Agency, has prepared principals for Jewish schools outside of Israel. These are important developments that nevertheless do not begin to meet the shortage of qualified principals.

35   According to Twersky, Maimonides assumes that it is natural for human beings to ask philosophical questions. Untrained in philosophical thinking, however, they will arrive at erroneous conclusions. Therefore, a school that adopts Twersky's vision must teach philosophy.

36   Greenberg, "On Teaching the Bible in Religious Schools," 45.

37   See Greenberg Supplement, Parshanut *in Practice.*

38   "On Teaching the Bible," 46.

39   Another example of such a program is the Teacher Educator Institute (TEI), which was established by the Mandel Foundation in 1995 to develop a national cohort of teacher educators for Jewish education. The program includes initial intensive training and continuous learning.

40   In this chapter, Scheffler describes a process of learning that begins with educational policy formulation and continues through execution and evaluation. Israel Scheffler, *Of Human Potential: An Essay in the Philosophy of Education* (Boston: Routledge & Kegan Paul, 1985), 99–126.

41   The commission was under the auspices of the Union of American Hebrew Congregations–Central Conference of American Rabbis (UAHC-CCAR).

42   Michael Meyer, *Response to Modernity: A History of the Reform Movement in Judaism* (New York: Oxford University Press, 1988), 301.

43   In Israel, the Rothschild Foundation (Yad Hanadiv) has established some very important educational institutions, such as the Open University, educational television, and the Center for Educational Technology. The Sacta and Rashi Foundations make large contributions to programs that attempt to close the gap between advantaged and disadvantaged students, and have encouraged the development of promising programs to improve the curriculum and pedagogy of schools, particularly in the area of

science education. The Andrea and Charles Bronfman Philanthropies have launched programs with the Ministry of Education to lengthen the school day with enrichment for various subjects in the curriculum. In 1999, Yossi Beilin, Israel's minister of justice, suggested to Michael Steinhardt that a program of educational trips to Israel be established for young Diaspora Jews (ages 18 to 26). The result was "birthright israel," a partnership among philanthropists, the government of Israel, and local Jewish communities that has sent 30,000 young adults to Israel for the first time.

44   In *The Shopping Mall High School,* the authors describe the risks to high schools that, lacking a clear vision, attempt to meet everyone's desires. They claim that "in most American high schools, almost everything is available in small doses, and everything tends to have the same weight, the same ranking." In trying to anticipate every possible desire that a student or parent might have, these schools have turned into the academic equivalent of shopping malls. "Both types of institutions," the authors write, "are profoundly consumer-oriented. Both try to hold customers by offering something for everyone." They conclude that such high schools "take few stands on what is educationally or morally important." Arthur G. Powell, Eleanor Farrar, and David K. Cohen, *The Shopping Mall High School: Winners and Losers in the Educational Marketplace* (Boston: Houghton Mifflin, 1985), 3.

45   CLAL and the Wexner Heritage Foundation have developed adult education programs that introduce community leaders to the regular study of Jewish sources and their relevance to contemporary life.

46   In Joseph J. Schwab, "Community: A Mission for the Schools" (unpublished manuscript); and "The Practical 4: Something for Curriculum Professors To Do," *Curriculum Inquiry* 13:3 (1983): 239–65, where he developed this point.

47   See Seymour Fox with William Novak, *Vision at the Heart: Lessons from Camp Ramah on the Power of Ideas in Shaping Educational Institutions,* 35–38, on how the partnership has been viewed in the past.

48   Joseph J. Schwab, "The Practical: A Language for Curriculum," in *Science, Curriculum and Liberal Education: Selected Essays,* 287–321.

49   Chaim Adler, at the NCJW Research Institute for Innovation in Education at the Hebrew University, documented how many of these students came from large families of low socioeconomic status. Parents, particularly mothers, had limited education and scant time to devote to helping their children adjust to and succeed in school.

50   James S. Coleman et al., *Equality of Educational Opportunity.*

11

Before the Gates of the School: An Experiment in Developing Educational Vision from Practice

DANIEL MAROM

Background: The Goals Project

From the beginning, our project was intended to contribute to re-form efforts in Jewish education as it is practiced.[1] The project's argument for a conversation about vision assumed that such a discussion would not be confined to the academy but would take place in the settings where policy decisions are made, professional development takes place, and programs are planned and implemented.

In placing vision at the heart of the work of education, our approach differed substantially from current "visioning" efforts. We assumed that in order to improve Jewish education, educators and other policy makers would have to design their programs in relation to a broader philosophic conception of "the educated Jewish person": For their vision to be realized, the human being nurtured in their school, synagogue, or camp would exemplify the qualities, knowledge, dispositions, and skills of their shared ideal.

The goal of "increasing the number of post–Bar/Bat Mitzvah students in our program," for example, would be informed by an answer to the question, "What kind of Jewish learning do we see as meaningful and compelling for twenty-first-century life?"

The goal of "knowing Jewish history" would be delineated by answers to such questions as

"At what point can we say a person 'knows' something about history?"

"How does this knowledge affect a person's thinking, feeling, and action?"

"What in Jewish history is more and less important to 'know' in this way?" and

"How should this knowledge of Jewish history be integrated with the learner's knowledge of other histories or with his or her religious or scientific knowledge?"

296

The goal of developing Jewish video games – to provide an alternative to a popular children's activity – would be checked by the question of how central Jewish text study should be to any conception of the educated Jew.

Our project's emphasis on the substantive content required to meet an educational goal did take into account issues of feasibility and the importance of sound educational strategies. Nevertheless, we were convinced that a reform effort based on new methods of teaching or a new curriculum that did not also raise the question "To what end?" would not be transformative.

To try out our approach, the Mandel Foundation, in collaboration with Harvard's Philosophy of Education Research Center (PERC), launched the Goals Project. Its purpose was to encourage communities and institutions of Jewish education in North America to pursue a "vision-guided" approach to education.

The Goals Project would ask participants to scrutinize their current goals and to study alternative visions of Jewish education. In the process, they would formulate new goals to guide their practice. This inquiry would address such questions as

"What vision of the 'educated Jew' is assumed by these goals?"

"What are the attributes, behaviors, and values of this person?"

"What is the justification for the adoption of this vision over alternatives?"

"How does this vision address the reality of contemporary Jewish life after the Holocaust and the establishment of Israel?"

Other questions would examine the alignment of content and methods:

"How is the study of each subject matter meant to contribute to the development of the 'educated Jew' of your vision?"

"How are educators trained to teach subject matter for this purpose?"

"How are these efforts integrated into a coherent approach to education at each stage?" and

"What indicators would allow you to gauge your success or failure in fostering this kind of Jew?"

In some cases, the process might involve an attempt to deepen understanding of the goals of a specific program and to link content and methods more effectively to those goals. In others, the process might result in a profound revision of current goals, content, and methods. In both, the effort would require the institutionalization of frameworks, modes of discourse, and practice so that such an inquiry could take place.

We made no distinction between institutions of formal and informal education or between programs for youth, adults, families, or educators themselves. In our idea of vision, everyone is a partner in the educational process. When vision is an effective force in an institution or program, we argued, community leaders, administrators, professional and adjunct staff, evaluators, and others will be committed to it, understand its mandate, and cooperate in pursuing its realization. The result will be an institutional culture that expresses its vision in new and compelling ways.

"A vision is a vibrant entity," we contended.[2] Its articulation cannot be limited to a mission statement or a manual. The ideas of a vision must guide, infuse, animate, and energize practice.

In 1994, a large group of Jewish educators and community leaders met in Jerusalem for the first Goals Project Seminar. During the meetings, the president and the director of the Magnes School, a nondenominational community day school, and the director of the board of Jewish education in the school's community turned to the Mandel Foundation with a proposal to undertake a "goals project" at Magnes.[3] These three participants offered the school as a laboratory site in which we could explore together what it might mean to formulate guidelines for the development of educational vision.

The agreement was that I would serve as a planning consultant and facilitator, with the assistance of Seymour Fox, from whom I had learned this approach and with whom I codirected the project that produced this book. I would keep a record of my activities, so that the staff of the Goals Project and our consultants at PERC could study it, make suggestions, and share it with others engaged in developing and actualizing their own visions of Jewish education.

The Setting: A Nondenominational Community Day School

From the school's founder, Martin Spivak, I learned that Magnes was established in 1967 by a group of trustees who were looking for an alternative to the Orthodox educational institutions in their community. Magnes, a school from kindergarten through eighth grade, would be open to other forms of Jewishness, with a strong emphasis on general studies and the arts. It was named after Judah Magnes, a Zionist leader who symbolized nondenominational Jewish identity.

For those who established the school, there was a defining difference between Magnes and the denominational schools, even if they could not articulate it. Magnes also distinguished itself from the non-Jewish private schools that attracted Jewish parents who were disenchanted with suburban public schools. Although many Magnes graduates attended these schools at the middle and high school level (because, among other reasons, there was no non-Orthodox high school), their parents felt the school offered something that even outstanding private schools could not provide.

The current administration had initiated a new chapter in the school's history. When Jon Kagan had proposed his candidacy for the director's job, he was the director of curriculum projects and associate director of teacher education programs at a private non-Jewish school; he had no background or training in Jewish education. Jon saw the Magnes School as an opportunity to explore his own Jewish identity. He was attracted to the idea that at Magnes he could enhance his experience of belonging to a community and embark on a quest – through Judaism – for values and spiritual content, while remaining within the liberal and pluralistic framework he needed in order to feel at home in any school. A group of Magnes teachers concerned about the rigor of the general studies program became involved in the selection process and strongly supported his candidacy.

Jon's tenure brought not only the anticipated emphasis on excellence in general studies but an attempt to raise the standards of the Jewish studies program, as well as integrate the general and Jewish studies curricula. Over time, these commitments energized the school. The result was an ennobling environment and a rapid increase in enrollment. I teased Jon by calling him "the Moses of Magnes."

Jon's journey, I discovered, was shared by other members of the Magnes community, including the school's president, Dave Reiter. A Harvard Law School graduate and federal prosecutor, he, too, lacked a strong Jewish education and yet chose to send his three children to Magnes and to devote many hours to its leadership.

Dave's perspective on America was striking. He saw Americans as overcome by economic and social fears provoked by "downsizing" and illegal immigration, fears that were eroding people's sense of community. America was becoming a place whose citizens survived by looking out for themselves, resulting in prejudice against immigrants, even when they gained legal status.

Despite his secure and comfortable life in the suburbs, Dave was not ready to acquiesce to this perspective, but he did not see the public or non-Jewish private schools as providing a sense of community or instilling strong social values, concerns he recognized as stemming from his Jewish background. Jewish education, he argued, can give students a positive experience of belonging to a community, leading them to respect community as necessary for a worthwhile life. This belief can make students more responsible citizens and more sensitive to the values and concerns of other communities.[4]

I teased Dave, too, by pointing out that his commitment to Magnes's liberal views was the only way he could slip compulsory prayer into his children's education without conceding what he shared with the American fundamentalism he distrusted.

Jon's desire to be a more informed Jew was echoed by a member of the general studies staff, Sandra Schwartz. In recent years she had deepened her attachment to Jewishness by studying Jewish symbols and introducing them into the art curriculum. Similarly, the possibility of exploring Judaism in a pluralistic framework had enticed Rabbi Robert Leder, whom Jon had astutely hired to be the school's "Director of Spiritual Life." "Rabbi Rob" was a recent graduate of the Reconstructionist Rabbinical College who preferred the primary school to the pulpit and was more comfortable with the challenge of bringing Judaism to a nondenominational setting than in trying to attract Jews from across the community to his denomination.

A day school was an attractive context for a goals project. Although vision is critical to universities, community centers, Israel experiences, and many other institutions and programs, a day school offers a unique opportunity. Its activities are comprehensive, and its mandate relates the long-term development of young learners to their future as members of the Jewish community.

At the same time, the nature of a school poses particular challenges. Logistical and administrative concerns, and the bulk of the work, are often so pressing that they leave little time for reflection and deliberation. The time for people to meet and work toward consensus on urgent issues is scarce, and it is often easier to rely on existing patterns of behavior and let the school "run on its own." Institutional inertia is a major problem for a goals project in any educational program.

Even so, the Magnes School was a compelling choice. Its eleven-year program meant that, beginning in kindergarten, hundreds of children spent most of their hours in a day school environment. Its program allocated two hours a day to the formal study of Judaica and additional informal study through the integration of Jewish studies with general studies, the arts, and other activities. Guided by its relatively new director, Magnes was trying to unify its curriculum both "vertically" and "horizontally," so that what took place in the preschool was related to what would eventually happen in eighth grade and what students learned in science would bear on what they studied in Bible.

Furthermore, since Magnes was nondenominational, its members were especially eager to define its vision. Their school was different from other Jewish schools in their community, even though Magnes, too, included prayer as a compulsory component in the curriculum, strongly emphasized the study of Hebrew and the Bible, and developed policies on issues such as kosher food and the wearing of *kippot* in the school. Magnes's nonaffiliated status reinforced the need for clarity in its educational identity.

In addition, the 1990 National Jewish Population Survey, conducted by the Council of Jewish Federations (CJF), suggested that a majority of Jews in America define being Jewish as belonging to an "ethnic" or "cultural" group and/or "nationality" rather than a religion, and that more Jews do not belong to synagogues than do.[5] These data suggested that North American Jews might be moving toward a postdenominational identity, one that would make them more comfortable in educational settings such as Magnes.

Although most of the families at Magnes were affiliated with a synagogue, they looked to the school to give their children spirituality beyond the sanctuary in such areas as citizenship. Since the number of "community-based" Jewish primary and high schools was increasing throughout North America, we would be able to explore nondenominational Jewish identity in the context of Magnes's emerging educational vision.

The goals project was supported not only by the school's leadership but by two important factors. Because of Jon's incessant efforts, both the professional staff and the trustees had developed a culture of reflection that provided a stronger base for our project than might have been available in other schools. Jon already used outside consultants routinely, and so I would not be perceived as a nuisance when I asked for time and receptivity to my questions and suggestions.

Furthermore, the terms "the Magnes family" and "the Magnes community" were often used by faculty, students, parents, and even consultants. The school seemed to engender a measure of trust among those affiliated with it.

These advantages could be drawbacks as well. Magnes's lack of denominational affiliation could make the defining of its vision more difficult. Its distinct climate of reflection and devotion might make the extrapolation from an experiment there to other settings more complex. The goodwill of members of the Magnes community was already being expressed in many extracurricular activities; people were overloaded and frantically busy. The trustees, administration, and even some of the professional staff were also heavily involved in raising funds and constructing a new wing. One argument against our working with Magnes was that no one would be able to devote enough time to the soul of the school while its body was being overhauled.

My participation was also conditioned by the fact that although I grew up in North America, I had been a citizen of Israel for many years. My immersion in the life of the school would be limited by geographic and cultural differences. This problem could be overcome in part by regular e-mail exchanges, telephone conferences, and weeklong site visits. I could also work with people from Magnes during their visits to Israel, since each summer Jon brought large groups of his staff and trustees to Jerusalem for professional development at the Hebrew University's Melton Centre for Jewish Education in the Diaspora.

Perhaps the cultural differences might not be so significant, I reasoned, since the Magnes experiment might also be instructive for the increasing number of Israelis concerned about how to integrate the study of Judaica and general education within a nondenominational framework.

Taking into account all the advantages and obstacles, we decided to undertake the experiment.

The Nature of the Task

"Almost all schools have an on-site psychologist. Why not have an on-site philosopher as well?"

From the moment I heard Seymour Fox make this intriguing observation many years ago in his course on educational planning, I thought the prospect of being a "blackboard philosopher" very appealing. Philosophers have been on-site resources in business, medicine, and other professions.[6] In education, philosophy is essential to such decisions as the relative priority of subjects in the curriculum: Why emphasize the natural sciences over the humanities, Jewish ritual over Jewish history, sports over a second language, art over community service?

Philosophy is even more important in decision making about such complex issues as admissions policies regarding children of mixed marriages, guidelines for hiring and dismissing staff and trustees, budgets, interfaith and interethnic programs, and disciplinary procedures in the event of substance abuse – all of which require a precise definition of terms and clear rationales.

My assignment was to enter into the culture of Magnes in order to raise issues and facilitate initiatives relating to the development of educational vision. In one of the consultations with PERC, Israel Scheffler had suggested that rather than make an abstract case for vision, a consultant might attend to it through day-to-day practice, making its import self-evident. I took this as a guiding principle for my work. Instead of declaring "Stop, everyone freeze!" and then trying to sell a plan of action, I would have to immerse myself in the activities of the school – in the classroom, the teachers' room, the boardroom, the director's office, the prayer hall, the gym, or the lunchroom – and infuse a vision-related perspective into whatever was taking place. If my work ignited interest and a desire to explore the meaning and role of vision, I might be able to propose more focused activities.

While it was important for me to be a Socratic "gadfly," I would also try to deepen Magnes's vision by serving as its spokesman. Here, I could draw on the resources of the Visions Project. In addition to my asking "What would you like to accomplish by teaching the Bible as a means to launch the student's spiritual journey," I could bring in, for comparison and deliberation, alternative approaches that emphasized Jewish literacy (Brinker), transcendent spirituality (Greenberg), and an authoritative introduction to the ideas and desired behaviors of Judaism (Twersky).

Goals project activities began at Magnes in the summer of 1994 and continued through 1998. In reporting this experiment, I have organized my work into five categories. Although the details are unique to Magnes, these categories will, I hope, be applicable to other settings:

1. Decoding the implicit vision
2. Establishing readiness
3. Introducing vision as a framework for everyday practice
4. Deepening vision through study, and
5. Developing strategies for sustaining vision in practice.

I have also illustrated each category with a vignette or two.

These categories are not a formula for intervention. The activities I describe often took place simultaneously, or even in reverse order. The complex work on vision, in which the detail stands for the whole even as the whole is larger than the sum of the details, is dynamic and unceasing.

Five Categories for Doing the Work

1. Decoding the Implicit Vision

Since almost everything could be relevant to the project, I first had to become familiar with the school. To facilitate a profound discussion on the question "what ought Magnes to be?" I had to gain an intimate understanding of "what Magnes is."

The case for educational vision would be most compelling when I could demonstrate that a school's practice inevitably reflects a set of commitments. It is one thing to ask, for example, "What are your goals in teaching about Israel?" It is quite another to ask, as I did on one occasion, "From reading a series of lessons on Israel, I see that you seem to want students to view Israel as the authentic setting for Jewish history. Won't they then see Jewish life in their own community as less authentic?"

To begin my assignment at Magnes, I drew on Seymour Fox's idea of "content analysis."[7] Content analysis is an investigation of an educational institution's culture, policies, curriculum, and pedagogy for the purpose of exposing its implicit vision. It is a method by which to uncover the philosophical assumptions and aims that, de facto, guide educational practice. In trying to decipher "what Magnes is," then, I would have to interpret the school and community as the enactment of a set of tacit assumptions about education.

This effort would differ from an ethnographic study. Like an ethnographer, I would enter the halls, classrooms, and meeting places of the school to study its culture from within, but my inquiry would not end with a description. Rather, I would have to define that culture in terms of its educational ideals in order to work with them subsequently.

Nor would I undertake a large-scale, systematic study of the school's educational program, pedagogy, student perceptions, and so on, followed by a presentation to decision makers and educators so that they could ask themselves, "Is this what we are aiming for – and, if not, what should we do?" At such an early stage my aims were much more modest. I simply wanted to learn enough about Magnes's implicit ideals so that they could be a focus for discussing and rethinking school practice.

Visiting Magnes for the first time, I was inundated with a wealth of "texts" and experiences. I met over half the school's trustees; shadowed Jon while he worked; attended classes and activities; interviewed teachers about a summer session I would direct in Israel on the goals of the Israel curriculum; talked with consultants, parents, students, and others; and wandered through the building and inspected materials displayed on walls. I also accepted Jon's invitation to stay at his home during my visits so that I could learn more about everyday life in the community.

In the midst of this intense immersion in the Magnes culture, I attempted to formulate a working hypothesis about "what Magnes is" and then to test it against my observations and interactions. This "rolling content analysis" provided me with a frame of reference within which I could make sense of what I encountered. A continually revised picture of "what Magnes is" informed my work in two or three yearly visits of three to six days each. The more I came to know the local Jewish and American community, the more my understanding contributed to the analysis.

In examining the results of this "rolling content analysis," I had to ask myself some difficult questions:

Were my impressions distorted by overexposure to any one aspect of the school's practice?

Was I imposing some of my own biases on Magnes?

Was I looking for more coherence among the ideas implicit in Magnes's practice than was really there?

I tested my hypotheses regularly by voicing them in the school community and assessing the consensus around my formulations.

Vignette: The Tu bi-Shevat Poster

A Tu bi-Shevat (the Jewish new year for trees) poster, which I noted ten seconds after I walked into the school for the first time, served as a point of departure for my content analysis. The poster, designed by students, hung at a central and highly visible point in the hall. Anyone at Magnes would probably walk past this poster several times a day. It was surrounded by other student work, which covered the hallways of the school. Each set of artworks had a theme; the Tu bi-Shevat poster was associated with "the world around us."

The poster depicted a huge tree, its hefty brown trunk rooted in the ground, with many leafy branches extended in all directions. This pleasing and harmonious image may have been informed by students' knowledge of Impressionist artists who created a scene from myriad dabs and dots. Accompanying the image was a written statement in English inviting readers to look west of the school in order to see Tu bi-Shevat trees.

The poster seemed more than a celebratory or commemorative placard. It explicitly asked the learner to experience Tu bi-Shevat by relating the tree it depicted to trees in the vicinity of the school. The artwork was trying to make a special ecological new year accessible to passersby by linking a Jewish holiday to the students' own environment. The difference between the Zionist Tu bi-Shevat focus on trees in *Eretz Yisrael* (the land of Israel) and this poster's focus on trees in a local American city was very telling. It revealed the school's intention to make being Jewish a matter of the here and now, emphasized by the lack of any reference to Tu bi-Shevat in Jewish sources.

To decode the poster's assumptions, I felt it would be useful to explore Menachem Brinker's phenomenological definition of Jewish identity. According to Brinker, a person is Jewish because he or she lives naturally in a Jewish society and environment. Brinker assumed that his definition of Jewish existence would have limited application to the Diaspora, whose society and environment are largely non-Jewish.

At Magnes the language of the poster was English, and the trees to which it directed the viewer were in an American context. Was the American orientation of the poster an attempt to compensate for the lack of a "natural" Jewish society? Or could it be a bold attempt to create in the school hall a "natural" Jewish environment (as "naturally" Jewish as elementary schools in Israel)?

2. Establishing Readiness

Both common sense and research into other reform efforts in education pointed to "readiness" as a critical precondition for any successful intervention. A recently published five-year study of the Coalition of Essential Schools revealed the complexity of this criterion. Readiness for change had seemed a precondition for affiliation: A school could join the Coalition only after 70 percent of its lay and professional constituents had voted in favor; and a team consisting of the director, a lead teacher, and either a trustee or another lead teacher was prepared to give much of its time to learning and implementing the Coalition's program for change.

Despite these requirements, the study showed that

"In most of the schools there was not a consensus that fundamental changes in school structure or teaching practices needed to occur";

"The changes that occurred or were considered when a school joined the Coalition forced the issue of what constituted the school's philosophy and revealed differences in faculty members' perceptions of their jobs, of the school's mission, and of the best ways to educate students";

"At most schools, a core of faculty members became active in their school's reform, but their efforts often ended up dividing the faculty";

"Most Coalition supporters were naive about the degree to which school reform could be effected by focusing on academic concerns and about issues of power and politics within their schools"; and

"Schools assumed that once the faculty 'accepted' a reform program, there was little need for further reflection on this decision."[8]

The Coalition experienced difficulties even when its program was spelled out in nine clear strategic goals.[9] The aim of the goals project at Magnes was to engage constituents in a discourse that was less concrete than the nine-point platform of the Coalition but might be more threatening. As Israel Scheffler pointed out, people often feel uncomfortable and even resistant to the philosophical. How much more so when one's professional practice, one's children's education, or the future of one's community is at stake?

My work suggested several factors that might contribute to a school's readiness for a goals project.

(a) Support from Leadership. The director and the president of the school were committed to an inquiry into the vision of Magnes because they believed it would increase the quality of the school's practice. It was their job to impart this belief to other constituencies, especially the staff leadership team and trustees. Their confidence was bolstered by their experience at the 1994 Goals Project Seminar and by the support of the Mandel Foundation Goals Project staff. The rapport among the three of us was also a factor. In addition, Jon and Dave had already established a measure of readiness before my work with them, a readiness they deepened and augmented between my visits.

These two thinking people were "seekers" committed to the power of ideas and capable of bringing the message to others. When asked by the board of trustees if a goals project would distract Jon from his administrative responsibilities, he responded that he saw this work as typifying what he was hired to do. In working on the plans for the new wing, for instance, Jon sat with the architect to consider what kind of structure would express and facilitate Magnes's guiding vision. Similarly, Dave decided that he wanted to continue being the trustee in charge of the Magnes goals project even after his term expired.

(b) A Climate of Reflection. As director of the school, Jon defined much of his work as the fostering of a reflective orientation among his staff and trustees. Particularly with teachers but also with parents, consultants, and others in the Magnes community, Jon had created forums for thinking analytically about the school's program and for launching new initiatives in light of that thinking. By convening teachers during lunch hour, hiring groups of substitutes to take over the teaching load for several hours every few weeks, having evening meetings, holding retreats, or even arranging for Israel trips, Jon had always found ways for people to sit around the table and discuss their roles and activities. To their credit, they responded to Jon's leadership with a willingness to volunteer their time.

Without this effort on both sides, it would have been very difficult to move from reflection to a discourse on educational purposes; most of my time would have been spent in setting up such forums. A school's members need time, energy, and a congenial place to think in order to articulate and implement a vision. Instead of my having to build this infrastructure, I would be able to work within already existing patterns and frameworks.

(c) A Measure of Trust, Devotion, and Care. The feeling that Magnes is a community was unmistakable to any visitor. As in most communities, there could be squabbling and gossip. It was evident, however, that various constituencies had a stake in what transpired in the school. Jon was indefatigable in his willingness to think and rethink issues, teachers worked well beyond their time in the classroom, and trustees lent their talents with the same devotion they gave to their own professions and businesses. For them, doing something for the school was a way of belonging to a community or even of expressing their Jewishness.

In addition, those who demonstrated their commitment to particular activities at the school, especially when they made positive contributions, were granted credibility. Although trustees and staff did not always express the admiration and attention they deserved from one another, innovators were not automatically distrusted. Whether insiders (such as Jon and the Hebrew studies director, Gila Levi) or outsiders (such as David Ben Dror, who led the summer experiences in Israel, or Dr. Rachel Marsden, an expert in professional development from the neighboring college of Jewish studies), people with new ideas were welcomed, if only because they expressed a desire to belong.

Taking this into account, I accepted, whenever I could, requests to participate in Magnes activities beyond the explicit scope of my project – teaching, observing, helping to clear up at social events – and found that this investment did allow me more easily to engage people in a conversation relating to goals.

The more involved I became, the more I learned to appreciate the significance of these three factors.

Later, Jon explained that a key to his planning was to bring together people he felt would have "chemistry" with one another. He had chosen many of those I would meet with this consideration in mind. Here was another factor in readiness.

Still another perspective surfaced well into the process and was inspired, in part, by my reading Seymour Sarason's *The Culture of the School and the Problem of Change.*[10] Sarason begins by asking the critical question, "Who owns the school?" The seven-page document I received in response to my posing this question to Jon became the subject of hours of mutual deliberation.

To understand a school's "readiness," one had to consider factors beyond the walls of the building. Influenced by Sarason's perspective on what determines the culture of a school and by Jon's realization that no single constituency "owned" Magnes, I came to think of schools, and Magnes in particular, as governed by a set of common aspirations. As Jon saw it, each constituent had some power over what went on – decision makers could define policy, Jon could hire and fire, teachers could determine what happened in the classroom, parents could enroll or withdraw their children, and students could participate or refuse to learn.

Because these sources of power checked one another, any cooperation among them had to develop from a sense of shared purposes. True ownership of the school was fostered wherever there was genuine agreement over its educational raison d'être. No matter how much such agreement may have appeared to be the result of power politics, it was actually a consensus around the aims of education.

A school, I realized, can be understood as the act of a community that wants to regenerate itself through the education of its youth in its image.[11] Beyond the exercise of bringing philosophical ideas and educational practice to bear on one another, the generation of vision was a matter of building community by developing agreement around educational aims.

If a group of people chose to send their children to the Magnes School or give their time, talent, and energy to it, that devotion likely reflected a particular view of being Jewish in America. Magnes seemed ready to examine its educational vision because it was confident that it was "onto something good" and wanted to know more about what that "something good" was.

This kind of readiness meant that I would try to get various constituencies to acknowledge their common aspirations, while inviting them to transform those aspirations into a more explicit and dynamic vision and program. To move from shared hopes to a guiding vision of education would indeed be demanding; constituents would have to confront their ambivalences, make hard decisions about how they defined themselves as Jews and as Americans, and invest resources of all kinds in reshaping the school's practice.

The work of decoding the implicit vision and establishing readiness does not in itself result in a strategy or specific plan of action. Rather, it provides a framework for discourse within and across constituencies in the school. I viewed establishing readiness as an ongoing component of all activities, rather than as a distinct goals project initiative. In every encounter, I would contextualize the conversation as the challenge of moving from aspirations to vision. Paradoxically, my work would be an attempt to build community in a community that already existed. As a result, we would also need to create a special forum for talking about the aims of the school as a whole, rather than those of a particular department or activity.

The challenges abounded. As evident as the aspirations were, equally visible was a map of "camps" within the school, each with a different conviction of what Magnes should be – for example, those who wanted a greater emphasis on Jewish studies versus those who did not. Instead of providing an opportunity for these camps to move closer to each other in their quest for a shared vision, the conversation between any two camps could turn into a tug-of-war. Another risk was that in their search for consensus, the disputing camps would generate an amorphous, bland vision, rather than a vibrant one.

This risk was not unique to Magnes. While attractive to many, pluralistic visions of education often evade explicit and rigorous directives for practice, thereby lacking, for the sake of tolerance, the forcefulness to be compelling.[12]

However exciting the effort to build community through educational ideas, it was also tempting for some at Magnes to perceive the work as "belonging" to certain figures or groups. Some felt that if they were not invited to participate in the project, they would pay a price in their own lower status within the school.

In one instance, Jon tried to explain to a group of teachers that although he did indeed have the power to fire any of them, if he could not justify a firing in terms of the school's educational vision, such a decision would be unacceptable. He pointed out that he, too, could be fired, or a trustee could be pressured to resign.

Often when a consensus was emerging around an element of the school's vision, a trustee, educator, parent, or student would feel threatened, thinking, "If this is what the school is about, I don't know if I belong here." In some cases, the goals work revealed to certain constituents that they did not subscribe to the vision and preferred a denominational or secular one.

Vignette: Helping Constituents to Identify with One Another

An opportunity to establish readiness across constituencies presented itself at a discussion on the goals of teaching about Israel with a group of Magnes teachers who were attending the Melton Centre summer program in Jerusalem. After I claimed that a school without a shared educational vision was in danger of being experienced by students as a "cacophony,"[13] a heated debate ensued about the commonality of purposes at Magnes. When one of the teachers pointed out the hypocrisy of parents who enroll their children at Magnes when they have no real Jewish commitments at home, I asked the speaker if she might think of a way to explain the choice of these parents that would allow her to love, respect, and identify with them.

The question was posed as a theoretical one, but I knew that any answer would make explicit the shared dreams of the Magnes community. Silence suddenly descended upon those who had been arguing. It was an admission of guilt in their settling for a critique rather than following their curiosity about what had drawn such parents to the school. The fact that two of the teachers were parents of children in the school may also have been significant.

In responding to the comment on parent hypocrisy, I drew on one exchange I had had with Dave Reiter in which it became clear that for him an educated Jew is one whose Jewishness is grounded in knowledge rather than mere sentiment. My task now was to restate this perception so that it linked the teacher's hopes to those of the parents she was criticizing.

Fortunately, I had a text I often use to stimulate discourse on American Jewry. In this brief passage, Philip Roth tries to explain his Jewish identity to a forum of Israeli and American intellectuals called together in 1963 by David Ben-Gurion to discuss their Jewish identity:

> I feel in my own instance and, I think, with some of my friends too –
> [that what has been] inherited has not been a body of law and it hasn't
> been a body of learning. (My familiarity with Bible is practically nil. I
> studied it in a college that identifies itself as a Baptist college; until then

I'd gone to a Hebrew School, where I had learned what I thought was history – perhaps it is – nevertheless, I didn't associate it with the Bible.) So there is no body of law, no body of learning and no language, and finally, no Lord – which seems to me a significant thing to be missing. But there were reminders constantly that one was a Jew and that there were *goyim* out there. . . .

What one received, I think, was a psychology, not a culture and not a history in its totality. The simple point here is, I think, that what one received of culture, history, learning, law, one received in strands, in little bits and pieces. What one received *whole,* however, what one feels whole, is a kind of psychology; and the psychology can be translated into three words – "Jews are better." This is what I knew from the beginning: somehow Jews were better. I'm saying this as a point of psychology; I'm not pronouncing it as a fact.

There was a sense of specialness and from then on it was up to you to invent your specialness; to invent, as it were, your betterness. . . .

There's always that hope that somehow all those fingers were pointing, and all that pride had some reason. But I think the amazing thing – which sort of brought the blessing and burden of having been brought up in America – was to have been given a psychology without a content or with only the remains of a content, and then to invent off of that.[14]

Philip Roth's statement about having a "psychology without a content" expresses the feeling of many American Jews who are parents today. Like Roth, they reject this psychology. Some avoid the Jewish education of their children; others seek to give their children a Jewish identity based on a psychology *with* a content.

Perhaps parents with scant Jewish knowledge sent their children to Magnes to give them what they themselves felt they had missed, while remaining confident that the Judaism transmitted at the school would not be dogmatic, intolerant, or one-dimensional. The strong core of Magnes parents who already had "a psychology with a content" and were looking for new avenues to give this psychology expression reinforced the ideals of the parents with less defined aspirations.

Before I could hear an answer to the question "Would that sort of reasoning make it easier for you to love, respect, and identify with these parents?" a teacher cried out, "That's why I sent my kids to the school," and heads nodded.

I then suggested that the group consider what it meant to have "a psychology with a content" and to imagine a Jewish studies curriculum accordingly. I was not sure I succeeded in making my point at that moment, or that the phrase "psychology with a content" would stay with the participants. However, I repeated the message, each time in a new formulation, to establish readiness for a discourse on vision.

Vignette: The "Core Values" Group Retreat

Given all the separate vision-related discussions that were taking place, we needed a cross-constituent group that could think together about the overarching aims of the school. The group of more than twenty members that was convened included trustees, the professional leaders of the early childhood, lower, and middle school programs, administrative staff, and any teacher who wanted to participate.

At the first meeting, the group studied a short passage from a draft of Michael Rosenak's essay, in which Rosenak distinguishes between communities that are held together by a common history and fate and those unified by a "core universe of values." The consensus of the group was that Magnes had always identified with the first, but that it was time to see if the school community did not also share "core values."

The group decided to meet every six to eight weeks for a few hours to explore and articulate Magnes's core values. The purpose of this process would not be to produce a mission statement that would dictate school activities. Nor would it be an exercise in arriving at consensus through compromise. Instead, it would be an honest attempt to make more conscious the values that members of the Magnes community wanted their children to embody. Even a small success in this context would be a significant resource for the ongoing consideration of Magnes's schoolwide educational vision and a focal point for efforts to develop its policy and curriculum.

This process was not easy, often leaving members of the group confused, suspicious, disappointed, and sometimes angry. Nevertheless, participation remained relatively constant. Two years after the group began to meet, its members decided to hold a summer retreat so that they could address their ambitious task with greater intensity.

By that time, there was already a draft of a document on the core values of Magnes consisting of a series of one-page statements on the school's commitment to "integrity," "lifelong learning," "habits of community belonging," "respect for the dignity and worth of ourselves and others," and "integration."

This draft, which reflected a tension between the school's commitment to individual freedom and to strong involvement in society, included very few applications of these values to specific settings or practices in Jewish and American life and did not support its articulations with sources from either the Jewish or American tradition. Although the document had not been designed to avoid painful realities and questions, the result was a "motherhood and apple pie" formulation. Since the group had begun to assume the responsibility of a community that endorses educational vision, I hoped the retreat might help clarify these still abstract values.

A number of factors worked in favor of a modest but real breakthrough, leading to a refinement of the core values document. The setting – a large house in a beautiful woodland area an hour from the city – provided a relaxed atmosphere for reflection. Under the guidance of Rabbi Rob, the group also held a prayer service for participants in a grassy area near a stream.

The critical point in the retreat occurred when representatives of various views responded to the seeming neutrality of the core values document by passionately but honestly and apolitically voicing their concerns. The first comments came late at night from Donna Shiff, a former trustee and now Bible teacher at the school. She began by speaking poignantly about the need for the document to have "a Jewish soul" and suggested new rubrics for the core values: "In the image of God," "community," and "lifelong learning." Donna claimed that she spoke as a member of a growing group of young Jews who rejected "institutional" Judaism as diminished, impoverished, and isolating and did not want their children "to be restricted by what we got." Limited by their own upbringing, however, they could not sufficiently transmit to their children what Judaism had to offer, and so they were turning to the day school to immerse their children in the Jewish tradition. These parents sought an education that would make their children Jewishly literate and informed enough to decide what kind of Jews they would be. At the same time, because they also wanted Magnes to give the children "the best of America" – a progressive and liberal education – they did not want the school to impose a single interpretation of Jewish life.

While the next three speakers strongly affirmed Donna's commitment to the Jewishness of the school, each offered a different version of their Jewish ideal. The first, a general studies teacher, emphasized her fear of assimilation. In her family she was "the only Jew left." She was sending her child to Magnes so that he could make responsible decisions about being Jewish, and she was teaching there to offer the same opportunity to all the children at the school. She believed that the school should convey the unique story of the Jewish people – not only educating students religiously, but also giving them the tools to feel comfortable in any Jewish setting.

The second speaker was a leading trustee. She had reserved her remarks for a long time until she burst out with a twenty-minute sermon of impassioned, if flustered, comments and a long reading from a text. She apologized repeatedly for her zealousness and confusion, but felt a strong need to make her statement. This trustee wanted Magnes to inculcate students unambivalently into traditional Jewish life and practices. She came from a Reform background and claimed that she was not concerned about the question of the Orthodoxy of these practices. "Three thousand years of history is possible only if there is an ongoing conversation among Jews about how to behave, even if they disagree," she argued. She wanted the school to initiate learners into the "intuitive circle" of Jewish heritage, developing in them a deep emotional commitment to the symbols and folkways of their people. For her, Magnes was not only an academically excellent school with strong values but also represented an opportunity for children to grow up in a warm and familiar public Jewish space, to become acquainted with a thousand basic Jewish concepts, to internalize a sense of Jewish authenticity, to develop a bond with other kinds of Jews, and to want to participate in the great Jewish project of mending the world.

The third speaker seemed appalled by the idea that the school and her teaching were not doing everything possible to achieve exactly what the previous speakers were advocating. A leading general studies educator, she claimed that things Jewish "infiltrate everything we do!" She felt that Jewishness pervaded the seemingly neutral language of the core values document. The question was how to find the right balance among the various components of the Magnes program. The balance itself is the point, she claimed. To overemphasize any one element would distort the beauty of what the school had already accomplished.

This comment provoked strong reactions. The director of family education, a committed Jew by choice, claimed that he had sought alternatives to his Catholic upbringing precisely because it had been so closed and monolithic. What he discovered at Magnes, and the reason he was sending his children there, was both the experience of living in a well-defined community and an exposure to "the great big world," where surprises and challenges abound and are welcome.

Then a general studies teacher spoke quietly but incisively, arguing that if she and many of the people around the table were the product of a failed Jewish education, it was because that education had not been prepared to deploy the same guidelines and methods for the teaching of Judaica as those utilized in general studies. Magnes was special because just as it gave students tools in general studies to make autonomous and independent choices, so, too, they were being educated to make choices about their Jewish lives. She saw the core values document as a very honest statement of this integrity and concluded with a forceful case: Only by nurturing literate, cultured human beings with an interest in the broadest and most profound issues would Magnes enable its students to find something of value in their Judaic studies.

At the end of the conversation, which continued at this level of intensity for hours, Jon brought the discussion full circle. The school and the core values document needed to accommodate the variety of personal journeys represented by people at this retreat, he said. He wanted to include his own, which he felt had gone unmentioned, perhaps because it was different. Whereas the focus of the discussion had been on preserving what was valuable in Jewish life, he had been ambivalent about certain aspects of American life, which had led him to reexamine Judaism. "My journey in this respect is as yet incomplete," he said. If people were not afraid to look at the question of their alienation from aspects of American culture, the results might be very revealing.

In light of all the comments, the group accepted Dave's suggestion to revise the document with a new introduction. Dave delivered a script for the introduction with great inspiration. A few generations after the Holocaust and the establishment of the State of Israel, he claimed, there was a search for a new basis for Jewish identity, beyond guilt, nostalgia, historical inertia, and external pressures. The challenges of the twenty-first century are freedom, openness, and a multiplicity of available paths: "No one is going to stay Jewish if forced to do so. Nor do we copy our parents' traditions anymore, but rather we reshape them to make them our own, like Jacob's wrestling with God. The goal is to initiate children into this process, not to let them drift, but to aim for a 100 percent commitment." America, he continued, is a religious country, constitutionally "under God." There are times when this fact clashes with our being Jewish and times when it is complementary. We must teach our children to find their way.

The experience of listening with integrity to one another had allowed the group to move forward in its deliberation. Now the educational vision and program of the school had to reflect the quality of the discussion.

My fear was that the opposite would happen – that once we moved back into the "real world," the magic of the retreat would be lost. It was not the intense debate that needed to be replicated, Jon and I agreed in subsequent conversation, as much as the character of the discourse.

A month later, he reported the results of various ad hoc meetings among members of the group, including requests by trustees to include teachers in meetings on important issues, plans for a board retreat, and much more.

After the core values retreat, an important meeting of trustees and teachers was dedicated to the question of how big the school could grow. Jon was very pleased by the tone and nature of the discussion, which was set by those who had participated in the retreat and was "infectious." His feeling was that "we could never have had this kind of discussion had it not been for the retreat."

Another outcome was the plan to replace the board of trustees' education committee with a core values group, which would oversee an in-depth study of educational issues at Magnes, soliciting feedback from those responsible for various elements of the curriculum.

3. Introducing Vision as a Framework for Everyday Practice

What was the nature of my work with Magnes constituents? To raise issues relating to educational vision "from within," I had to be privy to everyday discussions in the school and to ask questions, make comments, and suggest alternatives.

Most frequent were discussions with Jon before, during, and mostly after long periods of shadowing him through his workday. I had many opportunities, both formal and informal, to talk to teachers, trustees, parents, students, graduates, consultants, and others about their lives at the school. There were also group meetings for policy and planning decisions; professional deliberation and study; and special forums for consultation, public announcements, and cross-constituent discourse about the school.

The challenge was to find appropriate moments for intervention. A natural opportunity would arise when a statement or suggestion seemed based on assumptions about the broader aims of education.

In a meeting on the teaching of Bible, for example, one of the teachers suggested that the syllabus be arranged so that students would become familiar with portions from each of the five books of the Torah in consecutive order. I then asked such questions as

"Why is it so important that the portions be studied in order?"

"Are you saying that the goal of your *Tanakh* (Hebrew Bible) program is to familiarize the students with a sample of texts from each of the books in the Torah?"

"What sort of familiarity are you aiming for?"

"What level of understanding and retention of the biblical text will suffice for this kind of familiarity?" and

"What are your criteria for deciding which portions should be offered?"

When, at a meeting of science teachers, one suggested that the goal of science education in the primary school was to arouse students' curiosity about the world around them and how it works, I asked such questions as

"Are you speaking only of the physical world?"
"What would be the incentives for this curiosity?"
"What price would the student pay for not being curious?" and
"Where is this curiosity supposed to lead the student?"

These kinds of questions could seem to their recipients like an exercise in logic rather than an effective strategy for planning. Although greater theoretical clarity about goals did sometimes lead to an "Aha!" experience, it was hard to assess the ultimate impact of these conversations on practice. What seemed more important at this stage was to expose the fact that something was always at stake in choosing a particular goal, that there were other possibilities, or that one choice might contradict others.

I therefore asked the Bible teachers, "Could this 'familiarity' be achieved by learning the same text each year but in a different way, or by learning samples of texts by type of biblical literature [e.g., narrative, legal, historical], rather than in their current sequence?"

I asked the science teachers, "How does this curiosity about the world align with the strong emphasis in the school on the mystery of art and the power of spiritual experience?"

The immediate purpose of all this activity was to generate a resonance between ideas and practice in as many contexts and with as many people at Magnes as possible. The results could not yet be translated into a plan of action, but could lay the ground for a more serious and systematic inquiry into the goals of the school. I hoped that this "combustion energy" would lead to a desire to raise and analyze alternative possibilities, resulting in responsible decisions and creative ways of arriving at them. Since I could not involve enough people enough of the time in this discourse, even in a series of intense visits, I had to serve as a model for senior staff, rather than to pretend that I – or indeed any one person – could orchestrate a process of school transformation.

The long-term aim was to help people redefine their roles in terms of educational vision – to habituate them into thinking about what they were doing at Magnes by continually asking themselves the same five questions, as if they were a musical refrain with five notes, or a kind of mantra for practice:

1. What am I trying to achieve?
2. Why is this goal important?
3. How is what I am doing designed to attain this goal?

4. How does the goal fit into the larger aims of the school? and
5. How do I know I have succeeded?

The project's success would be measured not only by the engagement of various members of the Magnes community in specific aspects of educational vision, but also by their feeling comfortable with and driven by the school's vision as a defining factor in their work, until their asking such questions became a reflex.

The obstacles were many. An obvious one was time. To make an impact in such a short time, I would have to be professionally "intimate," to take chances in confounding and challenging people in their modes of work. As a teacher myself, I know it is much easier for school people to "hide" in their isolated roles than to be confronted with this sort of discourse. Jon made sure to back me up, but his imprimatur was not going to work without trust. Even so, I was often perceived as a threat, since this kind of conversation often called into question both personal and professional commitments.

The work led, for example, to very painful, if candid, discussions with Israeli immigrant teachers whose assumptions about Jewish education were often based on a critique of American Jewish life that arose from their nostalgia for Israel. The question of identifying the "red line" beyond which the discussion would get too personal was a difficult one, especially when people's stake in school policy was so high that they could be brought to tears in arguing for their commitments (as I discovered at the core values retreat). At times, this riskiness could be very awkward. At others, it was immensely rewarding.

This intellectual and introspective activity posed another problem. For some, the level of abstraction was too high. Others felt overwhelmed by the demand that they address matters for which they had few answers or which they had not been given sufficient opportunity to consider. People sometimes felt "put on the spot" rather than empowered. Still others did not grasp the practical ramifications of the discussion and preferred to be given a formula, procedure, or plan for "what works."

Seymour Fox had warned me that the question of which level of discourse is appropriate for teachers versus trustees versus administrators needed serious consideration. People might mechanically engage in the discussion of educational vision in this or that context without adopting this orientation in their practice.

A related problem was the singularity of each successful effort. What if all these little successes did not add up to anything more than an exciting experience? A sense of frustration often accompanied people's perception of success: If only we could have written down this conversation or videotaped it, so that it could be shared with others. On the other hand, they acknowledged that such a document might have been too inhibiting to their freedom to explore new ideas.

Vignette: Goals Statement on the Eighth Grade Trip to Israel

In planning activities for an inquiry into Magnes's goals on a particular subject, I found among various school documents already written "goals statements," which I would keep in a file to use during discussions of educational vision.

These statements themselves could be the object of close study. Specific words could be "exploded" to reveal assumptions, ideas, and guiding principles, then examined critically in light of alternatives. My aim was that participants in such an exercise would then reexamine the original text and realize that goals statements need to be drafted with more precision. Wary of seeming overly critical, I would in each case ask the permission of the authors and present the exercise as ennobling their efforts through collegial inquiry.

An opportunity to try this method presented itself during the week that the teachers visited Israel. This professional development program was designed so that the Magnes group engaged in two related activities. They were grappling with the case for inquiry into goals and examining its implications for the programs on the teaching of Israel. At the same time, through carefully designed tours they were experiencing alternative views of what Israel might stand for in Jewish life and considering the educational advantages and shortcomings of each – for example, Israel as an archaeological site proving the authenticity of Jewish history; Israel as a defender of Jewish life and source of Jewish dignity in the face of threatening adversity; Israel as a framework for the practice of Jewish tradition; Israel as a comprehensive and complex modern Jewish democratic society; Israel as a cultural theme in Judaism, other monotheistic religions, and Western civilization; and the Promised Land as a cherished theme in American life or American Jewish life. The two activities were meant to bear upon each other.

In the middle of the week, we spent two sessions studying a paragraph in a document two teachers had written about the annual trip to Israel of the eighth grade class. The trip, regarded as a climax of Magnes's program, provided a great opportunity for understanding the school's vision. The teachers who wrote the statement had agreed to its being studied by the rest of the group, especially since one of their assignments was to plan the eighth grade trip collaboratively. The particular passage read:

> The Jewish people was born and matured in the environment that is *Eretz Yisrael*. The connection of the Jewish people to the Jewish land permeates the curriculum at every grade level at the Magnes School. As we work with children through the years at Magnes, we help them make connections between the concrete land – its geology, topography and importance throughout history – and Jewish texts, identity and spirituality. We want to provide our eighth grade students with the opportunity to discover the Land with their own hands, eyes and ears. It is important for them to see the tangible expression of the learning they have done in Hebrew. This trip will serve as a culminating experience for their years of study in a Jewish day school, and the beginning of a more personal relationship with their Jewish heritage.

In preparing to study this text with the teachers, I worked closely with associates at the Mandel Foundation. We found that while the words seemed to convey an authentic desire for a meaningful encounter with Israel, they were informed by many different and even conflicting assumptions. Here, Israel was conceived of as the birthplace and incubator of the Jewish people; there, it was a tangible expression of the Magnes Hebrew curriculum. Israel's importance was first expressed in its geology and topography, and then in its being a reflection of Jewish texts. Israel was a means to the learner's developing a more personal relationship with Jewish heritage, and yet its distance from the learner's everyday life was evident. The text provided an excellent opportunity to make the case for precision and coherence in the definition of goals.

The pedagogy I chose was to direct attention to "loaded" words and phrases in this paragraph and to ask the teachers (including those who drafted the language) to explicate their meaning – for example, "connections," "importance throughout history," "spirituality," "tangible," "Hebrew," "culminating," and "beginning of a more personal relationship."

I also pointed out formulations that could have been used and suggested the implications of their having been excluded. For example, they could have added to the sentence "The Jewish people was born and matured in the environment that is *Eretz Yisrael*" the phrase "and has again placed it at the center of Jewish existence." Without the addition, the words stressed Israel as the place of origins but not necessarily the only place where Jewish peoplehood must be expressed today. What, then, was the conception of Jewish life outside Israel that should guide the teaching of local Jewish history, and how should it be related to this conception of Israel as the "origin" of all Jewish history?

As the distinctions and debates surfaced, I noted confusions, contradictions, and incoherence, while inviting the group to consider what might nevertheless be the overriding approach to the teaching of Israel. When alternatives were proposed, I asked the group to consider each in light of previous conversations about the relative educational advantages of different perspectives on what Israel might stand for in Jewish life.

I then suggested an exercise for the next session in which participants would suggest three distinct, clearly defined, and coherent goals for the Israel component of the Magnes curriculum.

The outcome of this series of experiences was a standard for the definition of goals in general, rather than the particulars of the Israel curriculum. The link between this standard and the curriculum was not clear until I met with each teacher to help plan the actual lessons. Then I saw that this approach was both practical and necessary for professional development. By themselves, these exercises might make teachers think twice before (and after) they formulated goals in the future. In the context of a larger "goals-clarifying environment," however, the exercises might be galvanizing.

Indeed, those who had been planning the eighth grade Israel trip decided to redesign the program around newly defined goals.

Vignette: The *Tefillah* Curriculum

The *tefillah* (prayer) curriculum presented one of the more significant tests of the Magnes School's nondenominational orientation. Jon was dissatisfied with the program he had inherited; he did not feel that enough educational thought had been invested in it. Rather than their gaining a special perspective or more profound meaning through the regular morning prayers, students were experiencing *tefillah* as a dry and rote activity that was forced upon them.

The compulsory status of *tefillah* was a solid foundation of Magnes's vision of Jewish education. The school wanted its students to go further than to study *about* prayer. It wanted them to experience Jewish life and acquire the tools for continuing to participate in it on their own. To achieve this goal, *tefillah* had to be compulsory, but students repeated the same prayerbook formulas every day with diminishing fervor. By telling them "This is what being Jewish is about," the school might inadvertently be fostering an estrangement from Judaism.

Jon was surprised to discover the same problem in Jewish schools throughout North America, most of which make prayer compulsory. His first step was to find someone with the appropriate expertise to tackle this dilemma. Jon wanted to learn about *tefillah* himself, working with a knowledgeable person who could also help him arrive at a conception and program that suited Magnes's vision.

This plan came to fruition at a meeting Jon held regularly with Rabbi Rob. Jon's role was to sharpen Rabbi Rob's pedagogical talents and sensitivities and build his confidence as an educator. Rabbi Rob's role was to deepen Jon's understanding of this mode of Jewish spiritual practice and to explore its possibilities for the school. The two embarked on a deliberative journey in education, searching for a way to make spiritual ideas, texts, and practices accessible to students while remaining faithful to their commitment to pluralism.

From time to time, I was invited to be part of these conversations, which I saw as an important context for the infusion of vision at Magnes. In various discussions, I had characterized the search for an appropriate *tefillah* program as an educational rather than a political decision. At first, people seemed to be thinking about the *tefillah* curriculum in terms of satisfying those in the Magnes community with diverse denominational commitments to issues of text, gender, and authority. My rolling content analysis told me that the existing curriculum was an expression of a "transdenominational" platform in a school that was actually groping for a "non-" or "postdenominational" identity. I assumed that Magnes would have to be liberated from paying allegiance to each of the denominations in order to arrive at its true educational aims for *tefillah*. Of course, there would be political consequences to the school's embracing a "non-" or "postdenominational" vision of education, but they would have to be treated *after* the school's aims for *tefillah* were explicit.

I repeatedly tried to neutralize the political element by posing questions about the school's seeming commitment to "transdenominationalism" against what could be achieved by embracing a "non-" or "postdenominational" educational vision:

"If all the denominational Jews at Magnes were satisfied that their particular denomination was well represented in the *tefillah* curriculum, but the students graduated without their having discovered *tefillah* on their own terms, would that be satisfactory?"

"Is it possible to understand the alternative denominational approaches to *tefillah* without first having been introduced to traditional prayer as it developed and was practiced?"

"What is the stance of unaffiliated members of Magnes and the Jewish community toward *tefillah,* and how should their position be represented and addressed in the program?"

"Is the option of choosing none of the denominational approaches to *tefillah* acceptable so far as the 'educated Magnes graduate' is concerned?"

Although not always easy, this persistent inquiry into the goals of *tefillah* from different angles did eventually make it possible for Jon, Rabbi Rob, and others to absolve themselves from having to answer to denominationalists. Slowly there emerged the sense that Magnes was an "educational denomination" in its own right, looking more for an appropriate way to learn about *tefillah* than to legitimate any or all denominational approaches to Jewish prayer.

Rabbi Rob proceeded to design an innovative *tefillah* curriculum. Each morning would include some basic prayers from the Siddur (prayer book), but only two of the five weekly sessions would be group services. On the other days, students would study the Siddur text, the history of prayer, and the exploration of spiritual issues through storytelling, consideration of current affairs, and more.

Rabbi Rob wanted students to begin the day by entering a personal and spiritual realm of a different quality than what they were used to in the rest of their lives. This daily excursion into a domain of meaning beyond the world of appearances would ideally be integrated into their lives as an ongoing and worthwhile activity, one that could compete with the superficial aspects of American life. Rabbi Rob paid special attention to the transitional moment at the start of each *tefillah* session when students would go from the hustle and bustle of their morning into the realm of the sacred.

To facilitate this transition, he usually began *tefillah* with a musical piece that invited the learners to slow down and turn inward. True to the Magnes vision, he also offered a choice of *minyanim* (quorums or prayer groups) and *tefillah* topics (with the option of rotation from time to time), so that students could explore many paths of engagement.

The new *tefillah* curriculum was so different from its predecessor that it was bound to have its successes and failures. Rabbi Rob was wise enough to supplement these innovations with other elements.

First, he continued to study literature on prayer and the teaching of prayer and to reflect on his own practice. He did so in his regular meetings with Jon and in professional exchanges with experts and Magnes staff. These exchanges included a full-day seminar that he and Jon organized for the entire staff with Dr. Saul Wachs, a specialist in the teaching of *tefillah* who was made available to the school (and to other Jewish schools) through the local Jewish community college, itself a nondenominational academic institution.

Second, Rabbi Rob encouraged staff members in both Jewish and general studies to help him. He asked teachers to participate in *tefillah* classes, and, when they wanted to, to experiment in their own classes. The art teacher, Sandra Schwartz, began to use images to explore and enhance the students' spiritual experience. Rabbi Rob also put the *tefillah* curriculum on the agendas of the Magnes board, Jewish studies staff, and the school's professional leadership team to get their input.

Third, he included an evaluation at the program's end that let students respond to the changes. To make sense of the data was a real challenge for him and all those who supported him in developing the new program. The risk was that the students' comments would be used as a kind of "market survey." The opportunity was to discover how an audience of learners was experiencing this new approach to *tefillah*.

In fact, the majority of students reported an improvement over former years. The feeling of treading in uncharted territories, however, was pressing upon the conscientious Rabbi Rob, as were statements of criticism and disenchantment made from time to time by various traditionalists at Magnes. One perplexing finding was that students preferred that *minyanim* be led by trained staff rather than learning how to run them on their own; yet the art teacher's experiential emphasis seemed to leave a deeper impression than the study of the prayer book text.

Ultimately, these initiatives burgeoned into a full-year inquiry into the *tefillah* curriculum by a group of educators, trustees, parents, graduates, rabbis, and consultants. Its aims were to articulate the goals of *tefillah* and to make curricular recommendations.

4. Deepening Vision through Study

Even if I succeeded in engaging people at Magnes in the formulation of vision, in redefining their roles, in asking themselves constantly "what are our goals, how can we attain them, are we indeed working effectively towards their attainment," it did not yet mean that the resulting vision would be dynamic, compelling, and operative. The stance could be right, the questions could be important, but the vision itself might still need to be enriched.

Just as parents want to be confident that their child's doctor is informed by rigorous scientific research, so a community educating its youth needs to formulate the vision that guides their children's education in consultation with outstanding scholars and thinkers. To articulate vision "on an empty stomach" would be, in Seymour Fox's expression, "like undertaking surgery without first sterilizing the scalpels and tools." And so I encouraged the Magnes community to expand its reach to include thinkers or scholars whose ideas represented the broader constituency of nondenominational Jews.

Few educational reform strategies emphasized such study or could provide models for our consideration. It would also be hard to convene people for sufficient time and in the appropriate frame of mind to learn together. Finally, without constant reminders, the link between ideas and practice could easily be lost, rendering the study exercise overly abstract or irrelevant to participants.

We did not have to look far for expertise. The Magnes School shared its campus with the Jewish community college and could benefit from the input of its staff, many of whom had the training to lead study sessions on texts that might help elicit the school's vision. Together, we could have to devise learning experiences to convince people at Magnes of the qualitative difference in the formulation, understanding, and application of their goals to practice when study was part of the process. Here, the visions of Jewish education in this book might also be valuable.

Vignette: The Visiting Professor

Two other study initiatives were launched, both benefiting from the talent and wisdom of Daniel Pekarsky, a scholar of philosophy of education at the University of Wisconsin at Madison, with expertise in the educational ideas of the French philosopher Jean-Jacques Rousseau. Pekarsky was also codirector of the Goals Project.

The first initiative was a two-day conference for the staff that Jon and I convened on issues that had emerged during the school's goals project. The meeting itself was an administrative feat. Jon had arranged for a battery of substitute teachers in order to release members of the teaching staff. He and his administrative assistant had cleared up all pressing matters so that the school was basically "running on its own." With a $5,000 grant he received for professional development from the local board of Jewish education, he invited several scholars and educators, and set up a special meeting for them with the staff. The crowning event was an evening lecture by Arthur Green, a scholar of Jewish thought at Brandeis University and pioneer in the *Havurah* movement. The lecture was open to everyone at Magnes and to the local Jewish community.

In these two days, members of the Magnes community were able to

1. compare educational visions with leading educators from two other "non-" or "postdenominational" programs;
2. familiarize themselves with new and compelling ideas and texts about Jewish identity in America presented by Green;
3. explore, with an expert, the idea of "multiple intelligences," which Jon had introduced to the design of the Magnes curriculum;[15] and
4. deliberate among themselves about the implications of all these activities for the school's goals project.

Pekarsky's address at the core values group dinner meeting was another component in the program. (This event took place before the retreat.) His assignment was to take drafts of the various core values statements that had been formulated over the preceding few months and to respond to them critically, using his expertise in philosophy of education.

In a forty-five-minute presentation, he dissected concepts in the documents, such as "respect," "integrity," and "community," showing that they could have multiple interpretations, some of which were at odds with others in consequential ways. Pekarsky's talk was followed by a lively exchange with trustees and teachers.

Although the content of any presentation, no matter how compelling, cannot be so immediately and thoroughly internalized that it can subsequently be used systematically by a group, the important achievement of this evening was that a discourse with a scholar about the school's vision had proved so captivating. People seemed to be participating not out of a sense of duty but because they trusted Pekarsky and found the exercise informative and significant. We were encouraged that similar exercises would be well received in the future.

Indeed, the second initiative with Pekarsky, which took place at the core values group retreat a few months later, was welcomed. The atmosphere for study had already been established: All participants had read Seymour Fox's *Vision at the Heart: Lessons from Camp Ramah on the Power of Ideas in Shaping Educational Institutions.*[16] This time, Pekarsky's input was of a different nature. He was asked to direct a study session on the topic of "individualism," as one of the references in the core values document was to the American tradition of "rugged individualism." I encouraged this choice because of Dave Reiter's comment that American life was vulnerable to the excesses and extravagances of individualism and that being Jewish and belonging to the Jewish community might offer a corrective.

Pekarsky had studied individualism in American thought extensively. Within minutes, he exposed the group to three different conceptions of the interrelationship between the individual and the community. In summary, Plato's conception was that the needs of each are the same. John Locke's view was that it was the community's role to maximize each individual's freedom to believe and behave as he or she chose. Rousseau's idea was that the individual could be fulfilled only through his or her involvement and contribution to the community. All this, Pekarsky explained, was an introduction to the American tradition that had placed a strong emphasis on the individual's interests, rights, and freedoms.

Pekarsky brought texts by Ralph Waldo Emerson, Henry David Thoreau, John Stuart Mill, and William Graham Sumner and then invited the group, after studying them, to explore such questions as "What are some of the justifications for individualism?" and "What could be wrong with individualism?"

Participants then broke into small groups to study the texts, reconvening to report what they had learned. Unsurprisingly, there was not nearly enough time to give the topic its due. The program was, however, an important attempt to explore the richness of text study for the development of vision.

Vignette: Greenberg's Conception of Prayer and the Magnes *Tefillah* Curriculum

Rabbi Rob was particularly concerned about identifying the "building blocks" of the prayer experience. He felt that while early learners were taught the alphabet before they began to read, Magnes students were asked to pray before they had their "spiritual ABCs" in place. No wonder prayer was an onerous activity for many of them.

In one of the study sessions between Rabbi Rob and Jon on *tefillah,* I came into the room as they were reading a passage from a book that attempted to identify the basic components of Jewish prayer. While this activity was important and useful, it also raised intriguing questions. I began by asking Jon and Rabbi Rob to explain why, from among all possible readings, they had selected this one.

In the ensuing discussion, they realized that there could not be an "objective" description of Jewish prayer. Any description would assume some "normative" view of what Jewish prayer should be. The educational leaders of Magnes needed to explore a range of perspectives on Jewish prayer – including the one espoused in the book they had chosen – as they searched for their own "theory of prayer." Then the Magnes community could evaluate its program in light of this theory, designing new methods and experiences accordingly.

In response to my questions, Jon and Rabbi Rob asked me to give an example of what I saw as a compelling theory of prayer for Magnes. I offered the one presented by Moshe Greenberg in his powerful work *Biblical Prose Prayer as a Window to the Popular Religion of Israel.*[17] Greenberg sees all human culture as spiritual, but he distinguishes between religious and other forms of spirituality. For him, religion is a form of spirituality consciously aimed at an encounter with the transcendent. In the case of Judaism, this encounter is with God, who created the universe for a purpose – to sanctify life and demand that human activity be governed by justice. In comparison, pagan religions in biblical times saw the universe as determined by an unceasing struggle among the gods, each of which represented a force in nature.

The difference between these two views expressed itself in prayer. In pagan religion, prayer was a magical incantation uttered by a priest to influence the balance of power among the gods in a direction favorable to the worshipers. It was performed by experts on specified occasions and was not motivated by ethical concerns. In the Bible, prayer was characterized by its universality and spontaneity and based on the worshipers' expectation of a moral universe. Although there were the poetic psalms that the Levites sang in the Temple at fixed times to praise God, individuals in the Bible pray at any time and place, appealing directly to God or offering thanksgiving, with no functionary to intervene on their behalf. The point of biblical prose prayer was the accessibility of the transcendent realm to all human beings in all circumstances. Prayer is a form of intimate existential and spiritual dialogue between the world of the here and now and what is of ultimate meaning and value.

This theory of prayer, which they found appealing, allowed me to ask some vision-related questions. The main one was whether spiritual education at Magnes assumed religious spirituality – that is, a relationship with the transcendent – or whether it was an attempt to introduce a cultural or simply nonmaterial element into the curriculum. Rabbi Rob and Jon both knew that much of what would happen at Magnes depended on this distinction. A "spiritual" *tefillah* program would be entirely different from a "religiously oriented" one.

Both found the question personally and professionally salient. Rabbi Rob believed that Jewish religion and experience had been emptied of its spiritual content. He saw his goal as reintroducing spirituality into Jewish life through education. Jon, on the other hand, said that for him, spirituality assumed a relationship with the transcendent, which is partly what he had been looking to understand in the journey that had led him to Magnes.

The questions became more probing: Was Magnes's thinking about prayer more rabbinic than biblical? How could obligatory and spontaneous prayer go together? Was God really a significant figure in the lives of Magnes students? Was it necessary for education to generate moral expectation and the sense that everything had a purpose? Could biblical passages describing spontaneous prayer be used in *tefillah* classes?

This was no routine professional meeting. We were already half an hour late before we noticed the time.

5. Developing Strategies for Sustaining Vision in Practice

The incremental approach to developing vision at Magnes raised a troubling question with each activity. How could we know if all this effort was having an effect? One weakness of the goals initiative was that it did not establish from the start a mechanism for evaluating its impact systematically.

Even so, there were certain indications of success. Members of different constituencies reported a transformation in their way of thinking and practice. People across constituencies were talking to one another. The language of the core values document was being used in other contexts, serving as a justification or critique of practice in the school and a way of presenting it to the world. New programs were being proposed and adopted in light of Magnes's larger aims. Goals project activities seemed to energize people and generate a hunger for more.

Most important, new frameworks were being created so that the school's educational vision could be addressed. Notably, the former trustees' "education committee" indeed became the "educational goals committee" and now included members of the administrative and teaching staff, as well as other experts, parents, and graduates. In addition, the committee dedicated to developing the *tefillah* program proposed that each year a group be convened to explore one area of the curriculum in order to make recommendations about its goals, as well as suggest new programs and methods, possible areas of overlap and conflict with the school's vision, and modes of self-evaluation.

It was not possible to know how many of these activities were direct outcomes of the goals project. For instance, the yearly eighth grade trip to Israel was scheduled for the period immediately before the Israeli elections in 1996, a particularly vulnerable time. Three horrifying bomb incidents had already taken place, as had the murder of Prime Minister Yitzhak Rabin. Two of the bombings were in Jerusalem, both in the vicinity of the hotel where the Magnes group would be staying for over half the trip. Parents started expressing doubts about sending their children.

In response, the trustees made a concerted and unified effort to contact and encourage the eighth grade parents. In the end, the trip's attendance rate was over 75 percent; among those who did not send their children were also parents whose reasons had nothing to do with the bombings. Jon attributed this success partly to the fact that he had brought a number of the trustees with him to Israel for professional development seminars, but more significantly to the goals project. He believed that the project had impressed upon them an obligation to stand behind the values of the school's vision. The claim of the trustees to the parents, he reported, was that the school's strong sense of community had to include the larger Jewish community and Israel. How could it convey this value to the students if its commitment was suddenly weakened by threats that other Jews had to confront every day?

Although this argument certainly demonstrated the power of vision at the school, we could not know if parents indeed sent their children to Israel that year because of the goals project.

The project, as I had implemented it, had other shortcomings. People had different perceptions of what they were invited to do. Some were confused. Others had no sense of how the pieces fit together. Few fully understood the direction in which the project was supposed to move. This deliberate lack of definition was exacerbated by the fact that, apart from the core values statement, there was not much the project could demonstrate in writing. In fact, there was a sense that vision could be undermined if reduced to paper.

This fear led to our repeated warnings that the core values document should not be seen as a mission statement or as a school constitution, but as an input or means toward greater explicitness about Magnes's goals. Nevertheless, some people felt that until each component of Magnes's program had a written statement of its aims, justified in relation to the school's vision, there would be little assurance of the goals project's impact and no way of knowing which areas needed further development or how to assure coherence among the various elements.

The feeling of never knowing or always being "in between" the implicit and explicit was ever present. Under these circumstances, I wanted to force the issue of writing. Doctors record every exchange with their patients in writing, I thought to myself. Why shouldn't those involved with education be asked to do the same? I imagined Jon's hiring one of his staff to be a roving editor, who would coach constituents to write up their goals and explain how the programs were designed to attain them. This effort would lead to the formulation of a schoolwide goals document created by bringing together various groups in the school to address vagueness and contradictions.

Jon adamantly opposed this suggestion. He felt that, at least at this stage of the school's development, a demand for writing would be problematic for most people, whose schedules were already overbooked. Rather than empowering them, such a requirement might be experienced as the introduction of a "program police," dampening openness and creativity.

The bottom line was that even if Jon did want to proceed, he had no budget to hire an "editor-coach." While he took the suggestion seriously, he argued convincingly that it would take five years of work on vision before writing could become central to the school culture.

His response to the idea did not preclude other ways of sustaining the momentum. A rolling or improvisational principle that contributed to the school's growth was preferable to a systematic and rational plan for change that could not be implemented. The goals project had not been presented as a mechanism for change. Although its implementation made change inevitable, the project's emphasis was on setting standards for ongoing practice.

One advantage of this improvisational approach was that it kept alive the capacity to "feed" into the rhythm of the school's daily life. It is striking how many opportunities there are for work on educational vision when one looks for them carefully, rather than imposing them.

A good example was the evaluation process Magnes had to undergo to be accredited by the state's independent schools organization. Keeping in mind Seymour Fox's claim that evaluation could be a strong gateway for a discourse on vision, I thought this accreditation might allow us to explore vision more deeply, since, in preparation for the evaluation, the school had to create a self-study that included a report on the attainment of instructional goals in each subject-matter component of the curriculum.

After much thought, and considering the coincidence of the completion and publication of the core values document with the beginning of the self-study, Jon requested that representatives of each subject-matter area describe and evaluate its educational goals and practice with reference to the core values statement. He would then collate the documents and submit them, with introductory and concluding comments, as the major unit of the self-study.

The purpose of the self-study was to prepare a team of educators associated with or recognized by the independent schools agency to visit the school, observing and evaluating it in light of the study's contents. Since Jon was permitted to choose the members of the team, he proposed the appointment of Daniel Pekarsky, as well as the director of a community Jewish elementary school (from another city) whom he highly respected. Their familiarity with the Goals Project and its local version at Magnes would enable them to make useful suggestions from "within."[18]

Other opportunities for vision development suggested themselves from time to time: for example, when teachers were hired or dismissed, when special requests were presented to the board of trustees, when there were changes in the parent body, or when significant events occurred in the community. The gamble of this improvisational approach was that all these activities would not only animate the vision of the institution but set in place mechanisms for renewing its vitality in the future. But the improvisational mode could as easily lend itself to the school's adopting an alternative, less content-focused strategy of change.

Did the goals project achieve a measure of success sufficient to affect the infrastructure of the school?

Did the project's approach pervade the school program as a whole, rather than depending on a small number of gifted teachers and students?

Would new staff and trustees by inducted into the process we had begun?

Would all the activities we had generated set a standard for the creation of new programs?

Would the school invite scholars and thinkers to help deepen its vision?

Would there be any worthwhile goals the school would nevertheless rule out in the understanding that an effective educational program cannot be all things to all people?

Would an intense preoccupation with the vision of the school survive changes in staff, administration, or the board of trustees?

We need to learn from many more experiments like those undertaken at Magnes, local goals projects that try a range of approaches to the development of educational vision.

At the 1994 Goals Project Seminar in Jerusalem, Seymour Fox suggested to members of the various communities around the table that when people from diverse backgrounds commit themselves to discussing a pluralistic, community-based vision of Jewish education, they might discover that they are more willing to accommodate other perspectives than they would have anticipated. If the experiment at Magnes does not necessarily lead to the conclusion that a "non-" or "postdenominational" vision is the most immediate challenge for the Jewish community today, it certainly demonstrates that it is possible to begin confronting it, and that there is a strong motivation for people to join the conversation.

The Magnes experiment also has implications for those who belong to more traditional or ideologically defined communities. The nature of a vision and the strategies for developing it may vary, but the principles that guide the work are applicable to many educational settings. The five principles that informed my work need not be bound to the mode of "on-site philosopher" I adopted.

The Magnes experiment taught me that the success of efforts to improve education through attention to vision will be commensurate with the degree of energy and wisdom a community is willing to invest in its future.

Concluding Vignette: From a Journal Entry, Midway Through the Project

As I stand once again before the gates of the school, I realize how profoundly my definition of this institution is changing. Yes, this is a place like many I have seen, with classrooms, hallways, and offices, where teachers stand before blackboards and students sit behind their desks, raising their hands or writing in their notebooks. But now I understand that it is also a setting where a compelling social drama is taking place.

The main character in the drama, ever present though never fully visible, is a community, a social consensus. This community shares values as to what, from among the infinite range of possibilities, is significant and useful in this world, and it asks those involved in education to nurture its youth accordingly.

The community stands behind every activity in the school. As the kindergarten teacher instructs children in the art of cake making, the community stands over her shoulder, asking her to teach them that whatever they appreciate in the world is often the product of knowledge and industry.

As teachers engage in a professional deliberation over the case of a child whose classmates refused to play with him at recess, the community presides over the meeting, making sure that the value of respect for each human being as made in God's image is not neglected.

While the director has a private telephone exchange with a concerned parent about the changes in compulsory prayer, the community echoes his voice in order to explain why the new program is more likely to lead children to a profound experience of Jewish spiritual life.

And as the board of trustees sits down to establish the scholarship policy for applicants who do not have the means to send their children to the school, they do so with deference to the community's view of itself as being more than an economic class.

All in all, a school is a place where a community boldly makes a promise to its youth – "Learn as we suggest and you will fare better. We believe that what we have to teach you is profoundly significant, that if you master it you will fulfill yourself more completely, grapple better with the challenges of life, and contribute to the good of others in our world."

Here is a place where the community mandates and oversees those involved in daily educational activities to deliver on this promise. To the degree that this mandate is clear, that it does indeed inform all aspects of the programs, the school is really a school. When the mandate is unclear or invisible, the school is a cacophony of voices, a melee of pedagogical stimuli, and a marketplace for the transmission of skills. It is then a place where the community abandons learners to figure out the important things for themselves, without giving them the means to do so.

For all the novelty of what we are trying to accomplish at Magnes, the education of our youth is an age-old Jewish commitment. The Jewish community is the oldest on record to make education universally compulsory. The Bible stipulated that one must "teach the commandments diligently to one's children" (Deut. 6:7), and by the period of the Second Temple there were already halakhic injunctions castigating any community that did not appoint teachers for its children (Shabbat, 119b). Indeed, the Talmud suggests that such a community abets the destruction of the Temple.

I cannot say that at Magnes we are rebuilding the Temple. But I do feel we are correcting something that has gone wrong in Jewish life in America.

I am reminded of the ironic comment made by Lloyd Gartner, the historian of American Jewish education, as he described the passion with which Jews in America embraced their country's educational systems – and the resulting void in Jewish education.

"Study," he wrote, "that ancient Jewish cynosure, inspired Jews in almost every field except that in which it originated."

Here at Magnes we are trying to reverse the process, aiming not only to revive Jewish learning but to extend the profoundly Jewish commitment to education so that it encompasses all areas of study.[19]

NOTES

1   See, for example, Seymour Fox, *"Prolegomenon le-Filosofiah shel Ḥinukh Yehudi"* in *Kivunim Rabim: Kavanah Aḥat* (Jerusalem: School of Education of the Hebrew University and Ministry of Education, 1969), 145–54; "Towards a General Theory of Jewish Education," in *The Future of the Jewish Community in America,* ed. D. Sidorsky (New York: Basic Books, 1973), 260–70; with Israel Scheffler, *Jewish Education and Jewish Continuity: Prospects and Limitations* (Jerusalem: Mandel Foundation, 1993, 2000) and, with William Novak, *Vision at the Heart: Lessons from Camp Ramah on the Power of Ideas in Shaping Educational Institutions* (New York and Jerusalem: Mandel Foundation, 1997, 2000).

2   *Vision at the Heart,* 5.

3   The names of the Jewish day school and of the educators, trustees, and others who were active at the time of this experiment have been changed. I am grateful to all participants for their cooperation.

4   A school of American sociology corroborates this view of citizenship. See, for example, R. N. Bellah, R. Madsen, W. M. Sullivan, A. Swidler, and S. M. Tipton, *Habits of the Heart: Individualism and Commitment in American Life* (Berkeley: University of California Press, 1985), and Robert D. Putnam, *Bowling Alone: The Collapse and Revival of American Community* (New York: Simon and Schuster, 2000).

5   Barry Kosmin et al., *Highlights of the CJF 1990 National Jewish Population Survey* (New York: The Council of Jewish Federations, 1990), 28.

6   Israel Scheffler introduced us to this idea and suggested ways in which young philosophers could be trained to work in Israel's Ministry of Education and other educational institutions. He also referred us to *Proceedings and Addresses of The American Philosophical Association* 58:2 (November 1989), whose entire edition was devoted to the topic "Careers for Philosophers."

7   See Leah Adar and Seymour Fox, *Nituaḥ Tokhnit Limmudim be-Historiah u-Vitzuah be-Vatei Sefer* (Jerusalem: Hebrew University School of Education, 1978); and Miriam Ben Peretz, *"Nituaḥ Mashveh shel Kamah mi-Tokhniyot ha-Limmudim be-Biologiah ha-Nehugot be-Veit ha-Sefer ha-Tikhon be-Yisrael"* (Ph.D. diss., Hebrew University of Jerusalem, 1977), and *Skimah la-Nituaḥ Tokhniyot Limmudim be-Mada'ei ha-Teva* (Jerusalem: Hebrew University Amos De Schalit Israeli Center for the Teaching of Science, 1980). I also used Fox's "five levels" to analyze and develop educational content. See *Vision at the Heart,* 27–34.

8   Donna E. Muncey and Patrick J. McQuillan, "Preliminary Findings from a Five-Year Study of the Coalition of Essential Schools," *Phi Delta Kappan* 74 (February 1993): 486–98.

9   See Theodore R. Sizer, *Horace's Compromise: The Dilemma of the American High School* (Boston: Houghton Mifflin, 1985), 225–27. In short, the nine goals were: (1) A "focus on helping young people develop the habit of using their minds well"; (2) Simple goals; (3) Universal goals; (4) Personalization of teaching and learning; (5) Pedagogy of coaching the student "as worker"; (6) Documentation and assessment of learning and graduation by exhibition; (7) Family participation; (8) Generalist staff with multiple obligations; and (9) Budget allowing 80 or fewer students per teacher, time for collective planning, competative salaries, and per pupil costs no more than 10% higher than at traditional schools. Since the publication of *Horace's Compromise,* the Coalition has added a tenth goal: nondiscrimination and inclusion.

10 Boston: Allyn and Bacon, 1971.

11 My articulation was informed by Werner Jaeger's introduction to his *Paideia: The Ideals of Greek Culture,* vol. 1, trans. G. Highet (New York: Oxford University Press, 1945), xiii–xvi.

12 See, for example, Ronald Reynolds, "Goals and Effectiveness in Jewish Education: An Organizational Perspective," in *Studies in Jewish Education* 3 (1988): 91–116. On the basis of his empirical study of Jewish schools, Reynolds suggests that vague articulations of educational goals are often used as a strategy to encourage participation and avoid conflict.

13 Lawrence A. Cremin, "The Cacophony of Teaching," in *Popular Education and Its Discontents* (New York: Harper and Row, 1990), 51–84. See also Patricia Albjerg Graham, "Schools: Cacophony about Practice, Silence about Purpose," *Daedalus* 113:4 (1984): 29–57. Cf. David Cohen's comment on intellectual "bankruptcy" in American high school education expressed in an inability among teachers to rule out the pursuit of any educational goal. See David K. Cohen, Eleanor Farrar, and Arthur G. Powell, *The Shopping Mall High School: Winners and Losers in the Educational Marketplace* (Boston: Houghton, Mifflin, 1985), 305–08.

14 "Remarks at 'Second Dialog in Israel,'" *Congress Bi-Monthly* 30:12 (September 16, 1963): 21. I found this reference through Charles E. Silberman, *A Certain People: American Jews and Their Lives Today* (New York: Summit Books, 1985), 81.

15 See Howard Gardner, *Frames of Mind: The Theory of Multiple Intelligences* (New York: Basic Books, 1983). The expert was an associate of Gardner's who staffed a project designed to implement the multiple intelligences idea in schools.

16 See note 1.

17 Berkeley: University of California Press, 1983.

18 On the integration of evaluation and development in teacher evaluation practice, see Lee Shulman, "A Union of Insufficiencies: Strategies for Teacher Assessment in a Period of Educational Reform," *Educational Leadership* (November, 1988): 36–41.

19 Bernard Zelechow first introduced me to the conception of education as a promise in his description of his own public school education as a child of Jewish immigrants in New York. The quotation by Lloyd P. Gartner is from his essay, "Jewish Education in the United States," in *American Jews: A Reader,* ed. M. Sklare (New York: Behrman House, 1983), 392.

Conclusion: The Courage to Envision

The visions we have recounted and discussed in the foregoing chapters are not to be taken as finalities. They are intended, rather, as exemplars of the way educational programs might best be conceived, exhibiting various attempts to weave authentic strands of our heritage into the growing fabric of our children's learning. Such attempts must continually be made if our educational efforts are not to relapse into superficiality, incoherence, or rote. We must try again and again to meet the perennial challenge, set us by the changing contexts of our educational efforts, to clarify the purposes that ought to animate such efforts and the principles embodied in our consequent practice. In sum, the visions of others we have considered here should spur us to undertake the ever-present task of educational envisioning in our own circumstances, and by our own lights.

This continued work of envisioning cannot be expected to culminate in a uniform outcome. As is illustrated by the array of visions in the preceding pages, this work yields not one vision but many. Pluralism is thus the rule, not the exception. But pluralism does not necessitate an acceptance of all the visions resulting from reflection, nor does it sanction a relativism that allows us to choose just any vision we like. Each of us needs to work out the principles, purposes, and practices that commend themselves to us as most sound and persuasive, while according the respect due to others who have, sharing the same task, followed a different path.

Pluralism, emphatically, does not imply that each vision is segregated from the rest by an impermeable barrier. Different visions within a shared community are inevitably in contact with one another, and their proponents are capable, as well, of respectful communication.

Our hope is indeed that Jewish individuals and communities may take this book as an invitation to project, compare, and debate their several visions of Jewish education, engaging in conversations that treat not merely of resources, strategies, and improved efficiency in following current directions but also of competing conceptions of such education, the overriding purposes it ought to serve, and the values it should embody in our time. Our book is thus, as we hopefully conceive it, not an end but a means, not a stopping point but a starting point for creative reflection on our educational heritage and an envisagement of its very shape and content in the coming years.

The Visions Project: Participants and Forums

The Visions Project was developed by the Mandel Foundation in 1991.

A. Scholars

The project began with seminars in which the scholars presented and discussed their essays (May 1991 at Harvard University; July 1991 at the Mandel Institute in Jerusalem; August 1994 at Harvard University). Written summaries of these deliberations were given to each scholar and used as a basis for the reformulation of their essays.

MENACHEM BRINKER is Professor of Hebrew Literature and Philosophy, Emeritus, at the Hebrew University and Crown Professor of Modern Hebrew Literature at the University of Chicago. Brinker has published books and essays on philosophy, aesthetics, literary theory, and Hebrew literature, most recently *Last Jews or First Hebrews: M. Y. Berdyczewski's Appeal for Re-evaluation of Jewish Culture* (Hebrew). He edited the Hebrew literary journal *Massa* and the political-social monthly *Emda* and was president of the Israeli Philosophical Association. A spokesman for the peace movement in Israel, Brinker has participated in public forums on contemporary Jewish life. He has also taught at teacher training seminaries in Israel.

SEYMOUR FOX, founder and director of the Visions Project, is Director of Program of the Mandel Foundation worldwide. He is Professor of Education, Emeritus, at the Hebrew University of Jerusalem, where he directed the School of Education. Fox has written and edited works on curriculum theory and practice in general and Jewish education, including *Freud and Education* and *From the Scholar to the Classroom: Translating Jewish Tradition into Curriculum*. He founded several institutions of Jewish education in the United States and Israel, including the

Melton Research Center for Jewish Education at The Jewish Theological Seminary of America; the Melton Centre for Jewish Education in the Diaspora at the Hebrew University; the Mandel Jerusalem Fellows program; and the Mandel School for Educational Leadership in Israel.

MOSHE GREENBERG is Professor of Bible, Emeritus, at the Hebrew University, where he held the Professor Yitzhak Becker Chair in Jewish Studies. He was awarded the Israel Prize for Bible in 1994. Ordained as a rabbi at The Jewish Theological Seminary of America, he contributed to the Bible curriculum project of the Melton Research Center for Jewish Education and served as a scholar-in-residence at Camp Ramah. He has also been an advisor on Bible curriculum to the Ministry of Education in Israel and was cofounder and coeditor of *Mikra le-Yisrael*, an Israeli Bible commentary series.

DANIEL MAROM is associate director of the Visions Project. He is a Senior Researcher at the Mandel Foundation and editor of the *Monographs from the Mandel Foundation* series. In addition, he is a faculty member of the Mandel School, where he has developed the tutorship program. Marom has published essays on Zionist history and education and has designed curricula for Jewish education in Israel. He directs a program to disseminate the ideas and methods of the Visions Project.

MICHAEL A. MEYER is Adolph S. Ochs Professor of Jewish History at Hebrew Union College–Jewish Institute of Religion, Cincinnati. He has published books and essays on modern Judaism, Jewish identity, and Jewish historiography and teaches these topics at universities in America and Israel. Among his books are *The Origins of the Modern Jew: Jewish Identity and European Culture in Germany 1749–1824* and *Jewish Identity and the Modern World*. A voice within the Reform movement, he has also written *Response to Modernity: A History of the Reform Movement in Judaism*.

MICHAEL ROSENAK is Mandel Professor of Jewish Education, Emeritus, at the Hebrew University and is head of the Department of Education and Jewish Education at the Mandel Jerusalem Fellows program. He has published works in Jewish educational thought, particularly its theological aspects. His book *Commandments and Concerns: Jewish Education in Secular Society* won the Jewish Book Prize in 1989. Rosenak was the Samuel Rothberg Prize Laureate of the Hebrew University for 2001. He developed the Jewish Values Curriculum at the Melton Centre for Jewish Education, which has been used in Jewish schools throughout the world.

ISRAEL SCHEFFLER is Victor S. Thomas Professor of Education and Philosophy, Emeritus, at Harvard University, where he directs the Philosophy of Education Research Center (PERC). A founding member of The National Academy of Education, he is author of *Four Pragmatists, In Praise of the Cognitive Emotions,*

Symbolic Worlds, and other works in philosophy. He has also written a memoir on his early Jewish education, *Teachers of My Youth.*

ISADORE TWERSKY (d. 1997) was Nathan Littauer Professor of Hebrew Literature and Philosophy and director of the Center for Jewish Studies at Harvard University. Author and editor of numerous books on Jewish philosophy and law, including *Introduction to the Code of Maimonides (Mishneh Torah),* he was also Rabbi of the Talner Bet Midrash in Brookline, Massachusetts. Twersky participated in the Continuing Seminar on Jewry under the auspices of the president of Israel and in the Commission on Jewish Education in North America. He played a central role in the development of the program of the Maimonides School in Boston.

B. The Educators Group

AMI BOUGANIM directs research and development and leads staff training at the Department of Jewish and Zionist Education of the Jewish Agency for Israel. He has served as the director of the Mandel Jerusalem Fellows program. He also directed the Education Department at the Alliance israélite universelle in France. Bouganim compiled *Sites and Sources,* a text anthology for the education of tourists in Israel. He has published books on Jewish and general philosophy and has worked extensively in settings of informal Jewish education.

RUTH CALDERON is founder and executive director of Alma, a liberal arts college for the study of Hebrew culture in Tel Aviv. Calderon won the Avi Chai Foundation prize in 1997 for cofounding the Elul Beit Midrash in Jerusalem for joint text study among religious and secular men and women. She hosts a popular Jewish text study program on Israeli television and has published interpretations of midrashic literature.

JONATHAN COHEN teaches philosophy of Jewish education and curriculum theory at the Melton Centre for Jewish Education at the Hebrew University. He is also head of Jewish and Humanistic studies at the Mandel Jerusalem Fellows program. He has developed many curricula in Jewish studies for Israeli schools and has published and edited works in Jewish thought and theory. Recently he published *Reason and Change: Perspectives on the Study of Jewish Philosophy and Its History* (Hebrew).

HOWARD DEITCHER is director of the Melton Centre for Jewish Education at the Hebrew University, where he also teaches Bible education and philosophy for children. He has written on the teaching of Bible, focusing on its applications to children's education. He directed the Mandel Jerusalem Fellows program and the Mandel School's Intensive Development Programs for educational leaders.

SHLOMO FISCHER is the educational director of *Yesodot* – the Center for Torah and Democracy. He has published essays on Jewish historical sociology and religion and society in Israel. He was the director of the History Project at the David Schoen Institute–Gesher Educational Affiliates.

MICHAEL GILLIS teaches curriculum and theory of Jewish education at the Melton Centre for Jewish Education at the Hebrew University and is on the staff of the Mandel Jerusalem Fellows program. Gillis was the director of Jewish studies at the Mount Scopus College, Melbourne, and directed the Senior Educators Program at the Melton Centre. His doctoral dissertation was on the application of contemporary theories of interpretation to the teaching of rabbinic literature.

BEVERLY GRIBETZ is principal of the Evelina de Rothschild Secondary School for girls in Jerusalem. She was previously a headmistress at Yeshivat Ramaz in Manhattan. Gribetz's doctoral dissertation was on the theory and practice of teaching Talmud.

NERIAH GUTEL teaches Jewish studies and education at Bar-Ilan University and in teacher training colleges. He has written extensively on Jewish law and on the teachings of Rabbi Abraham I. Kook. His book on the halakhic category of *Shinui ha-Teva'im* ("changes in nature") won the 1998 Tel Aviv Prize for Torah Literature. In 2000 his book on the correspondence of Rav Kook won the Aminoaḥ prize.

AMNON KARMON teaches in the Department of Education of the Mandel School. He came to the field of education from an academic background in the philosophy of science. Karmon is currently writing a doctoral dissertation on the relationship between epistemology and education.

LESLEY LITMAN is the regional educator for the Reform movement's UAHC Northeast Council and the UAHC national day school liaison. She guides change processes in day schools and congregations.

ZEEV MANKOWITZ, a past director of the Melton Centre for Jewish Education at the Hebrew University, is currently a senior member of its faculty. He also directed the Mandel Jerusalem Fellows program and the Institute for Youth Leaders from Abroad of the Jewish Agency for Israel. Mankowitz has written on the history and teaching of the Holocaust, including a recent book, *Life between Memory and Hope: Survivors of the Holocaust in Occupied Germany.*

MARC ROSENSTEIN directs *Makom ba-Galil,* which provides educational seminars and tours in the Galilee. Ordained as a Reform rabbi, he was principal of Akiba Hebrew Academy in Philadelphia before immigrating to Israel. Rosenstein has written on the history of Israeli education.

DEBORAH WEISSMAN is director of the Kerem Teacher Training Institute for Humanistic-Jewish Education in Jerusalem. Her doctoral dissertation was on the history of Jewish education for girls. She taught courses on Judaism and gender at the Melton Centre for Jewish Education and the Rothberg School for Overseas Students at the Hebrew University. She also served as officer in the education division of the Israeli Defense Forces, which develops informal educational programs.

SHMUEL WYGODA directs the Yaacov Herzog Teachers College at Yeshivat Har Etzion in Gush Etzion, Israel. He was the principal of the Montreal Hebrew Academy in Canada and on the staff of the Mandel Foundation and the Mandel Jerusalem Fellows program. Wygoda is completing a Ph.D. at the Hebrew University on the talmudic philosophy of Emanuel Levinas and has published essays on this topic.

C. Consultants

The Visions Project benefited from the contributions of various consultants. Some worked on the project on an ongoing basis, others on specific topics.

GAIL DORPH is director of the Mandel Foundation's Teacher Educator Institute (TEI), a program that prepares participants to design and develop cutting-edge learning opportunities for teachers in Jewish classrooms. Presentations of the Visions Project were made to various cohorts of TEI. Dorph has written on teacher education and was part of a national team that developed the Melton Graded Curriculum Series. She is also former director of the Fingerhut School of Education at the University of Judaism, in Los Angeles.

ANNETTE HOCHSTEIN is president of the Mandel Foundation, Israel. A policy planner by training, she served as the founding director of the Mandel School and established its Department of Policy Studies, where she teaches. Hochstein has contributed to major policy analysis projects, including the West Bank Database Project, the Commission on Jewish Education in North America, and many social and economic projects for public agencies. She was cofounder in 1980 of Nativ Policy Planning Consultants, a Jerusalem-based consulting firm, which she directed until 1990.

BARRY HOLTZ is Theodore and Florence Baumritter Professor of Jewish Education at the Jewish Theological Seminary in New York. An expert on Jewish text study and teacher education, Holtz has written and edited many publications on these topics for both academic and general audiences, including the forthcoming *Textual Knowledge: Teaching the Bible in Theory and in Practice*. Holtz is a consultant to the Mandel Foundation and lectures at the Mandel School. He played a central role in the presentation of the Visions Project to various groups in North America.

VERNON A. HOWARD was a codirector of the Philosophy of Education Research Center (PERC) at Harvard University from 1983 to 1998 and is currently a faculty member of the Harvard University Extension School. He is the author of books related to the arts and education, including *Artistry: The Work of Artists* and *Learning by All Means: Lessons from the Arts.*

STEPHANIA R. JHA is a research associate at Harvard's Philosophy of Education Research Center (PERC). She is author of *Reconsidering Michael Polyani's Philosophy.*

CHARLES LIEBMAN holds the Yehuda Avner Chair in Religion and Politics at Bar-Ilan University. His research on the Israeli and American Jewish communities and Israeli-Diaspora relations has informed the community of scholars and policy makers working on these issues. Liebman offered challenging sociological insights in response to the essays presented at the Jerusalem meeting in 1992.

MORDECAI NISAN is Professor of Educational and Developmental Psychology at the School of Education of the Hebrew University of Jerusalem. He was dean of the School of Education and a member of the Higher Education Authority in Israel. Currently, he is academic director of the Mandel School. He has published extensively on moral behavior and development and on human motivation, including his articles "The moral balance model: Theory and research extending our understanding of moral choice and deviation" and "Beyond intrinsic motivation: Cultivating a sense of the desirable." Nisan's monograph, *Educational Identity as a Primary Factor in the Development of Educational Leadership,* considers the implications of the Visions Project for the training of educational leaders.

DANIEL PEKARSKY is Professor of Educational Policy Studies at the University of Wisconsin-Madison. He has written various philosophical-educational works for both general and Jewish education. Pekarsky is former director of the Cleveland Fellows, a graduate program of the Cleveland College of Jewish Studies. He is a consultant to the Mandel Foundation and lectures at the Mandel School. He played a central role in presenting the Visions Project to various groups in North America.

D. Forums

More than seventy presentations of the Visions Project were made to groups from Israel and Jewish communities across the world. At these presentations, the project's staff argued for the importance of educational vision, using one or more of the visions developed in the project as an illustration. The presentations often included meetings with the scholars who had conceptualized the visions.

Participants included educators – teacher trainers, Jewish curriculum special-ists, administrators, researchers, and professors of Jewish and general education – as well as rabbis, scholars, federation planners, and policy makers.

Summaries of the discussions at each of these presentations also informed the scholars' reformulation of their essays.

Presentations of the project were convened by the Mandel Foundation; the majority of these presentations took place at the Mandel School. There were also special presentations of the project, such as the meeting of Reform educators in Los Angeles (see Supplement: Michael Meyer).

Others included:

The Fiftieth Anniversary of the Tarbut Hebrew College in Mexico City, Mexico (1993): Tarbut, a leading day school in Mexico City, convened a con-ference for educators from South America on the topic of educational vision. Brinker and Greenberg presented their visions at this conference.

The Goals Project Seminar (1994): Delegations from communities in North America met in Jerusalem to consider the topic of educational vision. They studied the visions of Greenberg and Rosenak.

The Wexner Heritage Foundation Alumni Retreat (1995): The Wexner Heritage Foundation convened 242 alumni of its leadership education program from 14 communities for a weekend retreat on the role of educational vision in the work of the alumni.

Atlanta New Jewish Community Day High School Initiative (1995): Members of the Jewish community of Atlanta considered Greenberg's vision of Jewish education as part of their effort to articulate a guiding vision for the community day high school they were in the process of establishing.

Academy for Torah Initiatives and Direction (ATID): Based in Jerusalem, ATID is an independent training program for junior educational leaders in the Modern Orthodox community. Founded by Rabbi Chaim Brovender and di-rected by Rabbi Jeffrey Saks, ATID has explored Twersky's vision of Jewish education with cohorts of ATID fellows in Israel and day school educators in the Diaspora.

Index